CW00733274

Also by Jim Crumley

SEASONS
OF STORM
AND
WONDER

JIM CRUMLEY

with a foreword by
KATHLEEN JAMIE

Saraband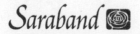

Published by Saraband
3 Clairmont Gardens
Glasgow, G3 7LW
www.saraband.net

ISBN: 9781913393533

1 2 3 4 5 6 7 8 9 10

Printed and bound in Great Britain by Clays Ltd, Elcograf S.p.A.

Many chapters in this book are drawn from the individual books in Jim
Crumley's Seasons Tetralogy: *The Nature of Autumn, The Nature of Winter,
The Nature of Spring* and *The Nature of Summer*. This is a new edit, along
with supplementary sections drawing the themes together.

Remember well
David Craig
1932–2021

Contents

Foreword

WHO IN THE LATE 1980s would quit a decent day job and become a "nature writer"? It was an extraordinary vocation at the time. It meant a leap out into the cold, a literal journey into the wilderness, but Jim Crumley did it, and with complete success. For thirty-odd years since, Jim has been our predominant writer on the natural world. For the first of those years, his books occupied a lonely corner of the bookshop, but boy – look now. He wasn't alone for long.

Jim is a naturalist with a great gift for observation, and he is a Scot. Scotland flows into him, and he breathes it out. Other landscapes and seascapes attract him (his inner compass needle points North), but his homeland is the one he knows and loves best. He spends a lot of time alone out in the hills, but he is not lofty. He can walk a lonely shore, but he has a knack for conversation and friendship. Jim is a great engager. (If I use his first name, it's because, as a reader, I feel that I know him.) His work engages us in the best ways – it addresses us as equals. We are drawn alongside him, to appreciate what he appreciates. In Jim's company, we can spend a long day searching for eagles at the top of a glen – and finding them – or watching whales in the Firth of Forth. His prose is lyrical, but he is no literary show-off.

He can also be emphatic, sharp, political. How to "cure" nature? Simple. Stop harming it. How to rebuild fully functioning upland ecosystems? Get out of their way (and add a few missing wolves). How to restore our raptor population? Don't muck about with ringing and satellite tags, just stop shooting them out of the sky.

Of all Jim's books, *Seasons of Storm and Wonder* is probably his *magnum opus*. Convened from his four original, individual books of the seasons, this volume gives us the year's round in one, a cycle marked by the two solstices. Within are all the storms and wonders one could wish for. There are adventures, diary entries, conversations, mullings-over and encounters with almost every creature we are privileged to share our lives with.

Much is going wrong; sometimes it seems like every day brings new dismay, and Jim knows these things. Modern nature writing has no option but to grapple with the breakdown of natural systems, with the declines and climate crises we are causing and witnessing. We cannot go to nature merely to "escape", because the worst of our problems are unfolding in the seas and woodlands, among the insects and birds.

And yet, and yet … as Jim constantly reminds us, the natural world is still there, right there, still astonishing. Planet Earth is still as beautiful as it is broken, and we have it in us to fix it. What must we do? "Listen to the land."

KATHLEEN JAMIE

Introduction

A Moment of Beauty

THIS BOOK WAS CONCEIVED in a moment of beauty. There had been a few fiery autumn days on Skye, then the reluctant drive back. Return journeys from Skye are always reluctant. There was a bend in the road above Loch Garry.

Between the outside of the bend and the loch shore was a stand of aspen trees, gold on gold, shaded by Scots pines but gilded and back-lit by sunlight that bounced off the surface of the loch below. A gasp from the driver.

A layby 200 yards further on, stop the car, find notebook a pen, write this: "Twice-gilded aspens, Loch Garry, a book about autumn." Drive on. That was the moment.

True, it lay in the notebook unexploited for a year or three, but in that time it was photosynthesising, as befits a book about autumn. I would come across it from time to time when I was looking for something else, and then I might linger over it for an hour. Always, I thought it was still a good idea. Eventually, the right time and the right space coincided and it put up a green shoot into the daylight, felt sunlight, bore trunk, limbs, branches, foliage and fruit.

The resultant book became *The Nature of Autumn* which in turn became the first of a quartet of books, for it was followed by *The Nature of Winter/Spring/Summer*, four books in five years, an endeavour that – crucially – came to feel like a single piece of work. This book is the final phase of the evolution of that moment above Loch Garry, a reworking of those four books into one, a final harvesting, and that too befits its autumn roots.

These are also Scottish roots, for Scotland is my country where I have lived all my life and where I go to work, and Scotland colours and informs much of this book. But Scots were always an outgoing, internationalist tribe, and in these pages you will also find tidings of nature from the Lofoten Islands of Arctic Norway, narwhals in the Arctic Ocean (and mysteriously on a Trossachs skyline), an Icelandic glacier that died, the largest glacier in Greenland in a kind of gruesome tailspin towards oblivion, a fracturing Antarctic ice shelf that has the capacity to drown the low-lying shores of much of the southern ocean; oh, and I tiptoed over the border to lovely Lindisfarne.

Re-reading all four books in the cause of producing this edition, the ghosts of climate chaos, global warming and nature in crisis lurked in all their shadows, a troubling presence in the wings that would occasionally shoulder everything else aside and declaim from centre stage.

Its essential message is that the well-being of the global economy is a piddling endeavour alongside the well-being of the globe itself. The colossal scope of human energy and our wealth, down to the last pound note and euro and dollar bill, is needed by the planet itself, to restore its health, its biodiversity, its fully-functioning ecosystem, its forests, its wetlands, and to heal and cleanse its oceans. Achieve that and the Earth will modify its increasingly turbulent temperament of storms and restore to nature the rhythm of seasons. Life for the people will also transform, for the better. We will never make a more profitable investment.

Fail to achieve that while we pursue instead relentless economic growth at the expense of fast-depleting natural resources, and our days on the face of the Earth are numbered. So, our task is to find the means, not just of survival, but of a quality of survival – not just for our own species, but for all nature. As a mission, it is so much more important than anything else you can name, because the health of the planet is a definition of life itself.

The planet is broken. Our species – yours and mine – has broken it. But we are, as yet, in the fortunate position of knowing what is wrong and how to fix it. And as we apply ourselves to the task, we do well to remember this: Planet Earth is still as beautiful as it is broken. Hugh MacDiarmid's "Bonnie Broukit Bairn" is still as bonnie as it is broukit. There is still wonder as well as storm. The aurora still shines and shimmers, rainbows have not lost the art of the arch. Deep in December, great oaks still confound the calendar by clinging on to much of their foliage. The wingsong of mute swans in flight still resounds and beats out the wild pulse of nature, and the grimmest of January days is still transformed by the display flight of golden eagles and the winter anthem of mating foxes. The miracle of migration in all its forms still recurs. Skylarks still sing. The moon still rises and commands the tide to ebb and flow, the sun still sets and ignites the west. Mountains still stand upside down in still waters. Rivers still beckon to streams, waterfalls still whiten, firths still widen to the sea and beckon to dolphins, to whales. Seal song has not lost its power to enchant and still turns the heads of storytellers. Snowdrops still fend off winter and daffodils still gather in spring hosts to disturb poets. Summer bog myrtle still smells like the nectar of the gods. Autumn aspens can still seduce a passing nature writer.

And the howl of a wolf pack still commands our heads and hearts to look inward and examine the wildness that remains within, the still-functioning animal instinct that shaped our species; and to look outward and reappraise and tend thoughtfully towards wildness and beauty. It is nature's summons, it asks us to be aware, to take heed. It says to us: "Listen to the land."

That sequence of four words recurs more often than any other in these pages. Listen to the land. For thousands of years, humankind has attributed wisdom and knowledge and elements of spirituality to non-human creatures and to the land itself. Without necessarily advocating a return to placing our gods on mountaintops (although if you must have a god in your life, it's not the worst idea), I still think there is a lot to be said for American architect Frank Lloyd Wright's response to a question about whether he believed in God. Yes, he said, he did believe in a God, then added, "but I spell it Nature". The crucial disconnect of these early decades of the twenty-first century is that between nature and ourselves. Our behaviour confirms an unavoidable truth: we are thirled to a belief that we are somehow other than nature, beyond nature, even better than nature, that we have the omnipotent right to control nature. Therein lies the fault-line. As it fissures, fractures, widens and deepens, it threatens all nature, including ourselves, and the well-being of the Earth.

Perhaps it is still possible to heal the fault line, to step back from the abyss, and perhaps the way to begin is to try and relearn the lost art of listening to the land. And by healing the fault-line, perhaps it is also possible to heal our beautiful, broken Earth and ourselves.

It is not a new idea. One of its most thoughtful articulations came from American nature writer Barry Lopez in *Arctic Dreams* (Scribner, 1986). He was briefly in the company of a drilling crew "far out on the sea ice north of Melville Island in the High Arctic". He was astonished by the sudden appearance of a seal which surfaced in "a moon pool, the open water directly underneath the drilling platform that lets the drill string pass through the ice on its way to the ocean floor". Man and seal looked at each other in complete stillness until his parka hood moved slightly and the seal "was gone in an explosion of water".

Then there was this: "To contemplate what people are doing out here and ignore the universe of the seal, to consider human quest and plight and not know the land, I thought, to not listen to it, seemed fatal. Not perhaps for tomorrow, or next year, but fatal if you looked down the long road of our determined evolution and wondered at the considerations that had got us this far."

That long road is now staring its journey's end in the face.

Rachel Carson wrote in *Silent Spring* (Houghton Mifflin, 1962) that "Man is part of nature, and his war against nature is inevitably a war against himself." Two years earlier, Gavin Maxwell wrote in *Ring of Bright Water* (Longmans, 1960) that "Man has suffered in his separation from the soil and the other living creatures of the world; the evolution of his intellect has outrun his needs as an animal..."

And more than a hundred years before that, there was this: "We need the tonic of wildness – to wade sometimes in marshes where the bittern and the meadow-hen lurk...to smell the whispering sedge where...the mink crawls with its belly close to the ground. At the same time that we are earnest to explore and learn all things, we require that all things be mysterious and unexplorable, that land and sea be infinitely wild, unsurveyed and unfathomed by us because unfathomable. We can never have enough of nature..."

There it is. We can never have enough of nature. Henry David Thoreau knew that when he wrote it in *Walden* in 1854. So, we can hardly protest now with conviction that we didn't know what we were doing, that we didn't know there would be consequences.

*

Because I am among those who can never have enough of nature, because I am among those who need the tonic of wildness, I was sitting on a rocky edge of the North Sea on a December afternoon three days before the winter solstice of 2021. "Cold" is the polite word. Unusually for me when I am watching wildlife, I had company – my friend Leo du Feu, landscape and wildlife painter, who lives just down the coast, and near enough to have brought Christmas cake. We were whale-watching. Leo sketched. I just watched, thinking how I might write it.

Somewhere out there, between Fife's northmost outer edge of the Firth of Forth and the Bass Rock about thirty southward miles away across the firth and just off the East Lothian shore, there was a humpback whale. One or two turn up most years in January. This one was early. When you settle and study that immense tract of firth and open sea, it looks a forlorn hope, but there is a whale-watching network your phone can tap into for news of latest sightings, and the willingness to share is somehow touching. Given my long habituation to solitary fieldwork, this was rocket science technology made suddenly relevant by whales, and Leo was plugged into it. We talked too much at first, exchanged pleasantries and information with a handful of others who were there for the same reason, then we found our own watching spot and permitted the necessary stillness to unfurl. Time stalled.

Then there was a familiar face on the path, a smiled greeting: Kathleen Jamie, Scotland's Makar – our national poet – and furthermore, a writer of intensely thought-provoking nature essays, and, as it happens, a friend; and a friend of whales. She joined us for a while. It was a pleasure to introduce the poet to the painter.

Then the first blow. A voice called out: "Just left of the green buoy!"

The sharing thing again. So, you drew a bead on the green buoy and hunted left from there with the binoculars. On the surface, a dark curve that looked black. The curve wore a crown, a small, backward-leaning pointed curve, the dorsal fin of a humpback whale. Then…nothing at all.

But it had begun again. My addiction to whales – and humpbacks, in particular – that began in Glacier Bay, Alaska in 1998, had just laid claim to me again. Over the next two hours the whale showed again and again and came closer and closer to our shore. And between sightings there were long-tailed ducks for entertainment, sleek black and white and grey birds from north of the Arctic Circle whiling away their winters around our coasts, the male with an exotically long black tail that looks more tropical than Arctic. And densely packed swimming clouds of eiders.

The whale blew yet again, then materialised as a long black log and just lay there on the surface, and I started willing it to lift a pectoral fin (anything up to fifteen feet long on a humpback) and "wave", but then it dived, and the sublimely sculpted wedge of the tail folded in last and with a quite enormous dollop of grace and we all muttered things like "ah" or "nice" or "beautiful" or "perfect". I wonder at moments like that if a whale picks up any of the admiring vibes and compliments (for water is such an efficient conveyor of sound over distance and a humpback whale knows that better than anything else alive), and if it does, does it recognise them as the voice of the same creature that terrorised the whale tribe for centuries with harpoons?

My favourite whale book is *Among Whales*, by Roger Payne (Scribner, 1995). He wrote:

Whales and humans seem to have an interesting kind of bond – call it a bond of mutual curiosity – which appears to form automatically and surprisingly often when whales and people find themselves face to face. This bond also seems to occur when people hear the songs of whales for the first time.

It is as though our two mammalian brains have more in common than we are aware of and that we really may have significant things to

say to each other…if only we could find a communication channel…
Meanwhile, we are signaling to each other with every gesture, every
sound, every hint of what may someday qualify as meaningful communication but for which meanings are not yet known.

There is an essay in Kathleen Jamie's book *Sightlines* (Sort Of Books,
2012) called "The Hvalsalen", which is about a visit to the Bergen
Natural History Museum in Norway. *Hvalsalen* means "Whale Hall".
It is a huge space more or less crammed with whale skeletons. "Whales
like sardines," she observed. The gist of a passage from that essay came
back to me while we talked on the Fife coast waiting for the humpback
to grace us with its company. That evening, I would take the book
down from my shelves and refresh my memory:

> *…But despite the weight of the bones, the effect of the Hvalsalen
> was dreamlike. The vast structures didn't seem to offer any
> reproach. Rather, they drew you in. Undisturbed for a century,
> they had colluded to create a place of silence and memory. A vast
> statement of fact: "Whales is what we were. This is what we are.
> Spend a little time here and you too feel how it is to be a huge
> mammal of the seas, to require the sea to hold you, to grow so big
> at the ocean's hospitality."*

Whales and humans had a common ancestor sixty-five million
years ago. It may be that we do still have things to say to each other.
Race memory is a thing of incredible endurance. Back on the edge of
the North Sea, the Bass Rock grew yellow then smoky gold in the setting sun, though by then the sun itself was lost to us somewhere under
the horizon. And at that moment I remembered the backlit aspens
of Glengarry, for they too were the reflection of the sun that lit them
from below and beyond. It is the beauty of the Earth that makes it
worth fighting for. Truly, we can never have enough of nature.

Part One

AUTUMN

One

A Child of Autumn

I WAS BORN IN MIDSUMMER, but I am a child of autumn. One September day in the fourth or fifth autumn of my life there occurred the event that provided my earliest memory, and – it is not too extravagant a claim – set my life on a path that it follows still. I was standing in the garden of my parents' prefab in what was then the last street in town on the western edge of Dundee. An undulating wave of farmland that sprawled southwards towards Dundee from the Sidlaw Hills was turned aside when it washed up against the far side of the road from the prefab, whence it slithered away south-west on a steepening downhill course until it was finally stopped in its tracks by the two-miles-wide, sun-silvered girth of the Firth of Tay at Invergowrie Bay. Then as now, the bay was an autumn-and-winter roost for migrating pink-footed geese from Iceland; then as now, one of their routes to and from the feeding grounds amid the fields of Angus lay directly over the prefab roof.

I can remember what I was wearing: a grey coat with a dark blue collar and buttons and a dark blue cap. So we were probably going out somewhere.

Why am I so sure it was September and not any other month of autumn or winter or early spring? Because it was the first time, and because for the rest of that autumn and winter and early spring, and ever since, the sound of geese over the house – any house – has sent me running to the window or the garden. So was established my first and most enduring ritual of obeisance in thrall to nature's cause. And so I am as sure as I can be that the very first time was also the first flight of geese over the house after their return from Iceland that September; that September when I looked up at the sound of wild geese overhead and – also for the first time – made sense of the orderly vee-shapes of their flight as they rose above the slope of the fields, the slope of our street, up into the morning sunshine; vee-shapes that evolved subtly into new vee-shapes, wider or longer and narrower, or splintered into smaller vee-shapes or miraculously reassembled their casual choreography into one huge vee-shape the whole width of childhood's sky.

But then there were other voices behind me and I turned towards them to discover that all the way back down the sky towards the river and as far as I could see, there were more and more and more geese, and they kept on coming and coming and coming. The sound of them grew and grew and grew and became tidal, waves of birds like a sea, but a sea where the sky should be, and some geese came so low overhead that their wingbeats were as a rhythmic undertow to their waves of voices, and that too was like the sea.

When they had gone, when the last of them had arrowed away north-east and left the dying embers of the their voices trailing behind them on the air, a wavering diminuendo that fell into an eerie quiet, I felt the first tug of a life-force that I now know to be the pull of the northern places of the earth. And in that silence I stepped beyond the reach of my first few summers and I became a child of autumn.

And ever since, every overhead skein of wild geese – *every* one – harks me back to that old September, and I effortlessly reinhabit the body and mindset of that moment of childhood wonder. Nothing else, nothing at all, has that effect. I had a blessed childhood, the legacy of which is replete with good memories, but not one of them can still reach so deep within me as the first of all of them, and now, its potency only strengthens.

It would have been about thirty years ago that I first became aware of the Angus poet Violet Jacob, and in particular of her poem, *The Wild Geese*. It acquired a wider audience through the singing of folk-singer Jim Reid, who set it to music, retitled it *Norlan' Wind*, and included it on an album called *I Saw the Wild Geese Flee*. I used to do a bit of folk singing and I thought that if ever a song was made for someone like me to sing it was that one, but I had trouble with it from the start. My voice would crack by the time I was in the third verse, and the lyrics of the last verse would prick my eyes from the inside.

The last time I sang it was the time I couldn't finish it.

Years later, I heard the godfather of Scottish folk singing, Archie Fisher, talking about a song he often sang called *The Wounded Whale*, and how he had to teach himself to sing it "on automatic pilot", otherwise it got the better of him, but I never learned that trick. Even copying out the words now with Violet Jacob's own idiosyncratic spelling, I took a deep breath before the start of the last verse, which is the point where the North Wind turns the tables on the Poet in their two-way conversation:

THE WILD GEESE

"Oh tell me what was on your road, ye roarin' norlan' Wind,
As ye cam' blawin' frae the land that's niver frae my mind?
My feet they traivel England, but I'm deein' for the north."
"My man, I heard the siller tides rin up the Firth o' Forth."

"Aye, Wind, I ken them weel eneuch, and fine they fa' and rise,
And fain I'd feel the creepin' mist on yonder shore that lies,
But tell me, as ye passed them by, what saw ye on the way?"
"My man, I rocked the rovin' gulls that sail abune the Tay."

"But saw ye naethin', leein' Wind, afore ye cam' to Fife?
There's muckle lyin' 'yont the Tay that's dear to me nor life."
"My man, I swept the Angus braes ye hae'na trod for years."
"O Wind, forgi'e a hameless loon that canna see for tears!"

"And far abune the Angus straths, I saw the wild geese flee,
A lang, lang skein o' beatin' wings wi' their heids towards the sea,
And aye their cryin' voices trailed ahint them on the air –"
"O Wind, hae maircy, hud yer whisht, for I daurna listen mair!"

★

It is the 31st of August, 2015, and the weatherman on the BBC News Channel has just said:

"Tomorrow is the beginning of Meteorological Autumn."

I am unprepared for this news. I have never heard of Meteorological Autumn. I was unaware until this moment that it occurs in the calendar every year, like Lent or National Chip Week. I am wondering whether or not to believe the weatherman. After all, he is often wrong about the weather. I consult the window without moving. There *are* yellow leaves on the one birch tree I can see, and is it my imagination or are there more of them than there were at this time last year? It has been a rubbish summer and maybe that encourages the leaves to do their autumn thing early? Or maybe he's right, and maybe I should begin my autumn tomorrow just as he is obviously beginning his?

A book about autumn has been photosynthesising in my brain for a few years, painstakingly metamorphosing at its own speed, changing shape, changing colour, drinking in moisture from the air around itself, the way it has always seemed to me that a book about autumn should. Why autumn? Because it is my preferred season of the year, my preferred portion of nature's scheme of things, nature's state of grace. Because autumn, in my mind, is a tapped kaleidoscope, a shifting sorcery of shapes and shades, a revitalising of the wild year after the too-long dirge of late summer, a maker of daring moods. Because if a human life can be represented by the poets and the songwriters as a year, and I am in the autumn of that year myself (it is undeniable), then what better time? And because now I have the BBC weatherman poking me in the ribs, and I had better not be late if autumn shows up tomorrow, the first of September, 2015.

Besides, autumn is a magic trick. Science will scoff at such a notion and confront you with the vocabulary of photosynthesis (the synthesis of organic chemical compounds from carbon dioxide using radiant energy, *especially* light; *specifically* the formation of carbohydrates in the chlorophyll-containing tissues of plants exposed to light – or, at least, so says my *Penguin English Dictionary*), which will include super-efficient evaporation, carotenoids, anthocyanins, decomposition of carbohydrates, oxidised tannins, soluble sugars, starches, cellulose, lignum and a complex exchange of gases. But science doesn't know what I know, and what I know is that autumn is a magic trick we call "leaf".

Two

Autumn Leaves

LEAVES MUST PRODUCE FOOD out of thin air, or else there is no tree. Luckily for nature and all of us, they are extraordinarily good at it. There is, for example, a stupendously beautiful oak tree at Ariundle, within the Sunart Oakwoods of coastal Argyll, that is perhaps eighty feet tall and of a still mightier girth of limbs. It is also an old acquaintance of mine. Consider first that the whole edifice is the work of its leaves, and that no leaf lives longer than six months. Then marvel at nature. Then believe in magic.

Leaves begin life tight-packed in a bud. In spring, they start to expand, then they start to draw the sap up through the tree.

How do they do that?

That is absolutely my favourite tree question. Because the answer is that no one knows. We can split the atom and fly to the moon and find water on Mars but we don't know how a leaf drags a tree up into the air. I find that profoundly reassuring.

The containing scales of the bud respond to the pressure from within and hinge backwards allowing the leaves within to open, at which point they go to work, which is food-shopping. Look again at the eighty-feet-high oak tree and take a wild guess at how many tons of timber it holds aloft in a crazy fan shape of idolatrous sun-worship. Almost all of it, perhaps as much as ninety-five per cent – the fabulous girth of the trunk and almost every bough, limb, branch, twig and twiglet – is nothing more than carbohydrates ensnared from the air by leaves. Before any one leaf is even half-grown, it has stored up more sustenance than it will need for the rest of its life, but it goes on food-shopping because that is what leaves are born to do, and it donates everything else throughout its life to the tree.

Photosynthesis insists that the action of sunlight on the leaf impregnates its water-filled vessels with chlorophyll (which, incidentally, is why leaves are green), a process that in turn exchanges hydrogen from the water with carbon and oxygen from the air. Photosynthesis needs a certain amount of evaporation to take place, but leaves are so super-efficient at evaporation that they deliver infinitely more than photosynthesis needs. As they lose water to the air they also draw it up through the tree, up through that trunk, through those boughs, limbs, branches, twigs and twiglets; they circulate sap all through the tree, they even draw water through the roots and out of the soil (dissolved soil minerals are the tree's other source of food). Trees consume unimaginable quantities of carbon dioxide. This is why planting unimaginable quantities of trees will save the planet. Carbon is the tree's primary food source, as well as the source of soluble sugars and starches that can be stored or converted to cellulose strengthened with lignin, which makes the thing we call wood, adding a ring to the girth of the trunk every year. This is why we can tell the age of a felled tree.

Then autumn kicks in, and all that stops. It stops because the leaf stops producing chlorophyll, with the immediate result that the green starts to fade. If you make a study of turning leaves on an autumn tree, you will see that the green survives longest in the veins. Green is replaced by a yellow pigment called carotenoid, or a red one called anthocyanin, or both, (and often it is noticeable how the sunniest parts of the tree change colour first and those in deeper shade linger greener for longer). When the yellows and the reds and the indeterminate pinks and oranges have had their fling, decomposed carbohydrates and oxidised tannins turn autumn leaves brown. In a tranquil and all-but-windless early autumn like 2015, huge clusters of leaves turned brown on the tree, and they would come away in your hand in their dozens and flutter uselessly at your feet, their show over, their race run. Or so you might think.

But I am getting ahead of myself. The TV weatherman has told me that tomorrow is the first day of Meteorological Autumn, and I, with a book about autumn to write, don't want to miss it, just in case he's right. So I went out into one of my friendly neighbourhood oakwoods, and although it was still as green as it was on the last day of summer, there on the ground were my first two brown leaves, except that one still had a single green lobe and the other one was still half yellow. I picked them up and took them home, where I write on an oak table. Both were a lighter shade of brown than the table. It took seven weeks for the yellow half to fade to brown completely, although it is still paler brown than the rest of the leaf, and there is still the faintest green discolouration on the other leaf. Both are beside me as I write and both are now darker than the table. They have curled up at the edges, but rather than become friable, as I had imagined they would, they are waxy and tough. They were joined a couple of weeks later by a tiny vee-shaped twig, two inches long with one green acorn still lodged in its cup and two empty acorn cups; and on the table the acorn soon fell out and also turned brown. And these have become emblematic of the endeavour, emblematic of the magic trick. The acorn is the length of my thumbnail and half as wide, yet it has an eighty-feet oak tree inside it. When this book is written, I will plant it somewhere it can fulfil its potential.

There is a second magic trick to the Ariundle oak. As its leaves thin at the height of autumn and dance to boisterous, salty onshore winds, the inner tracery of branches and twigs hidden away since early spring begins to reappear, and the sky beyond the tree begins to re-emerge as fragments wedged between the branches and twigs, as thousands of shards a dozen shades of blue, grey, white, sunrise red and sunset purple. Here, in such a tree was surely the genesis of stained glass, and the teeming tracery, black against the sky, became the black lead of stained glass windows. The oak tree in question stands on a hillside so that you can look up into it from below the level of its roots, a viewpoint from which the analogy of great cathedral east windows is irresistible.

The forest is like a cathedral. How often have nature poets reached for that too-ready metaphor, too-ready and wrong? Wrong because the reality is the other way round – the cathedral nave is like the forest. How long ago did a stonemason with a visionary cast to his trade walk home with his tools on his shoulder through a grove of tall, straight trunks, and, looking up, see in his mind's eye not trees but columns of stone?

And how long thereafter did he, or another in another town or another land, stop before an oak tree like this giant of Ariundle with late autumn tints among the thinning leaves, a thousand patches of sky ensnared among the branches, and shafts of sunlight prodding apart the canopy, so that he fell to his knees and dared to give voice to his vision: "Stained glass!"

It was an idea that would travel the world. Chartres, Cologne, Kirkwall, Washington, Amsterdam, Salisbury, Edinburgh, Durham, York. And in 1960s Coventry the whole idea was spectacularly reinvented by Basil Spence and Graham Sutherland as tapestry.

With all this swilling in the nature writer's mind as I wrote it down at my oak table with the leaves and acorn and the three empty acorn cups, the miracle – the magic – of the whole improbably, blindingly astounding process lit up the whole room. The stonemason who turned trees into columns of stone believed, so did the stained glass artist. The cathedral is like the autumn forest.

*

The first day of autumn exhales with a berry-breath and all nature catches the scent. It is always the air that announces the change. It sharpens, cools and gently startles. It smells of hedgehogs. The light yellows, a pale yellow that will deepen as the season settles into its stride. Yesterday was not like this. Yesterday was the last rites of summer – old, done, defeated, frayed-at-the-edges, holed below the waterline summer. Good riddance.

And the first day of autumn is the beginning of everything, the first stirrings of rebirth. The forest fall (it is better named in America than on this side of the Atlantic) thickens the land with limitless tons of bits and pieces of trees. The earth is hungry for these, for they break down into food: all spring, all summer, it has been thrusting life upwards and outwards, and by the last day of summer, it is tired. Autumn is the earth's reviver and replenisher, the first day of autumn is the new beginning of everything and the last day of autumn is the beginning of next spring. Autumn is the indispensable fulcrum of nature's year.

So I was summoned by the oakwoods, for oakwoods are the first theatre of autumn. The oaks at Woodland Trust Scotland's Glen Finglas reserve in the Trossachs are steeply clustered along the lower slopes of hills that reach 2,000 feet. It was there that I chose to go to test the weatherman's theory, my first destination on what would become a long and more or less non-stop journey through autumn.

Infant trees were all around: ankle-high rowans (new-minted greens and cracked rust and every photosynthetic shade in between -- autumn is a madcap, haphazard season in the undergrowth), knee-high hollies (friend of wren and ladybird) rooted in fat, lime-green blancmanges of moss that clustered around shady oak roots, birch saplings (thousands and thousands of these – a birchwood is nature's default position here-abouts) whose crowns narrowed the path and rubbed my shoulders and whose leaves were as golden as they were green. In the midst of so much burgeoning infant life, an eight-feet-high, limbless, headless and all-but-dead-on-its-feet sycamore torso still stood, still summoned the paltry life force that thrusts spindly twigs directly sideways without the intervention of branches; these twitched right in front of my eyes in a hidden and shadowed bend in the path and they wore a thin coat of leaves – washed-out and yellow, and freckled with black and brown, and fragile, the last gesture of a last gesture. The wind shivered among them for a moment and they danced fitfully to its soft, sad song. However long autumn allowed them (and it would not be many days now), theirs had been a dance in a beautiful coat.

A tree fifty yards ahead, partially obscured by a dozen others and their networks and clusters of branches and leaves, just moved in an eye-catching, instinct-rousing way. Eye and instinct fused to form my indispensable life-support system, my all-season-all-weather shadow. I never go out without it and it is forever muttering in my ear. What it had just told me was that the movement in question was not the tree itself, but rather something *of* the tree. It had come to rest and it was hidden, and it would have to move again – or I would – to reveal its meaning. But stillness is the most useful tool of my trade, and I knew that what-ever just moved was on the move and I was not, so I told myself, "It *will* move first" and that in moving it would justify my strategy and answer – or fail to answer – the unarticulated question in my head.

Wait.
Watch.
Listen.
Learn.

*

I had seen nothing arrive, nothing that flew in or ran up the trunk, but that does not mean that nothing flew in or that nothing ran up the trunk, it just means that I didn't see it arrive. And there is always the possibility, of course, that it was there all the time and there had been no arrival for me to see. But it was there now, however it may have arrived, and its movement had an effect on the tree and *that* was what caught my eye and roused my instinct.

A stand-off like this, if it is not resolved quickly, creates a kind of tension that stems from simultaneously knowing and not knowing. I know that something moved and that oak leaves rippled outwards and downwards in response. I do not know what moved and I do not know if whatever-it-was knows I am here and, if so, whether it is troubled by my presence. Instinct says no, it does not know and is not troubled, and therefore its subsequent stillness is relaxed, rather than a stillness that is terrified to move.

And then it moved.

And then it laughed.

It appeared from behind the tree's trunk no more than a yard off the ground and in that tree's shade, but almost at once it burst into sunlight. Precisely at that moment something odd occurred, and I began to see it with a quite startling clarity and apparently in slow motion. It was as if the perceptive resources of all my senses were simultaneously heightened and I had acquired the power to control the pace of events as they unfolded. I cannot explain the circumstances any better than that, although, occasionally, I have been the subject of such a visitation before, or at least of something similar. Each time I have been alone, each time I have been prompted by instinct into an awareness of something about to happen, and each time (I have used the analogy before and have found no better way of expressing it) I have felt as if nature was tapping me on the shoulder with an implicit instruction: "Watch this."

So I had stilled myself in response to the rippling oak leaves and waited, and waited, and then it moved and then laughed and then it appeared much lower than I had expected, and then it flew from shadow into sunlight, and then it inexplicably slowed down. In this new state of heightened awareness I saw its head crane sideways with a twist of its neck and almost at right angles so that it looked directly down the line of the path in my direction. I saw one wing-tip dip, the other rise then the whole sun-glittered body of the creature fell into line-astern behind the new course of the head and neck and every vivid and clearly defined colour swayed into place – raven black, maple-leaf scarlet, snow-bunting white, larch green, aspen yellow, oak-bark brown. The green woodpecker is a living emblem of early autumn, a fusion of all the shades of photosynthesis with added black and white details, a pop-art, yah-boo, guffawing mocker of the oakwood canopy and the airspaces between the trees.

It began to fly down the path towards me and no more than a yard above the ground, but because I was downhill a bit, it flew exactly at my eye level, even as the path fell away below it. It also flew with that jaunty, bouncing gait of all the woodpecker tribe, from the sparrow-sized lesser-spotted to the crow-sized black woodpecker of Norwegian pinewoods, and I became conscious of my own head nodding in time to the rhythmic fluctuations of altitude and attitude as it rose and fell a few inches with every flap and glide. The overall effect was one of level flight but, in truth, not a single yard of it was level.

At that stage in its flight, there was nothing to indicate that the woodpecker had distinguished my tree-coloured shape from among the many trees massed at my back and to my left and right. Then the head craned left again, that same twist of the neck, the same re-alignment of body to neck as the bird turned again at right angles, a sudden down-thrust of wings and the bird tilted abruptly back-wards and in an attitude more vertical than horizontal, rose into tree shadows again, wings working like a giant, ungainly humming-bird. It perched vertically against the trunk of a rowan well laden with berries. I might have assumed that this was simply a speculative kind of perch from which to re-evaluate the day and the wood and the possibilities of the next meal, which in the green woodpecker's world usually means ants. I *might* have made that assumption were it not for the fact that suddenly I was aware of recent history repeating itself, because ten months before and no more than a quarter of a mile away, something happened that introduced me to this jazzy bird's taste for improvisation.

★

That old November day from last autumn had been playing at volcanoes up on the mountain, lathering its flanks with mist that lolled and rolled and tumbled unpredictably at the whim of a lazy wind. The sun was lazier still, and by mid-afternoon the day was going headlong downhill and sunless and ever deeper into the greyest grasp of deepest November. Meanwhile, as befits volcanic inconvenience, all air traffic was grounded. I had seen one robin in a bramble bush and a hunched pair of bullfinches with their backs to me, which is not a lot to show for two hours of walking in country this wild.

So I crossed the glen's lower-lying and more open side, climbed a short slope through oak trees cluttered with clusters of old foliage the colour of cold tea, much of which will cling on right through the winter. (Why do oaks do that? And why do only some of them do that?) The mist was thinner beyond the trees from where, on any day when views are possible, there is a wide prospect of Trossachs hills. Holes appeared in this thinning veil, through which I could see back across the glen to the mountain mist, so the view was of thin mist and thick mist.

Near the edge of the wood – and this is the point of this historical diversion – there is a fine rowan just where the trees give way to open ground of undulating rough pasture, so I stopped to look at it as I have done many, many times. Something of the day's lethargy had infiltrated my bones and spirit by this time, so I sat on a rock and decided to drink coffee while I looked at the rowan, and then I would go back. The rowan held a few old leaves, pale-yellowy-gold-mottled-with-brown by now, and also a surprising amount of berries, although these were dark and far past what a rowan-jelly-maker might call their best. But without them, what happened next simply would not have happened.

I scoured the tree and what little I could see of the open ground beyond with the binoculars, searching for something to focus on, some vagrant scrap of life to thwart the evil twins of cold and lethargy, which had taken the day by the throat.

But then I became aware in a vague sort of way that something seemed to have changed out on the grass a dozen yards or so beyond the rowan. Something small and low-down and, as yet, shapeless, and not obviously different in texture and tone from the rough pasture hillside, except that it seemed to be moving, furtively and head-down (much of the movement of the whatever-it-was was obscured by grass in clumps and tussocks and humps; I was rather assuming at this point that the thing would have a head). Then all discernible move-ment ceased, and I suspected a trick of the half-light. Then something galvanised, there was a flash of fire that seared through the lowest air-space just above the grass, then came straight towards me at eye level, then veered abruptly upwards and left into the rowan tree, where it perched vertically and metamorphosed into a green woodpecker.

"Flash of fire" is a better description by far than "green wood-pecker", and I wish I could claim that I and I alone had invented it. In fact, all I have done is to translate it – from Gaelic. *Lasair-choille* is the Gaelic name. *Coille* is simply a wood. *Lasair* is fire, flame, flash; in any combination that fits the context. In the context of that moment on that stone-grey hillside, a "flash of fire" was exactly what had just illuminated my stone-grey day. Besides, as I now know, if your green woodpecker arrows up from obscurity on the ground and comes at you at eye level, it is not a green bird at all that you see but a red and white one – red skull cap (and cheeks in the male) and white chest.

Meanwhile, up in the rowan tree, something stirred. Almost every bird book you ever saw will inform you with absolute certainty that all green woodpeckers eat is ants, that ants control every facet of their well-being or otherwise, especially ants like the ones that throng the top few inches of the earth beneath the grass of old, unimproved pas-ture, like that one beyond the rowan tree. If the ants prosper, so do the green woodpeckers. A dearth of ants is likewise a dearth of green woodpeckers. It's one of nature's fundamental principles; the well-being of predators is determined by the well-being of prey species. Bird books will also tell you that the green woodpecker is purpose-built to eat nothing but ants: a stabbing beak to open the earth in cone-shaped grooves; and a secret weapon, a cunningly stowed-away, four-inches-long tongue designed to unearth the ants in improbable numbers. The same technique also works in rotten trees where the woodpecker's huge feet allow it to perch vertically, and again, ants are the essential quarry. If the bird book happens to specialise in Scottish birds, it may add that the green woodpecker is open to occasional forays into the Speyside pinewoods, where catching ants around the waist-high anthills is its equivalent of shooting fish in a barrel. The book may not use those words, but that will be the gist. I have yet to see a field guide acknowledge the possibility of a non-ant diet. Yet this one at the far end of my binoculars was eating rowan berries. It also proved remarkably adept at the berry-picking, which suggested to me that it had done it before. Even out-on-a-limb, even out on the outermost edges of out-on-a-limb, the woodpecker negotiated the slenderest of twigs in a slow, sideways glissade to reach the berries at the end, perfectly poised, sure of itself and its technique, and clearly relishing the non-ants that clustered there, the fruits of its labours.

So as I watched I thought about this, about the why and the wherefore, and it took about half a minute of thinking to come to the following conclusion. The green woodpecker is accustomed to ground-feeding – for ants – but in the course of ground-feeding for ants all it has to do is to stray somewhere near a rowan tree in summer or autumn to find windblown bunches of downcast, eye-catching rowan berries in its path. One speculative stab of that expert beak yields the delightful taste of rowan berries, so it eats all the berries on the ground. It then turns its head sideways to look up (it is a great sideways-and-upwards turner of its head, and this, remember, is a bird that nests in trees, and therefore understands perfectly that berries and nuts and leaves lying on the ground mostly come from above, from trees). And there was the rowan tree, one grey, misted November day when the ants were few and far between, and there were enough berries to keep body and soul together, and it stands to reason that if the bird scavenged that fretwork of branches often enough, it would get very adept at it.

It is equally possible, I suppose, that the green woodpecker has watched its spotted cousins gather autumn stashes of pine cones by carrying them individually to an "anvil" rock where it thrashes them open, plucks the seeds and chucks away the cones. This the spotted woodpeckers do in the lean months when the oak trees are not as replete with ants as they are in the spring and summer. Might not the greens resort to the same food source for the same reason? I don't know because I have never seen it, and if the compilers of my bird books know, they're not saying.

But here's a thing: the Gaels distinguish between green and spotted woodpeckers not by their utterly different colour schemes but by their characteristic behaviour, the flash of flame for the green, but the great spotted woodpecker is *snagan-daraich*, the knocker on wood, and specifically on oak. They were good, were they not, the old Gaels, when it came to naming the creatures that shared their world? My favourite is the jay – *sgreuchag-choille*, the screamer of the woods, and I know from the luminous writing of my friend Jim Perrin that it has its mirror image in Welsh – *sgrech coed*. In that spirit the Gaels might just have come up with something like the giggler of the woods in honour of the green woodpecker, for its far-carrying, manic guffaw that sounds as if it might have escaped from a 1950s recording of *The Goon Show*. But luckily for me, the bird-namers came up with *lasair-choille*, and the flash of flame that briefly turned my day of stones into a day of diamonds.

*

So that was the history lesson I brought to bear on the green woodpecker as it angled up from the woodland path to a vertical clasp on the trunk of a shadowed rowan, where its cramponed feet bit into the bark and its rigid tail angled in to the trunk too, so that the stance was well belayed. The moment bound bird and me together in our two stillnesses about twenty yards apart. The bird's stillness amid tree shadows was ill-suited to that heightened, mercurially slow-motion vision I had somehow contrived out of that brief flight from shadow into sunlight and back into shadow by way of two right-angled turns. Then my own stillness began to feel awkward itself, and that was more troubling. So often in my nature-writing years, a gift for stillness has been my saving grace and it had just handed me that small insight into the nuances of woodpecker flight, but without moving at all I felt the mood splinter and the woodland resumed its natural way of moving in normal time. I am aware that sometimes I try and immerse too deeply into nature's scheme of things and come up short. There are moments, especially in familiar landscapes, when I can see with the clarity of mountain spring water, moments of rarefied access to nature at work. It is tempting to contrive imaginary constructs to explain it away, but the only explanation I believe in is that because I have watched so much for so long, once in a while the quality of the watching rises above the norm on a buoyancy of accumulated experiences, and briefly achieves a kind of perfection. And because it is inevitably a momentary phenomenon, what follows immediately afterwards is – also inevitably – something of a letdown.

And yet almost nothing had changed. The light – the sacred light that graces autumn from its first stirring until prime October – had not changed from those few seconds when it chanced on the luminosity and the palette of the flier. No cloud troubled the sky, no alarm troubled the denizens of the woodland, no breeze nudged the oaks into silence-scarring whispers. But the flight's denouement was in shadows and that ended the privilege of the encounter, and I noticed at once that when the woodpecker's landing induced two slender rowan branches to quiver so that they discarded a dozen pale yellow ready-to-go leaves, these fell at the regular free-fall speed of all downcast autumn leaves.

Three
The Far East

DRIVING ACROSS THE TAY ROAD BRIDGE from Dundee, the low green hull of Fife's north-facing hills was noticeably patched with the tawny and faded yellow shades of standing crops and cut crops, and with newly ploughed fields the red-brown shades of fox. In other words, the entire palette of oakwood photosynthesis had been laid out like a colour chart on the face of the land itself – chlorophyll to carotenoid to anthocyanin and all their intermediate shades.

Like an Australian Aborigine tracing songlines across the ancestral homelands in search of the Dreamtime, I am helplessly addicted to a migratory route to Scotland's Far East, which threads the low-slung contours of east Perthshire or north Fife along the Firth of Tay to Dundee, and to a frontier of North Sea coast, from Auchmithie in the north to St Monans in the south, that resounds to the three-syllable poetry of kittiwakes and the baying of seals.

Of all the landscapes of my life, this is their common ancestor. Dundee is where I was born and grew up and for all that I have written about Scotland's Highlands and Islands (and I love them dearly), at rock bottom I am an east coast mainlander by birth and inclination and I belong to that cast of Scots who think the sun should rise over the sea, not set in it. I grew tall craning to see mountains in the north and the north-west, and it has long been a source of comfort to me that from the summit of Dundee's centrepiece hill (variously known as Dundee Law, the tautologous but widespread Law Hill, or the local vernacular's preference for The Lah), on the right kind of day, I can see Schiehallion, even as I inhale the salt-laden air on a wind off the sea.

The Tay would lure me west in time and my writing life eventually settled on a tract of Perthshire and Stirlingshire between the upper reaches of Tay and Forth. But all my life I have hankered after the sea, and from the mid-point of the country I have worn a groove from coast to coast between Dundee and Mull with such instinctive longing that surely I am a slave to some age-old, tribal, songline-like ritual. I have heard that, historically, the name Crum was a sept of the MacDonalds of Benderloch, which is Argyll coast opposite Mull, and I have traced my own branch of the Crumleys back to Donegal in the 1790s, whence a couple of them made their way to Dundee around 1840. In the Dundee enclave of Lochee they dug in for the next 120 years. Throughout the centuries-long sea-going heyday of Scotland's West Highland seaboard, Benderloch to Donegal was no distance at all, and the Benderloch MacDonalds thing is perfectly plausible. A consequence of all that is that whenever I weigh anchor and sally forth from the edge-of-the-Highlands heartland, and if my destination is one coast or the other, something of the air of pilgrimage attends the journey, although the nature of the pilgrimage varies radically depending on its direction.

A few days after the green woodpecker in Glen Finglas, and with the glowing gouache of its finery still undimmed in my mind, I travelled east along the north bank of the Tay in the lee of Errol's waving walls of reed beds, dawdling in their shadow because the road was narrow and empty and the whole day was at my command, and the wind in the reeds was a soft roar at my elbow as it leaned on the open car window. I drove into the emblematic sea-born sunrise that burnished the widening sea-going miles of the Tay beyond the reeds, and these were back-lit and topped with shades of flame. At that point, the river is a boulevard between reed-smothered banks, for these are the largest reed beds anywhere in Britain, and a very specialised micro-habitat all of their own with a unique wildlife community. Hefty, agile, vee-winged marsh harriers and furtive packs of bearded tits are the star attractions through spring and summer, but it is the reed beds themselves, their sheer quantity and extent and stature, that turn heads. They planted a momentary image in my mind of something exotically Middle Eastern that had me rummaging among half-remembered imagery from Gavin Maxwell's masterpiece wrought from the water-world of Iraq's Marsh Arabs, *A Reed Shaken by the Wind* (Longmans,

1957; Eland Publishing Ltd, 2003) Later that day, back among my own bookshelves, I would correct my careless remembrance with the real thing in my hands:

…we were moving through open blue lagoons fringed and islanded with giant golden reeds growing dense and twenty feet high. They were as ripe standing corn must appear to a mouse, huge and golden in the sun, with only a tiny fringe of new green growth in the blue water at their feet…the confining reed beds at the farther side looked like long yellow cliffs of sand…

I had a short meeting in Crail on the Fife coast that day, but either side of it the day was given over to a leisurely exploration of the first stirrings of a Lowland autumn. So I had edged slowly between the river and the flat fields of the Carse of Gowrie that sprawled away northwards to the feet of the first of all my hills, my forever-friends, the Sidlaws. At Dundee, I turned south across the Tay Road Bridge, and there was autumn at its far end. I turned east again to follow the river towards the coast. Estuary becomes open sea at Tentsmuir, a pinewood that wades into a fringe of sand dunes. These, in turn, relent into a vast sandy beach. Its outermost reaches are huge sandbanks internationally renowned as breeding grounds for both grey and common seals. The autumn seascape – and the waters of the estuary – had just begun to adjust to the arrival of vast numbers of waders and wildfowl, including densely packed rafts of eider ducks thousands strong. By midwinter, anything up to 20,000 will have gathered, an unforgettable and indelible presence. You never quite know what to expect when you step from the trees onto the dunes and thread a way through them and finally step out onto the open beach to confront the triple expanses of sand and open sea and open sky, arranged in immense horizontals: the tricolour of nature's national flag. I imagine someone like Mark Rothko confronting it for the first time and thinking to himself:

"No, I need bigger canvasses. Much, much bigger canvasses." And when he got them he filled them with immense horizontals. As far as I know, he was never here, but he was one of the New York School so he had the western Atlantic seaboard at his disposal, so who knows? Besides, he was famously reluctant to explain the motivation behind his huge abstracts. A retrospective of his work at the National Gallery of Art in Washington offered this perspective, which corresponds (albeit in slightly more academic terms than I could muster) with what happens to me when I step out onto Tentsmuir beach:

> *Alternately radiant and dark, Rothko's art is distinguished by a rare degree of sustained concentration on pure pictorial properties such as colour, surface, proportion, and scale, accompanied by the conviction that those elements could disclose the presence of a high philosophical truth. Visual elements such as luminosity, darkness, broad space, and the contrast of colours, have been linked...to profound themes such as tragedy, ecstasy, and the sublime...*

I stepped from dunes onto beach and raw space came at me in waves, an almost physical force whose ingredients were as Rothko intended, "colour, surface, proportion, and scale". It is not just the sunrise that distinguishes east coast beaches from those on the west coast, there is also the conspicuous absence of islands. The sense of proportion and scale is overwhelmingly intensified by the absence of a focal point. The pale tawny sand runs away from you across immense distance to south and north. At low tide the sea is far, far out and barely audible. The sand darkens by degrees as it marches eastward towards the rippling line of surf. The sea in the morning is pale and electrified by sunlight. There is almost too much light. I decided to walk out to the edge of the sea and head north to look for seals, knowing that if I did that, and whether I saw seals or not, all kinds of other things would cross my path. I knew that, because they always do.

The approach to the forest from the landward side had felt benevolent and warm, still suffused with souvenirs of old summer. Out on the edge of the land there was a surprising wind blowing up and a surprisingly big sea running, an energising intoxication. It occurs to me again and again as I travel the length and breadth of my own country how eagerly I respond to edges – island shores, the edge of the Highlands, the edge of the land – a sense I first became aware of right here. This is my source country, and so much of this nature-writing life, which has taken me to Alaska and back, has its identifiable origins within the force field of the Tay estuary. The debt I owe to my upbringing and its landscape is eternal and unrepayable.

I found seals much sooner than I had expected. Or, rather, I found one seal.

There was a single grey seal bull out on the water, his blunt head and his ruff of chins a kind of marker buoy, indicating the hazard to shipping posed by the better part of one thousand pounds of flesh and blubber and muscle slung beneath him, beneath the waves, a living iceberg of trouble. He stared directly at me across fifty yards of wavetops, his eyes a mask behind which he concealed one of the more bizarre relationships with which we bespatter our dealings with nature. Celtic and Norse storytelling is awash with selkies and sirens who cast their sealskins to come ashore as beautiful women and fall for a young man who steals her sealskin, locks it away somewhere safe and traps her ashore, marries her, and they live happily enough until the day she finds the hidden sealskin and returns with it to the sea, leaving bereft husband and children behind; or else they pose on rocks as women and so enrapture helpless sailors that they are lured to their doom.

But the biological reality is *that* out there, that preposterous hunk of seal meat afloat off the Tentsmuir coast, that is what really lights the fire of a grey seal cow, and autumn is their spectacular – and often vicious – mating season. The apparently benign bull, scratching all his chins at once as he gives me his most appraising stare, will become, literally, monstrous in defence of his chosen battlefield and his chosen harem. A fight between two half-crazy bulls turns the surf red with shed blood; their bellowing voices laced with equal parts of fury and pain can momentarily drown out the sound of the surf itself. The victor and vanquished blunder ashore to try and impress the cows, and to lick their many wounds. It is all a ferocious output of energy, so recklessly discharged that newly born pups are often crushed to death in the chaos.

Nothing much of grey seal mating makes much sense to human eyes, and perhaps that in itself explains why, hundreds of years ago, we felt the need to reconcile our response to the admittedly alluring song of the grey seal by concocting the selkie-siren mythology. George Mackay Brown was still working magical new variations on the ancient theme into his stories and poetry in the 1990s, and Perthshire author Linda Cracknell reinvented the genre in her 2014 novel, *The Call of the Undertow*.

A particularly rare characteristic of Tentsmuir is that it accommodates both grey and common seals. The vast area of sand on the beach and sandbanks offers almost limitless scope, and the very different breeding patterns of the two species help to minimise conflict; not that it doesn't happen – it does – but the Tentsmuir situation works better than you might think, and it confounds the theories of many a guidebook writer. So growing up in nearby Dundee offered, among many other things, an early-years education of the whys and wherefores of the seal tribes. It was a long, long time after those early nature study lessons in primary school, or leaning over the railings of the "Fifies" (the long-extinct Tay ferries that plied between Dundee and Newport) to watch the seals basking on the banks or flirting with the bow wave, that I would learn just how much seal blood my home city had on its hands. People have killed seals forever and wherever in the world they have coincided. But the scale of the killing inflicted by 19th-century whaling fleets, including Dundee's, makes grim reading in the 21st century. Dundee eventually accommodated the biggest whaling fleet in Britain, but it was the whaling ships' secondary target of seals that helped the whaling companies to make ends meet. In one year alone – 1881 – the fifteen ships of the Dundee whaling fleet killed more than 150,000 seals on the whaling grounds of Greenland and Newfoundland. The total number throughout the whaling years was well into millions.

Times and attitudes change. By the time Frank Fraser Darling was researching the grey seal colonies on North Rona and the Treshnish Isles just before World War II, the tone of his writings was markedly different from much that had gone before.

"We had come to watch seals and were full of eagerness and joy when the great beasts began to collect about the place in increasing numbers," he wrote in *Island Years* (G. Bell & Sons, 1940; Little Toller,

2011). He wrote with undisguised affection for one colossal bull he called Old Tawny:

> *His personality soon became evident to us...what a magnificent head and proud bearing he had! Never since, either on the Treshnish or on North Rona, have I seen a bull seal to equal him in size or majesty.*
>
> *His movements ashore were delightful to watch – the way he would make himself comfortable on the rock and then the expressive movements of his forelimbs...you would see Old Tawny scratch his belly delicately with his fingernails, waft a fly from his nose, and then, half closing his hand, draw it down over his face and nose just as men often do. Then he would smooth his whiskers with the back of his hand, this side and that...You might see him scratch one palm with the fingers of the other hand, or close his fist and scratch the back of it. A seal's movements are often a most laughable travesty of humanity, but considered more carefully as seal movements, they have great beauty.*

The science of conservation has also taken up the seals' cause, and seal culls amid Scottish waters are mostly a thing of the past. And the educational aspect of National Nature Reserves preaches considerate behaviour towards the seals at Tentsmuir, signs that further symbolise the evolution of our attitudes towards nature. If you are a nature writer born and brought up in a city that once flourished its whaling credentials all over the northern hemisphere, it's not before time.

*

The bull seal slid beneath the surface, and when I saw him again he was a hundred yards further out and easing north towards the seal sandbanks. The long beach and the nearest wave-tops were suddenly thronged with wader birds, and scanning the sea itself with binoculars revealed the autumn's first seriously large raft of eiders. The birds rose and fell through the crests and troughs of the waves, but every rising wave seemed to reveal more and more birds. Counting seabirds is the stuff of ornithological nightmares and I don't even try. But this kind of sudden appearance at the edge of the sea and the edge of the land is characteristic of the restlessness that besets much of the natural world as autumn's summons demands drastic changes of the established order of spring and summer. That awareness, and the unrelenting rituals and sounds of sea and sea winds (these were now making themselves heard among the pines), contributed to the sense of an un-still landscape, a place possessed by an organic restlessness as old as the Earth. Beneath that colossally arched tract of sky (and east coast skies are bigger than anywhere else's this side of Orkney), sea, sand and trees are forever realigning themselves, pushing against each other, testing each other out, reshaping themselves and each other. The effect of all that is of a landscape frontier constantly on the move, both unsettled and unsettling. I turned north and went to look for seals.

I found them out on the furthermost reaches of the fluctuating banks beyond Tentsmuir Point, several hundred greys but not a single common seal in sight. A lingering scrutiny with good binoculars offered an object lesson in colour-coding those seals biologists call "grey", for these ran through the spectrum from almost white to almost orange to as-near-to-black-as-makes-no-difference. There were only a handful of seals in the water. The mass of animals was at rest yet it was also restless. Heads rose and fell and turned to observe every compass point, jaws snapped at other seals and at nothing at all, flippers scratched and groomed, tails wafted or just arched up into the air and paused there with no obvious purpose or means of support. The individuals within the herd constantly changed place or readjusted the space around them, often with bickering, sometimes with biting, yet the collective will of the herd insisted on cramming as many seals as possible into as small a space as possible, safety in densely-packed numbers.

The big black-backed gulls were intrigued by the mass, although it was not clear to me why. They drifted against the wind, slowing almost to stalling speed within inches of the seals' upturned heads. The seals responded with upward lunges and snapping jaws, and the gulls responded in turn by rising a foot out of reach, then dropping again. I wondered if this was a game, a ritual enjoyed by both parties, but it still looked to my admittedly inexpert eyes as if the gulls infuriated the seals for the hell of it and without the possibility of profiting by it.

For the two hours I sat there the gulls maintained their tormenting presence the whole time, while dozens of turnstones ran in among the seals, apparently trying to find food on the seals' bodies. Fraser Darling had spotted the same thing more than sixty years ago, writing in *Island Years*:

> *Turnstones…remained in my memory as the little companions of the great seals. You would see a seal snap at a gull which might come near it, but the busy little turnstones ran among the seals lying on the rocks or high on the island, pecking morsels from the bodies of the great beasts themselves…*

It was good to have Fraser Darling's confirmation of something I had just noticed for the first time, but there was no explanation from him, and there is none from me, about why turnstones alone, of all the wader tribes that throng seal coasts like this one, have identified a seal colony as a source of food, and are tolerated by the seals at such intimately close quarters.

*

Fifty miles to the south, on a hidden cliff-girt, boulder-strewn Berwickshire beach one late-November a couple of autumns ago, a sodden gale was flaying the land with sheets of rain, a huge sea was running, and the noise where it head-butted that broken shore was fearful to human ears, fearsome to human eyes.

Yet it was precisely there in the fearful, fearsome midst of that headlong sea's landfall that the grey seals played.

Played?

Yes, I think so. They hauled themselves over shattered, angular and chaotically stacked rocks, but they turned in their own length and heaved into the sea where they were at once fluent and wonderfully agile. They stayed among the breakers and they stayed on the surface, which is not the way of a hunting seal, and they relished the shattering of huge waves, and apparently relished the roar in their ears. In the rarefied world of the grey seals, this is what passes for a nursery. This is where the females gave birth and suckled and taught their young to swim. Everywhere among the rocks there were pups. Most were alone, a few suckled, a handful seemed impossibly far-flung from the centre of that broken bay where the adults congregated. Some looked impossibly trapped, and the next time I checked on them they would be a dozen yards away or back in the water.

I was looking for a secure foothold among the highest rocks, a secluded refuge to settle in and watch the nursery at work, when I almost stood on a pup that was further out and higher up the beach than any I had seen. Its immediate response to my sudden arrival was to slide down the rock where it had been reclining, to push itself deeper into a natural cavity among the rocks. Then it turned its back so that instead of its white face I was presented with the grey shades of its back and the back of its head and neck, and at once, it was not a seal but another rock on a beach of rocks. I found a different place to settle and watch.

Several bulls waited for the females just offshore, for mating had begun within a few weeks of the pups being born. As they waited they sparred, and sometimes they sparred so vigorously that they fought, and when they fought the sea reddened around them. The females too were not slow to draw blood if a bull was too enthusiastic before they were ready to receive his enthusiasm. It is difficult to imagine a more untranquil theatre of nature than a grey seal nursery on such a shore and with such a sea running.

The pups grow strong and learn quickly (the ones that are not crushed to death by the mad heavyweight dance of the mating cows and bulls), for not to grow strong and not to learn is to die young. They are improbably young when they abandon the nursery and the adults leave them to their own devices, and they travel improbable distances. Some of these very pups will have travelled to Norway by next spring. You look at them, apparently helpless, you look at the brutal sea that awaits them, and you ask yourself two questions:

How?

Why?

The answers, of course, are known to every grey seal that ever spilled from its mother's milk into such a shore and with such a sea running.

"Luminosity, darkness, broad space, and the contrast of colour have been linked to profound themes such as tragedy, ecstasy, and the sublime..." Whether the base of a Berwickshire cliff or the sand-sprawl of Tentsmuir or a hidden bay on a skerry-strewn shore of west Mull, the autumn sights and sounds of a colony of those seals we call the Atlantic grey live up to that assessment of Mark Rothko. But it is the Tentsmuir landscape that pays truest homage to his art.

*

Late lunch at Crail in the early September sun was based on one of my simplest of food philosophies. If you're going to eat seafood, eat it where they catch fish. At Crail's too-picturesque-for-its-own-good harbour (every Scottish calendar photographer since the dawn of photography has paused here, most more than once) there is a wee wooden shed that sells live lobsters and dead crab rolls. I sat on the harbour wall with a fresh coffee and a fresh crab roll, re-ran the morning in my head, and the uncharted months of autumn that lay ahead, and all was well in my world. Few things taste of the sea the way fresh crab does, and what with that and the salt air and the coffee and the sun on my face and a few still-lingering terns gatecrashing the sea a few yards offshore with all the style of an Olympic medallist and twice as much grace, and a headful of seals, I was in no hurry to go anywhere.

Ahead lay the inland drive back to the edge of the Highlands, the land-locked heartland of Scotland, and whenever I go to my native coast and have to drive back west again I start cross-examining my motives, and wondering why the hell I don't return to where I unquestionably belong. Still looking for answers.

*

Driving back among neat and gently contoured farms, I stopped to watch a ploughed field. The earth here is an exquisite shade of deep red-fox-red and the lowering afternoon sunlight ennobled the art of the ploughman, for it burnished the crests of the furrows and shadowed the depths. The fall of the earth from crest to shadow was briefly immortalised. I wondered what the ploughman Burns might have made of it. There is a Gaelic word for the swathe of earth turned by the plough – *sgrìobh* – but as far as I know Lowland Scots has no equivalent. I sense a missed opportunity, for there is no denying the artistry of the endeavours of a good ploughman when the soil he has to work with is as textured and toned as this. There should be a word that arose out of its own landscape to acclaim the result.

The ploughed earth had a further embellishment, for it was starred by hundreds of black-headed gulls that had just floated up from the sea and now waded the crests and troughs of these earthen waves and trawled the invertebrate shoals of the soil. I had been watching for about twenty minutes when a hefty buzzard (a female, I guessed from its bulk) crossed the low skyline of the next field and put every gull to flight. The buzzard is more of a small mammal predator than a birder, and in any case a gull is probably a level or two above its prey grade, but that eagle-shaped silhouette against the sky is an ancient enough symbol of adversity to activate the ritual of the first line of defence among flocks of grounded birds, which is not to be a sitting duck. Clustered fliers in large numbers confuse the predator and the manoeuvre tips the odds in favour of the prey species. The buzzard crossed the ploughed field without pause or deviation while the gulls swirled loudly above. In five minutes all was restored and the gulls gleamed gluttonously among the furrows.

A yellowhammer started calling from the topmost sprig of a hawthorn hedge. I like yellowhammers, like their poise and their vivid here-I-am bravado that fires to a particularly rich canary shade in sunlight. The species does have a specifically Lowland Scots word of its own – *yellayite* or just *yite* – which I also like. It may not possess the musical prowess of canaries (its single phrase is repeated *ad infinitum* bordering on *ad nauseam* and ends in a strung-out metallic *ziinngg!* as if it was constantly surprising itself), but something in the moment made me reach for a pencil and a notebook and a sketch of half a poem spilled over the paper, and I have just found it again.

And oh the yellow light
And the caller air

And the yellayite zinging
On the wire there, bright

In autumn-leaf-yellow-and-brown
And thistledown

One day I'll finish it.

Four

The Unexpected Eagle

THERE ARE FEW PLACES I KNOW BETTER or set out for more readily than Balquhidder Glen. It used to be in the old county of Perthshire but, without moving one inch, in recent years it has drifted into (so the road signs say) "The District of Stirling" and into the Loch Lomond and the Trossachs National Park. I think of it as none of these things but rather as a kind of still centre of the Southern Highlands. It is a well-wooded east-west glen that wilders as it westers until its single-track road stops in its own tracks at Inverlochlarig, the end of a cul-de-sac memorably furnished with elegantly sculpted mountains – Stob Binnein and Stob a' Choin.

There is a quality of softness about the particular beauty that pervades these hillsides, lochs and hidden side glens, one that is immediately absent the moment you breast the watershed on the north side of the glen and stare north to a spreadeagle of mountain landscape that grows ever harder-edged into northern distance. That quality fosters a wider diversity of wildlife that harsher Highlands lack. I lived nearby for some years; my windows were full of its charms.

My particular way into the hills climbs through forest, mostly spruce, some larch. Birches and rowans (their leaves already flecked with yellow) flourish anywhere they can find a toehold. Handsome, limb-flexing, broad-crowned, deep-dark-green Scots pines gather loosely under the mountain, as historically significant a reminder of the old order of this glen as the Ring of Brodgar is to Orkney. In the dense shadows of the spruces, frost had crept out onto the track in the night and now as the sun began to warm the morning after, the unmistakeable tang of the dawn of one more new autumn seasoned the air.

Two ravens started calling to each other in the pines and from three trees apart, and a fluke of their rocky hinterland threw echoes at me, so that echoes and real-time voices overlapped again and again over several minutes. Ravens are always worth watching at the best of times but here, when they give loud and frantic voice, it can mean they are discomfited by the presence of the neighbourhood golden eagles, so I stopped and scanned the glen with binoculars, because the eagles were why I was in the glen. For years, I was involved in an organised watch on their eyrie to counter the worst excesses of egg thieves. In the course of those years I became a willing apostle for the gospel of eagles. What had been an enthusiasm weaned on the masterworks of Seton Gordon became a crusade. "It was a long time ago – April, 1904 – since I photographed my first golden eagle's eyrie," he had written in 1955, thirty years after his first golden eagle book, and he was still writing about them twenty-two years later just before he died in his nineties. My idea of a role model. I never shared his passion for photographing from hides the intimacies of eyrie life, never enjoyed being in a hide at all, but his writing had stirred something in me and my mission became to try and understand more about the eagle's life *out there* on its territory, in flight, for in flight is where the nature of the bird reveals itself. In my book *The Eagle's Way* (Saraband, 2014), I wrote:

> *I started to watch eagles being eagles. These were no longer the chance encounters that every mountaineer knows, but rather they were the direct consequence of the fact that I was looking for them with eyes wide open and a new thrill in the back of my throat. In the course of two or three years I also lost any interest in climbing a mountain to reach the top. Instead I was lured by eagle-thraldom into a different relationship, first with the mountain world then with all wild landscape, a relationship whose objectives became the unravelling of nature's secrets, a better understanding of the wild world.*

Eventually the spruce forest relented and the glen opened into its high alpine-meadow-like upper chamber, a kind of box canyon dignified by a mountain birchwood. The grass was knee-high now and still green, albeit a faded green, a jaded green. The high mountain grass had begun the same process that coloured the oakwood, the leaves have given up on chlorophyll. A few weeks hence, and for a few mesmeric days, the floor of the upper glen would be orange, as would mountainsides all across the land, the earlier the further north, like autumn itself. A few late marsh orchids were still in flower, and grass of Parnassus (loveliest of all mountain flowers) basked in the sunlight. Grass of Parnassus is *Fionnan Geal* in Gaelic, and one little field guide I know translates it as "pleasant little pale one" and I suppose you cannot say fairer than that, although I can't help thinking that Gaelic is a more accomplished language than that.

But mostly I was watching the sky (unclouded Californian blue, but paling to white only in the north above the headwall), the three sides of the skyline and all their buttresses and trees, and especially I scanned the middle distances, which is the hardest part. "If you want to see eagles," Mike Tomkies told me more than once (and he was another accomplished champion of golden eagles), "you must learn to scan the middle distance." I duly learned, and he was right.

I know the eyrie ledge, at least I know where it is, I have never set foot on it. There are rules about these things. I know the ways the eagles come in to the eyrie, I know some of their favourite perches. But by early September, the young have flown, if they have had young this year. Their track record is not particularly good. Much of my spring and summer had been spent furth of here and no intelligence reached me via the grapevine about their nesting season. The simple way at this point in the year is just to spend time in the glen and up on the watershed with long views over the eagles' territory and see what turns up. And I am well versed in the art of dealing with the disappointment of the many days when nothing turns up at all. Over the years of the organised watches I had all the views of golden eagles at the nest that I could ever wish for, and now I mostly avoid the nesting season altogether. In *The Eagle's Way* I wrote about my ambition to become a part of the eagles' landscape and to be accepted as such, and that remains the be all and end all. Two things induce eagles to desert the nest: a protracted, cold, wet spring and human disturbance. I can do nothing about Highland weather, but I can remove myself from whatever accumulation of human disturbance comes their way.

But even when eagles don't reveal themselves, there are no dull hours in the glen. I found a young peregrine falcon against the sky, one of this year's, autumn-shaded, and much more prone to hovering than the adults. They can all do it, but seem to discard the idea when they discover how fast they really are. There was a kestrel up on the watershed too, and which hovers for a living, copper in the sun, fan-tailed, flicker-winged. There were red deer stags crossing the west skyline high up, moving from shadow into sunlight, girding their loins and growing sleek and ready for the imminent rut, when their voices will provide the mountain anthem of every Highland autumn. But I was seeing no eagles.

I was dawdling back down through the upper part of the glen, following the burn for a while, enjoying the sun. The walk back down through the spruces would be in shadow, and quite a few degrees colder. I stopped to watch some small trout in a pool, and just as I began to rebuke myself for my lack of knowledge about fish, a crow started to call. At first I was more absorbed in the fish and the voice only half-registered. Then, as it kept on and on and on, I decided to pay it some attention. The problem was that I couldn't see it, for it was hidden behind the spruces to the south-east. There is a high crag over there where I have seen eagles before. If the crow was there...

But, of course, as with ravens in such a glen, so with crows. The voice was stationary so the bird was perched, and its persistence suggested at least the possibility of a perched eagle either on the crag or in a spruce. The other possibility was no eagle at all and a crow that liked the sound of its own voice. Back on the forest track I pounded down through the trees to a place where I could see the crag, the crow, and whatever else it may or may not have on its mind. Halfway there, it fell silent.

When a sightline finally opened up, there was, inevitably, no crow to be seen and nothing else to confirm my suspicion. But crows and eagles can cover distance in no time at all when they put their mind to it, and it seemed worthwhile hanging around for a few minutes. Then a rock just below the skyline decanted a large bird I had simply not seen, and which promptly disappeared over the skyline. The thing to remember about a skyline is that it is only a skyline where you are standing. Climb up or down and the skyline changes. Beyond this one there lies a broad hill shoulder where a golden eagle might hunt, and if it was hunting there it might reappear just as easily as it disappeared, and especially if it decided to gain a bit of height. Then I heard a raven.

It was the raven that appeared high over the skyline, and perhaps a hundred feet above the crag where I thought the crow had perched. It dived down, giving voice, disappeared behind the skyline and reappeared almost at once in a steep climb. This was more promising. Not for the first time in my thirty-something eagle-watching years, I saw the eagle shadow before I saw the eagle, for the sun had planted it out on the open hillside before the eagle emerged from a small gulley just below the skyline's rock outcrops. What followed was snatches of the confrontation, infuriatingly brief and distant even for good binoculars.

The eagle climbed as the raven fell, the eagle in silence, the raven falsetto-croaking to the rhythm of its wingbeats. But as the eagle climbed, something in the way it was flying gave me pause for thought, for it seemed to be making rather hard work of it, huge air-swatting wingbeats with wings almost vertical at the top of the stroke. It didn't look right. Then there was a moment against the sky's deep-blue cloudlessness when the two birds were no more than a few feet apart, and at that point I took the first of two photographs with a camera that was hopelessly inadequate for the purpose, photographs which I knew would be hopelessly blurred, but they might just confirm something. I have the equally inadequate result before me as I write this, and I have blown them up on the laptop screen to the point just before the image disintegrates entirely. There are the eagle's wings almost vertical, the further one hidden behind the nearer one. The raven's wingspan is at its fullest extent, and it is barely as wide as a single eagle wing. The other unmistakeable characteristic that confirmed what I wanted to know was the huge size of the eagle's beak in relation to its head. It was unquestionably a young sea eagle.

In the two years since I wrote *The Eagle's Way*, I have often wondered when this might happen, when sea eagles might begin to find the Balquhidder landscape to their liking. That book's proposition was that ever since the reintroduction of sea eagles on the east coast of Scotland, and birds from there began to find their way right across the country to the established west coast population around Mull, a kind of two-way, coast-to-coast highway had begun to evolve between the Tay estuary and Mull, and that through fraternising with young sea eagles on their travels, the golden eagles too had become travellers along this same highway. What I did not know at the time was whether this was completely new behaviour or very old behaviour indeed that had lapsed with the demise of the sea eagle, but now the circumstances had begun to recur that made it possible again. As time goes by, I am more and more convinced that the latter is true, and that as more sea eagles cross the country in both directions, they are attracted back into historic sea eagle landscapes by the presence of golden eagles there.

In every respect, Balquhidder Glen is perfect sea eagle habitat, and in *The Eagle's Way* I described an encounter between the established golden eagles and a wandering sea eagle several miles to the north, beyond the watershed and down in Glen Dochart, which had always seemed to me to be the northern limit of the Balquhidder golden eagles' territory. But the setting of this new encounter was in the golden eagles' heartland, and if it has been around for a while, there must have been some spectacular face-offs during their nesting season. My own experience has been that if such face-offs happen in the air then the golden eagle can outfly the sea eagle every time, but if they happen on the ground, say around the carcase of dead deer, the sea eagle can out-muscle the golden.

Over the next few days, as I prepared to head north to the Isle of Harris Mountain Festival, I wondered often what had been going on in this glen I know and love so well while my back was turned.

Five

Twenty-four Hours on Harris

HARRIS HEAVED INTO FOCUS as the ferry barged through the final onslaught of short waves whose crests were whipped off by a sour north-westerly. A gannet seemed drawn to the boat, a moving cliff of possibilities. Nesting responsibilities would be over. This one could have been on an away-day to Harris from St Kilda, forty miles out into the Atlantic. The gannet's long-winged stride devours distance. During the nesting season, round trips of 500 miles to the feeding grounds are not unusual. Forty miles is an hour's cruise at wavetop height. All kinds of birds are forever making that journey. When I was on St Kilda for two weeks in 1988 researching my first book, among the birds that turned up were a golden eagle (almost certainly from Harris), four incredibly scruffy turtle doves (from God knows where), and a cock snow bunting.

The gannet inspected the boat from every angle, from stem to stern, and from waterline to bridge. In the glasses it looked as white as sunlit snow against the many greys of ocean and island landfall. My good omen bird. But as the MV *Hebrides* slowed to ease its relatively ponderous bulk through the rocky wiles of Loch Tarbert, the gannet all but stalled above the stern, dropped a starboard wingtip and glided away from her on unbeating wings through a huge arc that dropped towards the sea, where it straightened and levelled out inches above the surface to resume its fishing foray among the dark east coast bays of Harris, a foray which the arrival of the *Hebrides* had interrupted. The only land in which it has any interest of any kind throughout its life is the square yard of stinking rock that accommodates a sitting female and her egg.

The entrance to Tarbert, the island's only town, demands that the ferryman executes a sustained gentle curve. The moment recalled the skipper of a small eagle-watching boat out of Ulva Ferry on Mull on which I had had a memorable sail three years before (see *The Eagle's Way*). He was a droll man in English and Gaelic and in his practised commentary and off-script conversations with passengers (though I imagine that from one boatload to the next they ask the same questions). I heard one woman ask, with a hint of wonder in her voice:

"And do you know every rock along this stretch of coast?"

"No I don't..." – pause while she took this news in – "but I know all the places where there aren't any."

Knowing the places where there aren't any and putting your boat in them is, I further imagine, what sailing in Hebridean waters is all about. When your boat is the MV *Hebrides* and the all-purpose lifeline between Harris and Skye and thereafter the rest of the world, there is arguably a little more to it. Actually there is a lot more to it, for she is 5,506 tonnes, ninety-nine metres long, her draught is 3.32 metres, she is 15.8 metres across the beam, and she can carry 612 passengers and ninety cars. And it's not as if mooring offshore is an option. She must berth alongside in Tarbert so that she inches into the vehicle ramp with the ease and precision of fingers in a cashmere glove. The rocks glide past wondrously close, and never at any stage from my vantage point leaning over the rail on the top deck does the feat look possible. That it is possible and happens routinely seven days a week is surely mostly because the skipper knows all the places there aren't any.

I turned away to look out at the island. After Skye, Harris looks unfinished. Its rock skeleton still grows, so that it bursts through what is clearly an inadequate covering of vegetation. Evidence of autumn at work and far advanced was everywhere and ubiquitous as rock. Even under the colour-sapping burden of such an oppressive and sodden grey shroud, it looked as if the whole island had been brushed with a thinly applied patina of rust.

I drove from the belly of the MV *Hebrides* the few hundred yards to my hotel, checked in, deposited my overnight bag in my room, turned round and left the building. I had a handful of hours of wind-fretted, rain-soaked early autumn daylight before I had to prepare for a talk about eagles at the Isle of Harris Mountain Festival. I pointed the car towards the west, to maybe the best beaches in the world. It had been a long time, and as I drove I realised that I had forgotten the jolt-in-the-solar-plexus impact of the Harris landscape on unaccustomed eyes. This would be my third time, the second had been at least twenty years ago, the first about ten years before that. The place is a ribcage, a geology of broken bones. Rock heaps up like crouching armies, and here and there it infiltrates the edge of the road where you drive, as if it rather disapproves of the idea of tarmac and is hell-bent on reclaiming it. One day, I have no doubt, it will succeed. Nothing is flat, nothing straight, nothing tame, nothing domestic. The land itself is dark, and yet it accommodates a savage species of beauty. More than anything else, Harris is its own place, and the entire repertoire of Scottish islandness knows nothing like it.

I don't like treating islands this way. It strikes me as disrespectful. I would be here for not much more than twenty-four hours, do my job of work, sleep, and tomorrow make what I could of the few hours at my disposal, and it appeared they would be seriously circumscribed by a hostile weather forecast. But the least I could do was to pay the island what respects I could, beginning half an hour after I had landed.

What is not rock is water. There is heather and there is half-hearted grass that seems to be perpetually pleading for mercy from the weather or being eaten by sheep, and the trees are rarer than milestones and they have given up pleading and they are low and wiry and bent because the salt-smothered wind insists on it. But mostly there is rock and there is water: lochs, lochans, pools, burns, and fast, fitful and slender rivers; and sea lochs so long and languorous that they are tidally indolent at their heads, much to the delight of sudden hundreds of birds. Knee-deep in shallowest of shallows are the wader tribes – lapwings, golden plovers, redshanks, greenshanks, and curlews towering over them all like a tribe of Gullivers among Lilliputians. The shock is the clarity of the water (I had forgotten that too), and where it languished over the pallor of sand and even at a distance, the legs of every bird were clearly visible underwater.

After crossing the island from Tarbert, the first of the west coast beaches appeared to my unfamiliar eyes like a cold mirage or a landscape in a dream or a glimpse of Tír Nan Óg (which I had always assumed would be much further west than Harris), or just an out-and-out miracle. First the ocean appeared, and on such a day it was grey on grey and darkening towards the almost black line of the horizon, but then the road fell away in front of me so that the inshore ocean and its startling sprawl of sand drew an audible gasp, and seeing was barely believing at all. And that suddenly deep, deep green ocean with a mysterious blue undertone (where did *that* shade derive from under such a ponderous greyness of skies?) edged the whole towards turquoise but never quite got there. And the low coastal hills in the north were purple.

Enchantment set in where the final – the only – breaker unfurled. I had anticipated an ocean in a rage that reflected the weather, and the intemperate crossing of the Minch, but instead I met an ocean in a dwam. The breaker, having broken, advanced on the shore in a low, wide band the white of new snow, and in the form of a perfect arc. Ahead of it, between its leading edge and the shore, there were three more arcs that fitted the white water and each other with all the precision and perfection of rainbows. The first of these was a pale greyish blue, the next a line of white as thin as a lace, and that marked the last reach of water up the beach. But the tide was newly turned, so there was a fourth arc, a yard wide, and it wore the lightest dusting of lilac, and that was damp sand that showed where the sea had newly departed from the high water mark.

And yet the chief glory was the sand itself, a pale blaze of sand, especially on such a day; not white exactly, but after Skye, where the few scraps of sandy beaches are black-ish, these were so exotic I felt entitled to expect palm trees. And they were so unbesmirched, so perfect, so untrodden, it was as if the ice age had just finished the day before yesterday and the provider of sand, following everywhere in its wake, had just finished the west coast of Harris, and no creature – neither bird nor mammal of two legs or four – and no camper van, had found the place yet.

Travel south down the coast and beaches imbued with that same surreal quality of organic mesmerism keep materialising round the next corner, until finally the road swerves away south-east and the bemused traveller is done with his dalliance in Tír Nan Óg. I spent hours with notebook and camera, writing in the rain (use a pencil!), and photographing (as I saw it) Rothko-esque compositions with horizontal bands of sand and ocean and sky in thirds and fifths and sevenths. And after all that I found a rock and sat on it and poured coffee and stared and marvelled and soaked it up. Sometimes you get days, or rather moments within days, when something parts or slips aside – like a screen or a door you never saw before – and what lies beyond is nothing less than an intimate exposition of the lie of the land. Confronted by such a moment, my response is always the same – look at it, listen to it. Such thoughts that cross my mind then are elemental and huge and soon I put them down again and settle for thoughtlessness and the free rein of instinct, for all smaller thoughts are impossible.

*

I had been asked to talk to the Isle of Harris Mountain Festival about eagles following the publication of my book, *The Eagle's Way*, which concerns itself primarily with a swathe of land clear from the Tay estuary to the Isle of Mull, its slowly increasing sea eagle presence and the golden eagle's response. I had been vaguely uneasy that some islanders might have detected a coals-to-Newcastle tendency, given that Harris and neighbouring Lewis have good populations of both eagle tribes. As it turned out, the unease was completely groundless, and besides, I had already rationalised my approach to myself, and to the Harris audience. In a country the size of Scotland, no community of distance-devouring eagles can exist in isolation. For example, a wandering sea eagle from the Tay estuary that travels west and arrives on Mull has reached not so much a destination as an eagle distribution hub that lays out the entire western seaboard at its disposal, from the Mull of Galloway and the Mull of Kintyre to the Butt of Lewis, Cape Wrath, and beyond even to Orkney, where 6,000 years earlier men and sea eagles had such closely co-operative lifestyles that they were buried side by side in the same tomb, the so-called Tomb of the Eagles. My book's story begins there, and in the second chapter there is a detailed account of the first sea eagle I ever saw, on Mingulay, which is a few links down the chain of the Western Isles from Harris. And Harris is now writing its own chapter in the glittering success story of the return of the native. Two of the more remarkable of my friend Laurie Campbell's photographs that grace *The Eagle's Way* are the fruits of his long-term fascination with the wildlife of Harris. And it is fair to say that by now all Scotland is once again a realm of eagles: every mile of coast knows its eagle shadows, and as with my notional eagle highway between the Tay estuary and Mull, wandering sea eagles are finding ready company among wandering young golden eagles and some are luring them on forays furth of their Highlands and Islands strongholds.

Sitting in the hotel bar with a nightcap whisky, an open notebook, and a head full of the events of an extraordinary day that had begun with a pastel dawn over Broadford Bay, I thought I might find one more insight and write it down. An hour and another whisky later I called it a night. The notebook page was as untroubled as the sands of Luskentyre.

*

The next morning the weather had turned really dirty. The wind was up and the wee burn below my hotel bedroom window had developed a hoarse energy in the night. I had a few hours before lunch and the afternoon queue for the ferry back to Skye, and decided to spend them on a leisurely exploration of the C-road to Roghadal at the south end of the island. Sunday morning on Harris is q-u-i-e-t. Of the island's 2,000 souls, more than sixty per cent are Gaelic-speaking and the Sabbatarian philosophy is still alive and well. I would go softly down through the island along one of the most beautiful, bold, brass-necked, berserk roads I have ever travelled. It also marked the moment in this book's journey when I met full-blown autumn head-on and saw the morning's storm ram it down the landscape's throat.

Such a blasted landscape as now unfurled before me had clearly no memory left of even the latest of late summer. This salt-scented gale hurdled the crests of the smaller hills then dived down what had been leeward slopes yesterday, there to feed and whiten the burns into instant waterfalls. These were suddenly as thick on the ground as a gentler landscape might accommodate trees. I swore some of these burns were not even there yesterday, but most of them rumbled over rocks and tossed stallion manes of white water arcing into the air so that they tumbled heads over their own heels and spent themselves, exhausted, among chains of hissing lochans whose occasional sheltered shores (usually under an overhanging black buttress or beneath a wind-cheating gorge) were thickly layered with flowerless water lily pads. In high summer tranquillity (I brought the most outrageous stretch of my imagination to bear on recreating that lost scene) they must have been as exquisite as they were outrageous. *Water lilies! HERE!*

I had the road utterly to myself, and whenever possible I stopped by the ends of sea lochs and the edges of inlets (the road helpfully swerved and dipped down to water level to greet every one of them and embrace the high-tide rocks) to scan water and shore in the less than optimistic pursuit of even a glimpse of another of nature's creatures other than myself. There was not much chance of birdlife picking morsels out of the teeth of the storm, and if there was to be anything at all, the chances were that it would be raven, for it takes the vilest of weather to ground a raven, and such is its inclination to fly in the face of storm, I suspect a hint of masochistic endeavour lurks deep within that likeable blackguard. The thought had barely registered when I negotiated one more blind summit, with a lethal hairpin built in, to be confronted with two ravens in the middle of the road about a dozen yards away reducing a few bloody inches of meat and fur to a sodden pulp. They accorded me a two-second appraising stare, giving me (as I fancied it) the benefit of the doubt that I might not actually run them over, but even at my Sabbath dawdle they were simply too close. One flew left, the other right (and the morsel of whatever it had been flew with that bird). I was able to pull the car off the road a few yards further on, and when I opened the door to look back, both birds and their bite-sized snack were back on the road, and they were sharing it amicably. They behaved as if I was not there.

I like ravens. I found myself wondering if they responded to life in a more or less treeless landscape the same way their Icelandic kin do when it comes to sourcing nest material and nest sites. I found a nest there on a glass-less window ledge in an old outbuilding. The nest was built entirely with little pieces of barbed wire fence instead of twigs, but it had the most sumptuous lining of sheep's wool of any nest I have ever seen.

The rest of that little expedition, I saw only two other birds, a meadow pipit and a stonechat. What I was really hoping for on the water was otters. Otters are indifferent to weather and the east coast of Harris is pretty well perfect for them. And while this stop-and-start morning was diametrically opposed to my preferred otter watching methodology, you just never know. Sometimes, right time, right place, is all you need. But mostly, nothing was moving at all. Blackface sheep hunkered down behind rocks, at the bottom of banks, under bridges, in the doorway of a broken shed, in the lee of outbuildings, diggers, tractors, vans and in the ditch beside passing places, though all they were passing was time. They are the last survivors of a doomed way of life, for there is little interest in shepherding left among the islanders and even less money. I am no fan of sheep (their capacity to wreck landscapes and their historic symbolism as an instrument of Clearance get in the way), but on days like this one, it is hard not to admire their stoicism, at the very least.

Below one croft house, down at the water's edge of a long, quiet and deep-sided inlet, a small dark brown horse and a slightly paler donkey stood motionless and shoulder to shoulder under the imperfect shelter of that rarest of Harris phenomena – a willow tree. Two hours later, having been to Roghadal and back, I passed them again and neither had moved an inch.

In the long, lifeless lulls of the morning I reconsidered the road, wondered idly if there could be a more torturous man-made object on earth. The shortest of straights felt like mistakes, as though an opportunity to throw in an extra gratuitous hairpin had been wilfully spurned. It gathered in un-numbered and still skinnier roads, coastal cul-de-sacs every one, tributaries to its own chaotic mainstream. I wondered at the townships it visited, wondered what the inhabitants do (the ones that live there, that is, as opposed to the second home owners and self-catering holiday letters), for they can't all be crofters and artists and postmen and nature writers.

One more blind summit flipped into a bend round a small buttress. The whole island is more or less a conglomeration of buttresses, some of which gather into wondrous 2,000-feet mountains (not that I would see them on this trip, but I remembered). Whatever their size, they are all parties to a dark-toned conspiracy hell-bent on out-witting the weather and on clothing the island with its rare strain of savage beauty. There was a brief lessening in the rainfall's volume. I slid down the driver's window, the better to execute one more sideways glance at one more seaweedy bay, and there was an otter staring back at my passing glance from where a tiny shrug of the Atlantic Ocean heaved a few inches of orange tangle up the flank of a low, flat-topped shoreline rock, a rock with an otter on top; then the ocean sucked and the orange drapery subsided.

There was – of course – nowhere to stop. The road demanded that I rounded the buttress, where I judged that a patch of roadside was wet rock, not bog. It turned out to be both, but at least there was no ditch. My car is small and light and blessed with very good four-wheel-drive. This is why. The car and I took our chances, we did not sink, but I jumped out into a bog.

Two minutes later I was clamped to the side of the buttress, being flayed by the wind and stared at by an otter with one forepaw pinning what looked like a lumpsucker to its rock. Its other front paw was raised, a gesture with an interrogatory edge, like a pet dog cravenly quizzing its human about the possibility of Bonio. We were twenty yards apart and I was twenty feet higher. If anything, I was wetter than the otter, and certainly colder, but right there, right then, there was nothing I would rather be doing, nowhere I would rather be doing it. A primitive connection fell into place. A thin thread bound us – otter and otter-watcher – to that moment, that crossing of paths in that most elemental of landscapes. Hail fellow, well met.

★

The MV *Hebrides* crept out of Loch Tarbert in the late afternoon, assiduously adhering to the places where there weren't any. She spun round to face the Minch and the disturbingly corrugated waters. It would be a crossing sponsored by Stugeron. The more open water the *Hebrides* put between herself and Harris, the more the island seemed to recede back into itself, and to darken to almost black while its hills snored through the Sabbath shrouded in a collapsed sky the most hodden of greys. It was not how I wanted to remember Harris. I sought out a quiet corner of the lounge for a while to try and write down something of the morning. Strange, I thought, how ferryboat coffee always tastes like bilgewater. Half an hour crept past, but my mood of darkness was a contagion I had brought aboard from the island and I seemed to have been incubating it ever since. I was like Burns's sulky, sullen dame:

Gathering her brows like gathering storm,
Nursing her wrath to keep it warm.

The miracle, when it happened was as sudden as whirlwinds, as startling as rainbows. It began in the south. A far headland of Skye appeared where none had been visible moments before. A hole appeared in the dark smother of cloud, and sunlight poured through in a tilted column that smote the headland and lit it from stem to stern. It was the precursor of a kind of Hebridean rebirth that made all the visible world new again. The sky fissured open and began to leak sunlight with the energy it had recently channelled into leaking rain, and in a hundred different places at once. The ocean that had been dull grey was suddenly ablaze, then slowly turned deep green and deep blue, and an unbroken band of molten white light as vivid as a Luskentyre breaker lay all along the horizon.

Ahead, Skye basked. Astern, Harris smouldered. Other islands sprang up all along the western skyline to resume their accustomed positions in the ocean. The air filled with birds. The effect among the passengers was to galvanise them out of a huddle of torpor. Voices were raised, extended hands and arms pointed out the bleeding obvious, eyes squinted, sunglasses appeared, cameras and phones gorged on the spectacle like gulls on a dead whale. The mood of everyone and everything was transformed.

Arriving at Uig on Skye and driving up the hill on the road south to Sligachan and the rest of the world was a thing of constantly unfolding and expanding marvels, an instant festival of distance. At the summit I stopped in a lay-by to let the ferry traffic breenge on by. I stood outside the car, felt warmth on my face, heard swallows and martins, and the sense of having changed planets for the second time in twenty-four hours was utterly, utterly complete.

Six

Daylight on the Dream

THE SUNLIGHT IN THE AFTERNOON that first day of October had a quality. Wherever it shone directly on to the trunks of the trees, wherever it negotiated its way through the slowly thinning canopies of hundreds of oaks and their sporadic underlings, the rowans and the hollies, that I could see without turning my head, wherever it lit a long and ragged-edged strip of forest floor or a grassy clearing a dozen yards wide, wherever it fell on the darkest bark and blackest roots, it struck notes of bright white in them all, notes so vitally defined that I felt I might hear them. Any moment, the oakwood might resound to the silvery voices of vibraphones or woody wind chimes, and every note would sustain and ripple and hang on the air in layers of tremolo echoes. Their pitch would change every time a sliver of a breeze wafted a holly spray so its shadow shifted on an oak trunk, beginning new notes, silencing old ones with its prickling dance.

I became aware that I was walking very, very slowly, military-march-slow but without its insistent rhythm of ostentation, "pibroch-slow" I said aloud to myself and smiled at the memory of Finlay MacRae playing the *Desperate Battle of the Birds* in the pinewoods of Glen Affric. I have seen cock capercaillies in just such terrain, treading with the same dignity and certainty and strut, and I saw a man embody both landscape and bagpipe music and make them an indivisible and organic whole, and I had never seen it done before and never seen it done since, and forty years after the event I can see him slow-slow-slow-slow-slow marching as he played. I was a young journalist at the time, just beginning to flex my muscles on environmental themes, and something I had written about forestry produced an invitation from the Forestry Commission to meet Finlay, who had just won an award from the American Society of Travel Writers for his work on native pinewood restoration. That day in Glen Affric, there were half a dozen journalists from a variety of newspapers, but as the music moved like smoke through the trees, and as it rose and fell through the careful ground-and-variations structure of pibroch, I was the only one with tears in my eyes. I shook his hand afterwards, but I couldn't say a word. He smiled and nodded and put a hand on my shoulder. To this day, a good piper and a great pibroch puts me in mind of Scots pines and capercaillies.

Twenty years later I would discover that we had a great friend in common. His name was Pat Sandeman, whose life evolved around three passions – birds, Gaelic and piping. His day job had been in the family wine and spirits business. He was much older than I am but late in his life we became great friends and he would recruit me as his "eyes and ears" on various birdwatching missions. One day he mentioned Finlay MacRae, and I said: "The piper?" "Yes," he said, "why, do you know him?" So I told him the story of our Glen Affric encounter, and from his pocket he produced a letter from Finlay he had received that day, and it was clear from the odd paragraph he read out that they were great friends indeed. Pat had been, by his own admission, a "ropey" piper, whereas Finlay, by international agreement, was a genius, and a pupil of one of the greatest of all piping tutors, the Head of Army Piping at Edinburgh Castle, Pipe Major Willie Ross. But, as I was about to discover, so – very briefly – was Pat. He told me this story.

He had tried and failed several times to get an interview with Willie Ross, then he got "an introduction", and I fancy I now know who had done the introducing. They had talked for a while at the Castle, and eventually Ross had said he was just too busy and didn't have room for Pat. Then, as he was leaving, he asked Pat what line he was in. Wine and spirits, said Pat. A pause. I think I might just be able to squeeze you in, said Ross. He was duly squeezed, but struggled to make headway. One day, making "a right hash" of a pibroch during a lesson, Willie Ross had stopped him in his tracks and said:

"No, no, no, you're playing it all wrong. You'll never be a great piper. All the great pipers are dead, and to tell you the truth, I'm not feeling very well myself."

*

So that was why I was smiling to myself as I realised how the mood of these Trossachs oakwoods had infiltrated my mind and slowed my stride to the soft stealth of a Finlay MacRae. And I was walking along an animal trail not half a yard wide, and I knew by now that the trail builders included roe deer, fox, badger, red squirrel and pine marten, for I had seen all of them use it over the years and at different hours of day and night, and different seasons of the year. The trail wound between tree trunks and through clearings and spawned offshoots down to the river from time to time (all mammals must drink and most swim), and although I know the place as well as I know anywhere, it seemed to me that on that particular afternoon I could look at it with a new way of seeing. There was the sunlit wood and the shadowed wood and one was bright white and the other a deep ebony dark, and both were restless because of the movement of trees in the wind and the image occurred to me briefly of a kind of dance like the movement of chess pieces, and I wondered if this was how Ansel Adams ever saw woodland, and whether it explained his utter mastery of black and white landscape photography.

My favourites among his woodland images include one of aspens and one of redwoods, and in one you can see the sunlit gold of the leaves and their tremulous shimmer, and in the other the deep dark red of the bark and the colossal reach from soft ferny undergrowth to open sky, yet the achievement is rendered in shades of grey and black and white and the framing is tight and sunlight and sky are elsewhere, but the sense of what is not shown, and the colours of what is shown, are palpable. And I was looking at a sunlit wood and I was seeing in a kind of monochrome the essential elements that pinned it together and fastened it to its earth. And then, by setting something free that I could not possibly put a name to if I sat here and thought about it for a fortnight, I could allow in the canopy and the woodland floor and these were of fading green and paling yellow and darkening oak-leaf tans, and all of that gathered about me in such a slow whirl of pin-sharp detail that to write it down that way sounds dizzying. But its effect was the opposite: I had slowed and slowed without thinking about it, and then I stopped and I sat at the base of a sunlit oak with my back to its trunk and face to the sun and I felt becalmed, at rest and at ease with the wood itself. And this is how I go to work.

At various times I have been called a wildlife expert, a nature expert, a naturalist, an ecologist, a conservationist and disciple of biodiversity (I am none of these, I don't even know what the last one means and I also don't believe that it is possible to be "expert" in wildlife, let alone all nature, such is the limitless scope of the subject); nature is simply my preferred field, and when I go to work in its field, I go to write. And it has been my experience – and it still is – that if you go often enough and in an open frame of mind, and if you take the trouble to win a degree of intimacy with your subject whenever that allows, then there will be moments when you see something other in the familiar. All you have to do then is find a way to write it down.

An oak leaf fell on to the open page of my notebook. It was green and yellow and brown, and when I held it up to the light I could see many small holes and each one was haloed in sunlight. I put it back down on the page where it had landed and photographed it. I decided it looked a bit like a satellite image of Lewis and Harris, complete with their characteristic freckling of dubh-lochans. My habit of writing out in the woods, or in the hills, or by lochs and rivers and waterfalls and the edges of bogs, is fundamental to my ambition of effectively *becoming* nature, so that – however briefly – nature treats me as a part of the landscape. When I am sitting writing I am still and silent, and over the years all manner of things have landed on or chosen to explore the notebook in my lap. The majority of the leaves have been oak, but also birch, rowan, willow, larch needles and more robust bits of trees – acorns, pine cones, beech nuts, various catkins, twigs and, once, a piece of pine bark loosened by a treecreeper. Bugs seem to be attracted to its bright white glare with the blue ink doodles, especially butterflies. Once, I had just written down the words "they have more to fear from us than we have from them" (I think it was something to do with wolves) and had then laid the notebook aside on the grass for a moment, at which point a tortoiseshell butterfly landed on the page and its shadow fell over the two lines of handwriting, "embracing" it, or at least so I chose to interpret it at the time. Dragonflies have turned up too, as have ladybirds, pinewood ants (a marching column, too many for the comfort of a sitting writer; some of them carted off a sandwich crumb), spiders, bees, a burnet moth and, once, (and still the only bird) a robin, again while the notebook was on the ground rather than in my lap.

"Write in the very now where you find yourself," wrote Margiad Evans, "...there is no substitute even in divine inspiration for the touch of the moment, the touch of the daylight on the dream." I have quoted her many times, but nothing like the number of times I have been grateful for her priceless advice. How often, too, I have invoked her to myself, and that would include every time something of nature landed on my open notebook whether by accident or design; how often I wished I could have thanked her, how often wished our paths could have crossed, but she died (on her birthday) in 1958 and I was still a child, but a child of nature even then.

*

After ten days of high pressure and still, warm days, October finally cracked and threw a cloak of grey and rain over the woods and sent furious, scurrying salvoes of short-lived winds through the trees. There are few facets of nature I enjoy more than walking in the still centre of a wild wood while the winds torment the tree tops and set tree against tree as trunks are bowed against each other and limbs interlock amid thin screeches of protest. Deep in the oakwood and down near the river, I was stopped in my tracks by a broken runt of a tree I had never noticed before, but now it caught my eye because it was waving a crimson flag. It had been unexceptional as oak trees go, its girth was modest and it had forked at about seven feet high. What remained of the tree was the trunk, one limb hoisted from the fork at a shallow angle – about thirty degrees – and a skinny, broken-off branch where the rest of the fork must once have been. From the fork to the outermost broken tip of the surviving limb (surviving in the sense that it still exists, though it does not live) was perhaps another seven feet, certainly no more. The limb itself divided into two branches that had also broken apart but twisted rather elegantly and tapered to fine points. Much of the trunk was swaddled in thick moss, light and dark shades of green, but the scene-stealer was not of the tree, but rather a fly-by-night opportunist. Rooted in the moss and deadwood on the top side of the broken fork, a small cluster of stems of rosebay willowherb had rooted, and prospered, and now flaunted a pretty show of autumn-crimsoned leaves, conferring on the entire oak remnant a jaunty, rakish air that made me smile. I stopped to sketch it and take a few photographs. Moral: deadwood is the lifeblood of living woodlands, whether standing or prone.

Half a mile away in the same wood, a larger oak had succumbed to the previous winter's storms, crashed sideways across the path so that a new diversion was initiated, which navigated round the now vertically realigned mass of roots that faced out towards the river like a huge, dark satellite dish with a hundred antennae. But the tree had declined to die completely. For although what had been its canopy was now smashed and bare, a frieze of around twenty leafy oak saplings a few inches high had sprung vertically from the horizontal trunk, and these made a kind of loose-knit hedge in shades of green and yellow and brown. I was looking at it from about twenty yards away when a great spotted woodpecker materialised on the very topmost claw of the upended roots, and from there dropped nimbly down onto the trunk and began to thread a tricky progress through the saplings with an ease that suggested this was not the first time. At any one time, the various components of its black and white and bright red plumage appeared through gaps in that inches-high screen of leaves, often revealing no more than the bird's head with its black crown, red nape and white cheeks, but other glimpses showed a bird apparently on tiptoe and craning its neck to see over the leaves. Once, in a bare patch of horizontal bark between saplings, it appeared to be discomfited, and stretched its entire body into a low-slung and elongated parody of a woodpecker's normally upright posture, and proceeded in tiny steps of its huge feet as if horizontal progress were an ordeal, and not a manoeuvre to be undertaken lightly.

At the far end of this unlikely journey, it astounded me by turning in its own length and retracing its steps. The point is that at every few steps it would pause and very clearly find food there, for not only was that dying oak tree determinedly fostering new oak life for as long as it produced any sustenance at all, but it was teeming with invertebrate life, and the woodpecker was not about to miss out, even if it meant having to improvise a new hunting technique. In dying as in death as in life, there is no more endlessly resourceful living organism than an oak tree.

Seven

An Audience with the Great Shepherd

IF THE FIRST OF SEPTEMBER is the first day of Meteorological Autumn, and if therefore the 30th of November is the last day, then the 16th of October is midautumn day, the centrepiece of autumn, the fulcrum, when all that is wondrous about this pivotal time of year alights on ultimate pitch-perfect notes of harmony, a moment of sublime equipoise. Yet midautumn day, when you write it like that, looks unfamiliar, even weird, while midsummer day is not really the middle of anything at all, but rather the end of something, in this case the Earth's annual but half-hearted approach towards the sun. We should do something about that; make Midautumn Day a national holiday with capital letters. Until then, it seems to me that the least I can do is to make a kind of pilgrimage to the heart of autumn. A pilgrimage needs a destination, so I chose the perfect mountain – Buachaille Etive Mòr, the Great Shepherd of Etive. And as luck would have it, I also chose the perfect day.

*

Traveller, you must always wave to the Rannoch Rowan! If you are unfamiliar with this first commandment of the A82 between the Black Mount and Glencoe, you should know that the Rannoch Rowan stands just yards from the road: you can't miss it, for it grows directly out of a large rock, a glacial erratic carelessly dumped there a few millennia back down the line by a passing glacier. (There are many such rowans scattered across the Highlands that know how to get blood out of a stone, and some are befriended by golden eagles, which carry off sprigs of their leaves to weave with some delicacy into the colossal

endeavour of the building and maintenance of their eyries. I have
seen them do that every month of the year in which there are rowan
leaves to be plucked. It is not clear why they do it, at least it isn't to
me, nor why it is thought fit adornment for both the inner and outer
walls. And while it is true that they use other greenery too, especially
birch leaves, it is surely no coincidence that so many eyries have rock-
rooted rowans for neighbours. The very word "greenery" is not always
accurate; I have watched an eagle carry a September sprig of bright
red rowan leaves to an eyrie, which if it had any use at all so late in the
nesting year, it could only have been as a roosting ledge. Golden eagles
like rowans and perhaps it is as simple as that. So do we: the rowan
before the door of Highland houses, both lived-in and ruinous, is as
ubiquitous as the rowan at the eagle's door.)

But something in the erect stance of the Rannoch Rowan, its often
brutal isolation, and its blatantly conspicuous roadside situation has
endeared it to drivers on the A82. And it is the only one I know that
has a name. I first came this way as a child on family holidays to the
West Highlands in my father's car, and he waved to it. I do not remember exactly how he replied to family questions about the habit, but I
think the gist was that it's the Rannoch Rowan and that's what you
do. It would not surprise me to learn that the tradition made its way
in among the rest of us by way of Scotland's Traveller families. My
father certainly knew quite a few of them from his years as a telephone engineer among the backroads of Angus and east Perthshire.
But somehow or other, it was impressed into my impression-eager
young mind that it was a good thing to do to wave to the Rannoch
Rowan each time you passed and to ask for a safe journey. I have done
it ever since. Over the years the greeting has contracted to a kind of
shorthand. I say: "One more time – safe journey" on the way north,
and: "Until the next time – safe journey" on the way back. And I've
always had safe journeys.

So in my mind, and for many years now, Glencoe in general and
the Buachaille in particular, have begun with the Rannoch Rowan as
if it were a herald the mountain gods had sent ahead to announce the
imminent presence of the Great Shepherd of Etive, and the particularly rarefied mountain realm of the Coe that lies beyond its mighty,

graceful profile. Even if you know what's coming as you top the final crest in the road and the Buachaille begins to rise up out of the land, it is still quite impossible not to succumb to anticipation's thrill. Whatever the weather, what unfolds is Scotland's mountain masterpiece. On that particular Midautumn Day, it was a mountain out of a dream. The sky had slowly emptied of cloud as I drove north and west, and now it was utterly cloudless. The Buachaille looked enthroned in a way that was new to me, one perfect mountain whose very standing in the landscape is so overarchingly dominant *and* beautiful that only prime autumn adds a daring, zesty, burnt umber frisson to the foreground grasses and even flirts with the hems and pleats of the mountain's skirts, and the sense of nature as a seductress is utterly complete.

My plan was characteristically ill-defined and optimistic. I would park on the Glen Etive road, wander up the River Coupall, find a sunny nook on a bank, and sit at the mountain's feet. Then I would watch it for a while with a notebook and sketchbook, empty my mind, and see what rubbed off. Sometimes, when I don't have a better idea, that's what I do.

The name puzzles me. Why "Shepherd"? And why is the same name afforded to its next-door neighbour, Buachaille Etive Beag, the lower hill simply being named as the diminutive of the Great Shepherd? If, as seems likely, they were named from settlements at the head of Loch Etive, where the two mountains appear cheek-by-jowl, there is nothing shepherd-like about their appearance. Perhaps they were named from a time when the people placed their notion of a god on mountaintops, and they had already imbued that god with the notion of a guardian of the flock, which was later attributed to Christianity. Or maybe something fundamental was lost in translation over the millennia. I'm going with that as the most likely explanation. And anyway, the first thing that struck me when I found my sunny nook on the banks of the Coupall was that the Buachaille, from that vantage point, is the most feminine of mountains, a Great Shepherdess. There again, back in the days of the namers-of-the-landscape, perhaps their language made no distinction between "shepherd" and "shepherdess".

I began by just sitting and looking. I am an admirer of this of all mountains. I have climbed it four or five times and circumnavigated it once. With the help of a former newspaper colleague I climbed it by way of Curved Ridge, the beginning and end of my rock-climbing career. It is rock-climbing for beginners, but a sensational way to climb the mountain, for it leans close to the Rannoch Wall (famed rock-climbing theatre) and it unlocked for me something of a sense of the inner mountain, something of the workings of nature as sculptor that created such a work of art of the highest order. It is such an individualist, such a landmark of such raw, incomparable beauty, and it is in moments like this that I find fault with the Munro-bagging fad that has shaped modern Scottish mountaineering. I have trouble with the idea of Buachaille Etive Mòr as something collectable to be ticked off and lumped in with every other mountain in the land because it happens to qualify on the grounds of a spurious height limit. To climb such a mountain, just to "collect" it, is not a good enough reason.

Then I remembered that I had sat right here years ago now, sifting my way through a similar train of thought, and that I had written down the result in an old book, long out of print, called *Glencoe – Monarch of Glens* (Baxter, 1990). I had considered the Buachaille's work-of-art status then too, had mischievously re-categorised it, not a Munro but a MacDiarmid of a mountain, and had quoted the great poet in support of my argument:

> *...and the principal question*
> *Aboot a work o' art is frae hoo deep*
> *A life it springs – and syne hoo faur*
> *Up frae't it has the pooer to leap.*

And then I summoned my favourite painter to my cause:

Paul Cézanne said: *"What art is primarily about is what the eye thinks." His eye thought so much of one mountain, Mont St Victoire at Aix-en-Provence, he thought it worth painting again and again for ever, the mountain growing in stature and abstraction the more he painted it, the more his eye thought about it. My eye thinks much the same when I sit under Buachaille Etive Mòr, studious and seduced. It is a mountain to satisfy a Cézanne. Circumnavigate the Buachaille, shape and re-shape it, build and re-build all its landforms, let your eye paint its every profile again and again forever until it is a familiarity you crave, until you must breathe the Buachaille, not air. Know then what love impelled Cézanne, intimately alone with his mountain, what Buachailles we'd have seen if only Glencoe had a climate like Aix-en-Provence...*

Now, the better part of thirty years later, and without consciously making that old association, I was reaching out to the same mountain as the symbolic embodiment of autumn. The simplicity of its shape from the banks of the Coupall is central to the notion, an almost perfect isosceles triangle, such a shape as children would reach for if you asked them to draw a mountain. The shape is a deception, of course, because what you see from here is only the Rannoch-inclined east face of Buachaille Etive Mòr, beyond which (and out of sight) a long ridge runs westward, a heady highway slung through the airspace that binds Glen Etive and Glencoe. But the pyramidal aspect is so persuasive that it perfectly represented what I had envisaged when I considered the possibilities of a destination for this book. I saw it as a meandering journey to a particular time and place that turned out to be this time and this place, not just the summit of this particular land but the summit, the highest endeavour, of autumn itself. From here and now, this autumn journey would lead back again by way of lesser summits and foothills to the land of the Highland Edge where it began. I have always enjoyed descents more than ascents, and from this zenith of the endeavour, the sense of what still lay ahead between Midautumn Day and the last day of November excited me. I sat warming myself in early afternoon sun, watching a blue-black swathe of deepest shadow creep round the mountain as the sun westered.

I shifted my focus to more immediate surroundings for a while, which is the kind of diversity that a long stillness encourages. In the right circumstances it can lead your eye from the golden eagle crossing distant watersheds to the wren at your feet, or from an island-strewn ocean to a clutch of plover eggs in a nest of stones. Under the Buachaille, I shifted my gaze from the mountain and started to explore the grasses themselves, this high watermark of that moorland-sea called Rannoch, an image which is greatly strengthened just by turning to look behind, to where the land opens out into Scotland's most spectacular land-locked space, at the far edge of which it is possible to make out the tiny blue shape of Schiehallion. The sheer scope of the space is what assists the notion of a moorland sea.

The grass was enlivened everywhere by the fading, withering stalks and leaves and heads of wild flowers that a month before still brushed the land with their own hot and cool shades of sparks and flames. Finally I reached for notebook and pen, made quick and ill-considered reference sketches, then out of one more thoughtless stillness came patterns of words.

BUACHAILLE (SHEPHERD)

At my feet the flotsam
of the moor: the bog triptych
– cotton, myrtle, asphodel –
and bluebell, sundew, tormentil,
mountain grass, heather, lichen, moss,
finished fragrance of orchids.
And glaring down from within
the upgathered robes of Etive
the Shepherd saw my pencil hand
measure a sundew with a thumbnail,
then raise the same thumb
at arm's length to measure
the whole Shepherd from robe-hem
to mountainous pow.
And in the evening the Shepherd
enfolded all that grew there,
and the quiet deer, golden eagle,
raven, owl, lost wolf howl;
but I remained unfolded, beyond
the Shepherd's reach. I must
go on or coldly wait the dawn.

Have you ever simply sat and watched a mountain over, say, three hours, long enough to observe the evolving action of sunlight and shadow, and to realise how these alone affect your own sense of the nature of the mountain? Drive past the mountain, or pause just long enough to take its photograph and drive on again, and your souvenir is nothing but a moment in the mountain's life. Climb it and you are too close to achieve a sense of the whole mountain as it eases through a succession of moods. But sit – just sit – and make no gesture towards it beyond your complete engagement with it so that you begin to fathom in your long stillness what it might take to be a rock.

The sky above the Buachaille had emptied of cloud hours ago, and the utter blueness was at its deepest directly above the summit, and that shade seemed to seep into the very buttresses on its sun-smitten flank, and into the shadow that edged towards the middle of the mountain as the afternoon dwindled down. The foreground was the river, whisky shaded, its midstream rocks pale grey and fawn. The far bank was embellished by the deep bronze of withering bracken. Beyond and between the fronds, blue-black banks of peat in deep shadow were topped by friezes of vividly lit heather, blaeberries and bog myrtle bushes. The tallest, wispiest grasses were pale pink, and these shimmered above tussocks of citrus shades – orange, lemon and lime green, and all these harmonised into distance and relentlessly rising eddies of that burnt-umber cloak that fed the lowest reaches of the mountain. Finally, a single tiny white cloud appeared and came and stood by the summit for a few minutes, during which it slowly dematerialised before my eyes. I photographed it, and somehow even that least intrusive of actions damaged the palpable magic, the mystery of what persuades a cloud to form alone in an empty sky, to drift as if by design to this of all mountaintops, and then vanish as if it had never been. The photograph shows it had been, of course, but it doesn't tell me anything I didn't know.

Then, far over my shoulder, a red deer stag roared, and changed the nature of the moment, the hour, the afternoon, the day.

★

The red deer rut often bursts into full-throated, anthemic pageant with the first frost. But September and early October had produced barely a whiff of frost, and I had encountered nothing but half-hearted overtures on my travels. But this sounded more authentic. I had spent the better part of four hours in the mountain's company, and now what promised to be a memorably lingering late afternoon and early evening (the light was already yellowing delightfully) turned my thoughts towards the deer, and how – and where – I might make the most of such a golden opportunity. I like woodland and red deer together, and so, for that matter, do red deer, for they are – they *should* be – woodland animals. They prosper in woodland. What stops them from being woodlanders over much of Highland Scotland is the human perversion of nature's scheme of things known as the Highland deer forest, in which the only thing that grows branches is a set of antlers. Centuries of treating both the red deer and the red grouse as economic sacred cows, and manipulating the land and all the wild creatures that live there (not to mention the ones that should and could still live there, which the "sporting estate" mentality has rendered extinct) have impoverished the natural landscape. Absence of anything like natural predators means that red deer are routinely fenced out of new woodland projects, and one way or another they have been banished to the open hill, and there they suffer a most unnatural way of life.

But I had in mind a theatre of the red deer rut where at least the illusion of some interaction between deer and woodland is intact. It is also perfectly placed for the reintroduction of those missing species that would make a truly significant, benevolent impact on the biodiversity of wild Scotland, notably beaver and wolf. The stag voices that now began to reach me from both Rannoch Moor and Glen Etive put the place in mind. I packed up, I said my farewells to the mountain, and headed back down the main road to Bridge of Orchy, thence on the single track towards Inveroran and the woodland-and-loch-and-mountain sorcery of Doire Darach.

It is a strange name. *Doire* is Gaelic for an oak copse; *darach* is an oak tree. But Doire Darach is an ancient pinewood remnant with a few larch and a lot of birch. Just to the south-west is another pinewood remnant at Glen Fuar and just to the north-east yet another at Crannach, all the proof anyone needs that Scots-pine-dominated forest cover was once nature's preferred option hereabouts. The particular attraction of Doire Darach is that it stands on the shore of Loch Tulla and the lovely wetland flourish at its west end, and it looks out beyond the loch to the mighty ridge-and-corrie mountain showpiece that is Stob Ghabhar. A few decades ago now, Doire Darach's owner was something of a pioneer in pinewood restoration using small, fenced plots to expand and enhance the surviving woodland. The results so impressed the old Nature Conservancy Council that it adopted a policy of encouraging further restoration projects.

I slipped inside the inevitable deer fence and the first thing I saw was what looked like the disembodied head of a red deer staggie lying in the grass beyond an inlet of the loch. It confirmed that it was not disembodied by twitching awkwardly at my arrival, then twitching the other way when an unseen stag roared from the trees. So was it stuck in the mud? Or was it just dying? Or was it comfortably resting on a warm and sunlit couch of firm ground that I couldn't see? I tended towards the idea that it was in some kind of trouble, but without a boat there was no way for me to get anywhere near it. I found a dry pine root to sit on, to watch it for a while, and to let the drama of the red deer rut unfold as evening began to ease in across the landscape, scattering shadows and low-slung beams of yellow light. There was a beautiful twisted spray of yellow bracken beside my pine tree, and all the blueberries I could eat. For the second time in a single day dedicated to some sense of autumn's high water mark, I found myself becalmed by a kind of idyll. Nature was gilding its own lily, and the effect was bewitching. My favourite lines of Seton Gordon crept into my mind. They are from *The Cairngorm Hills of Scotland* (Cassell, 1925):

> *In the immense silences of these wild corries and dark rocks, the spirit of the high and lonely places revealed herself, so that one felt the serene and benign influence that has from time to time caused men to leave the society of their fellows and live on some remote and sun-drenched isle – as St Cuthbert did on Farne – there to steep themselves in those spiritual influences that are hard to receive in the crowded hours of human life.*

My book about the return of Scotland's beavers, *Nature's Architect* (Saraband, 2015), had been published earlier in the year, and I was constantly reappraising the landscapes of Scotland with beaver potential in mind. I thought how perfect this end of Loch Tulla would be. That book's predecessor, *The Eagle's Way*, had alighted on this very shore with sea eagles in mind, for a tiny rocky islet in the loch with a couple of defiant trees was identified by John Love as a historic sea eagle nest site. Love had spearheaded the very first sea eagle reintroduction project on Rum in the 1970s and he had trawled the country for evidence of known sea eagle nesting sites. And Seton Gordon, who died aged ninety just three years after Love's project had begun, wrote of another sea eagle nest on a birch tree on an island in Loch Ba, about five miles away. Ospreys have already returned to Loch Tulla, and given that suitable conditions for ospreys are often suitable for sea eagles too, and given the young sea eagle's tendency for wandering among its historic heartlands, it is only a matter of time before it nests around these waters again.

By the autumn of 2015, beavers from the unofficial Tayside population had already reached the far side of Rannoch Moor under their own steam, and beavers from the official trial release in Knapdale were within easy reach of Loch Tulla. Here is where they will meet someday soon. And this vast landscape both behind and ahead of me, from the Black Wood of Rannoch to the shores of Loch Etive and Loch Awe, and with Doire Darach and Loch Tulla as a kind of lynchpin where east meets west, is one of limitless potential for innovative nature conservation on the grand scale. From the re-foresting of Rannoch Moor to the reintroduction of Scotland's wolves (their demise was 200 years later than that of Scotland's beavers), thereby implementing nature's ancient method of controlling deer populations and enabling the co-existence of native woodland and native red deer herds, and to the beaver-fuelled expansion and restoration of Scotland's desperately depleted wetlands... all that can be achieved right here, and can serve as a showpiece for enlightened nature conservation for landowners to copy and the rest of the world to admire.

An hour drifted past, the light evolved from lemon shades to deep gold. The rut began to give voice, and to intensify. I became aware of at least six stags calling from six different compass points, although as yet I could see none of them. The nearest voice was in the woods across the loch. I stared through the binoculars at those trees and once caught up with a moving shadow that must surely have been a deer, but looked like nothing more than a mobile piece of woodland. Slowly, the realisation grew that the voices were all closing in on the loch. I looked for the staggie's head, and found it in exactly the same place, still turning from time to time to follow the stags' conversation of challenge and counter-challenge. Suddenly a ten-pointer with a grey muzzle and neck appeared splashing across the river to the west of the loch and climbing its far bank onto a level patch of turf, and less than 200 yards away. There he stopped and stared along his back, and in that pose, unleashed an unearthly roar, which was matched at once by an unseen beast in the trees, unseen but closing. These, I guessed, were the voices of vanquished and the victor in that order.

There was an immediate and astonishing consequence. The staggie with the disembodied head suddenly sprang effortlessly to his feet and edged away from the old bruiser beyond the river. I thought I might call him Lazarus.

The evening began to drowse, the hearing was becoming easier but picking out the individual stags was almost impossible, and I had an eighty-mile drive ahead of me. I drove south with a headful of shapely mountains rising from a lightly woven blanket of native forest, of roaring stags, of beaver muzzles furrowing a still, pale watersheet and, from the edge of the highest pines, the woodwind discords of wolfsong. If you cannot dream such dreams in such a landscape on such a Midautumn Day, you shouldn't be allowed to dream.

*

A few days later I watched a television programme that featured a deer farm and showed staff sawing off the antlers of red deer stags so that "the animals don't get hurt".

Eight
A Storm Called Abigail

THE AUTUMN OF 2015 proved to be a benign one until mid-November when the Met Office made the bizarre decision to start naming storms in the way that the world names hurricanes, after which all hell broke loose. The first snow of autumn almost always baptises the big mountains in September. In the six years when my writing desk sat at a window that faced west up Balquhidder Glen with the graceful profile of Stob Binnein at its far end, not once did that mountain dodge September snow, nor did its higher (but unseen from my window) Siamese twin, Ben More. Both are the better part of 4,000 feet, both are wide open to east and west and north-west winds, and both seem to catch snow earlier in the autumn and hold it longer than anywhere else south of Ben Nevis. But in the autumn of 2015, it took until the middle of November, and the arrival of a storm called Abigail.

Abigail was preceded by skirmishes between big winds and troublesome rains, the support act to the main event that more or less set the tone for most of the winter that was to follow. There were immediate implications for the trees on my reasonably regular morning walk. Take, for example, a beautiful big ash by the bridge. In the last few days it had shed perhaps a third of its leaves, leaving an airier, sunnier canopy. And the leaves had begun to change colour in a remarkable way, for they paled to a shade of bright green that embraced a hint of yellow but never became yellow. Rather, it resembled nothing so much as a tree full of sunlight. And on the grass the fallen leaves gathered in a pool of the same shade. The tree stood in its own slowly thickening and widening pool of green sunlight.

No phase of leaf-fall endures for long, and there was a sense of fluttering fragility for a few days as the pool deepened and the canopy lightened and brightened, but then there came one night of big winds and the next day the tree was utterly bare. After the two days of heavy rain that followed, the "pool" was dark brown and the few feet that use the path had reduced the leaves there to something the colour and consistency of French onion soup. And then the Met Office (whose very existence I had never given much thought too before, but which now assumed a sinister presence in my life) announced the imminence of its first-ever named storm. They christened it Abigail and suddenly the news bulletins were full of weathermen and weatherwomen beaming like proud parents and explaining the significance of the new christening policy, which I confess still eludes me. And as Abigail trundled in from the Atlantic she was depicted on our TV screens with worrying weather-map swirls straight from Van Gogh in his maddest Wheatfield-with-Crows phase, and with isobars packed tighter than beans in a bean-can, and she was accompanied by those colour-coded Met Office warnings that skipped quickly through yellow and amber to red, which indicates prepare-to-meet-thy-doom.

Well, the wind topped ninety miles per hour over the Western Isles and Shetland, Abigail dumped snow on the mountains, the windspeed on Cairn Gorm gusted to 120, which is not that unusual at 4,000 feet in autumn and winter. (The record gust of 194 miles per hour was achieved by an anonymous storm in 2009.) There were storms along both the Atlantic and the North Sea coasts, but it looked as though, in the middle of the country, the earth had failed to move. On the other hand, walking out past the big ash from where a wide view of the Ochil Hills revealed new snow down to about 1,500 feet, the thing that impressed me most was the change in the air. It was not just that it was colder, it had been supercharged by Abigail's icy breath, and she had dragged along in her wake an untidy brawl of camp-followers, wind-driven squalls of rain, sleet and snow that bashed holes in the clouds through which sudden suns scattered fast rainbows. All this seemed to have energised clouds of birds, especially freewheeling jackdaws, their voices ricocheting through the squalls like bullets. And where the path follows the edge of a wood, the sunlit edge was crammed with small birds keeping their heads down but raising their voices in unbroken, querulous chatter.

The afternoon after the morning after felt worse than the storm itself. Lured by occasional breaks in deep, dark rain, I saw an opportunity to find proper mountain snow. The small back roads of Stirlingshire were awash with prolonged deluges of water and leaves. Every small field burn declined the culverts under the roads provided especially for them, and they burst open walls and fences and sprawled over the tarmac, depositing bits of trees and tons of leaves on the road, and rearranging stones by liberating them from the insides of potholes. Abigail would prove to be an expensive date.

There is a forest track just off the hill road that bridges Lowland and Highland here, and where I routinely pause to look at a posse of the local mountains – Ben Ledi, Beinn Each, Stuc a' Chroin and Ben Vorlich. If there was snow to be found that day, that's where I would find it. And in what proved to be the final respite from the rain, and the final few moments of anything like daylight (at 3p.m.) the lower two-thirds of the mountains emerged blearily – and whitely! – through the murk, and I greeted them like the father of the prodigal son. These are my snow mountains that were lost and have been returned to me. Whatever else might lie in store in the second half of November, my autumn palette was finally complete.

*

As I drove home in semi-darkness through squalls that rocked the car and challenged the windscreen wipers to keep up, it occurred to me that what I had seen and felt and experienced of Abigail's wrecking spree was surely a tiny symptom of something much, much larger, something oceanic, and beyond oceanic she was herself a small symptom of something global. I wrote in a notebook: *Nature is restless.* The next day, I drove out to the core area of my working territory, that Highland Edge land I have studied and written down for more than thirty years. I walked among familiar woods, my favourite lochside and the lower slopes of the mountain I know best, and the whole place seemed to dance with wild energy. Even as I write this, I am hard-pressed to pin down a physical idea of what I mean, and perhaps it was more a phenomenon of the nature-writing mind, but that's not how it felt at the time; it felt much more like a thing of the land itself. I don't believe that the land is neutral. I do believe that it reaches out to us, that it is capable of a kind of language couched in terms we might understand if only we are prepared to *listen*. It offers guidance, a better way of coexistence between it and ourselves, because right now our relationship with it is not in the interests of either the land or ourselves.

There is also this: the value of a core working territory for a nature writer is that over the years you acquire a degree of intimacy, you discern recurring patterns, you sense the rhythm to which nature moves across the landscape, and when something new or at least unusual appears, you are in a position to pick up on it quickly and you can assess if its presence is permanent and how it will fit into the landscape, or if it is transient because the landscape will not accommodate it. The only thing I can say with any certainty about what I picked up on that day was that it felt like a part of something much larger than the physical confines of what I could see and where I was walking. My response to that thought was to do the only thing that I have learned to do in such circumstances. I found a place beside a waterfall on a mountain burn with a wide view over the upper glen where young Scots pines had been hand-planted a few years ago and which now have begun to fulfil the promise of a recreated pinewood. Above it, a shattered boulderfield soars steeply to within a few hundred feet of the mountain summit. And there I sat and listened.

My ambition for that hour was to become a part of the mountain. That sense of nature in a mood of distressed restlessness was still there and, if anything, it was more marked than it had been the day before, or at least I felt it more keenly. It felt as if nature itself was approaching some kind of fundamental watershed, and again it felt that I was being confronted by a small symptom of something immense. Then, that evening, I read for the first time about Zachariae Isstrom, and I shuddered with a kind of recognition.

Scientists at the University of California had just published a report about Zachariae Isstrom, a huge glacier in the north of Greenland. Remember the name, for it is surely difficult to overstate the significance of what is happening there. It is calving into the Atlantic Ocean, a force with almost limitless potential at its back to raise the world's sea levels on a scale that would make the most ostrich-headed climate-change sceptic choke on the ice cubes in his gin and tonic. It's a flawed metaphor, I know, for not even a climate-change sceptic can drink with his head in the sand, although it would account for why both his eyes would be blind to the glaringly obvious. Everything about the present and future condition of Zachariae Isstrom is going to stand climate-change thinking on its head.

The glacier is melting at the rate of five billion tons a year. The number is meaninglessly large enough to impress me. What does five billion tons of ice look like? How does science measure it? Mine must be among the least scientifically inclined of all minds. But I understand the next bit: ninety-five per cent of the sea-based part of the glacier has been "lost" (the scientists' choice of word) since 2002, and the ice is now steadily retreating inland. They then raised the possibility that the glacier will retreat twenty to thirty kilometres in the next twenty to thirty years, which means, incidentally, that it will retreat *northwards* into the *coldest* part of northernmost *Greenland*.

The scientists explained that Zachariae Isstrom is being compromised from above and below. Steadily increasing air temperature melts the top of the glacier while warming ocean currents erode the underside. "And the glacier is now breaking away and retreating into deeper ground." Nor is this an isolated incident in the north of the world, although it is possibly the largest. Besides, its near and equally huge neighbour, Nioghalvfjerdsfjorden, is suffering a similar fate, although the presence of a sheltering mountain means it is melting more slowly. But, between them, they account for twelve per cent of the Greenland ice sheet. How long before we contemplate building artificial mountains to protect the last of the world's glaciers in order to stop our world from drowning us and all we stand for?

Listen to what the land is telling us. Glaciers are the easiest of barometers of the world's health to read and understand. The intelligence they lay before us is simple and unmistakeably visible. When they vanish, it is because they melt, and when they melt, ocean levels rise and climate change accelerates because the darker surface of the land that replaces ice absorbs more of the sun's heat instead of reflecting it back, the way the ice did before it vanished. I have met glaciers in Iceland and Switzerland. I was amazed to hear how vocal they are. We have to listen to them.

All of which made me wonder about that land-restlessness I detected a few hours earlier sitting by the waterfall under the mountain in the glen of the recovering pinewood. It was as if that storm called Abigail had stirred something slumberous, shaken up an old order into the beginnings of something new. But it did not stop there. Abigail was the first of a relentless series of storms that charged through much of the winter, flaying the land and piling floodwater on floodwater, so that when it all finally stopped, the very land itself seemed to gasp in the aftermath. That is what began in a quiet mountain glen in the heart of the country and hidden among the southernmost mountains of the Scottish Highlands, the same day that a Greenland glacier made headlines all round the world, an event that characterises the state of affairs we call global warming, climate change, or Zachariae Isstrom or Nioghalvfjerdsfjorden, or Abigail. And that quiet glen was shaped by a glacier too, a glacier that melted utterly away 10,000 years ago when the last ice age's rule came to an end, when ice relented and freed up the world for new life. But what is happening now is not moving at the pace of change of the last ice age. Now we are seeing the last tracts of ice in the world diminishing *at speed*. The speed of Arctic ice-melt in the whole of the 20th century was outpaced in the first decade of the 21st. We have to listen. One way or another, I won't forget Abigail.

Nine

The Carse

THE CARSE OF STIRLING is the upper Forth's mile-wide, flat-bottomed valley and floodplain. But it curls up at the edges to the south, the west and the north, where hills and mountains gather round. Even the eastern end is barricaded by Stirling Castle on its rock, by the western "gable end" of the Ochil Hills and by the Abbey Craig with its preposterous but somehow agreeable Wallace Monument. The Forth only escapes such a noose by writhing through a berserk course of loops – "the Windings", a dozen of the most eccentric river miles in the country either side of Stirling itself. I was intrigued to observe the parallel fates of Forth and Tay as Abigail and her retinue of named storms smothered the country in floods.

The upper reaches of the Tay, with its vast river basin, gather ferocious power from overgrazed deer forest and grouse moor hillsides, and exacerbated by wind farms and commercial plantation forest, both of which wreck natural drainage and hurl water down onto the low ground through industrial scale drainage channels. Downstream, the river's course and that of many of its tributary rivers have been straightened or otherwise tampered with over the years. The Forth's upper reaches are well wooded, notably in the Trossachs, and its course has largely been left to its own devices through the Carse, where miles of loops slow the flow and mitigate against flooding. From time to time it sprawls far and wide across the grassland fields of autumn and winter, but never for long. Add beavers into the mix, with their capacity to slow watercourses and their common-sense wisdom in the matter of manipulating river systems (and they have just begun to find their way over the vital watershed between Forth and Tay just south or west of Loch Earn), and you have a useful tool at your disposal to counter some of the worst excesses of global warming with its increasing tendency towards Abigail Syndrome. It is worth pondering that every decision we have made about watercourses in this country over the last 400 years was based on rivers without beavers. We have some serious homework to do in the matter of rectifying that omission.

The Carse puts its own individualistic imprint on the landscape, a legacy of the geological and human histories that have sculpted and sandpapered the land and which lie just below its well-tilled surface. It is the corpse of a glacier, a dried-out sea loch and a drained bog. Flanders Moss towards its north-western corner is a souvenir of the landscape that was, a raised bog, a National Nature Reserve that somehow escaped arguably over-zealous agricultural reforms. Nature loves it. Every time I go there, I think of the Carse as the mile-wide, miles-long wilderness of bog and wetland and woodland that must have evolved out of the ice, home to wolf and beaver and eagle, seafarers gingerly threading a course through the loops of the river, pausing under the black shadow of the volcanic plug that sat in the throat of the valley – where one day a thousand years of castle-building would begin – then easing westwards into a majestic land. Oh, to have seen that Carse then in any guise other than my own imagination.

As it is, I must have logged thousands of driving and cycling and walking miles across and along the Carse in the many years I have been its near-neighbour, and when I got round to the idea of establishing a writer's territory (an idea I borrowed from watching golden eagles a couple of watersheds to the north), the Carse was an essential component, for that meant that I would travel constantly back and forward across the Highland Edge, Lowlands into Highlands and back, and there is no richer terrain for nature in my own country than that overlapping of mainland Scotland's defining realms.

The autumn speech of wild geese on a certain watersheet under a mountain skyline and layered with the deeper grace notes of whooper swans is a cacophony of peace, especially if, like me, you incline towards the dusk rather than the dawn. Dawn dispatches the geese in a single tumultuous salvo, followed by a more or less day-long silence. But the dusk weeds them out of the farthest reaches of their feeding forays, lures them home in ones and two, in tens and hundreds, and occasionally in thousands at a time. They come in over the mountains, the trees, out of the shrouded east at your back or out of the ashes of the sunset west, and they settle in a thick, dark band of water half a mile long and gossip all night about the day's doings, about the night's dangers. And just as you think the day is done, the wind throws you a snatch of a single whooper swan, bugling home alone. There is no end to the spell of autumn nightfalls on such a loch, and your presence is limited only by the deepening cold, and by how long you can stave off the pangs of hunger and thirst. But perhaps the last thought that occurs to you as you pull out for the night is of the golden eagles you left behind you, hours ago now, in that glen beyond the first of the mountains, the adult female and her newly fledged chick on a ledge near the eyrie buttress, her mate a hundred yards away and a hundred feet higher, perched on a rock with the longest, widest view across land and sky of any rock in their home glen; that glen where the eagles taught you the wisdom of a nature-writing territory and how to unearth its secrets, its intimacies, and you saw eventually why it must embrace Highland and Lowland so that you might better understand your own place on the map.

*

Mist flattens the land. The mountains and the foothills vanish and the Carse is defined not by their bold upthrusts but by a grey blur under a clamped-down grey hemisphere. These are the close-quartered days, the inward-facing days, and November is something of a specialist in sprawling handfuls of them across your path in slow, quiet succession. You rein in your vision, you slow your step. Or you inch the car along the empty, narrow roads among farms with window down and the heater up a notch.

A big old roadside birch was already midwinter-bare in early November. A small burn beneath it defined the edge of the field. I saw bird movement right up at the crown of the tree and pulled onto the verge a hundred yards away for a better look. For a few moments after I switched off the engine I heard the murmur of the burn as it dipped in under the road, but at once it was lost under the muffled roar of several hundred wings. The tree emptied, discarded its dense foliage of fieldfares and redwings.

The birds had not gone far. After about a quarter of an hour they began to drift back up into the birch. Any flock of migratory birds is restless, more often than not. Travel is their natural habitat, and restlessness is their natural state whenever they gather and perch. Three vehicles passed in the next half hour and they filled the air each time. I watched their flights. The limits seemed to be a hawthorn thicket to the north and a rowan tree halfway to the thicket, and on the other side of the road they flew to a single hawthorn tree and a telephone wire. At the centre of this whole area stood the birch and, directly across the road from it, a dog-eared old beech. After about an hour, in which small groups of birds came and went from the birch and the beech, it became clear that the day's main purpose for these birds was to pillage spilled grain from a stubble field a hundred yards to the south. Then, once I had got my eye in and begun a painstaking scrutiny of the field, I saw that they were not alone: a much larger flock was working the field from the edge of a wood to the south.

The Carse is a four-season thoroughfare for birds on the move, thanks to its clearly defined east-west course and its feeding opportunities. In a lull out on the stubble field I turned my binoculars on the hawthorn thicket, where I found these: redwing, fieldfare, mistle thrush, starling, chaffinch, linnet, bullfinch, yellowhammer, tree sparrows and house sparrows. The thrushes apart, these are the small bird natives of such a place. And on such a day, the male yellowhammers and the male bullfinches glowed in the dull light like fairy lights. In that hundred square yards where most of the bird activity unfolded, a throng of essentially grey-brown birds might not attract too much attention, but anything brightly coloured or white can expect to lodge in the eye of a speculative sparrowhawk or peregrine falcon at a considerable distance. I know the sparrowhawk is in the edge of the wood to the south, and I know the peregrine's base is a crag just up there in the mist, rather less than a minute's flying time away if he put his mind to it. And be sure that if I know it, every bird in sight knows it too. There are buzzards and kestrels to worry about too, and while these are happier hunting small mammals, they are not likely to pass up a birding opportunity if one crosses their path.

All over the Carse and on every day of the year, its vigorous and diverse birdlife is at risk from the very nature of the landscape itself – its wide-openness. The trees and the hawthorn thickets and the occasional small woods are sanctuaries, but mostly the food sources are out in the wide-open flat fields, and a predator with eyesight like a sparrowhawk or a peregrine can choose a target from a long way off and pick the best, the stealthiest line of attack. The predators' other commonly deployed strategy is to make themselves blatantly visible, to cruise the airspace and cause mayhem, and see what opportunities arise. A sparrowhawk appeared, fifty feet up, drifting with menace above the stubble field. It was still a hundred yards from the big birch when the fieldfares and redwings reacted, fled en masse for the hawthorn thicket. So far, so good.

At that point, I had been more or less still for two hours, more or less screened by the open rear door of my car, and right in the middle of the open-air theatre the birds had designated for themselves that afternoon. And then one of nature's unlikelier little dramas took the stage. Just as the sparrowhawk reached the solitary hawthorn tree in an eerily slow glide that even I found ominous (so I'm guessing it was designed to terrify the birds), there was a burst of high-octane activity at the edge of the small burn that headed towards the stubble field before taking a right-angle bend towards the hawthorn tree, which now hosted the perched hawk. Two birds were locked in tumbling, squabbling, cartwheeling combat, in which blows were struck with claws and beaks, until one of them broke free and sprinted away down the line of the burn. Immediately the second bird followed in furious pursuit. They were the unlikeliest of foes – a redwing and a yellowhammer.

I was so enthralled, not to say bewildered, by this turn of events, so absorbed in trying to keep the combatants in focus in the binoculars that I made the same mistake as they did – we all forgot momentarily about the sparrowhawk. Just as the redwing reached the right-angle bend, with the yellowhammer a yard behind, the hawk appeared from below them, coming in the other direction, for it had used the banks of the burn for cover and flown just above water level. The redwing twisted sideways and dived for cover in the longer grass of the banks, but nothing twists sideways faster than a hunting sparrowhawk, and when the redwing hit the ground it was already in the hawk's talons. The yellowhammer flashed above them, hurtled round the bend, and inexplicably perched in the hawthorn, where it was as conspicuous as a flag on a flagpole. I switched my attention back to the hawk just as it eased into the air with the now headless redwing tucked neatly beneath it, and turned away south, low across the fields until I lost it against the background of distant woodland. It has occurred to me from time to time when I have been watching redwings that that diagnostic underwing patch of dark red looks like a bloodstain. I now know, having seen my first headless redwing very clearly in good binoculars, that redwing red is much darker than redwing blood. I turned back to the hawthorn but the yellowhammer had gone.

I turned again to look at the hawthorn thicket in the north and counted over a hundred fieldfares and redwings there. A few minutes later, they flew back to the birch tree and there were at least twice that number. There was also a pair of mistle thrushes right in the topmost branches. Throughout the two hours, with all the alarms and excursions of the flock, these two birds had not moved. They were, I guessed, seen-it-all-before natives, and therefore immune to that restlessness that so characterises the autumn and winter lives of nomadic migrants.

*

The interaction between predator and prey is a recurring theme of the Carse. The place is a favourite haunt of waders whenever floodwater patterns the fields with pools. Driving across the Carse on the way home from somewhere further north, and pausing often to scan floodwater pools, I saw a dark stain a long way out in the fields. It could have been anything or nothing, but the years have taught me that when something catches my eye in an unfamiliar way in a familiar landscape, it is always worth stopping for a look. If it's nothing, all that's happened is that I spent half a minute finding somewhere to stop and focussing binoculars, which is not a great price to pay. So I stopped, and the "dark stain" turned out to be more than a hundred golden plovers. I have a soft spot for golden plovers because, among other things, they embrace the lowest ground of my writing territory – like that flock in a wet field – and the highest ground, where they keep the company of golden eagles (and sometimes pay for the privilege with their lives).

There was a track nearby that headed out across the fields, and a hundred yards away there were two dead trees. I judged I might be able to reach one of these without alarming the birds, and I would have a much better view from there and I could pretend to be a piece of tree trunk for a while.

The plan went well. I made the nearer of the two trees, then chose a line that put the second tree between me and the flock that would help to break up my shape as I closed in. It took me ten minutes to cover fifty yards but eventually I was where I wanted to be and the flock was intact and feeding busily in the edges of the floodwater. Waders and wildfowl – and swans, in particular – are drawn to that combination more than any other inland situation. They appear to feel much more secure when they can feed through shallow water. Lapwings, curlews and oystercatchers all do it.

Sometimes the aesthetics of watching wildlife are simply an end in themselves. A dense flock of golden plovers in low afternoon sunlight appears to ripple as it moves, the way a high tide moves at slack water, an undulation of the surface rather than a wave, then the first hint of an inches-high surge running up the beach as the tide turns. And they are surely the most beautiful of our wader tribes. Over half an hour they edged closer to my tree until the nearest birds were only fifty yards away, and as I relished this moment of supreme birdwatching elegance, I reminded myself that this had been my "dark stain", and I reinforced my own belief in the essential ritual of taking the trouble to stop and look *every* time. Sometimes the dark stain will be a new scattering of manure on the field, but sometimes it will be a pot of gold.

Fifty jackdaws appeared from over my shoulder in a hurry, and announced their arrival in raucous chorus, and as they passed me I saw the peregrine at the top of the flock and the plovers took to the air in a single convulsion. They wheeled across the sun in a flock as tight and silent as the jackdaws were loose and chaotic. The jackdaws dragged the peregrine away with them, bullying it far out across the fields, and in their wake the plovers drifted back down within a few yards of where they had been, and every bird lifted its wings as it landed and pointed them at the sky before folding them away. But no sooner had calm resumed than the second peregrine struck a single bird on the far edge of the flock. It lifted off at once with the plover's wings thrashing the air beneath it, and landed again twenty yards away, where it pinned the plover to the earth until its convulsions stopped.

It's the oldest trick in nature's book, or at least it's one of them. The decoy flies over and allows itself to be driven off and the instant that calm resumes and the prey species is at its least wary, believing the danger is past, the second falcon strikes with exquisite timing. I shake my head in wonder at the beauty of the rippling plover flock. I shake my head in admiration of the tactical precision of the falcons. That's the way it is. Out on the Carse of Stirling, you get a better view than most places, but only if you have taken the trouble to stop.

★

The peregrines and the plovers are but two players in an eternal pageant, their roles unchanging over millennia, the plot lines and their denouements more or less predictable. The relationship between predator and prey species is set in stone. Unless… the predator happens to be your species and mine, for we are forever thinking up new ways to torment the creatures with which we share the planet. And sometimes our own imprint on a landscape like the Carse is as unpredictable as it is unwitting.

Whooper swans like the Carse. Sometimes they settle in the same field for days, weeks if the feeding is good enough and if the field sustains half an acre of floodwater. For several days I had marked the gradual build-up of swans in just such a field until they had mustered thirty birds, and these were joined by fluctuating hundreds of pink-footed geese and a handful of Canada geese, which are part of a small but growing native population. The field was in stubble. On a day of brightening weather I found all the swans and two or three hundred geese clustered quietly around a patch of floodwater around noon. Slowly, as the sun began to warm the early afternoon, the swans stirred. A group of six appeared to reach a consensus, got to their feet in unison, and walked in well-spaced single-file towards the north end of the field, where they began to feed on spilled grain. At first the other swans either watched or dozed on, but over the next half hour they followed, a few at a time, until every swan was head-down in the stubble.

The geese were unmoved. A few bathed, most dozed. The afternoon flowed then ebbed at the same serene pace. A mist drifted in and lay above the hidden river, the tranquil, looping meanders of the upper Forth. A sparrowhawk wheeled across the field. A distant tree fired off a fusillade of rooks. The hawk ducked down and vanished at speed, watched by thirty swans. The rooks dematerialised as if they had never been.

Then a mechanical drone sounded away in the west – a helicopter engine with a deep-throated throb. It grew louder over several minutes and as it did so, the swans stood tall and listened, staring westwards. Then the geese went slowly berserk. First they all stood, not just the crowd round the floodwater but also two more large groups in the adjacent fields. Then they began to give voice, an anxious mutter that swelled to cacophony then to bedlam as the helicopter appeared low over the farm buildings. The geese rose in clouds and headed straight in the direction of my car. The nearest birds passed a dozen feet above me, the air rocked with the rasp of wings. The flock climbed and circled and called out in hundreds of voices. It was five minutes before the first of them landed again, five more before the last of them settled among the crowd at the floodwater. By then, the helicopter was lost to sight and sound, having passed well to the north. In all that time, not one swan had moved, but they added their own brassy chorus of single notes to the goose chorale, each *woop?* apparently embellished with that rising, interrogatory edge.

The sun grew almost warm. The swans resumed their feeding, the geese their loafing. There was another gentle half hour of such tranquillity before the decisive moment of the day erupted. The catalyst was another engine, higher pitched, more strident, and far more alarming for the birds – a microlight. I can only assume that it was the appearance of such a huge wingspan relative to their own and so low over the field that so terrified geese and swans alike, but I was intrigued by the very different nature of their responses. The geese flew as before, criss-crossing hordes of them, for they joined forces as soon as they were airborne with their kin from the next field. But the swans did not fly. They ran.

They ran as I have never seen swans run before. Running whooper swans is invariably a prelude to take-off, body and neck stretched horizontally, wings beating vertically. Not this time. After the first few strides the swans brought their wings to bear much as an athlete pumps his arms. Their bodies and necks remained vertical and the wings beat horizontally, not to generate lift but running speed. Thirty swans made a flat-out beeline for the floodwater, where they gathered, wading or swimming, but with their heads still high and voices raised.

Questions for the bemused swan-watcher in his car at the field-edge:

1 – The microlight engine was quieter than the helicopter, albeit with that strident dimension, and it may have been that the tone rather than the volume unnerved the birds, but did the swans misunderstand that huge fixed wing as some kind of imponderable predator, an eagle from a nightmare?

2 – I have watched whooper swans for more than thirty years, and not only have I never seen such behaviour before, I have never even heard of it. But every swan reacted to the situation in exactly the same way at the same moment. Was there a signal? Did it specify "run – don't fly" because in that particular circumstance they considered their best option was to stay on the ground?

3 – And if so, what is the significance of a half-acre patch of inches-deep floodwater? What reassurances did that offer in the face of an attack by an eagle from a nightmare?

Answers were not immediately obvious. But sometimes, with a species you have watched so eagerly for so many years, it is good to be flummoxed. You reappraise what you think you knew, you scan the written records of others in your bookshelves to see if they have solved a puzzle that you have not, and when you draw blanks there you resolve to go out again to the field, to go back, to sit and watch again. And meanwhile, the landscape of the Carse endears itself to you a little more, and you think again how much the sum of the parts of your chosen writer's territory is exceeded by the whole thing.

Ten

Autumn into Winter

Trees have coloured every shape and shade of this pilgrimage through autumn. And if your mindset is generous enough to indulge the idea of an apotheosis among Scotland's trees, it is surely to be found in the Fortingall yew, deep in Highland Perthshire. You could be forgiven for thinking that there is very little new to say about the Fortingall yew and nothing at all of any certainty. Pontius Pilate may, or may not, have played in its shade before he mysteriously turned up in the Bible to determine the fate of Christ and the course of Christianity. It may or may not be the oldest living thing in the world. It is reasonably safe to say it is 2,000 years old. But it may be 5,000 years old. Or it may be much, much older. The new broom that was the last ice age still permits the possibility that it is 9,000 years old. Nobody knows. Nobody knows because, unlike the Californian redwoods, which we know can live to 3,000 years old, yew trees die back from the inside of the trunk. Their annular rings, by which most trees can be dated, have no protective rind, so they disappear as the trunk disintegrates. As Hugh Johnson wrote in his book *Trees*, "The Fortingall tree has no centre left at all: it is a palisade of living fragments."

So, just when we thought it had nothing new up its sleeve with which to scratch our heads and furrow our brows, in the autumn of 2015 it stunned silviculture's inner sanctum by producing three berries. Actually they're not berries, they're fleshy red cones that protect a single seed, but because they are red and roughly berry-shaped, that's good enough for most of us. The thing is that silviculturists had always presumed that the Fortingall yew is male, but now it has produced three berries, and only female yews produce berries. So it would seem that one of the younger fragments of the palisade is female, "younger" being a relative term.

The phenomenon of yew trees apparently changing sex is not unknown, although it is not common either, and when it does occur, usually only part of the tree changes. But the fact that this one has done it after somewhere between 2,000 and 9,000 years of being the alpha male of all yew trees – all trees for that matter – has rather caught the fancy of the silvicultural world, not to mention people like me who just like trees a lot.

I confess I smirked an inward little smirk to myself when I heard the news. I find it so reassuring when nature catches us out and slaps us across our superior faces, so that we are compelled to revise our thinking, and sometimes when we do that, we have to hold up our hands and admit we don't know as much as we like to think we know. My own first response was to wonder if this has happened before, to this tree. It has, after all, been around for a while, and we have no idea whether it began life as a female and changed to male after, say, a thousand years. We have no idea whether it has produced berries sporadically throughout its life. All we know is that, suddenly, within the very limited context of its recent history, this apparently male tree has grown a berry-producing branch.

I have never liked the Fortingall yew's imprisonment behind a stone wall and a locked metal gate just outside Fortingall's wee churchyard. I think it should be allowed to take its chances with all the other yew trees of the world, as it did for thousands of years before the prison builders came along. Tampering with nature, succumbing to our age-old instinct to control it, is one of the less endearing character traits of our species. In my beaver book, *Nature's Architect*, I quoted my American friend David Carroll's book, *Swampwalker's Journal*:

> *The term "wildlife management", often used in the environmental polemics of the day in reference to human manipulation, is an oxymoron. We should have learned long ago to simply leave the proper natural space, to respectfully withdraw and let wildlife manage wildlife.*

Yes we should, but the idea terrifies us. Besides, wildlife management is an addiction for which our species has yet to find a cure.

Indeed, we have shown no desire to find a cure. The Fortingall yew's berries have just provided one more manifestation of the addiction, for science has elected to cut the berry branch off the tree, and to plant the berries in pots under controlled conditions. If you have not visited the Fortingall yew, you may not know that inside its prison is a little green plaque planted to commemorate the Queen's Jubilee in 2002, so that it might proclaim the yew as one of Fifty Great British Trees, and adding that it is sponsored by the National Grid. By what preposterous arrogance does anyone get to sponsor a plaque to tell the world that such a tree is "great"? And what on earth has it got to do with the Queen? And now this. One more variation on the theme of managing nature has judged that the tree is not really fit to dispose of its own berries. No storm must be permitted to prise them free and scatter them where it will. No bird may be permitted to pluck the berries one by one and deposit the seed somewhere else nearby in the time-honoured fashion. And should it still be really necessary to point out the bleeding obvious, which is that however many thousands of years have passed since the Fortingall yew sprouted from a seed, there are only two ways that seed could have arrived at Fortingall and one of them is on the wind and the other is having passed through the innards of a berry-eating bird or beast? We used to be nature ourselves once. Now, every day, we find new ways to travel further away from it than ever.

Old trees dignify old built stone in a way that is rarely reciprocated. The prison-like incarceration of the Fortingall yew (the illusion compounded by iron bars set into the high wall and a fat padlock on a robust, iron-barred gate) is as unsympathetic an interpretation of that truism as you will find. But where nature has moved in on long-abandoned human architecture and is left to its own devices, the effect is more of a benevolent regime of enhancement than the rigid incarceration of the Fortingall tendency, which denies the tree dignity.

The news from Fortingall urged me out on a mission to restore my faith in the dignifying place of trees in our midst, and in the company of the phenomenon that is Scotland's lost broch. Bit by bit and with almost divine artistry, nature overwhelms it a little more each year, and renders it a little more verdant. Strictly speaking, it is not lost at all. It has not gone anywhere in the 2,000 or so years since it was built, and it is clear from the official register of such things that the archivists of our built heritage know where it is, how high its ruinous walls are (seven feet, ten inches), its internal diameter (about thirty feet), and what details are still in evidence (three cells and a staircase, and they might have mentioned the doorway and entrance passage too, but didn't).

It stands then, where it has always stood, on a low ridge among the rippling fields of rural Stirling and just above the level ground of the Carse, which is not quite what you might expect with brochs. Their stronghold, after all, is in the Northern Isles, the Hebrides and the Northern Highlands. There are a few in Argyll, two southern outposts in Galloway and the Borders (one near Duns is a monster by the standards of anything else in the land), and there are known fragments in Angus and Fife. And then there is this extraordinary Middle Earth survivor in Stirlingshire.

I think I must be its best customer. I have never once seen another soul there, although there is some evidence that badgers go in about the place. I go several times in each season of the year, partly because seasonal transformations make it feels like four different places, four different evolutions of a kind of natural seductive magic.

And now that I think about it, the broch no longer "stands" on its ridge at all (although it did once), but rather hunkers down into its ridge. It is so smothered in vegetation, so embedded in a spacious ring of big trees, that the sparse traffic on a minor road a hundred yards away would see only a dark field edge and a woodland edge beyond. Furthermore, there is no sign, no car park, and (mercifully) no neatly clipped Historic Scotland lawns. What there is, is a farm track that crosses the ridge then dives down to the flat fields of the Carse, and as you pass the edge of the ridge's woodland there is a discreet little gate in a discreet little fence, which is why, out of respect and gratitude for whoever owns the ridge and its half-buried treasure, I have declined to say exactly where it is or what it is called.

Some places are layered with what I think of as natural sanctity, places that seem to demand respect. Every time I push open the gate and take pains to close it soundlessly behind me and step into the trees that cover the ridge, I feel the weight of an unspoken commandment: walk softly. At the very least, the footsteps you tread in are 2,000 years old, and who knows what and who preceded the broch, and for how long?

Whether by accident or design (by design in the first place is my guess, but whose, and how long ago?), the narrow, half-hearted path along the crown of the ridge and the setting and the very walls of the broch are ablaze in their seasons with thousands of snowdrops, then daffodils then the deep smouldery blues of wild hyacinths. And when all these are done and summer has thickened the walls with more moss, more ferns, more wildflowers of myriad varieties, and filled the inner space with nettles (all of this much to the delights of butterflies and bees and the sporadic raids of spotted flycatchers), then the big beeches and the sycamores and the ashes smother the place with all the fallen shades of autumn, and the two majestic Scots pines that rise just beyond the broch's northern edge promise shelter from winter's north winds. It is as if nature has decided to dress the wounds of the crippled building, and to pay its architect the supreme compliment of treating his work as an organic fragment of the very landscape where it is rooted.

When that architect set the very last stone into the top course of the broch's tapering tower, it would have stood at least fifty feet in the air above what was surely a treeless ridge. Otherwise why build a broch on it at all? Why such a defensive structure and lookout tower of such massive proportions and so many hundreds of miles from the stronghold of the broch builders, unless it commanded a stupendous view in every direction, and (for it is widely assumed among historians that brochs were a status symbol of important people) unless it could be seen from a great distance? That great spotted woodpecker pounding its paradiddle into the topmost branches of the broch's oak tree neighbour... his is the view that the broch builders had in mind. In fact, the oak tree is a reasonable approximation of the building's height and massiveness. The most intact of all brochs, at Mousa in Shetland, survives to a height of forty-three feet, six inches, but its internal diameter is only a little more than half that of the Stirlingshire broch, so perhaps my lost broch stood over sixty feet high, in which case the oak tree is just about right.

The brochs continue to exercise historians' imagination and the best guesses of our intellect, but mostly they simply baffle us. They are routinely referred to as "Pictish brochs", for which misinformation we have Walter Scott to thank. We don't know who built them, but we know the Picts didn't. We do know that there is nothing else remotely like them anywhere outside Scotland; that they did not evolve from a humbler dwelling, but rather they were the fruits of an inventive mind, which came up with a design and then built it. It is also fair to say that that same design with its thick double walls that accommodated stairways and galleries, and the single, small and heavily defended doorway, informed much of Scottish traditional architecture right up to the tower houses of the mediaeval era. The design was a work of far-sighted genius. We just don't know whose.

So on a quiet November day, a lull between storms lit by an almost grey sun, I eased open the small iron gate, closed it (soundlessly) and stepped at once from sunlight into shadow as the trees clustered round. The ridge loses almost no height at all to the north, where small, neatly hedged fields edge away towards the distant mountains of the Southern Highlands. But to the south a steep and well-wooded bank plunges towards the flat fields of the Carse. I had walked less than fifty yards from the gate when a stoat appeared from behind a tree trunk and skipped down the skinny path towards me, the first stoat I had ever seen here. It stopped dead, stood on two legs, and tried to stare me out, as if I was an over-developed rabbit he might delude with his devilment and fell with a swift bite to the throat. I made the approved clicking and kissing noises that usually lures stoats and weasels closer, but this one was smarter than the average stoat, bounded left and vanished among the trees, and quite possibly among the old, overgrown badger holes of a cold sett, for although I lingered for a few minutes, it did not reappear. But it left a good set of footprints in a patch of wet mud.

The broch is surprisingly well hidden, and I was only a few yards away before it reared its grass-encrusted walls like a low and mysteriously curved cliff, except that here and there patches of old stone push through the vegetation, and you realise that the cliff is carefully constructed in wonderfully worked stone. Patches of that eerie sunlight knifed down through the trees and lit the stone with a dull gleam. In spring, there are daffodils everywhere here. They line the terrace that runs round the broch to the south, a narrow stone ledge that peters out towards the entrance on the east side. The walls at this point are head high, and so are the daffodils – head high, shoulder high, waist high, and knee high. If you step in through the short entrance passage (as short as the combined thickness of the double wall – about nine or ten feet) into the circular courtyard, where here and there the walls reach almost eight feet high, you find daffodils dancing there too. In November it was as if they had never been, and all was submerged under a smouldering, darkening pelt of fallen leaves.

The unmistakeable cacophony of jays cut into the late afternoon quiet high up in the oak behind my back. I turned slowly in the centre of the broch's circle to look at them, and was greeted by a sight I had never seen before. One of the jays was in mid-air, had just hurdled the wall of the broch and was approaching me at pretty well eye-level. It flashed left and passed my right shoulder so close that it left the sound of its wings in my ear, as indelible as a stoat's footprints in a patch of mud. By the time I had turned back to follow its flight, it had crossed the further wall with inches to spare and swerved away in a fast climbing diagonal between the two great pines, and there I lost it.

"And what the hell was that all about?" I asked the trees and the grown-over walls and the litter of leaves and acorns and beech nuts and pine cones. I will never know.

I am a fan of brochs. I have visited them from Shetland to Lewis to Skye and Glenelg, to Lismore, to Sutherland and Caithness and that vast Edenshall broch near Duns. I have never encountered one with an atmosphere like this. Somehow the sense of great age is more palpable because it offers itself only in fragments. The shape and stature of a broch is unmistakeable, but this one is cloaked and fattened and softened and somehow soothed by its greenery and the four-season colours of a kind of wild garden; and in the process of all that, its essential old stone skeleton is elusive. The occasional patches of bare stone are dropped hints of the structure beneath; its great age is safeguarded even as nature reclaims it. This is no longer a man-made artefact, no longer the fruits of the genius we call architecture, no longer the raw material of the science we call archaeology, but rather it has become the raw material of the science we call nature. The lost broch of Scotland may not be physically lost in the sense that it still roots where it always did, but it is in the grip of an inexorable process of reclamation by nature, it is slowly slipping out of the unnatural world of man and his built works, and back into the natural world which is, after all, the source of everything.

*

Most mornings of the working week when I am at home, the walk between my house, the shop where I buy newspapers and the café where I read them passes a row of larch trees. It's not the shortest route, but it's the only one with a row of larch trees, and that is why I choose it more often than not. The tenth larch is the showstopper, the tallest, the most widespread, the most profuse in its leaf-making. It was November before they started to turn, and it was the middle of the month before the storms found a way through the steep and deeply wooded sheltering bank that spares them most of the onslaughts of winds from south-west to north. By then, autumn had slipped across that watershed that divides its Indian summer from winter-waiting-in-the-wings. Since the first few days when snow had begun to camp on the mountains again, the air on the path by the larches had cooled noticeably, and the big larch had shed at least half of its needles. The effect was to reveal its true elegance, the more elegant because it was dressed in the softer-shaded seduction of a garment that now revealed more than it concealed. The legacy of all late-autumn storms is that softening of all their shades, cool fires wrought from the shades of flame.

The effect is nowhere more painterly than among larches. I had noticed it first a few days before when I had driven out to Loch Lubnaig under the first of the mountains to look at the snow, and found the loch – the epicentre of my writing territory, as I fancy it – in a particularly beguiling mood. It was flat calm, reflecting dark rock, dark bottle-green spruces, newly whitened mountains (but not their cloud-draped summits), and in the midst of all that the startling slashes and curves and twisted ropes of larches past their brightest autumn prime but still smouldering with embers of that shade of fire. Walking the forest road under the mountains, the surface would change colour every time it passed beneath a belt of larches, and their faded orange carpet had been badger-striped by the passage of forest vehicles, so that there were three orange stripes and two black. Now you know where Bassett got the idea for Liquorice Allsorts.

There was a small echo of that effect down the path by the ten larches, for the sparse foot traffic had made a dark stripe down the centre, between two wider swathes of that same faded orange shade. By the 20th of November, the big larch was the only tree that still held needles and they were now the colour of straw. I had the slightly out-of-left-field notion of a beautiful woman with grey hair, and how, in the right circumstances, that can add elegance and dignity to the beauty.

That day, the siskins arrived in the larches. They came in a cloud, and their voices sounded like rain in the trees. Larch trees have ripe seeds in autumn, a characteristic they share with Sitka spruce, and the spread of commercial plantation forestry across Scotland has boosted the Scottish population of siskins from around half a million to somewhere near five million in the winter when the natives are joined by swarms from mainland Europe.

I stood under the big larch watching these most engaging of small birds for so long that I started to shiver, and I dragged my thoughts away from the birds towards coffee.

★

The second last day of November, the second last day of Meteorological Autumn, I walked up through high woods to photograph the mountains as the snow thickened and crept down to the mountains' waists. The summits of Ben Vorlich and Stuc a' Chroin kept emerging from cloud then slowly dematerialising again through softening focus as new piles of snow-cloud drifted across from the north-west. Then the process reversed itself painstakingly slowly, like the autofocus on my camera lens when it struggles to find a focal point. The foreground foothills were brightly sunlit, and sometimes the sun would creep up onto the snow slopes, tantalise for a few seconds then creep back down again. A big herd of red deer had gathered under Stuc a' Chroin, just below the snowline. I could read their minds: browse up here while the going is good. I had heard the weather forecast – more snow and temperatures falling tonight to "as low as minus twelve in sheltered Highland glens", and I thought, "Sheltered Highland glens like this one..." Of course, the deer knew all that already, and I suspected they would be down among the trees just above the little frontier town of Callander long before morning.

On the slow drive back over skittishly slushy roads down to the Carse, I had already decided to divert out among the small roads through the fields to where I had been watching one more gradual build-up of whooper swans over several days. When I got to the field in question there was not a swan in sight. It happens. I turned for home, rounded a sharp bend and was momentarily dazzled by a sudden burst of sunlight on a small pool of floodwater. As I drove past, I realised there was movement in the midst of the dazzling water. I found a spot on the grass verge where I could open the car door and look back. There were two swans there. I acknowledged my satisfaction at that little last-day-of-autumn glimpse, and was about to drive off when instinct stayed my hand and suggested a closer look. I could get to within about thirty yards of them without being seen, and a tree there would afford some cover while I took that closer look. They were Bewick's swans, the little goose-sized swans from Siberia. They are very rare fly-by-night visitors to the Carse, and more autumns and winters than not, there are none here at all. But my autumn pilgrimage had just bowed out with a pair of Bewick's swans. The pilgrimage was effectively done, for the next day I had to go to Edinburgh, and I could think of no finale more fitting.

Eleven

Edinburgh: Summertime
in November

IT WAS THE LAST DAY OF NOVEMBER and he played *Summertime* on the trumpet. They told me it had rained hard for a week and the river was high. Edinburgh is apt to do that in November. No sooner is its long tourist season done than it doles out a loyalty test for the natives. Then, by way of reward, a day dawns like this one, the rain stops, the weary and wearying south-westerly holds its breath, trees straighten after a week of stooping and wading in mist. Up-tempo, the Water of Leith slaloms down from the Pentland Hills to the sea, booming and rasping through the city's canyons of built stone with their impossible bridges, pounding over its own weirs, surfing over its own rocks, plucking chairs from patios, footballs from gardens, saplings from banks; and a million leaves in every deep-fired shade of autumn are rafted seaward.

Herons stand on branches watching flotsam, waiting with the stalwart patience of their tribe for the river to relent, for shallows to resume. Kingfishers tremble on their accustomed perches in fear of drowning. Dippers, underwater foragers of distinction, are temporarily defeated. You may find any or all of these briefly crowding in on the swans and lesser fowl of the tranquil pond at the Botanic Gardens. They all carry accurate street maps of the city in their heads. And they are all neighbours and passing acquaintances of the trumpet player.

He played by an open window on the ground floor in Hawthorn Bank Lane, which is quiet and steep and closed off and traffic-free apart from the river traffic – the birds and the varying thrusts of the current – and the cool trumpet on a still afternoon, when gently robust notes harmonised with the riversong as agreeably as honeysuckle blossom and summer rain.

I saw him for the first and last time that November day, when the rain forgot to fall and the wind to blow. His window, as I have said, was wide open, and reached down almost to the floor. Naturally, I looked in as I passed, but without stopping, which would have been rude. I walked on a few yards *then* stopped and turned and looked back. I saw him from behind and over his left shoulder, but beyond him on the far wall a mirror framed his face and his eyes were closed.

I had walked the riverside pathway from Stockbridge towards Dean Village, and it was there, crossing the cobbled street by the Dean Bridge, that the first notes of the trumpet glanced among the river's hoarse choruses, the way seams of light from a full moon leak through the thickest midnight clouds; between the overwhelming river and the stone walls that towered above its banks and threw its voice back at itself, the sound of the horn spun in and out of my reach.

A steep, narrow, cobbled lane high above the river ends abruptly in a steep stone ramp with a built cliff of flats on one side and an open, terraced drop to the river on the other. It was there, down by the foot of the ramp, and almost at water level, that the window stood open, a second bell through which the trumpet sound issued as burnished smoke.

So I turned my head as I passed without stopping, walked on a few yards, stopped and turned. He sat alone in a small room a few feet from the window, almost as if he was inviting the gaze of passers-by. He was good. He played with a pure, rounded tone, the notes well spaced, room for silences between phrases, jazzy embellishments here and there, but mostly loyal to the melody.

I decided he was American. He had been the leader of a trumpet section in a big band, perhaps, rather than a true jazz soloist. He had some kind of keyboard beside him, one that had been programmed to play a backing track – a rhythm section and some muted horns. There was a chart open on the keyboard in front of him, but his eyes were closed.

He looked about seventy, his crew-cut hair silvered and thinned, his stomach thickened by too many years of too much Jack Daniels on the rocks, his back straight, his trousers well cut, dark green cords, his shirt loose, silken, grey, button-down collar. He was oblivious to the day outside and its few passers-by, uninterrupted by my lingering pause beyond his window. He played on while his phantom orchestra kept time. Inside it was *Summertime*, outside it was *Autumn Leaves*.

He began a third chorus, building, but building softly, and where I wanted it to rouse and gather and reach further, it held back, lengthened and softened its notes and silences and drifted to a close, as gently as falling oak leaves, and there the river took them both. It took the music as it took the pale sun, broke it into fragments and cast it across the city, and northwards to where the firth casts off for the sunrise, the North Sea and the coast of Denmark.

His eyes opened then, and in the mirror they caught and briefly held mine. He lifted the trumpet an inch or two in acknowledgement. I nodded, mouthed a silent "thank you", turned, walked on up the autumn river and in my head it was summertime and the living was easy.

Part Two

WINTER

Twelve
The White Bird Passes Through

THE NATURE OF WINTER is one of simplicities. The wild world is reduced to its barest essentials. It is a self-portrait worked in low light with a limited palette of pastels. Here, for example, is one such portrait.

You might come across it and think at first glance that you had wandered into the motif for a painting by Monet at the height of his Impressionist powers. Three quarters of the composition is given over to a soft-focus screen of trees at dusk, and this sets the tone, establishes the atmosphere. Individual trees are hinted at rather than rendered explicitly, because between the screen of trees and the viewer there is a second screen, flimsy and translucent, but essential to the startling effect of the whole: it is a screen of falling snow. The remaining quarter of this self-portrait of winter – the bottom quarter – is itself divided into three distinct and shallow horizontal bands. There is first a band of tall grass, which meshes raggedly with the lower parts of the trees. It is a pale, straw-coloured band; it speaks as eloquently as the falling snow of winter, and its shade contrasts sharply with the darkening bluey-greeny-grey of the trees. At the very bottom of the portrait is a slim band of water, pale and featureless and colourless, so the setting is defined as the bank of a river or the shore of a lake. And all these bands of colour – trees, grass and water – stretch from edge to edge as far as the eye can see. There is no vertical emphasis in this self-portrait. All is hunkered down and stretched wide and taut as ... well, as taut as an artist's canvas.

The falling snow has just begun, and as yet it clings to nothing, and there is no wind, for it falls straight down, yet it is the snow and the subdued light which impart the sense of the season and the hour of the day. Winter, at the very moment you stand before this self-portrait, is battening down in preparation for a long and very cold night.

It may not sound like much of a portrait (for the writer must always come up short when he tries to render the artist's visualisation with his palette of words), but I have not yet told you about the third horizontal band, the one between the grass and the water. Unlike the other horizontals, it stretches only seven-eighths of the way across the composition from left to right, and it is much shallower than the other bands. Yet the viewer's eye homes in on it at once with the certainty of moth to flame, which is of course precisely what the artist intended. It shows, hunched against the cold, a loosely spaced frieze of forty-four little egrets. A forty-fifth glides in to land just inside the right-hand edge. The whole thing is one of the most moving and enduring images of nature I have ever seen, and I have been carrying it around in my head for thirty years now. I was asked by someone in the audience at a book festival what I was working on, and when I said that it was a book about the nature of winter, she asked, "And what does that look like?" I said it was still a secret, but what I could have said was, "A long line of forty-four little egrets standing on the shore of a lake at dusk just as the snow starts falling, and a forty-fifth little egret glides in to land."

And it is not a painting by Monet, although the artist has clearly set out to achieve something like an Impressionist effect. In fact, it is not a painting at all, but a photograph. It lies on my oak table as I write, and even on a spring day of bright sunshine it contrives to thrill and chill me in the same instant, as it did that day in 1988 when for the first time I turned a page in one of the most remarkable and downright exquisite nature books I have ever owned, and there it was, and I probably gasped out loud. The book is *The White Egret* (Blandford, 1988) by a Japanese photographer, Shingi Itoh, and time without number in the intervening years I have taken it down from my bookshelves when I felt fed up or ill at ease or dissatisfied with something I had just written, and I have felt my mood lighten or my sense of perspective readjust to a more even keel in the reflected light of its quite magical aura.

Sometimes when I'm out and alone in the company of nature and the raw beauty of the setting takes over from whatever original purpose had led me there, I think about the elusive nature of what I aspire to as a writer, of the arrogance that underpins the ambition to incarcerate what lies before me within the covers of a book. Then I think of Shingi Itoh and his book, and I reassure myself of the merits of the endeavour, if you put in the work, if you approach it in the right frame of mind. In his preface to what is primarily a photographic essay, he wrote:

> I have taken more than one hundred thousand photographs of egrets ... the task of capturing the true beauty of the lustrous, snow-white egret on film has been completely beyond my capabilities, although I have continued to take pictures of them. As difficult as this task might be ... I have felt a need to understand the egret's movements and behaviour, their enduring existence, and to share what I have learned ...

One hundred thousand photographs! And one of these, shot at a pre-roosting gathering of little egrets – in what I imagine were agonising winter conditions for wildlife photography – travelled halfway round the world and fell into my hands by happy accident, and made an unlikely disciple in Scotland of the culture of white egrets (in Japan, the bird is a recurring motif in painting, literature, haiku, song and place names). Thank you, Shingi Itoh, for your work and for your sharing; it is a job very well done.

About the time that *The White Egret* was published in Britain, a recovering egret population in France had begun to send emissaries across the English Channel, where they established a pioneering presence along the south coast. The first British breeding record was in Dorset in 1996 and there are now around 700 pairs with more than 4,000 wintering birds. The slow drift northward continues, and solitary travellers have begun to turn up on some unlikely wetlands. For example:

Loch Leven, on the border between Kinross and Fife, January 2017, the day sunny and hazy, the RSPB's Vane Farm reserve drenched by a ragged, undisciplined choir of around 200 curlew voices, a gathering rare enough to be thrilling. It is also begs symbolic questions of where our country stands in its relationship with nature. Curlew fortunes are in steep decline right across Britain, numbers have fallen by two-thirds since 1970, and given that Britain hosts more than a quarter of the world's population, the bird has become a high priority for nature conservation. It is a victim of land use change in particular, the tendency towards commercial forestry and field drainage, the consequent loss of wetlands. In the short term, reserves like this are priceless, for the land is tailored to a perfect habitat for curlews and other troubled species, and it allows people to witness spectacles like this one at close quarters, so that they can watch and listen to nature making its own arguments. Such circumstances create the opportunity for people to see what can be done, and to win new friends for nature's cause. It is essential work.

The curlews moved in from the fields in a constant left-to-right drift low across open water, beyond which was a wide grassy mound where geese grazed. Many of the curlew banked round the far side of the mound and came back over its wide crown in a still-winged glide to the shore. As each bird landed it raised its wings before it settled, a heraldic pose of beauty and balletic poise.

Then one more wave of about thirty curlews came over the mound from the north, and right in the middle of them was a vivid white bird that blazed in the sunlight, and I shook my head in disbelief. Then as the curlews' wings stopped beating and they began to glide, the white bird stretched out a long neck, which I now realised had been tucked inside its shoulders, and I remembered something:

To maintain balance, the egret untucks its neck when taking off and landing.

It was the word "untucks" that had stuck in my mind when I read the line in Shingi Itoh's book, and I had smiled at the idea of being able to untuck your neck, like pulling your shirt out of your trousers. And here, after all these years of turning the pages of that book with a kind of reverence, here was a wild white egret not twenty-five miles from my doorstep. And of course the next thing that came into my mind was *that* photograph, which so summarised winter for me by reducing it to its essential simplicities.

It landed, not with the curlews, but alone and on a different shore, and in the instant of landing it re-tucked its neck. It walked a few yards, a snow bird on black heron-legs, and sought the lee of a small clump of tall, reedy grass and began to preen. At a distance of around a hundred yards, it looked like a flapping curtain in the wind, until it reassembled itself and became egret again. Then it ran a few steps, untucked its neck and flew down a watery channel and just above its own reflection. I took one photograph, which I will keep until I get a better one. It is over-exposed and out of focus, neither of which was surprising in the circumstances, but the pose is one that is familiar to me. The angle is different, but the attitude of the bird so low over water is uncannily like the forty-fifth little egret in Shingi Itoh's photograph, the one flying into the picture from the right-hand edge.

In my own photograph, the wings extend in a straight horizontal line from the head to the "elbow" of each wing, then angle down at about 120 degrees. It is a three-quarters view, so I can see most of the underside of the left wing and, because of a complete fluke of the light, the shadow of the bird's long, black bill is thrown onto the inside of that wing. One photograph – 99,999 fewer than the Japanese maestro – but it was my only souvenir of the moment when the white bird passed through my life (until I wrote this chapter).

I was back at the loch in early April and asked about the egret. The RSPB records revealed that there had been long gaps between sightings on the reserve, but that it had been back just three days before.

In its natural homelands (and, for the moment at least, Scotland is a long way from being one of those) it is a bird that lives in flocks. So why was this single bird so far from other egrets? Where did it come from and how did it get here? And then there is the more troubling question: was its presence here so far north of what I imagine is its comfort zone, and on what was by any standards an unseasonably mild January day, a small but beautifully formed symptom of our warming world, of climate change? Whatever the explanation, I am full of gratitude that our paths crossed and that it let in a little exotic light on my own idea of the nature of winter.

Thirteen

White Walls Weeping

WINTER IS THE ANVIL on which nature hammers out next spring. Its furnace is cold fire. It fashions motes of life. These endure. Even in the utmost extremes of landscape and weather, they endure.

Three thousand feet up in the Cairngorms, and deep in the nadir of the wild year, there is danger of a kind in simply being so exposed to the adrenalin of solitude and silence and the primitiveness of midwinter at its zenith. Strange how the season's zenith and nadir can co-exist in the same place at the same moment.

There is a brink somewhere just ahead. It is not a thing of the landscape, not a cliff edge or a *bergschrund*. It is a thing of the mind. Can you stretch the day's boundaries just a little more? And how much is a little more? How much of this rarefied distillation of solitude can you handle? What do you stand to gain? What do you stand to lose? Look around at the nothing that surrounds you, a nothing saturated in Arctic quantities of snow; surely such nothing-ness is inimical to life?

But a moment ago, a tiny scatter of movement caught my eye and vanished. I stopped in my tracks, literally in my tracks. There were no other tracks. All I could see was white walls weeping, the white walls of an amphitheatre of snow. Snow in billowing downdraughts, snow so solid you could build it into buttresses, snow so fozy and gauzy it hung on the air like curtains of iced steam. I remember thinking perhaps it should be colder at the winter solstice this high on loveable old Bràigh Riabhach. This is my sacred ground. Here in all the tormented, tumultuous geology of the mountain massif we call the Cairngorms is a piece of such singularly dishevelled ground that some unknown someone some unknown sometime ago christened it (with surely malicious understatement) "rough".

An Garbh Choire, the Rough Corrie.

Somewhere down below, down in the belly of the snow cloud that had squatted on these mountains for a week, was the boulderfield of the Làirig Ghrù, a place of underfoot treacheries at the best of times, and this, you could be excused for thinking, was not one of those. Not unless this is your idea of sacred ground; not unless, over the last forty years, this of all mountains has occasionally commanded you to stillness in its company and revealed to you one of its many secrets, leaving you spellbound and speechless; not unless it has mostly done so in winter and mostly when you have been alone; and not unless you are a nature writer for whom such a moment is the living, breathing definition of the Holy Grail.

Somewhere up above, up on the mile-wide summit plateau of Bràigh Riabhach, is where the River Dee liberates itself from the underworld of the mountain's dark red innards into the snow-lit overworld in a single convulsive shiver; and where, when the mood takes them, winter winds shudder and wail at 150 miles an hour.

Between these two fundamental phenomena of this most fundamental of lands is the corrie someone decided to call "rough". In that company it's some accolade. And something fleeting had just caught my eye, and I looked up towards the headwall and all I could see was white walls weeping. And the more I stared, the more I began to wonder if I had seen anything at all. So I stared harder, but the whole corrie was hung with unfathomable layers of snow. The headwall was curtained by teeming downdraughts, lavishly hung folds of falling spindrift. But from time to time, gaps in the curtain briefly opened and these showed momentary glimpses of the snow behind the curtain, snow that clung to the raw stuff of the mountain in bluegrey depths, the pelage of the hoary old remnants of Scotland's Arctic. That further-back snow had plastered the Rough Corrie worryingly smooth. It looked like far too much snow to cling for very long to something so vertical as the corrie headwall.

Choire Bhrotain, the enigmatically named Porridge Corrie, was missing. The glacier that had dragged its creaking, growling carcase this way 10,000 years ago, give or take a millennium, howked out the Porridge Corrie *en passant*, and made a corrie within a corrie there, a gratuitous roughening up of the Rough Corrie, an extra helping of *garbh*, a pinch of rock salt rubbed into the glacial wound. I knew it was there because I have often seen it before, explored its edges in less onerous seasons than this. I knew where it hung, like a picture of a corrie on a corrie wall, high up there on my right, because I was standing by the young Dee and I was facing upstream, and as long as I kept the river in my sight, the map of the corrie in my head would place its component parts on their correct compass points. Roughly.

My stance was a few hundred feet above the Làirig Ghrù, also roughly. I didn't count my footfalls or time my climb. It could be 300 or 400 feet – there are a thousand to play with here between the floor and the rim of the corrie, all of them rough, and mostly I could not see more than about fifty of them at any one time. Even when those gaps opened in the tumbling spindrift, they revealed no known reference points above or below to give them meaning. There was only the river to rely on. I had reassured myself earlier that if conditions should become too much for me (too much flimsy snow, too much mountain, too much Arctic, too much dreich), I would turn and follow it back down to the Làirig, and where it turns right for Aberdeen I would turn left for Coylumbridge. I would refine the process as I walked, but that was the gist.

Then I had started to ask myself if I should be there in such conditions, the familiar self-scrutiny of the solitary mountain wanderer. I had no intention of climbing the corrie walls to the plateau, not with the mountain happed in a fleece as thick as a polar bear's. I became the focal point of a quarrel between two truths. The first truth was that for the sake of my own safety I had no business being there. But the second truth was that I had put myself there because being there is exactly my business. I am more in the business of savouring mountains than climbing them. I do climb them, of course, but with a wanderer's gait rather than a mountaineer's. I don't much like beaten paths or recommended routes, I don't put ticks on lists of summits and I'm no rock climber. I don't frontpoint up frozen waterfalls. I never learned to trust a rope, far less another climber urging me to trust *his* rope. Here, in the Garbh Choire, the river was my rope. Trust that. Climb when you're ready.

And my business is to admire and applaud and marvel at this theatre of the wild, to question it, rather than to participate in it. I am not interested in measuring myself against it, but rather the height of my ambition is to taste it and to write it down. There you are, there is the honesty of my situation: I want to know all this to write it down. If I simply know about it and do nothing with the knowledge then I have no means of articulating my response to it, and responding to the wildest gestures of the nature of my native heath is the best reason I can think of for exploring it. I am a nature writer at heart, this is nature writing on the edge, and I like edges.

The cautionary voice, then, had been silenced by the edginess of the hour, and I had pushed on for the heart of the corrie. Far below and hours ago, considering the day as it dawned from the side of the road at Coylumbridge, a single thought: I wonder how the Garbh Choire looks and feels in this? So here I was finding out, jumaring up the fixed rope of the Dee, and all I could see was white walls, weeping. And all I could hear was the muffled river and the wind that dived down from the plateau and billowed the curtains drawn around the corrie wall. And then something moved that wasn't me and wasn't snow.

I found a rock where the wind was less boisterous, flattened a level shelf in the snow and sat on it. I like being still when nature is in a berserk mood. I like thinking about the natural forces at work on such a mountain on such a day when I am in a position to witness them at work. Being still assists that process.

Almost instantly, I saw spiders. They were tiny and red and they were moving on the surface of the snow, and being still had brought them into focus. They will have a name, these mountaineers for whom one of my footprints is an abyss. Biology will have considered them, mapped them, classified them and given them a Latin name. There was a curious comfort in the presence of another living creature with a purpose in the Rough Corrie that day, even a tiny red spider. I wonder if the Latin-name-giver paused long enough to ponder their purpose. I can only imagine they were hunting, but what the size and nature of their prey might be is beyond my imagining.

And where did they live?

And did they feel the cold?

But it was not little red spiders that had stopped me in my tracks, or made me sit on the mountain. I began to scrutinise the snow for focal points, tried to assess distance, looked for changes in the contours of the visible land where whatever I had seen might take cover or feed or draw breath.

And now I was in my element, in that state of mind which is unknown to the climber who insists on climbing in company. I was sitting on a mountainside where nature's mood pushed me to the extreme edge of what I had any right to handle on my own, but it was precisely because I was on my own that I could handle it, and that I could work at this pitch of profound concentration. And then fifty yards away I saw the inch-wide head of a bird move in the snow. I had my focal point, I unsheathed the binoculars, and I found a snow bunting.

Snow buntings are simply among my favourite things. Small squads of them live up here all year round, and not much of anything does that (spiders maybe). A handful of pairs breed on the summits of the land – the Cairngorms and the Ben Nevis group, where the terrain resembles their Icelandic origins – and on bare Shetland tracts. The numbers are guesswork but maybe fifty pairs all told. But migrating thousands flock to our coasts and stubble fields to while away the winter, and there are few more agreeable spectacles on a drab midwinter day than several hundred snow buntings in a loose flock, freewheeling over the machair of the west or the red sandstone clifftops of the east, thickening strands of fence wire to rest between feeding forays. And I once met a solitary brilliant white and glossy black male bird on St Kilda in early June, presumably a late migrant en route home to Iceland. John Love notes in his book, *A Natural History of St Kilda* (Birlinn, 2009), that the snow bunting has only been recorded once as a breeding bird there, and that was in 1913. He also compares St Kilda's origins to Surtsey, the island which rose out of the sea off Iceland in a volcanic convulsion in 1963, then he writes that the first bird to breed on Surtsey was the snow bunting. It is the sheer daring of the bird that delights me.

And now the unblinking black eye of one more male bird was watching me; a scrap of living, breathing warm-bloodedness at ease in the midst of that most demanding of landscapes in its most demanding winter demeanour. All I could see was the dull brown skull cap, the pale yellow beak, the black eye set in the off-white face, and a pale shadow behind and beneath the eye – for the bird has none of its midsummer splendour in midwinter. Ah, but then it bounced over a tiny rise into full view, and then so did twenty more, and as they bounced they stabbed at the snow, and as the distance between us closed I could see what it was they were eating: red spiders.

And then they flew in that loose-knit make-up of the flock, curved past me, rose twenty or thirty feet and landed again no more than twenty yards away, and as they flew, the snow-white of their wing flashes was a tribal badge, and they chatted in single down-curving notes. And they began again, scouring the snow for its tiny bounties, while the Garbh Corrie rose immensely above and around them, and all its white walls wept.

Suddenly the corrie filled with cloud, a cloud that seemed to consume daylight as it moved. I turned to assess my situation above and behind and below, and when I turned back to the birds they had gone. I stashed the binoculars, shouldered my pack and began to descend the lifeline of the river. Nature had stopped me in my tracks, and now it turned me in my tracks.

For an unbroken hour I walked down through grey-white silence, slipped into what I think of as a hand-in-glove relationship with the mountain, in which there are no distractions and no view, and no company other than the mountain itself, so that you feel the vastness of the massif gathered beneath your feet and reaching down into unimaginable depths below the very curved skin of the planet. You become aware of yourself almost as a creature you can observe from afar and moving minutely across that curving planetary skin, and of no more account in the mountain's scheme of things than a red spider or a snow bunting – less, because they are at home on the mountain whatever its mood, and you, you are a fleeting presence for a few hours, a few days at best.

The scale of the Cairngorms makes these demands on you, and demands of you the quiet patience of the unbroken hours. Then I felt the cloud stir. I stopped and looked around.

There were holes in the cloud below me, and through one of the holes the darkness of trees. There were holes above too, and through one of these a patch of blue that was roughly the shape of the Isle of Mull. And then, over one more afternoon hour, the Cairngorms shed their hodden grey rags to emerge in sunlight as rejuvenated as an adder in its new skin.

There was a sepulchral stillness to the pinewoods in the late afternoon, and all that crossed my path was a treecreeper and a roebuck. The pinewoods passed me on, tree-to-tree, my safe passage down through the dusk. I love the deep green pungency of these trees as I love few other facets of my native landscape. In the Cairngorms they lift you up until they part and offer you the unclothed mountains beyond their outermost shadows, then they reclaim you in the dusk and you feel reabsorbed into an ancient brotherhood of Nature, and I know of nothing else that treats you that way.

Late in the evening I sat in a bar with a fire, a whisky and a full stomach, and I wrote down the head of the snow bunting that emerged from behind an inches-high contour in the snow, and I raised my glass to the black eye at its centre. Up there at midnight, it was as cold as the Icelandic ice cap, but a small flock of snow buntings tholed the long darkness somehow and without fuss, and in the morning there would be more spiders.

There is a school of thought, and it is underpinned by a great deal of convincing science, that if climate change persists on its warming curve, it will remove birds like the snow bunting from our landscapes. If that happens, I might have to move to Iceland.

★

So what's this? I take two steps along my pilgrimage through winter, and each one stumbles over an obstacle on the path, an obstacle that manifests itself not as a protruding stone or an exposed root, not as something I can step over and march on unperturbed, but rather (it seems to me) a thing of dark moods and hidden depths. For the truth is that these two powerful savours of what we like to think of as an idealised winter ... the egrets in their blizzard, and the snow buntings in their high mountain world of winter at its most adversarial ... these are souvenirs of old winters, and in the second decade of the 21st century such moments have become the exception rather than the rule. Winter is in the throes of becoming something other: something less wintry, something much less predictable, and something infinitely more adversarial, not just for snow buntings and solitary nature writers, but for all of us, for the very well-being of the planet.

Fourteen
Sweet Medwin Water

THE MAP IN MY HANDS was published fifty years ago and 300 years after the event that lured me here. It is Bartholomew's "one inch and a half to the mile" map of the Pentland Hills and Edinburgh District. There is an old handwritten inscription on its cover in black ink block capitals, which was its writer's idiosyncratic way with treasured quotations. Even now, I read the inscription with a shiver of an emotion somewhere between recognition, gratitude and regret, for that hand was responsible for what must have been hundreds of letters, postcards, drafts of poems and captions for an endless stream of cartoons, all of which came my way. And drawings, of course, always drawings. What the inscription says is this:

> "THE SWEET MONOTONY WHEN
> EVERYTHING IS KNOWN, AND
> LOVED BECAUSE IT IS KNOWN"
> – GEORGE ELIOT

The map is frayed round the edges and broken at all its corners. The front is so stained on its margins and faded in the middle that it is now impossible to tell whether it was originally white (in which case that was surely as stupid a colour for a walker's map as cartographic mankind ever devised) and now tending towards sepia, or the other way round. When you open it out, you find that a large part of the map – the part occupied by the Pentland Hills – has been covered (not by Mr Bartholomew) in overlapping sheets of some kind of clear laminate, and that outwith that area, some of the more weathered folds have been belatedly sellotaped. There are also holes where the tape has succumbed. There are rainwater stains, sleet stains and snow stains, tea stains and coffee stains; and whisky stains for which I was responsible while trying to unite the contents of a hip flask with just the right proportion of sweet Medwin Water one old and dark December day. There are countless other indeterminate stains, the result of decades of manhandling in all winds, all weathers, all seasons. Other than that, it is in pretty good condition, considering the life it has led.

Strictly speaking, this unlovely document is not mine, and it was never in my possession until its rightful owner handed it to me more than twenty years ago, having reached that point in his life when he judged that he could make no further use of it. Thinking about it now, the significance of the gift begins suddenly to deepen, and I have never stopped thinking of it as his, as if he might one day materialise out of a thinning mist on a shoulder of Black Law and ask if he might reclaim the map he had lent me. It is just an old worn map of the Pentland Hills, but old worn maps amount to rather more than the sum of their taped-up parts, for they are the unwritten anthologies of the hill days of perhaps half a lifetime. For the better part of the last thirty years of that lifetime, the map's owner was the closest friend I ever knew. His name was George Garson and he was a shipwright-turned-artist (and there are not many of those), whose change of career so prospered that he became a senior lecturer at Glasgow School of Art, a mosaicist and stained glass artist with an international reputation. The Pentland Hills was his soul country, Dunsyre Hill was his Dunadd, and the Medwin Water was his *aqua vitae*.

The Pentlands coursed through all his lives – Edinburgh youth, National Service drill sergeant ("I used to like to make patterns with the marching men!"), shipwright at Henry Robb's yards in Leith and Burntisland, mature student (he went to art college at the age of thirty after a neighbour saw him in the National Gallery of Scotland in Edinburgh when he should have been at work and told Jean, his wife; she confronted him, it turned out it was far from the first time, then told him that if he was going to do art he should do it properly and go to college, and she took on extra work to help him through it), then professional artist, then latterly journalist, poet and author. His art was blessed by the fact that he had built ships, his journalism by the eloquence of his art, his poetry by the unashamedly working-class rootedness of his journalism.

He came from an endless line of Orcadian Garsons and he told me with some pride that the name means "son of the dyke-end". Orkney's horizontally striated bedrock, and the way the islanders worked with stone, was the seed from which his unique mosaics blossomed. He used slate to mimic the horizontally stacked stones of Orcadian walls, as consummated in the exquisite 5,000-year-old Maeshowe; and, inspired by these and the standing stones of such as Brodgar and Stenness, he fashioned a one-man art form. Its finest example, Black Sun of Winter, is in the collection of the Royal Museum of Scotland in Edinburgh. Two smaller slate mosaics hang on a wall of my house, as do drawings, paintings and pastels; and a first-year student piece of wood carving stands on a bookcase. He painted and drew more or less every day until a few days before his death in February 2011, just short of his 80th birthday and less than two years after the death of his beloved Jean.

Orkney was yin to his Pentlands yang. The words "I'm a Garson" were a mantra that opened many doors to him in Orkney, not least his long friendship with George Mackay Brown (and it was through his introduction that I met GMB, the writer who still means more to me than any other). The salt of the earth does not come any purer, any saltier, than George Garson, and I was never anything other than enriched by every moment of his company. He came into my life like an onshore gale while I was still a newspaper journalist, a gale which blasted many of my more timid ideas about writing, art – and life – into smithereens, and which urged me relentlessly along the path I have followed since.

*

It is the 29th of November, 2016. The low-slung, low-curving whale-backs of this south-west corner of the Pentlands are sunlit, snow-lit and frosted, and in the deepest recesses of the Medwin Water's banks, low-bowing blades of grass have been transformed by ice, the green sliver at the heart of each gleaming icicle as gloriously incarcerated as a pearl in an oyster. I have never seen these hills wear a fairer face than this. I am here because on this of all days I have business up the Medwin Water, but inevitably he is here too, in every whispering waterfall, in every fold of the ground, in every footfall. We have been here before, you see. The first time was when he told me the story and then showed me the landscape of the Covenanter's Grave. And this of all days is 350 years to the day since the Covenanter in question was laid in that grave.

Ah, sweet Medwin Water! A mouthful soothes the back of my throat. Another handful splashed in my face is a kind of renewal, a symbolic gesture of homage to what will always be George Garson's landscape in my mind. I simply borrow it occasionally, as I have done since the passage of time caught up with him, and he charged me with the responsibility of keeping an eye on the place and reporting back to him. Now, I mutter a word or two of thanks for all that was shared here, all that is gratefully remembered.

Walkers are fewer in this corner of the hills than in the over-promoted, mob-handed acres of the Pentland Hills Regional Park in the north. George was its sworn enemy, a regular and fluent curser of what "they" did to the hills he grew up with, for he was an Edinburgh south-sider by birth. The few folk you meet down here tend to be solitary chiels like himself, not given to walking the hills in parties, fond of the hills' solaces and silences, yet cheerful enough when you do pass the time of day with them because they know the chances are you are of the same cast.

We (I am something of a lone wolf in this regard too) like to think we take our cues from the hills themselves. They meet our needs. We mould our moods to theirs: if they are hunkered down through a week of anti-cyclonic gloom, we go deep and dark ourselves. And if they celebrate winter's early arrival with sun and frosted snow, see how we glitter in response! They are subtler hills than their northern kin, wide-open on the surface, and given to concealing the best of themselves among the smaller intimacies of cleuch and syke. It was a thick, Lowland Scots tongue that named this landscape – Black Birn, Yield Brae, Lingy Knowe, Bawdy Moss, Bassy Burn, Fingerstane Cleuch. The hills around the north-south course of Medwin Water – Bleak

Law, Black Law, Darlees Rig, Catstone Hill, Fadden Hill, Millstone Rig – rise easily in wide, airy curves until they are ultimately gathered in by the twin heights of Craigengar and Byrehope Mount. For all that these twins barely graze the 1,700-foot contour, they wear their overlordship of this land bravely enough, and in a glazed ermine of two-day-old snow they would pass for anyone's idea of mountain royalty. They despatch their various waters far and wide across the face of south Scotland: Medwin Water is a tributary of the River Clyde, Lyne Water to the east of it is bound for the Tweed, and to the north of that high ground, the first flickering burns of the Water of Leith set sail for the very heart of distant Edinburgh, thence to the River Forth at Leith.

There is a roof-of-the-world-ish feel to these wide-open heights. George Garson would tell you they are painted with broad brush-strokes and restricted palette. Then, warmed by my question, he would tell me what he meant, gesturing with an artist's hands at shadows that implied but did not reveal the hidden gully, and clasping an imaginary brush he reeled off the five different shades of grey on offer from almost blue to almost purple to almost black; then with his hand in front of his face he would rub a thumb repeatedly across the tips of two fingers to denote the landscape's texture, sinew, pith. He not only preferred these hills to the more sharply etched summits of the regional park like East and West Kip and Scald Law, he also preferred them to Highland mountains of the far north-west and the Cairngorms, where I had been his guide. At its root, the attraction of the Pentland Hills was one of kinship, of belonging. He slipped in among these hills with the ease of a hand in a cashmere glove; only Orkney endowed him with something comparable. I am as sure as I can be in his absence that he embraced with his artist's eye, as well as the twin strands of belonging, the comparable shapes of these low, whaleback hills and Orkney's low, whaleback islands. In his heart and his mind and his eye and his mind's eye, nowhere on Earth moved him like these Pentland Hills of home except for those Pentland Firth islands of home to untold generations of Garsons.

His favourite ploy in his hillwalking prime was a fifteen-mile-long circuit of his own devising, beginning and ending at Dunsyre, and stitching together all his preferences and prejudices into that singular journey among that herd of hills that gathers above and around sweet Medwin Water. He – and I (for he shared it with me occasionally) – loved it best in winter when the landscape wore an acutely primitive air and a smoky blue cast (but can you see the yellow within that smoky blue, I hear him speir at me, and in time I learned to see it), and when it necessarily consumed all the meagre daylight hours at our disposal. We emerged at the end of it all physically tried (but not found wanting) and spiritually supercharged by the terrain, the wide-open hilltop winds, and the old snow's tendency to linger longest and deepest between the hills where it smoothed over the ditches, burns, sykes and boggy holes, and it became something of a dishonour to escape without sinking at least one boot up to the knee, and preferably two. And that first time, then, he showed me the Covenanter's Grave, and told the immortal story of who lies buried there.

With the benefit of 350 years of hindsight, and especially on such a breathless late November morning as this (when nature will always provide the only religion I will ever need), the Covenanters' place in the history of Scotland strikes me as much ado about very little, and poor reason to shed blood, to kill and to die. It had all begun in 1637. King Charles I, a Stuart king of all things, had introduced the Book of Common Prayer, an episcopalian invention of all things, and decreed that it would be used throughout Britain. Opposition would be interpreted as treason. The Presbyterian Church of Scotland, for which episcopalianism was not too far removed from the work of the Devil, duly declared its opposition. In 1638 it drew up the National Covenant, to be signed by everyone who was opposed to the interference of the kings of Britain in the affairs of the Presbyterian Church of Scotland. Scots signed up in their thousands and thousands.

Sympathetic ministers, caught between a rock and a very hard place indeed, were evicted from their churches, and so they sought secret places where they could continue to preach, and so began the relationship between the Covenanters and the quiet places of the hills. But it didn't stop there. Those who failed to attend local church services were branded "rebels", and rebels were rounded up by Government troops. Many were fined or tortured, or both, and confronted with a simple choice: swear an oath acknowledging the king as head of the Church, or face execution. By the time Charles II took charge of things the land was pockmarked with countless skirmishes and battles. Among the hostilities, the so-called Pentlands Rising of 1666 consisted of a series of skirmishes that culminated in the hopelessly one-sided Battle of Rullion Green on November 28th of that year – 350 years and one day before I found myself slaking my thirst in the Medwin Water. The Covenanter army, if it can be called that, had mustered in the south-west of Scotland and travelled by way of Lanark to the Pentlands en route to Edinburgh. What they hoped to achieve there, only their God knows. There were 900 of them, and at Rullion Green on the eastern edge of the Pentlands near Penicuik, they were intercepted by a Government army of 3,000 men. One hundred Covenanters were killed in the battle, 300 more as they fled the battlefield, 120 were taken prisoner to Edinburgh where many were executed, while a handful were sent to be hanged in the south-west as an example to the natives.

So far, so very history textbook. But then there was John Carphin, and his story is the reason why I have come back, for he it is who lies in the Covenanter's Grave, up by on the summit crest of Black Law.

Carphin was an Ayrshire man, and he had marched with the Covenanters to Rullion Green. He was badly wounded, but somehow he eluded the mopping-up operation that killed the 300 fleeing men. From Rullion Green to Black Law is about twelve miles in a straight line, but any reasonable route between the two is going to be nearer fifteen miles, and as I have already explained, I have some experience of walking fifteen miles among these southern Pentland Hills in winter, and I hadn't just marched from the south-west of Scotland, fought a battle, then suffered a wound so serious that I would be dead within twenty-four hours; and nor were the hills awash with Government troops in a fever of bloodlust.

None of that deterred him. He had one idea in his head. It was that he should stay alive long enough and travel far enough towards the south-west so that he could reach, or at least see, the hills of Ayrshire; just possibly, he might make it all the way back to his own hills of home and die there in peace. Given where he ended up in the dead of night at Medwinhead on the Medwin Water, it would seem that he knew enough of the Pentlands topography to find his way back to the Lanark Road, but he was still four miles short of it when he stumbled into the arms of a Samaritan.

Adam Sanderson was a shepherd who lived at Blackhill, an isolated cottage on the banks of the Medwin. Carphin was far gone when Sanderson found him, and the shepherd made to take him in and tend his wounds as best he could. But Carphin declined. He reasoned that Sanderson's life would be endangered for harbouring a fugitive Covenanter – an amazing show of concern for his fellow man considering what he himself had just been through. One must assume that he knew by then that he was breathing his last, that the Ayrshire hills were out of reach to him, and it seems that he then asked Sanderson to bury him in sight of his homeland. The two men sheltered for a while under an oak, and it was there that Carphin died. Sanderson carried him up to the summit slopes of Black Law, a distance of perhaps half a mile and an ascent of 300 feet. From there, there is a sightline through a gap in the hills between Bleak Law and The Pike, and at its furthest reach, eighteen miles distant, is a glimpse of Ayrshire hills. He marked the spot with a rough stone, on which was carved a coded message, one the Covenanters would understand, but which would baffle the dragoons if any of them chanced that way. That stone is now in Dunsyre Kirk, and at the Covenanter's Grave there is a tombstone erected around 1840. By then, there had already been a bizarre sequel, which was reported in *Blackwood's Magazine* of October 1817:

> *An enterprising youth, a farmer's son in the Easdon district [Easton, a farm near Dunsyre], went to the top of the hill with a spade with a view to discovering whether tradition was correct in declaring that this spot was the Covenanter's Grave. He began to dig, and speedily found what he was after. He came home in triumph with a skull, some pieces of cloth, and a few brass buttons, but his father, a true-blue Presbyterian, indignant at the desecration of a spot hallowed to the mind of every patriotic Scotsman, first administered a severe thrashing to his son, and then went with him to re-inter the sacred relics ...*

A minister of Dunsyre, a Dr Manuel, eventually acted on a proposal to create a permanent monument, and at his own expense the tombstone was erected where it still stands. And around 1990, George Garson copied out the inscription and set it at the start of his own poem to Adam Sanderson: "sacred to the memory of a covenanter who fought and was wounded at Rullion Green Nov 28th, 1666, and who died at Oaken Bush the day after the Battle and was buried here by Adam Sanderson of Blackhill."

BEFORE THE BATTLE
Come first light, his commonplace skyline
ran mad with curses and pikes.

He had slept fitfully on his strae bed,
listening ...

The nocturnal raspings of stoat and rat
riven by the alien tongues and the yelp of steel.

A gaunt straggle:
some had guns with rusty ratches;
others the coulter of a plough,
scythes and spades.
Some had halbards, forks and flails.

'The Almichty bless the shiel, hird.
Nae ill tae ye guidman.
Oor fecht lies furth o' your bit dykes and fanks.
But pray for us.
For Presbyterian bluid micht weel smitch
your puckle knows gin dayset.'

Weaned on the moor's elemental creed,
he mumbled rough blessing on the day
and called his dog to heel,
flummoxed by the grim tenets of Kirk and Covenant.

Inching into sleep that night,
he pondered on the Westland man:
a shilpit chiel,
yellow hair slaggered to his brow
by winter's ceaseless blash,
legs clad in hoggers of strae
bound with rags.
Unaware that, come dawn,
he'd spade down the bairn's sword-bitten corpse
in a shallow hillside grave.

I concede that I am still as "flummoxed by the grim tenets of Kirk and Covenant" as Adam Sanderson was 350 years ago, and "the moor's elemental creed" is a surer star to steer by for me too, as it was for him. Yet it is impossible to be unmoved by his selfless response to the plight of John Carphin, as impossible as it is to be unmoved by Carphin's concern for his would-be rescuer; an exchange of mutual old-world courtesy between two such different men of the hills. And I am well aware that I used the word "Samaritan" back there to introduce Sanderson, and there are few more potent symbols of the Christian faith than the Good Samaritan. But to go to war over a book of prayer, to die and to kill because you believe your take on that faith is better – truer – than someone else's … "flummoxed" is the right word. Why not, for example, pay lip service to episcopalianism in the kirk building, and keep the old ways alive in those secret meetings in the hills until the fuss died down, until they could be reintroduced by stealth, until some other king from some other dynasty or other came up with another daft idea of the true faith, or an enlightened one who simply repealed the stain of the daftness?

But it is hard to deny the beauty and the tranquil atmosphere of the little kirk at Dunsyre, and I have never passed that way without pausing to push open the door and touch the old stone, the original one with its coded carving, and to acknowledge what passed up the valley of the Medwin Water that day and night in 1666. This was my starting point again, that earliest winter morning of 2016, in the shadow of Dunsyre Hill, which my old friend so revered. His God alone knows how many times he climbed it, drew it and otherwise committed it to the inner sanctum of memory. Ten years before, I had visited him and Jean at their home in the West Lothian village of East Burnside, and a decent stone's throw from the Lanark Road and the west flank of the Pentlands. He handed me a big charcoal drawing. Its title, written on the back, is *The Path to the Mountain*. It is a rough drawing, done quickly, and his instruction to me was that if I wanted to put it on a wall I should just stick it up with Blu-Tack, because it wasn't worth framing, and for a few years I did just that. He said it was a hill of his imagination but that Dunsyre Hill was in the back of his mind. But after he died, and a retrospective exhibition of his work was being organised, involving the framing of a considerable body of late work, I added it to the framer's workload, and now it hangs in a more digni-fied setting in my house, and I take it as a kind of constant injunction from the artist that I should keep following the path to the mountain, whether it's lowly Dunsyre Hill or Bràigh Riabhach or Suilven, or my friendly neighbourhood mountain of Ben Ledi, or, as on the morning of November 29th, 2016, Black Law. So I raised a hand to Dunsyre Hill and set off for sweet Medwin Water one more time. And when I reached its banks and turned north to fall in with its amiable company and downed a ceremonial dram of its water from my cupped hand, I guessed that the nature of winter would never taste sweeter than this, no matter where its journey took me.

Improbably, Adam Sanderson's Blackhill cottage still stands, or at least the footprint of it does. What survives is a low ruin, less than waist-high in places. I stopped there to look at the stonework and to see if I could still detect the places where a kind of rough restoration had been applied in patches. This was George's homage to Sanderson, long before he wrote the poem. His years of studying the architec-ture and the archaeology of Orkney, and applying what he learned there to his slate mosaics, not to mention his great enthusiasm for the Pentlands' repertoire of wonderfully worked drystane dykes ... all that had given him a certain easy familiarity with, and a fluency for the craft of setting stone on stone so that it "reads". He may have wrought his art and his poetry from Orkney bedrock, but he understood the timeless strength that underpins it too. And besides, he'd built ships.

The passing of time, the blessing of lichen, and the cold fire of many a winter wind, had absorbed his handiwork into the body of the ruin and I couldn't tell his stonework from the rest of what remains of Blackhill, and I dare say he would judge that I could pay him no higher compliment.

The Medwin is a heron's water, and in the same way, the heron is a Pentlands bird. The myriad burns, cleuchs, sykes, bogs and reservoirs fill these hills with small fish, frogs, toads and other heron food. I had been sitting for a while by Sanderson's ruin, and when I finally stood and advanced a few yards towards the water, a heron I had not seen and which had not seen me, rose from the burn with a ponderous heave of a wingspan that looks more than is strictly necessary to do the job. As it rose from shadow into sunlight, its unfolded legs scattered pinpricks of watery light, its shadow rippled across the decrepit stone walls of Blackhill, and suddenly my memory was turning cartwheels. I had seen that simple shadow-dance before.

George Garson and I were padding up the Medwin, rounding the scrap of a pinewood that clings there, dropping down through the worn-out bracken to the burn, when a heron rose from a pool, spread a grey-blue sailcloth of wings, and as he climbed, I saw his shadow fall across the walls of Sanderson's cottage. It was done within a few seconds, but it had caught my eye as it clambered the slope up to the ruin, and I had turned to George and shouted:

"The shadow!"

For the sight of it had stopped me dead, and the thought it implanted was this:

How many shadows of how many herons have fallen across these walls throughout the life and long death of the cottage of Blackhill? Say 400 years? When there was a roof on the walls, Sanderson would see the shadow slide down it whenever a heron dropped down to the pool. He would see an otter's wake bubbling upstream, and he would see the shadow climb the house again as the heron leapt in slow alarm with a Presbyterian oath of its own. I have no doubt that from time to time the shadow would wear the embellishment of an eel at the sharp end (the immortal Henry Williamson referred to it as "a two-pointed spear on a shaft hidden by long, narrow feathers"), as the bird was disturbed while it wrestled with its catch. There are few things in nature less willing to die than an eel in a Scottish hill burn. In that way, or some other, thousands of heron shadows have darkened Sanderson's window and scaled his walls and the pitch of his roof.

The particular heron George and I disturbed that day had, in its turn, disturbed a dipper from a mid-stream rock. There are few more eloquently displayed extremes of the diverse art of bird flight than these – the ponderous heave of heron wings and the tiny headlong blur of the burn-clinging dipper. Yet when the dipper goes under-water-hunting, his wings slow to a heron's gait as he dives down, effortlessly defying all the instincts of natural buoyancy, and he drags his shadow down with him to walk along the river bed. On the bank, we grounded bipeds watched with a kind of stupefied wonder.

I hefted a few stones as if I knew what I was doing and set them thoughtfully into the wall of Blackhill, but I don't know what I'm doing and they never seem to find a snug fit. It's the thought that counts now, as far as that particular ruin is concerned. It has ceased to be Sanderson's place, and instead it has become a landmark in George Garson's territory, in George Garson's Pentlands, which is how he thought of it himself. I headed off uphill into the sun and the cold, still air and the brilliance of snow-light. I paused at Carphin's final resting place, his plain stone graced by a thin arch of frozen snow, and here and there patches of the same snow still clung to the inscribed face of the stone like white lichen, eccentrically editing its text: *...and who di ... ... sh/ the day a ... ... e Battle/ and w ... ... uried here ...*

I hope he found his peace and his God, and I hope his God was generous to him. Whatever the nature of the reason why you died, John Carphin, there are worse places by far to be laid to rest, even if it isn't Ayrshire.

Fifteen

The Narwhal in the Sky

A STRANGE DAY DAWNED, a day autumn had stolen back from winter. En route for Glen Finglas, the Woodland Trust Scotland reserve and Ben Ledi's next door neighbour to the west, pausing on Loch Venachar's shore ... there, at noon, the day was *warm*, and so still that a hint of surrealism crept into the sunlit surface of the loch and the reflections of land and sky. There was no obvious join, no demarcation between reality and reflection, cloud and water seamlessly united, the western shore which includes Ben Venue was both suspended and afloat in sky and water simultaneously, neither the real land nor its reflection noticeably brighter or darker than the other, an equinox of the mind's eye. Was this autumn's revenge for winter gatecrashing autumn that day in the Pentland Hills? Do the seasons deal with each other that way? Is there a conversation, a negotiation, a deal, or just an uninvited raid, facilitated by one more foible of the jetstream?

The Glen Finglas oakwood was deep dark brown, mysteriously suntanned. All the leaves had turned, but they still clung to the trees in huge quantities. By early December 2015, four of those storms the Met Office likes to refer to by their Christian names (Abigail to Desmond) had already bludgeoned the trees bare and left quite a few of them prostrate on the forest floors of the land. But by early December 2016, the back end of the year had been utterly stormless. The result was an atmosphere within the oakwood of other-worldly tranquillity, as if the natural order of things had been suspended, as if time itself had been outwitted. The oakleaves had passed through all the phases of photosynthesis demanded of them by nature except the final one.

Sunlight was the saving grace of the place that day, for it lit and shadowed all that brown-ness. When a female buzzard and I surprised each other (she had her back to me and the sun, using it to spotlight fugitive prey by positioning herself on an oak limb so that the light came over her shoulder), she parted with the tree in such a way that it was as if a fragment of the oakwood cloak had been prised away from the whole and unwillingly cast adrift. For she flew so knowingly through that web of trunk and twig and branch and limb, and she bore in her plumage – and especially in the fluctuating revelations of upper and lower wings – every single shade of the winter oak; she was as much of the wood as every living tree and every fallen tree. The sense that my arrival in the wood had wounded some ancient peace lingered with me until I climbed up beyond the highest oaks and out into the more open-handed generosity of the embryonic birch wood above, then the broad expanses of mountainside with their splashes of tall, slender pines against the skyline.

These are survivors from the commercial forestry that predated Woodland Trust Scotland's benevolent rescue operation. The dense spruce was felled, birch and pine enclaves had somehow found a niche and with no room to fill out they survived by putting all their energies into growing tall. They may not look much, but they are seed-bearers and they beget more of their kin, and that is the object of the exercise.

I paused – as I always do – at the bench dedicated to the memory of William Butler. I like to sit and write there. On that December day of unseasonal warmth and calm I listened to far-carrying sounds: a dog bark at a distant farm, the woodwind sigh of bullfinches, and the one that made me wish I could spin my head through 180 degrees like an owl – the high-pitched, incongruous yet unmistakable terrier yap of a golden eagle. I found it in the glasses eventually, much higher than I had thought it should be and almost directly overhead. It was the fourth time I had seen an eagle from that seat in two years; one more reason why William Butler's thoughtfully-placed memorial endears itself to me, likewise his family who thought fit to put it there.

I watched the eagle climb out of sight (it simply became too tiny), but the arrival of the sound of its voice in my ear, fallen to earth like a discarded feather, had only been possible because of the stillness of the day, the clarity of the air, and the fact that whenever I am alone in wild places, I am increasingly intrigued by that idea I have mentioned before of *listening* to the land. It is the simplest of ideas and one of the oldest; it is the basis of a relationship with landscape common to many of the native peoples of the northern hemisphere.

You make a space in the day. You think only about listening. You give it time. Those are the essentials. Slowly, you can begin to reach beyond the surface sounds and detect the presence of something beyond them, something deeper. Then your eyes begin to assist the process of listening.

So, there was a moment within that hour of profound calm when every shallow curve and every deeper breast-shaped curve in the contours of the wooded hillside below became a kind of breathing, the breathing of the land itself, and there is at least the sense of something other: the speech that flows between land and forest and water emerged as a conversation on which I could eavesdrop. The American nature writer Barry Lopez hinted at something similar when he wrote of a conversation he had with an old Eskimo woman about a visual equivalent of that "something other" in his book *Arctic Dreams*, then interpreted it thus:

> *To put it another way, occasionally one sees something fleeting in the land, a moment when line, colour and movement intensify and something sacred is revealed, leading one to believe that there is another realm of reality corresponding to the physical one but different …*

George Garson would have nodded his head agreeably at that. I subscribe to it wholeheartedly.

I turned my attention back to the hillside below. I love the pines at this time of year, when every other tree is either brown or bare or both. They appear to glow, as if they are lit from within. That particular winter circumstance of dead calm (wrong expression – *living* calm), the air rinsed clean, the land lit by the afternoon sun low in the southwest … all that conspired to show off the finery of pines while every other tree on the hillside was smoored. At its most exhibitionistic, the phenomenon alighted on a small heathery knoll where two pines have flourished spectacularly in the years of their liberation from that old spruce stranglehold. One is twice the height of the other, but the other has twice the spread. The trunk of the taller tree forked about six feet off the ground, in order to send two perfectly parallel limbs shooting skywards, so that now it brandishes its double crown forty feet above its roots. I have seen many pine trees I would call handsome, but I have never seen another one with quite this elegance.

In the late afternoon, with the sun half in and half out of that realm of shadows beyond the hills in the south-west, I felt the air stir and knew it at once for the breath of winter. Then the air went immediately cold. One hour hence, it would be deep dusk and deep winter cold, the day's illusion done. It would prove to be the first of many illusions in which that particularly skittish winter would indulge itself. Global warming's southwards seepage down through the northern hemisphere from the Arctic is making mockeries of the very nature of winter itself. A thin, creeping, purplish band of cloud began to wrap itself across the half-sunk sun. Its progress across the sky held an indefinably ominous air and made for hypnotic watching. When I eventually turned my back on it, I was just in time to see my shadow fade into the hillside. At once, the cold rushed in around my neck. Then, there was that sacred thing again, a force of such quietness that I was compelled to linger and listen to its symphonic purity. My stillness felt like a kind of command. No nature writer worth the name is deaf or disobedient to nature's commands. It could have been moments or minutes or half an hour.

★

Sometimes I think I believe in omens. If that sounds half-hearted, that's because it is, because a belief in omens is a tough creed to commit to, because by the very unchancy nature of their appearance, they invite doubt, scorn, disbelief. What, for example, am I supposed to make of a whale that was about to appear in the sky?

I had just shared that landscape's brief era of quietude with eagle and fox, vivid embellishments to the day's tapestry of nature's moods from lochside to oakwood to open hill. I was already thrilled by a kind of lingering unease before that eerie cloud ushered the sun from the sky, and I watched the western sky as I dropped back down the hillside. It was then that a new cloud shape materialised above Ben Venue, the mountain which dominates the very heart of the Trossachs. It was the shape of a narwhal, complete with long, slender, tapering tusk, jutting out dead straight from its head. I stared and stared and stared. If I concede that the moment was attended by a sense of omen, I should also acknowledge that I was clueless about what kind of message it might be trying to impart. It is a long, long way from the landlocked Trossachs of the Scottish Highlands' most southerly mountains to the Arctic Ocean domain of the narwhal.

The narwhal is a kind of wolf of Arctic waters, if only in the sense that humanity has endowed it with bizarre legend and misunderstanding fuelled by ignorance of what it is and what it does. Stir into the brew of centuries the unicornish connotations of the tusk, and the narwhal has offered up one of the most fertile sources of legend-making ever to spew forth from some of the most irrational excesses of human imagination. It is comparatively recently that any reliable information at all began to emerge about where narwhals go and what they do in winter, and that has only been possible because of global warming, because the disappearance of Arctic sea ice has become as much of a threat to the very existence of the narwhal as it is to the polar bear.

Among the things we still don't know is the origin of its name, and there seem to be almost as many theories out there as there are whales in the oceans. One of the oldest and most persistent centres around a theme of death, apparently because its pallid skin is thought to resemble that of a human corpse. Old ones have been known to turn quite white. In some circumpolar societies, its appearance was an omen, and thought to presage a human death; or it became symbolic of human death. Happily, I was still unaware of this when my own narwhal omen loomed above its mountaintop.

And then there is the question of the tusk. What is it for? It is, almost exclusively, the preserve of the males, but it is not a weapon. They don't impale their prey on it (they catch fish, notably cod and halibut, in their mouths), they don't wound rival males with it, or fend off attacks from their predators, the killer whales and the polar bears.

It is, in reality, a tooth, their only tooth. It is one continuous spiral and crammed with nerve ends, and it appears to pierce the upper lip on the left side of the narwhal's head. Two males will sometimes cross tusks, like swords, but there is no clear evidence that it is a ritual pose with a purpose, or whether it is even a deliberate manoeuvre. One of the more persuasive possibilities is that in narwhal mating society, size matters, that the bigger the tusk, the more dominant the animal, the more impressed are the females.

The narwhal is one of the smaller whales. It can grow to about sixteen feet, but its girth can be eight feet and it can weigh two tons. Add on ten feet of tusk and you have a considerable presence. They can also dive to improbable depths, although science differs with itself about just how deep. Half a mile, perhaps. Its unique underwater life, and especially its under-ice life, is where the waters really start to muddy.

But when one appeared in a Highland sky to adorn a winter sunset, the effect was magical. The tusk extended levelly across the sky, tapering, to end in a perfect point above the sunken sun, so that it was tipped with gold. The head of the narwhal cloud flamed briefly, while its underside beneath the tail echoed that shade more palely, a gentler flame. I had never seen a cloud like that before, so I took some photographs, unaware for the moment that right then and a few thousand miles to the north-west, one more symptom of global warming had just dumped a new and life-threatening crisis on the narwhal's distinguished head, and then there was the coincidence of what followed. The particular nature of what a Highland winter has become, a disjointed series of the briefest fragments of snowy and frosty weather punctuating long and turgid swathes of mild grey gloom, and of which the winter of 2016–17 would prove to be the most convincing example yet, is global warming writ large and indelibly. Believe in it.

If you have been writing about nature for a living for more than thirty years, and studying it for rather longer, your perspective is arguably as valid as anyone's. If you weigh the verdict of those sources you trust among the world's biologists, ecologists and nature writers of, say, the last 200 years, then set that in the context of what you have seen and questioned for yourself, then there is only one reasonable conclusion. It is that global warming is no longer a disaster waiting to happen – it has begun, it is already happening, and it is travelling with terrifying speed towards the point beyond which it will not be reversible. Right now, I think that winter itself may be halfway towards extinction, that the wild year will soon be measurable in three seasons – a spring that lasts from February to May, summer from June to September, and autumn from October to January. There will be savours of those winters of memory from time to time, but they will be fragments that conjure up little more than nostalgia. We would get the storms, the fleeting shades of the season formerly known as winter, but no more seasons of sustained snow and ice, no more weeks at a time of a land locked up in sub-zero temperatures. In winter's place there has emerged a troublesome species of climate chaos. And the idea of four seasons will be reduced to a piece of music by Vivaldi.

Which brings me back to the plight of the narwhal. The narwhal is an Arctic specialist. Unlike many whale species, it doesn't migrate to warmer waters, but remains in Arctic waters all year where it can live under the sea ice. At the time the narwhal-shaped cloud appeared in the Trossachs sky, and quite unknown to me then, narwhal on the north coast of Canada's Baffin Island were having a specific problem. That problem was killer whales. But the reason they were having a problem with killer whales at all is global warming. In February 2017, the Canadian Department of Fisheries and Oceans published the findings of their study of the narwhal's particular problem. The presence of killer whales, said the study, "is intimidating the narwhal into drastically altered behaviour. It's another symptom of how climate change is remaking the delicate northern environment."

Most narwhal "overwinter" (if I am right about the near future, we are going to have to find a new verb for that idea soon) for up to five months under sea ice around Baffin Bay and Davis Strait. But 5,000 of them spend the summer in Admiralty Inlet on the north coast of Baffin Island and 500 miles north of the Arctic Circle. There, they have been accustomed to enjoy the protection of sea ice. Crucially, as far as the narwhal are concerned, killer whales don't like sea ice, so their presence in these, the narwhal's calving grounds, had always been limited. But the rapid decline of the summer sea ice means that the narwhal are much more accessible. So the killer whales have started to arrive in greater numbers, arrive earlier and stay longer.

"Inlet" is a deceptive word in the circumstances, inviting thoughts of tranquillity and landscape intimacy. Admiralty Inlet is huge – almost 200 miles long and thirty wide. Historically, the narwhal hunted between two and six miles offshore. But now, whenever the killers are present anywhere at all in the inlet, the narwhal "cower" (the revealing word used by the Canadian study) within 500 yards of the shore. They have a unique system of communication between groups which spreads the word of the killers' presence several miles out to sea, so they cower inshore, and they become easy pickings in what had always been one of the richest and safest of hunting grounds. One of the study report's authors said that "the narwhal are scared to death". Then he offered this chilling thought:

Most traditional science views changes from the bottom up – the food supply changes and it ripples its way up the food chain. A few of us believe the changes can happen from the top down and be just as significant.

It is hard to overstate the significance of Arctic sea ice in terms of nature's own ideas about what constitutes a healthy planet. The ice's underside is densely coated with algae, the essential original source of a chain reaction that reverberates out into the oceanic world. These feed zooplankton, unimaginably large clouds of which drift through the upper layers of the sea. They are, in turn, devoured in unimaginably large quantities by fish like cod. The fish feed seabirds and narwhal, and the ringed seals that feed the polar bears and (once the bears have had their fill) the Arctic foxes. Ice binds all this together. Ice-thirled seals, like the ringed seals, are not comfortable hauled out on a beach; they are vulnerable there. But out on the ice they can rest up directly above their feeding grounds. And ice is where they have their pups. And ice is also how the bears reach the seals.

Narwhal seem to be able to read the ice like no other creature in the Arctic Ocean. When a "lead" (a channel of temporarily open water in an ice field) is about to close, trapping them under an extent of ice too long for them to travel on a single breath, they sense the advent of the change and they leave. This kind of specialised sensitivity to their ice world is also communicated around different groups of narwhal by methods that are still not completely understood. Scientists have talked of tape recordings of narwhal being "saturated" with the tumult of their acoustic emissions.

Such intuitive genius is not lost on this Scottish nature writer, observing in some detail the nature of this winter of 2016–17 in his own part of the world and finding it bestrewn with admittedly smaller symptoms of the chaotic phenomenon that is climate change. But it bears repeating what John Muir knew 120 years ago when he was writing *My First Summer in the Sierra*:

> *When we try to pick out anything by itself we find it hitched to everything else in the Universe.*

We know that too, of course, but we forget we know it, or we choose to ignore that we know it, and then the facts get in the way and we remember again, when it's too late. Satellite records from America's National Snow and Ice Data Center showed that in February 2017, the extent of Arctic sea ice averaged 5.51 million square miles, "the lowest February extent in the 38-year satellite record", and 15,400 square miles less than 2016. The summer sea ice of 2016 reached a "statistical tie" for the second lowest Arctic sea ice minimum at 1.6 million square miles, and only 290,000 square miles more than the record low point in 2012. If these numbers sound comfortingly large to you, then consider this: in the first thirty-eight years of these records, two million square miles of midwinter sea ice simply disappeared – two million and counting. And how far away can we possibly be before the Arctic summer sea ice disappears altogether? And, because "when we try to pick out anything by itself we find it hitched to everything else in the Universe", it stands to reason that the consequences will be far-reaching.

Some more numbers for you to consider, courtesy of my Alaskan friend, the writer and teacher Nancy Lord, in her book *Early Warming* (Counterpoint, 2011):

I know these numbers: White sea ice reflects about eighty per cent of the sun's heat, blue water absorbs ninety per cent.
And these: Twenty years ago, eighty per cent of Arctic ice was at least ten years old; in 2007 only three per cent was that old.
And this fact: The Arctic has been ice-free in summer before, but, according to the National Snow and Ice Data Center, scientists have confidence that the last time was 125,000 years ago ...

The melting of the polar ice sheets may be seen as a kind of global shorthand for climate change at work, but I can perhaps be forgiven for wondering what nature was up to when it grafted a narwhal onto a Trossachs skyline.

Sixteen

Solstice

THE YEAR DWINED towards midwinter. The sun had been a fleeting, pale-faced stranger in the hills, the snow when it came was deep and wet high up, but the temperature never stayed low enough for long enough to stabilise it, so it leaked water by the ton into dark gullies wrapped in long, skinny and restless fragments of cloud that drifted and reshaped and disintegrated before a cold, clammy, listless wind. One morning, the mountainside was striped with white-foaming burns, hoarse and loud-mouthed. They charged down the gullies, rain hissed on the bent and broken tea-stained leaves of withered ferns and heather. In forty-eight hours, all that had eased down to a dripping, listless day of uneasy calm.

There is a rowan up there on that Glen Dochart mountainside which cleaves to a buttress, a skinny little runt of a tree going nowhere, especially not upwards. Yet it has clawed sustenance there for thirty years that I know of, and quite possibly for twice that long. I have seen a golden eagle pluck a sprig from it in its green portion of the year, for all that it is fully a mile from the rowan's buttress to the eagle eyrie buttress.

And there I sat, holding a one-sided *ceilidh* with the rowan, huddled under an overhang, hands clamped on the cup of my flask, drinking two-handed while the coffee still steamed, and happed in ridiculously expensive waterproofs and boots; and still the sodden air found a way inside the jacket's neck and hood the way spiders and slaters suddenly turn up mysteriously in your bath, as I explained it to the rowan. You can dress for weather like this, but that does not necessarily mean you can keep it out.

But sometimes it is simply part of the job, and the bizarre truth is that I was enjoying myself. There is a perverse satisfaction sitting on a familiar mountainside when most of the views are down and none of them are long, as secure on my chosen cleft of rock as that rowan, friend of the wind and the rain and fellow traveller of the snows, and intimate companion of the mountain itself.

"Intimate" is the essential word for a nature writer. It's why I work a particular landscape the way an eagle works a territory. And intimacy with a landscape, with how nature works in that landscape, is gleaned from a day like this as much as from a blue, shirt-sleeve day of late spring clarity and endless sightlines, of ring ousel song and a litter of orchids in long summer grass. I need them all, and I need to know how they are connected. So there I sat in the dripping snowscape, conversing with a rock-rooted rowan waiting for something to turn up, and five red deer hinds and three calves had just filed out of a slaister of screes and boulders a hundred feet below me, out into what on a better day you might call "the open".

I hadn't seen them coming. But there again, on such a day with no long sightlines in any direction, unplanned encounters like this one were very much part of the plan. Sometimes, just being there is all that matters, and you let the day take care of itself.

The deer were as unaware of me as I had been of them until a few seconds ago, but right now they were movement and I was stillness, so for the moment I had an edge. With luck, and if no unkindly wind sprung up, things might stay that way for a while.

They walked slowly and in single file, a trail-breaking matriarch with three younger animals directly behind her, then the calves and a grey-faced old veteran bringing up the rear. The snow was old, wet and deep, and I had stumbled knee-deep more than once on my way up. But I noticed the matriarch had chosen a contour where the snow was no more than three or four inches deep. So there is the kind of intimacy that *I* feel for this mountainside, and then there is the intimacy a mature red deer hind brings to bear on every living, breathing moment, so that it extends to the way the snow lies on any particular slope, the ledges where it deepens beyond what is comfortable, and the flat-topped bluffs and buttresses where the work of a particular wind from a particular airt over a particular number of days thins the snow to a workable shallowness. She reads and understands her mountain the way you or I might read and understand this page of this book. She is fluent in its language.

She angled up the near flank of a buttress directly below me, and where I had expected to see her struggle in deep drifts, she had found a runnel of water that oozed from the base of the buttress, and she stepped elegantly up there on almost bare rock. The younger hinds had stopped at the base and watched her for a few seconds. If I was inclined towards anthropomorphism, I would say that when they followed they did so with admiration and gratitude – but I don't care too much for anthropomorphism, so I will concede only that the gratitude and admiration were all mine.

On the top of the buttress she stopped and began pawing the snow until she bared a few square inches of mountain grasses, mosses and lichens, then she lowered her head to eat. The others went to work after the same fashion. The snow there was no more than two inches deep.

But where was the old one? She had not made the climb up the flank of the buttress. I took a long look down what I could see of their tracks back to the boulderfield, and of the wide slope below. So I was not looking at the deer at the precise moment when her grey head would have appeared from below and beyond the far side of the buttress. When I did look back at the deer she was already there, pawing the snow and feeding with the rest. Much later, once they had taken all that they could from the meagre offerings of the buttress-top (in a moment I was handed a vivid new definition of the expression "slim pickings", and these were on the skinny side of slim), I dropped below the buttress to look at the old one's tracks.

They were not hard to find. She had passed beneath the buttress and contoured about fifty yards beyond it, to where a venerable stalker's path zigged and zagged easy gradients into the slope, and where days-old boot prints had stamped the snow into a red deer walkway as flat and firm as bare rock. Intimacy, you see? That's what it looks like through her eyes.

I have a notion of my own that the hind which led the way up there had learned about the bite of old grass under the snow above the buttress from the old grey-faced one. When the deer finally moved on, they descended by the old one's route and resumed their original contour line and disappeared by degrees into the gloom. If they had registered my presence at all, they gave no hint of it.

I moved off downhill, for I didn't much care for the look of the sky in the north-east, and took easy slopes above the gully of a burn that slithered quietly away to the distant river. I was still thinking about the deer and what it must be like to carry that kind of map of the mountain in your head, when I heard voices from below, thin and high-pitched and just about carrying above the voice of the burn. From the edge of the gully the source was obvious at once – snow buntings again, a flock of about thirty, every one of them clinging to the swaying tops of the bleached hill grass that grew thickly in a sheltered corner of the bank of the burn, every one of them plundering seeds, and flickering palely in short flights from one grass stem to another, the air as vibrant with the white flash of wings and tails as with their voices.

Snow buntings are among the boldest of small birds, so I took a chance and simply sat down on the top of the bank a dozen yards away and watched. Once again, not one reacted to my presence. They were nearly all males, which is the norm for a winter mountain flock. Science thinks they are better insulated than the females and first-year birds, which tend to winter in Scotland around the coasts, and it seems as likely an explanation as any.

Eight red deer and thirty snow buntings. If anything else at all moved on that mountainside in the four hours I was out there, they left neither sight nor sound of their passage. The most compelling characteristic of the day was its utter quietness, a few soft mutterings from the deer, the thin havers of the birds, a half-hearted wind, a soft-voiced burn; not so much as a raven croak to disturb the equilibrium of late afternoon. The buntings were still there when I stood and left, still swinging and swaying with the wind and the tall grass.

In the night it snowed hard on the mountain. Eight red deer, thirty snow buntings and a rowan tree rooted in rock all tholed a night such as you and I can barely imagine; the deer and the birds finding shelter of a kind, the rowan leaning out from the rock into the storm like the bowsprit of the *Discovery* in her Arctic-going prime. The snow buntings would fly on and head for lower ground if things became too rough on the mountain. But the long winter of the red deer had only just begun.

Seventeen

Wolf Moon

SOMETIMES, WHEN I HAVE WOLVES on my mind, I go to Beinn a' Chrulaiste. By the standards of its nearest neighbours it is an unprepossessing mountain (it lives across the Glencoe road from Meall a' Bhùiridh and Buachaille Etive Mòr, and it rubs shoulders with the Aonach Eagach on one side and Rannoch Moor on the other). It even has an unprepossessing name – *crulaist* means "rocky hill", so Beinn a' Chrulaiste means "rocky hill mountain". The old namers of that landscape that fringes Rannoch Moor didn't burn the midnight oil of their creative imagination to come up with that one, did they? There again, perhaps there was a time when the mountain was just called An Crulaist because it had a particularly rocky profile when viewed from where the namers lived, then some academic twat with a degree in pedantry went on a Highland jaunt, paused a night in the Kings House Hotel, and decided to affix the prefix which was already built into the name; and once it was written down on a map, no one could be bothered to change it back, for the local folk didn't need the map and went on calling it An Crulaist, and the mountaineers who did need the map called it what it said on the map without much caring what it meant. But despite its name, Beinn a' Chrulaiste has rare qualities. I am predisposed to any mountain that assists the idea of an imaginative understanding of how the landscape works, and for that matter, the idea of wolf reintroduction into Highland Scotland, which is why, sometimes, when I have wolves on my mind, I go to Beinn a' Chrulaiste.

Mostly, when I do have wolves on my mind, it is midwinter. Winter is the wolf time. In countries where they still run free and where they are still permitted to make the rules which govern all nature there, winter is the season when wolves are at their most imperious. When all their prey species are weakened by winter, and especially the deer, wolves grow stronger. It can never get too cold for wolves; they are too well designed, too well insulated. On firm, dry ground, a healthy deer will always outrun a wolf, but in snow the deer struggle and the wolves are tireless. Snowy winters are when wolves effect decisive measures to adjust the balance between the deer herds and the well-being of the land. So they are not simply supreme hunters, they are also eco-warriors. One of the comparatively few human beings on Earth to grasp the true significance of that was an American ecologist, Paul L. Errington. In a book called Of Predation and Life (Iowa State University Press, 1967), published five years after his death, he wrote:

In my opinion, native predators belong in our natural outdoor scenes, not so much because they have a monetary value ... as because they are a manifestation of life's wholeness ... Predation is part of the equation of life.

Errington also wrote:

Of all the native biological constituents of a northern wilderness scene, I should say that the wolves present the greatest test of human wisdom and good intentions.

He was an enlightened thinker on the subject of wilderness, but then he had studied at the University of Wisconsin with none other than Aldo Leopold, who became his mentor and friend, and with whom he enjoyed a close working relationship. And Leopold had numbered John Muir among his friends, so there would have been conversations in the University of Wisconsin at which I would love to have been a fly on the wall.

And it was Leopold who wrote in *A Sand County Almanac*:

... I have lived to see state after state extirpate its wolves. I have watched the face of many a newly wolfless mountain, and seen the south-facing slopes wrinkle with a maze of new deer trails. I have

seen every edible bush and seedling browsed, first to anaemic des-
uetude, and then to death ... Such a mountain looks as if someone
had given God pruning shears, and forbidden Him all other exer-
cise ... I now suspect that just as a deer herd lives in mortal fear
of its wolves, so does a mountain live in mortal fear of its deer ...

In a Scottish context, this kind of thinking does not go down well, even today, with the manipulators of those two great oxymorons of our landscape, the deer forest and the grouse moor. The idea that "predators are a manifestation of life's wholeness" is not one that would sit lightly on the shoulders of most Highland estate land managers, far less that "predation is part of the equation of life". Unless of course the predation is done by human beings with shotguns who are paying dearly for the privilege, and who have no feeling for where they are and no sense of responsibility for the well-being of land and landscape, nor of nature and deer, nor of the native people; and to whom the idea of deferring to the wolf as top predator is an abhorrence. The economics of sporting estates are an affront to the land itself and to the deer. I love red deer, love to watch them thunder over a bealach from a high mountain perch, love to find them placidly browsing a sunlit woodland corner (they are woodland beasts at heart), love to come close and listen to their con-versations. But I despise what passes for Scottish land use policy has done to them. We have been accustomed for far too long to the reckless proliferation of deer, to pruning-sheared mountains and to the absence of wolves. We have lost the capacity, the inclination and the willingness to consult our mountains, to listen to our land.

Beinn a' Chrulaiste is unquestionably a mountain that lives in mortal fear of its deer, a mountain that makes its own eloquent case for the return of the wolf. The first time I climbed it was also the moment I began to piece together the case for reintroducing wolves into a majestic Scottish Highland heartland with Rannoch Moor as its centrepiece.

The plan is this: a new wilderness national park extending from the Black Wood of Rannoch and Rannoch Moor to the Black Mount, Glen Orchy and Inishail, and west to the shore of Loch Etive. The national park should mean what it says – a park owned by the nation, rather than the unwieldy conglomerations of often reluctant landowners that characterise Scotland's existing national parks. Its overwhelming priorities would be to serve the needs of nature. Its every native habitat would be enhanced, extended, restored; Rannoch Moor would return to the lightly wooded mosaic it once was. The first wolf reintroduction would be into the Black Wood and the Moor of Rannoch, and because the new national park would march with the Cairngorms National Park in the north-east and Loch Lomond and the Trossachs National Park to the south-west, the wolves would be well served with room to expand in both directions. We have nothing to fear. On the contrary, when the wolf's wholly benevolent presence is revealed to us, an ancient darkness locked deep within our psyche will be banished. For the wolf is a catalyst, an enabler, a provider of unlimited opportunity for nature in all its guises, all its tribes. Like aconites and snowdrops thrusting through frozen ground to burst into flower, wolves invigorate the land with new light, new colour, a new flowering.

All the obstacles are in our minds. We misunderstand the nature of the wolf. That ancient darkness from which the old stories emanated and elaborated their distortions (a devourer of babies, a despoiler of the battlefield dead) is the product of nothing more than a very old storytelling tradition. The real wild wolf is to be found elsewhere. And despite all that biologists now know about the wolf in many countries, despite all the literature and all the television documentaries, despite the Yellowstone reintroduction making positive headlines for wolves around the world, there are still far too many of us who believe, or think we believe, that the only good wolf is a dead wolf, or better still, an extinct wolf.

Even the myths are stubborn. There was a strange story in some British newspapers on January 12th, 2017, concerning the full moon that night. It said that the first full moon of the year is known as the wolf moon. I had never heard of a wolf moon, so with years of dismantling wolf myths under my belt I was immediately suspicious. The story explained that it was so named because in the deep snow of midwinter, wolf packs got hungry and came in around the villages of Native American tribes, scavenging for food. The implication, at least, was that the food walked around on two legs.

So far, so much bollocks. But why, I wondered, would British newspapers run such a story? Where had it come from? I sniffed around. I have a background of newspaper journalism, and although I quit my last staff job more than thirty years ago to write my books, sometimes it still serves me well. It turned out that the 2017 edition of an American journal called the *Farmers' Almanac* was its 200th, and so it had issued press releases and posted blogs in celebration. And because one of the ingredients was the wolf – and I can see no other explanation – it found its way into some very unlikely outlets, which you could be forgiven for thinking are normally furth of the fiefdom of the *Farmers' Almanac*. It said that native tribes among America's northern and eastern states used to name each full moon (which is true), and the first of the year was the wolf moon (which, it turned out, isn't). The *Almanac* elaborated on the reason why the first moon of the year was called the wolf moon:

> *Amid the cold and deep snows of midwinter, the wolf packs howled hungrily outside Indian villages.*

Oh did they, indeed? There are two problems here. The first is that wolves don't "howl hungrily". They howl to talk to each other over distance. And they do it at different times of the day and night and at all phases of the moon and when there is no moon at all. They do it when they're hungry, they do it when their bellies are full, they do it to announce their presence, their numbers, their state of health, their territorial boundaries. Howling is wolf-to-wolf conversation and it is pack-bonding. It has nothing to do with snow or hunger or January. Or the moon.

The second problem is that wolves don't go hungry "amid the cold and deep snows of winter" because as I have already explained, (a) it can never get too cold for wolves, and (b) deep snow is when wolves are at their strongest and their prey at its weakest. They feed sumptuously in midwinter, and the surplus from the unfinished kills they leave behind feeds many, many other mouths. They had no need whatever to go anywhere near a village in the north-eastern states in winter, and they know from a few thousand years of their history that there are very sound reasons for avoiding human settlements, the most pressing of which is that they get shot.

Even if there were tribes that referred to the first full moon of the year as the wolf moon, then that still doesn't explain the story. I went in search of those conspicuously unnamed tribes, and you will be less than amazed to discover that I found none. What I did find was a Native American Studies source that listed all the names of all the moons (for they are all named, in much the same way as we name the months). Then I narrowed the list down to the tribes of the northern and north-eastern states, and this is what I found for January, the first full moon of the year:

Abenaki – greetings maker moon; Algonquin – sun has no strength to thaw moon; Anishinaabe – great spirits moon; Cherokee – cold moon; Cree – moon when the old fellow spreads the brush; Lakota – hard moon; Mohawk – the big cold moon; Passamaquoddy – whirling wind moon; Potawatomi – moon of the bear; Winnebago – fish running moon; and Sioux – wolves run together moon, the only wolf reference. There was no other mention of a specific wolf moon for any tribe anywhere; this despite the fact that there were moons named for eagle, grey goose, snow goose, frog, ducks moult, and birds fly south.

I could be uncharitable and say that this was the farmers using their magazine to spread a little seasonal anti-wolf propaganda, but even if that were the case, it does not excuse newspapers in this country publishing such rot. But our 21st-century media, as in many other northern hemisphere countries, cannot resist taking a potshot at wolves. In general, basic journalistic principles – like a respect for truth and thorough research – are abandoned when the subject is nature, and when it is the wolf then the level of abandonment goes into overdrive. Exaggeration, misinformation, jokes and profound ignorance characterise the coverage. It has been that way for a long time. But there is no longer an excuse. It took me about fifteen minutes to pull the story apart. When I wrote *The Last Wolf*, it took me a day and a half to prove to my entire satisfaction that the story of the death of Scotland's last wolf up the River Findhorn in 1743 was a work of pure fiction. Yet it has been unquestioningly regurgitated since 1829 (when it was first written down) and still reappears even in some nature conservation thinking uttered by people who should really know better.

This is what the wolf is up against.

This is what champions of wolf reintroduction are up against, and ahead lies a lengthy struggle to overwhelm the forces of ignorance, indifference and downright hostility from much of Scotland's land-owning class.

But my best guess is that the wolves will be back. The climate has begun to inch away from the dark forces of Victorian prejudice to which much of Scottish land management practice still clings. Community buy-outs of estates have forced their way on to the political and social agenda of the land. In December 2016, the Arkaig Community Trust, in partnership with Woodland Trust Scotland, announced the purchase of 2,500 acres of Scots pine woodland above Loch Arkaig in Inverness-shire, having raised £500,000 in nine months. The woodland was described as "degraded", but the management strategy is based on the restoration and expansion of a key native habitat. The move is symptomatic of a new optimism that has begun to enliven social and political debate in Scotland, at the heart of which is a new relationship with the land, with nature.

And just a month earlier, the Scottish Government approved the formal reintroduction of beavers into Scotland after a five-year official trial in Argyll and the simultaneous emergence of a slightly less official population on Tayside accumulated from mysterious sources, but demonstrably thriving.

The precedent is a significant one for wolves. Reintroduction of bird species had always been regarded as a more straightforward process, but a significant mammal with a capacity to redesign its chosen landscape, creating and expanding wetland, slowing the flow of water-courses, making new habitats and opportunities for a vast range of species of fish, plants, insects and birds ... all that indicates a willingness in government and nature conservation to challenge the old order, to make a space for new thinking. All that must mean that there is a greater likelihood now than at any time in the last 200 years for the return of the wolf to Scotland.

It was in that frame of mind that three days after the last snowfall of the winter (so far advanced was March that it was also just one day before the clocks went forward), I headed back to the Rannoch-Moor-facing flank of Beinn a' Chrulaiste. As was the way throughout that winter, no sooner had the snow fallen than the temperature climbed again, and what I found was a land in transition again. There was sunlight, but there was also a high, thin layer of cloud. The mountains were zebra-striped with snow and dark rock. The Moor wore all the wolf shades from dark brown through all the shades of grey and the slate of pools and lochans, all of it shot through with the white of old snow patches, a confetti of white. It occurred to me that twenty wolves could walk across that spreadeagled land and I would be lucky to see one of them.

I mention this because Beinn a' Chrulaiste is a mountain which lives in mortal fear of its deer, and because wolves and deer and Rannoch Moor were part of my purpose on the mountain. And because of the red deer hinds clustered within yards of the car park of the Kings House right under Beinn a' Chrulaiste when I parked there. Such an occurrence is by no means unusual in Highland Scotland, which has been wolfless for more than 200 years now, and in that time the deer have forgotten how to behave like deer. Studies at Yellowstone have shown how deer quickly re-learn forgotten behaviour in the company of reintroduced wolves. The very presence of wolves keeps the deer herds on the move so that the impact on the land of their relentless grazing is reduced immediately. I asked Beinn a' Chrulaiste what it thought of the idea of a wilderness national park with wolves right here, and it agreed with me.

For nineteen consecutive weeks through the summer and early autumn of 2001, I paused under Beinn a' Chrulaiste at midnight. I had been asked to give a talk every Tuesday evening to a different group of American visitors on board a small cruise ship that was moored for the night at Neptune's Staircase, a majestic chain of locks on the Caledonian Canal. It was a delightful commission. The audiences were warm and engaged, the meal I shared with them was excellent, the job paid well, and the drive between Glen Dochart (where I lived at the time) and the ship's berth a little to the west of Fort William was hardly a hardship. Every week, more or less around midnight, my drive home wound up through the tight black-rock curves of the Pass of Glencoe, and then the road would open out to accommodate the broad miles of Rannoch Moor on my left, the mountains of the

Black Mount on my right. Immediately before that there was the small matter of passing between the scene-stealer (Buachaille Etive Mòr) and the unsung off-to-one-side mountain, Beinn a' Chrulaiste. And every week, I crept along that long, straight road among hundreds and hundreds of red deer. Just past Beinn a' Chrulaiste, I slipped into a layby, wound down the window, switched off the engine and tuned in to the midnight secrecies of the red deer.

As far as I could see, there were two reasons for the gathering. One was that the lush grass on the roadside verge was off-limits during the daytime because of the volume of traffic. After midnight, mine was often the only car on the road for miles at a time.

The second reason was that they liked the warmth of the road and lay down on it. Sometimes I had to treat them like roundabouts. Here was the living proof of Aldo Leopold's theory. Here were fearless deer in a wolfless landscape, deer which had long since forgotten how to behave like their ancestors behaved when they shared the land with wolves. And there was the mountain that lived in mortal fear of so many deer. If you climb Beinn a' Chrulaiste by the burn that feeds into the River Etive near the Kings House, you can count the number of trees on the mountain as you climb. One.

Such is the legacy of the wolfless years, the God-with-the-pruning-shears years.

I sought out the company of the burn which emerges into the over-world from the unknowable inner heart of the mountain among its summit rocks. The re-interpretation of that burn as a kind of pulmonary artery of the mountain was irresistible, ferrying lifeblood to the landscape's lungs, sustenance for all nature. Just below the water-shed I sat in pale sunlight on a rock in the middle of the burn and between two talkative little waterfalls, a notebook and a map in my lap, a sandwich in my hand and the makings of a cup of tea. I fished the teabag from the cup with a finger and in the process I spilled tea over a few square inches of the Ordnance Survey's idea of Rannoch Moor. I immediately thought of Sweet Medwin Water, of *that* map, *those* stains. I wiped the Rannoch tea, watched the residue darken, and left it where it was. The tradition is alive and well, George, on this off-to-one-side mountain between Glencoe and Rannoch, as it was in the southern Pentland Hills. The rock where I sat was pale pink, and the melting snow had imbued the burn with a hint of the green of glaciers in its pools and glimmers of yellow in its cataracts and small falls.

For an hour, possibly longer, I did nothing at all but look around, drinking tea and burn water, and drinking in that astounding land. Slowly I realised that the peculiarities of the light and that high, thin cloud conferred on the snow the frailest, the palest, the iciest shade of blue you ever saw. Yet that very frailty of that blue was all-pervasive, for it was held fast and underpinned in every large and small fragment of snow. And every snow fragment was in turn buttressed and secured by black rock and dark brown heather stems, but then again these seemed to be held in place by the snow. But the blue was as transient as eggshells and the whole effect was of a phenomenon that might crack apart in a million places at once and the whole palette of the landscape collapse, or slide away into gullies, burns, rivers.

The temperature climbed into the early afternoon, the wind drifted away, and I could almost sense the mountain shaking itself free of the warming, dwindling snow – like a wolf. On my way down, the change in the underfoot conditions was marked. The whole hillside was charged with the movement of impromptu burns and waterslides, so many of them that I was struck with an image of migrating eels, albeit it a downstream migration. They burbled and gurgled. They mumbled, rumbled and tumbled. They wriggled, giggled and jiggled. They croaked and joked. They glittered and chattered. They tripped and skipped. And the Allt a' Ballaich, the mountain pulmonary, drank them all and surged on its way down to the distant glen of the River Etive.

Back at the car park, a tourist minibus had decanted its passengers beside the deer, some of which had walked right up to the bus, clearly in expectation of being hand-fed. I have no doubt the visitors get a kick out of the encounter. God knows what the deer get out of it, but none of it will be healthy.

Once the bus had gone, they went back to browsing and drowsing. One grey-faced old hind lay in a flat-out curve on the grass. She hadn't moved to greet the bus. When she lay with her chin in the moss and her ears erect (and with the notable absence of a thick tail to wrap round her muzzle), there was a moment when I thought she looked like nothing so much as an old wolf.

If you drive south between the edge of Rannoch Moor and the mountains of the Black Mount, as I did in the late afternoon of the last day of winter, you should pause to have a look out at the Moor just where there is a cluster of lochans not far from the road. The islands in the lochans reveal the true nature of this land, which is that it should be lightly wooded. They reveal it only because no deer graze there. Any crossing of the Moor reveals the same thing, except that the only evidence of trees you encounter is their broken, long-dead bones protruding from the peat. Too many deer impoverish the land, and then because the land is impoverished and cannot sustain so many deer, the health of the deer herds themselves is also impoverished.

Remember Paul Errington, writing in 1967:

Of all the native biological constituents of a northern wilderness scene, I should say that the wolves present the greatest test of human wisdom and good intentions.

Watching the old hind with the wolf face I thought that, more than fifty years later, it's time to put our wisdom and good intentions to the test. It's long past time.

Eighteen

Hark the Herald Eagle

Mountain dark at the year's end
then hark! the herald eagle
(a golden ray):
"I am the Light."

THE PLANET WE INHABIT spins on its axis in deepest midwinter in such a way that it begins to draw closer to the sun, even as we tend to draw closer towards the fire. But regardless of what the thermometer may tell us, regardless of what winter may yet have to throw at us, an irrevocable process of warming and brightening is already dimly underway. The darkest days and the longest nights are already behind us, and nothing in nature misses the change, unless of course it's hibernating. You could be forgiven for thinking that the first place to mark the change would be somewhere mild in the west, perhaps a shoreline lulled by the Gulf Stream where palm trees nod agreeably in gardens. But it is not so. The first truly conspicuous indication that winter is on the wane is one of grand gestures, and high in the landlocked mountains at that, and even while winter still seethes.

At the rounded end of a dipping hill shoulder, I was pretending to be a small piece of the big rock at my back. It is at a little over 1,500 feet, and somewhere in that wild and roadless terrain between the glens of Balquhidder and Dochart. The rock is on more or less level ground, the first respite after the steep plod up from one of those small cul-de-sac glens that plough deep into the hills then abruptly seem to think better of the idea. The shoulder climbs away from the rock, rises in a series of false summits to a rough cairn a thousand feet higher.

I sat there because quarter of an hour ago now I saw a golden eagle climbing in wide spirals up through one of those vast internal spaces enclosed by the flanks of the big hills. Then as it reached some kind of zenith in its own mind, it drifted south on the north wind towards the summit of this very hill. As it happens, I know this eagle, or at least I recognise it: a male, almost universally dark, a kind of mahogany shade, except that those feathers on the nape of his neck that ornithology decided long ago were of a distinctive enough shade to christen the bird "golden" … that feathered headdress seemed to me to have a particular burnish. I know where it is accustomed to nest. I also have a rough idea (very rough – I have no grasp at all of how a golden eagle thinks) of how it defines its territory. After years spent watching the same two pairs on adjacent territories, I have begun to believe that the boundaries may be determined not by distance or geographical features but rather by flying time away from the nest, and so the boundaries of territory will fluctuate with the wind direction. But when golden eagles mark out their territories, when they begin to restate their claim, when they embark upon their own idea of the annual festival of New Year, they do so by display-flying above the same prominent landscape features. However flexible the boundaries of territory may be on a day-to-day basis, year after year they announce their renewed presence to the rest of the watching world in the same places, and these may (I'm guessing again) mark the territory's non-negotiable core.

So I sat with the big rock at my back because I saw the eagle climb and drift towards the summit of the long hill shoulder, and because I know from many hours spent here over many old winters, that this particular hill shoulder is important in that particular eagle's scheme of things. And as I sat, I told myself this: if the eagle in question is about to do what I think it may be about to do, then I am in the right place at the right time, and this could be good. I faced south, the rock shielding me from the north wind, and I prepared for the near certainty of getting very cold very slowly.

An hour later I *was* very cold, but still, I reassured myself, I *was* in the right place, and the right time would be along any minute now …

Another hour, still facing south, still scanning the sky, and trying to suppress the memory from one old spring not far from this rock of sitting watching a perched golden eagle do nothing at all for four hours. And then suddenly he appeared far in the south, very high and very small. I had found him by chance with a slow sweep of my binoculars across the sky, perhaps the 20th such slow sweep. And yet, it wasn't chance that led me here, it wasn't chance that commanded me to sit, it wasn't chance that imposed stillness and patience on the sitting and the waiting, and it wasn't chance that finally fulfilled my expectation of seeing him there, sooner or later. I write about what happens, of course, not about the hundreds of blank hours over thirty-something years when nothing at all happens except the slow seepage of awareness, experience, and acceptance between the mountain and the watcher.

"This way," I muttered aloud to no one at all, "this way."

I saw the eagle tilt, change direction, and vanish going *that* way, checked my watch, decided on a time limit. One more hour sitting still on this hill shoulder in this hazy grey weather and its persistent north wind would be quite enough. I don't know why I do that, because events inevitably determine the timespan of the vigil. Almost certainly, I will not notice the moment when fifty-nine minutes tick over to sixty. The passage of time will have nothing to do with it. I look at my watch when there is nothing going on. When things are happening, who knows where the time goes?

So the trick then is to find a way to renew the commitment to the watching. You have to intensify the scrutiny, you must learn to scan the middle distance. It's a tall order sometimes, and it is never as easy as it sounds, not least because there is often nothing in your middle distance to focus on. You must explore the three-dimensional space between you and the next piece of land. But you get the hang of it with practice. So I set about devouring the middle distance of the space between me and the limit of what I suspect might be the eagle's territory, and I tried it with and without the binoculars ... the narrow view and the wide view. If I was right, if I was still in the right place, one more cold hour (or whatever it took) would be a small price to pay.

A hint of brightness stole over the sky in the south-west. A single stag came and stood on a corner of a skyline buttress. I watched it for a while with binoculars and then without, putting it into the context of its colossal landscape. Then I rebuked myself, for I was watching a fixed point of land, not scrutinising the middle distance.

The middle distance became the centre of the world. There came a point in the passage of time when I started to see that space as a thing of its own, with colours of its own, a three-dimensional object as tangible as a mountain.

A new wind came, curving round the rock at my back, exploring my right cheek, a light gust that danced on almost at once, but leaving its mark on my cheek for a while. I heard a crow, then a raven, then both together. I sought them both out because of that ancient symbiosis by which golden eagle and mountain corvids are forever bound, and which has offered countless scraps of encouragement over several decades to this watcher of eagles. But these two appeared to be shouting at each other, the crow perched, the raven adrift close to the stag's buttress. Either that or I was missing something. It occurred to me then as my binoculars briefly followed the raven that the stag had gone and I had not seen it go, because it had not been part of the middle distance.

Then there was a sudden movement, a movement so sudden that its very suddenness startled me. It was a movement not of a golden eagle but of my own head, turning to the right. Suddenly.

Why turn at that moment?

There had been no sound, nothing lodged in the corner of my eye, not even that playful wind. Instead, there was … a shift, a waft of awareness.

And there was the eagle.

Falling.

Falling as nothing on Earth falls, and nothing in Earth's sky.

Falling as a state of grace.

Falling as an art form, with beauty and purpose.

The shape of a falling golden eagle is an abstraction, almost a diamond, but a diamond tampered with by nature's take on the science of aerodynamics, and squared off at the top and curved to a point at the base. In its falling, the eagle looked as dark as mahogany, except that the new brightness that had begun to infuse the sky also infused the nape of the eagle, that mercurially light-sensitive hood of feathers, that "golden". In different lights it can catch your eye as anything between tawny and auburn, and in almost no light at all it transforms again: an extraordinary photograph by my friend Laurie Campbell, and published in my book, *The Eagle's Way*, shows a golden eagle on the island of Harris asleep on a ledge near its eyrie at midsummer midnight, and that same mercurial hood is somewhere between ash grey and white. But on this falling eagle excavating an eagle-shaped shaft through the middle distance of mountain air somewhere above Balquhidder Glen in the Loch Lomond and the Trossachs National Park, that new light in the sky glanced upon the nape in such a way that it shone, it truly shone. The same light smote the base of the eagle's bill deep yellow. Mahogany, pale gold and deep yellow … but of course the thing was happening at a barely credible airspeed, so that from the moment it came into sight, high and to my right, until the moment it pulled out perhaps twenty feet above the hill shoulder where I sat, and well over to my left, no more than five seconds could have passed. Five seconds, but somewhere in their midst, that falling eagle breenged through the precise moment at the precise angle that caused the nape of its neck to flare with a pale gold sheen, and for what may have been no more than a second, no diamond ever shone with a finer lustre than that one.

Then it was ascending again in spirals, scratching its name on the blue-grey void of the northern sky, then it was holding up against the wind at the top of its climb, then it fell again but this time the flight took the form of a roller-coastering parade the whole length of the hill shoulder, a sequence of short wing-folded dives and towering climbs, and all of it in and out of sunlight, and all of it spilling air with brutal power and sustained elegance in perfectly equal measure. At such a moment, my sense of the world shrinks and my state of mind is one of helplessness, helpless admiration, helpless thraldom in nature's cause, helpless anguish that there are out there and not more than a couple of watersheds distant, examples of my own species who would rather poison such a bird than sit and watch it in silent wonder. It is a lot to take on, one cold afternoon of late January.

Amid the more or less limitless glories of natural flight, there are two examples of the art which astound me beyond rational thought so that they become the preserve not just of the mind but also of the heart. Both of them are at their most luminous in midwinter. One of them is this golden eagle festival by which it celebrates its own idea of a New Year, the beginning of one more long haul to establish one more new generation of its tribe; the symbolism is irresistible. The other could scarcely be more different, either in the execution or in the purpose, but both have in common that they deal in grand gestures and that they are events of extraordinary power and beauty and grace. The eagle flies to proclaim its place on the map of the world, its spectacle is solitary and silent. The whooper swan is a thousand miles from home, it moves from one wintering ground to another in low and level skeins, a restless, nomadic procession from the Northern Isles or the Western Isles to Slimbridge or the Fens and back again, then when it is satisfied that winter is done, back up the northern ocean to Iceland. The conversation of these flights is a constant exchange of snatches of muted brass. The glory of them is in low sunlight, which January and February assist, so that the white plumage of their wings takes on a variety of shades from blue to orange, depending on the strength of the light and the nature of the terrain where it is flying. A skein of whooper swans flying into a sunset is a constant rhythmic progress of flashing lights: overwings and underwings rise and fall and respond in a four-in-the-bar jazzy way to the impact of the light source.

With the eagle gone from my sky, these were the thoughts that rummaged around in the vacuum it left behind. Eagle and swan rarely coincide, and when they do, at least in a Scottish context, it will usually be out in the Hebrides where golden eagles nest much lower than they do in the Highland heartland mountains, and where whooper swans both migrate and linger on favourite lochs and lochans. On the rare occasions when whooper swans venture into the mountains, it will be perhaps because prevailing weather conditions persuaded them to cross a mountain pass rather than fly round the mountain, and there is no doubt that some will follow the course of major glens on migration.

Once, and only once, I watched a solitary whooper swan battle against a real Hebridean gale and apparently try to cross the ridge of the Skye Cuillin at upwards of 2,000 feet. The incident is as inexplicable to me now as it was then, more than twenty winters ago. An eagle can fly into a healthy headwind, half-fold its wings, and pick up speed. A swan in the same wind struggles to make headway and usually goes low and tries to fly under it.

Suddenly the eagle was back.

It flew so low and slow above the ground at that moment that I wondered if it had just risen from a perch, and if so, where had it perched and how long had it been there, and had it been watching me? The next moment I had at least some circumstantial evidence to back up that hunch. At no more than about fifty feet above the shoulder, the eagle held up in the wind again, and hung there, working wingtips and tail feathers, and I am as sure as I can be that the object at the far end of its gaze for a few moments was myself. This has happened to me three times before, and each time I had been very still for a long time, sitting against a rock that was deliberately chosen because I knew it was a landmark in a golden eagle territory. The feeling engendered by each occasion was one of profound respect, of being in the presence of one of nature's ambassadors, of briefly keeping the company of true, undiluted wildness. To a nature writer, these are scraps of gold dust.

The eagle banked away, leaned out into the void beyond the mountainside and began to climb, not in lazy spirals this time but straight up at an angle remarkably close to vertical, an ascent powered by a surge of huge wingbeats, hundreds of feet in a handful of seconds. At first, there was an audible pulse with each wingbeat, the sound diminishing as it climbed. Then from almost directly overhead, it began again. The eagle appeared to lean forward in the air so that its tail was almost directly above its head, then it folded its wings so that the tips were held close to the end of the tail, and in a mighty burst of speed it was falling again. The dive levelled out and curved upwards again without pause and in precisely the opposite of the position in which the dive had begun, the head now almost directly above the tail, the tail pointing back at the earth, at my rock, at me. This time the climb soared on and on, maybe a thousand feet, maybe 2,000, for the eagle was quite alone in that portion of the sky and any idea of its final altitude was far beyond reliable guesswork. Then it boarded the wind and raced south away from me.

Hark the Herald Eagle

So high up and far away a golden eagle began to sky-dance its way into my heart. It travelled a mile-long mountainside in a free-flowing sequence of power-climbs and free-falls, dismissing a thousand feet of air from its wings, ripping open the sky, climbing again, flipping over, diving down, the whole thing as rhythmic as waves, as seamless as winds. It reached the slope that dipped towards my rock. It was suddenly so close that I became more aware of the blurring hillside as I tried to keep the binoculars focussed on the bird, so I lowered them to watch with my eyes instead. Sometimes you see more clearly without binoculars. In this case, that simple action liberated everything. In particular, it restored the glorious perspective of the bird and its native heath, the mountains and all their intervening spaces and their overarching skies.

Nineteen

A Winter Diary

FAR OUT AMONG THE FIELDS of the Carse, the snow all but gone from the mountains, the river bloated, pools of standing water in the stubble fields, and the light in the early afternoon had a strange silvery quality. There was an alacrity in the air as if nature had tired of winter already and wanted to get on with the year. I had paused to watch two large flocks of birds that had just alighted in the same field. One was mostly the Scandinavian thrushes – fieldfares and redwings, about 300 of those, I guessed; the other was a mix of finches, yellowhammers, siskins, corn buntings, linnets, and goodness knows how many there were of them. As they fed, they seemed to establish a kind of no man's land in the middle of the field, with the thrushes on the far side of it and the finch-sized birds closer to the single-track farm road and its fringing hedges.

The birds were clearly nervous. They knew better than I that, sooner or later, such a gathering of so many small birds in a single field was bound to attract the attention of a predator. At every small or substantial alarm, as small as a dog bark and as large as a snorting tractor on the road, the finch flock fled to the hedges and filled the air with their voices. A shudder went through the thrush flock as they stopped to assess the threat then fed on. The finches poured back into their portion of the field and fell silent. Then there was a fox in the field, a patch of colour in the furthest corner. There is a small wood over there, then a deep and steep-sided ditch and a fence and a hedge, and if the fox had come from the wood it must have negotiated all three. There was a thin strip of longer grass by the hedge and the fox was there, half in and half out, dead still, assessing the possibilities. It was a big field, the fox had at least fifty yards of open ground to the nearest bird. But no bird flinched.

Except one. A heron of all things, and it appeared from somewhere beyond the corner of the wood, all wings and dangling legs, homed in on the fox and screeched, the way herons do when they are discomfited by pretty well anything. The fox turned in its own length and vanished beneath the hedge. The air above the field convulsed. The finches exploded up from stubble to hedge, a low-level, high-voltage retreat. But the fieldfares and redwings rose in silence and flew in disciplined order to a pair of tall ash trees, one each side of the road, and suddenly the bare branches were thickly clustered with a foliage of thrushes. I turned back to the far corner: the heron stood precisely where the fox had been.

Then I realised that the whole episode had been watched by a buzzard, huddled and fluffed up on a telegraph pole, and in that bulked-up form and from behind, it had the look of a crouching eagle. I decided to move on, edged the car towards the buzzard's pole. It put up with me creeping slowly past, but as soon as I stopped it stepped off and glided down to a yard above the ground, crossed the field beyond, then rose again to another pole a hundred yards away. There it perched side-on, fluffed its feathers again, trapping a cushion of air with which to fend off the north wind, and held its wings loose and unfolded, like a compact eagle. I was intrigued because it had not flinched when the fox and then the heron and then the small bird chaos intruded on its afternoon. It didn't even seem to be watching. Perhaps it was as simple as this: it had a specific prey species on its mind, vole most likely, and it was watching a known vole terrain (it carries that kind of knowledge the way you or I know where the good cafés are). Or perhaps it was even simpler: it was well fed, it was tholing a cold winter afternoon, and there was nothing on its mind at all.

Late in the afternoon I edged my car down the rough access track to Flanders Moss, a regular haunt towards the south-west corner of my working territory, and a few miles to the west of the buzzard pole where the flat fields of the Carse run out and give way to wetland and forest and the land starts to curl up at the edges towards the foothills of the Highlands. The Moss used to be a reliable winter roost for hen harriers, but in the early decades of the 21st century, nothing at all about hen harriers is reliable. They still turn up, but they are few and far between.

For that matter they are few and far between everywhere on the face of the land, and we have the grouse moor industry to thank for that.

The mountains had dragged new snow showers across their south-facing slopes, but low sunlight carved an eerie wedge of yellow light across the foothills and only the foothills, for it neither glanced off the falling snow nor flooded over the wide sprawl of the Moss, which lay robed in its own mysteriously tea-shaded shadow of winter heather and winter grass. Its hundreds of watery patches and its puddles, pools and ponds reflected no colour of any kind, yet there was an unearthly beauty in its utter colourlessness, a very rare thing in nature. There were pine marten scats on the path.

I followed the edge of a birch wood to the south-east corner of the Moss where the birches form a containing right angle. From here, the Moss offers the widest horizon in all the land of Menteith. Only lochs normally have this kind of spaciousness, but in the wider Trossachs area they are all hemmed in by forests, hills and mountains. The Moss is like a huge wheel laid flat on its tabletop of water and moss and heather and peat with only a thin "tyre" of rimming trees. The foothills and the mountains lean back and keep their distance.

In the last of the light I climbed the reserve's observation tower on the off-chance that a harrier or two might slip in under cover of dusk. I was just halfway up when I saw a harrier-shape through the timber spars of the tower. By the time I reached the top, it was not in sight. What I had seen was a female, which is to say it was brown, and in that light and against that bog-at-dusk background, the chances of finding it again diminished by the second. I simply scanned the land with the glasses, moving slowly from south to north and from east to west, hoping against hope of catching something which looked like a piece of the Moss that had taken flight. And that was exactly what I found, and for about twenty seconds and at the very furthest edge of reliable vision I saw its impossibly slow flight, its wingtips just inches above the ground, the white blaze at the base of its tail occasionally showing up to confirm that it was what I thought it was. Then it passed behind a screen of small birch scrub and I didn't see it again.

Every time I see a hen harrier out here, which is not often, or up on a quiet corner of the Ochil Hills, or above the trees at Glen Finglas,

I am reassured to this extent, and this extent only: it's one more hen harrier that has slipped through the net, one more that those who like to "manage" nature with a shotgun in one hand and a dose of poison in the other have not yet shot or poisoned or otherwise removed from the face of the land.

★

The blizzards charged eastwards across the land, leaving the mountains breathless and beautiful for a day or two. Then the temperature rose, the rains came, it grew too mild for anyone's winter comfort … by the end of January it had become an erratic pattern, a predictable sequence of events. Not even the rains set in for long, and the fitful appearance of watery sunlight became a kind of default setting, so that from time to time and day after day, the sodden land was briefly ablaze where the sun bounced and dazzled from every imaginable form of standing, running and dripping water. I lived in wellies, I ploughed a four-wheel-drive furrow around the backroads most afternoons, squelched among woods and fields and foothills in search of swans and foxes, hares and deer, river otters, restless and bewildered shoals of birds; and as I ploughed and squelched I tried to piece together a sense of how nature was facing up to this too-warm, too-spasmodic winter, writing down whatever turned up.

There was one upside to the whole chaotic mess: rainbows.

Seared in my mind even now is a moment when I had just clambered back into the car after a long wander by the river and the discovery of a family group of six mute swans finding the swollen current hard going. There can be few stronger swimmers in the bird world than mute swans, but again and again their attempts to make headway upstream failed and the cob would urge his brood up onto their feet then into a wave-thrashing, feet-pounding, running flight on the surface of the water, and in that way they would cover fifty upstream yards before subsiding back onto the surface, at which point they were once again incapable of headway. The process was repeated again and again, while I scratched my head trying to understand why they didn't just fly, or get up on the bank and walk. I don't know how long I watched, but when I eventually plodded back to the car and clambered in, started the engine, edged forward from a watery verge onto the road, I was no sooner mobile than something astonishing filled the driver's door mirror. I reversed the few yards I had just driven, grabbed a camera, and jumped out. Wedged between the bottom of the Ochil Hills and the Wallace Monument on its wooded rock was a fat lump of rainbow.

Not only was the sun very low, but it was working on two fast-moving showers of rain about a mile apart. One consequence was a double rainbow, but the main arch was also of a double thickness. Where the pot of gold should have been, between the monument and the hills, was one of the showers, and it was lit gold. It was that point of collision between the rainbow's double-thickness arch and the lit rain that produced that fat wedge of saturated rainbow colours, and even as I watched it, it contrived a ghostly twin image of itself.

Then, as the gold shower moved on towards the east, it had a curious effect on the base of the rainbow, as if it was nibbling into it from the edge so that from time to time, bits of the rainbow were missing. The arch had vanished, so that there was only this leaning-over wedge towering over the monument. The spectacle was as bizarre as it was beautiful, and it produced a somewhat bizarre response, for I suddenly had the notion of a colossal rainbow-shaded tree trunk being gnawed at by a golden beaver. I stood and stared and stared, and as nature-as-sorcerer went through its paces I started to laugh at the joy and the wonder and the sheer madness of it all.

★

Snow was promised by breakfast. I had heard this before on a dozen different weather forecasts, and none of them had delivered, at least not in my neck of the woods, not below about a thousand feet. I woke at four in the morning, peered round the curtains at a white street and heavy snow falling in a big wind. Oh joy. By breakfast time the sun was out of course, and although snow showers punctuated the morning they had already lost their fervour and I felt cheated again. But it was the first time in four years I had needed to select four-wheel drive to get out of the street, so that was something.

I travelled the Carse by its wee roads, and the Ochils and all of the lower hills were white, the fields were white, the wee roads were white. The mountains were lost, still snowing up there behind and beneath those piles of grey-black clouds. Birds were on the move everywhere, homing in on the stubble fields in huge numbers. The fieldfare and redwing flock had doubled in size in a few days, likewise the masses of small birds. Everything on the ground faced into the north-east wind. Everything that flew in over the hedges would reach a point in the field where they would wheel through ninety degrees, stall and land ... facing the same way as the rest. The feeding was conspicuously frantic, and it became clear that it was being plundered between brutal showers when the sky darkened, the wind (and the wind-chill) picked up, and everything bolted for cover. It evolved into the most restless of days. The weather was restless, the sky was restless, the birds were restless. Clouds tore along hillsides and packed themselves thicker and thicker against the mountains. The sun shone and vanished, shone and vanished. The moon arrived and stood over Stirling Castle, and vanished, and so briefly did Stirling Castle, briefly obliterated from its ancient stance, a feat which was never accomplished by English kings and Oliver Cromwell.

Sitting in the car, watching through an open window, I felt like the still centre of the wild world, as if I should be doing more. But my job was this. As one more shower thudded into the car, the hedge five yards away filled up with tree sparrows and linnets, and they burrowed deep inside it and gossiped loudly for every moment of the deluge. Then the sky lightened, the wind calmed, the sun stole out, and they were gone. Then suddenly everything was restored at once. The sun and the wind started to bore into the mountain clouds, making holes just above the foothills but never quite revealing the summits. Geese piled in, adding to the mayhem in the stubble fields, and perhaps they had been waiting out the storms on the river, keeping their heads down below the level of the highest banks. A big flight of rooks drifted over, sounding like heavy agricultural traffic, and launched dozens of dummy-run assaults on a solitary kestrel on a fence post. It finally tired of them and headed west, and so did I.

Out near Flanders Moss I found it again – on a fence post, being harassed by jackdaws. I had stopped to watch, but then I found my attention distracted by some odd shapes in the field across the road. They were dark and inert, they looked like sods of earth where the snow had melted (except that the snow had not melted), or lumps of spread dung (but there was no spread dung). The field had been partly ploughed before the snow came, and the shapes lay in the hollows made by the plough and partly filled in by the snow. None of them moved, and yet there was something about them that did not quite make sense. Nothing else in the field was free of snow. I reached for the binoculars and what snapped into focus was a flock of lapwings. But they were so hunkered down that only the broad dark curves of their backs and the slim curves of their crests showed.

A single sentry bird got to its feet. Otherwise, not one bird moved, this despite my very obvious presence standing by my car and my very obvious interest in them. The field at my back, which the kestrel had just crossed, seethed with jackdaws, sparrows and starlings. The field where I had stopped earlier was feverish with birds. All across the Carse, that winter bird highway thrummed with traffic. Yet there, thirty yards away, these lapwings were still enough to make me think at first glance that they had been sods of earth. It was three o'clock in the afternoon, the sun was out, there were two hours of usable daylight, followed by a long, cold night. Why were these birds and these alone not making hay while the sun shone?

They had the look of birds that had just reached journey's end after migration, probably from somewhere down the east coast, Northumberland perhaps. Behind them was a journey up the coast, into the Firth of Forth, then the long haul upstream. If you make such a journey, this is as far inland as you can get in this part of Scotland. Keep going west and you run into the mountains, and you start to close in on the long sea lochs of the west coast. Go north from here and its mountains all the way to Orkney. This was journey's end all right. If I'm right, these lapwings migrated about six weeks early. So, were they lured by an absurdly warm December and an all-but snowless January, nothing more than dropped hints of winter, a day or half a day at a time while the temperature swithered between ten and fourteen degrees? Is this, in other words, another symptom of climate change convincing enough to tamper with one of their most fundamental biological functions; convincing enough to delude them into migrating six weeks early, only to find that winter had turned up on the day they arrived? Can that happen? Yes, it certainly can. Was it happening right there in front of my eyes? I don't know. But I think so.

When I left them, I drove on to Flanders Moss (finches, linnets, geese and jackdaws again, wrens a-twitch everywhere in the woods). When I passed the lapwings again more than an hour later, it looked very much as if not a single bird had moved. In all that time, the sun had shone. That night, there was an almost full moon, the temperature had dropped below zero, and then it had started snowing again

*

Airthrey Loch on the campus of the University of Stirling is a swan water. All kinds of wildfowl use it, but it is owned by mute swans, or more specifically one mute swan, the resident cob. I have spent more hours watching swans than any other creature, and more hours writing about them. I have watched them all across Scotland, from Shetland to Solway and from the Western Isles to the east coast. And from Lindisfarne to Norfolk to a swan hospital in Surrey. And trumpeter swans in Alaska, and whooper swans nesting in Norway and on an Icelandic beach of black volcanic sand with the volcano in question – Hekla – for a backdrop. Over the years, I have learned among many other things to avoid generalising and to recognise individuality. I have met clever swans, stupid swans, brave swans, timid swans, reasonable swans, unreasonable swans, enlightening swans and downright baffling swans. I have yet to find a swan that turns into a beautiful swan maiden, but I haven't finished looking yet.

And sometimes you come across the mute swan cob from hell. Airthrey Loch has such a cob. To begin with, he is huge. They always are. He is also fearless. They always are. And when he does that thing that all swans do, "standing" on the water with head and neck held high and wings flourished and wide open so that they crack like sails in a big wind, it becomes a gesture intended to intimidate, and it succeeds. When he strikes that pose on still water so that it reflects itself and becomes an exquisite, two-headed, four-winged monster, it becomes difficult to overstate the impact. I have tried to imagine how that must look to a lesser swan or a mere duck or a swimming otter down at water level, and I think it must look as if the Celtic gods have moved in to terrorise all lesser beings.

Winter is a difficult time for swans, especially young swans in their first year. The mortality rate is exceptionally high. Some adults pairs look after their brood right through the winter and only evict them from the territory when they start entertaining nesting notions again. Other parents throw them out before winter sets in. Airthrey's cob is one such parent. Luckily for his offspring, the loch is effectively two lochs connected by a long narrow middle section. The larger of the two watersheets is owned by the cob and his mate, the smaller is where the banished offspring go, and there they can winter well enough, for their water is sheltered, there is good feeding both in the water and on large areas of mown grass. The reliable presence of humans with handouts also helps.

On a day towards the end of winter, with a fair bit of ice on the surface of the smaller loch and the narrow connecting stretch, I had wandered that way with a camera and my insatiable swan curiosity. The cob was already well fired up, and was clearing everything from coots to goosanders to geese from his path in a series of fast swimming charges with neck furled, head held low and wings hoisted like mainsails. Some of these sallies evolved into wing-thrashing lunges, his colossal black webbed feet and his wingtips thrashing the surface with fear-inducing rhythmic precision. So far, so predictable. Then I heard the wingsong of more swans in flight. If you ever had a humming top as a child and you remember the noise it made, and if you can imagine that sound broken up into rhythmic four-in-the-bar fragments, that is the song of a mute swan's wings in flight, a pulse of extraordinary beauty. When its echo bounces back off the frozen surface of a winter loch, then you know for sure you are eavesdropping on the language of one of nature's chosen tribes.

Three swans came low over the loch, undercarriages lowered, wings angled and gliding, but at the last moment they pulled out and went round again, and if the change of mind was instigated by the sight of the cob in full flow, they failed in that one moment of doubt to appreciate the full implications of what awaited them. For they circled again, and this time they landed on the water and by the time the water around them had subsided, the cob was twenty yards away and closing. Fast.

In this mood of more or less constant belligerence, nothing heightens it to a pitch of terrifyingly concentrated rage like the arrival of a new adult swan. And now there were three of them. As often as not, a cob's territorial sallies are designed to deter, to deliver a sermon about discretion and valour and all that. Physical contact is comparatively rare. What followed was all physical contact. After the first lunging assaults, two of the incomers fled. The third was either a little slow on the uptake or it was made of stronger stuff and was in the mood for a challenge. But this was David facing up to Goliath in a version of the story in which Goliath hadn't read the script. He first grabbed a beakful of the smaller swan's back and held on. The victim let out a yelp that could only be pain. Then he was simply unable to free himself as the sheer weight of the assailant bore down on him. Then the attack moved to the neck, and at every bite the victim yelped again and again. Finally, the cob drove his victim against the bank and then the attack really got going. How this might have resolved itself is not a pleasant speculation, but there was a fisherman on the bank, and he, brave soul, waded into the water, separated the swans and stood between them. He was a big man, over six feet and well built, and the cob didn't give a damn. He eluded the fisherman's defences and time after time he charged again at the swan on the bank, always going for the neck, always inflicting pain. But the fisherman hung in there and finally succeeded in ushering the injured bird far up the grass bank, at which point, honour more than satisfied, the cob withdrew a few yards on to the water, where he was joined by his mate, and they rose on the water together, flourishing their wings and calling loudly, as blatant a demonstration of triumphalism as you will ever see in nature.

Some swans are better at the "nuclear option" school of territorial rule than others. Here, it works. There are six very healthy-looking young swans on the smaller part of the loch, the cygnets from last summer, and now, at the end of their first winter, with the brown plumage of their nursery months giving way to their first coat of brilliant white, they look primed, ready to go out into the world, where it is just possible they will join forces with the seven cygnets that flew from here last year. Demonstrably, they have wintered well. Demonstrably, their parents know what they're doing, and any day now they will finally clear their offspring from their nursery waters, forcibly if necessary.

Twenty

Insh Marshes: A Waterworld
With No Half Measures

THE LONGER THE NIGHTS, the more precious the daylight. At the latitude of the Insh Marshes in the upper reaches of Strathspey and the lee of the northern Cairngorms, December rarely doles out more than six usable hours of the stuff. Between dawn and dusk, the daylight fliers cram the hours with hunting. These are the dark days, which the weak and the ill-starred rarely survive. At this time of year the Insh Marshes are a waterworld with no half measures, as uncompromising as Iceland, which may be why Icelandic whooper swans feel at home here. Their beauty and their arctic-toned music dignifies every Strathspey winter. Wetlands this expansive, this wide-open, this wild, are the stuff of nature's own dreams, and it is not possible to overestimate their value.

There should be beavers here. In nature's scheme of things, such a wetland should be managed and manipulated by beavers, because their presence is capable of increasing the biodiversity of such a landscape fourfold, so it becomes four times as priceless.

The marshes lie between two of the Highlands' set-piece mountain massifs, the Cairngorms to the east, the Monadhliath to the west, and every December the snow unfurls down their flanks by degrees, according to the depth of winter, the one in shadow when the other is in sunlight. It is a sorcerer's landscape. Birch woods, garbed in that mysterious winter purple that stows away their tight-packed finery of the seasons to follow, climb up and over low ridges between here and the Cairngorms' pinewoods. They also offer cover for a nature writer on a mission. Mostly when I have come here at this time of year my priority has been the swans, but I have also come in hope of renewing another old acquaintance.

An hour drifted by, drifted from one woodland-edge viewpoint to another, to another, to another ... each one opening out a different portion of the marshes, a different set of possibilities. A little elevation goes a long way on the Insh Marshes. A birchy knoll of fifty feet opens up the miles-wide world which is simply out of reach when you are down at water level. There are inevitable diversions: wolf-whistling wigeon flocks; a red squirrel on a birch trunk a dozen yards away, cramponing vertically upwards, three points of contact, one hind foot lifted to scratch some woodland irritant, hanging on; the whooper swans, of course, a handful swimming far out on dark pools, and one heart-stopper of a flypast – nine of them came low over the trees from behind me, then dropped almost to water level as they banked to fly south down the marshland miles. But such an hour, fascinating and sometimes enchanting as it was, reduced to five the workable, watchable daylight hours, and the particular old acquaintance I wished to meet had not shown up yet.

Realistically of course, you do not just drive a hundred pre-dawn miles, park your car at first light, walk down through the woods, focus your binoculars, and have the object of your day's endeavours manifest itself in the glasses, majestically lit by the rising sun, but you do try to harvest the fruits of the sum of your experience. You know what you are looking for and where you have seen it before. You know the kind of places it likes – low, solitary trees, fence posts. You fall back on proven techniques of stillness and moving through the landscape. If you don't like hides (I don't, although once in a while, needs must), you must become a part of the landscape. It all takes time. It all takes patience. That particular day, it would take two-and-a-half hours. Oh, and that was my third day of looking. It is, to say the least, an imperfect science. But after two-and-a-half hours, I focused my binoculars on a line of fence posts just beyond the edge of a long, narrow pool, and there on the third post from the left, in the sunlight, and perfectly reflected in the water, and exactly (down to the very fence post) where I had seen one two years ago, was a male hen harrier.

Apart from everything else that pushes the hen harrier so far up the list of bird conservation's priorities, it is a singularly stylish bird. Aesthetics alone would account for its superstar status in what you might call ornithology's pecking order. The male is the showstopper, and in light as uncompromising as a December noontide, and at a good distance, he looked white, and only a slightly darker white on his head and the tops of his folded wings, those wings which are ennobled by vivid black primaries. The legs looked bright yellow, and the face had a snowy-owlish aspect. No part of him moved. The male hen harrier is a master of stillness when he needs to be and he needs to be often because he is so conspicuous.

All stillness is a deception. It feigns disinterest. That particular manifestation of stillness in my binoculars was saying: don't bother about me, I'm a fence post. Such stillness also conceals the bird's true colours, metaphorically and literally, for the male hen harrier shares with the swans a quality in his plumage that absorbs colour from its surroundings. I stumbled on the phenomenon years ago when I was writing a book called *Waters of the Wild Swan* (Cape, 1992), in which I quoted the wildlife artist Charles Tunnicliffe. In his book *Bird Portraiture* (The Studio, 1946) he first dismissed the idea of a "white" bird, then there was this:

> *Notice the yellow tinge in the feathers of neck and upper breast, and the cold bluish purity of the back, wings and tail. Note also the colour of the shadowed under-surfaces and how it is influenced by the colour of the ground on which the bird is standing: if he is standing on green grass, then the underparts reflect a greenish colour, whereas if he were on dry, golden sand, the reflected colour would be of a distinctly warm tint; or again if he were flying over water, his breast, belly and underwings would take on a colder tint, especially if the water were reflecting a blue or a grey sky.*

But suppose the swan is swimming ahead of you, and straight into the sun:

> *... only his upper surfaces are lit by sunlight, the rest of him being in shadow and appearing dark violet against the bright water; in fact, but for the light on his back and the top of his head he appears as a dark silhouette in relation to the high tone of the water.*

Snow changes everything:

Now you can see how yellow his neck is, and to a lesser extent, the rest of his upper plumage. Note also the reflected snow light on his undersides which makes them look almost the same tone as, or even lighter than, his top surfaces ...

The best wildlife artists are the best observers of wildlife (and most of them are also masters of stillness). If you want to see the full range of possibilities in the repertoire of that "white" hen harrier on the fence post, look up the archive of Donald Watson, who was arguably the greatest observer of hen harriers, for he studied them throughout his life and he painted the results of his studies. One of the paintings that comes to mind shows a male bird flying very low over a snowy hillside in low mid-afternoon midwinter sunlight, and the bird is blue, for it has absorbed colour from both sky and snow (and the snow too has borrowed from the sky); and just as Tunnicliffe noted, the underside is lighter than the top surfaces.

It would be another hour before the Insh Marshes harrier flew, and what galvanised him was the arrival of the ringtail, the female harrier, a bird so different in plumage, so inconspicuously brown that it looks like a different species, until, that is, you see them flying in tandem. And she brought with her a retinue of small birds, a cloud of finches, siskins and tits all twittering their displeasure and dicing with death to make their point. They looked like blown leaves in a November gale as they bowled across the marshes. For the next half hour the harriers came and went in and out of my vision, but they were rarely out of it for long and I judged that stillness would serve me best. Watching two harriers at work, hunting as a pair, demonstrating such mastery of the art of ultra-slow, low-level flight (only golden eagles do it better), tormenting the small birds of the marshes, striking down two within half an hour, sharing the meagre spoils, then taking to the air again, the ringtail like a mobile fragment of the winter landscape, the male a wizard of flickering colour change, while in the background, a pageant of the country's finest mountain massif drifts by in soft focus ... watching all that is to be transported to a more rarefied realm than the one I was occupying an hour ago.

It remains then, the grimmest of paradoxes that these birds are public enemy number one in the eyes of the grouse moor fraternity, that their beauty and their uncompromising and stylish wildness are of no account, simply because they are judged inconvenient for the most grotesque of all the human rituals Scotland has inflicted on its own landscape. The industry has grown tetchily defensive in response to mounting and sustained criticism of the toll it takes on Scotland's hen harrier population. Representatives of both landowners and gamekeepers have loudly and repeatedly condemned illegal killings, but they still happen, and the hen harrier remains an absentee from much of the landscape where it should thrive.

The longer the nights, the more precious the daylight. Winter is the nadir for all our most vulnerable wildlife communities, the dark days for the weak and the ill-starred. Unless we find a new way to look after the land, we may be living through a hen harrier winter beyond which there is no second spring.

*

Suddenly in early February, winter appeared to have found its voice. The mountain rescue teams were at work on Ben Nevis, on Mount Keen, and in the Garbh Choire of Bràigh Riabhach. One of the Cairngorms rescue team spoke of "full-on winter". On Mount Keen, the rescued climbers had been "woefully ill-prepared … it's winter folks, don't believe the hype". But there were only three weeks of meteorological winter left and the first daffodils were out, and some climbers had got careless because even in the mountains, winter had hardly bothered to show up. One of the main Highland ski centres hadn't opened until February. A week later I took advantage of an encouragingly wintry forecast and headed back to the Insh Marshes, hoping against hope for the bonus of a snowy day in Rothiemurchus or Abernethy.

I awoke in a Speyside hotel room at 3a.m. I opened the curtains on a sky stuffed with stars, the Cairngorms basking in moonlight and barely a shred of snow in sight. At 7a.m. there was ice on my car and fog shrouded the land. Talking to the hotel staff at breakfast, it turned out that full-on winter had lasted three days. I was at the Marshes by 8.30, the sun was making next to no impression on the fog. The descent from the footpath to the Invertromie hide was a carefully negotiated, ice-encrusted, frost-bound transition down through primeval-looking woodland. Sunlight had not penetrated down there for, oh, weeks probably. If it had not been for the all-pervasive pallor of the frost, the depth of shadow could have intimidated susceptible mortals. The hide itself is right down at marsh level and right in the outermost edge of the trees, a place on the cusp of two landscapes. At the door, it has a subterranean feeling. If you turn round, the wooded hillside you have just descended rears steeply above and shuts out all other sights and sounds of the overworld. The fact that it was bewitched by that ghostly off-white ermine of frost did not endear me to the job in hand.

Inside the hide, it seemed to be colder than outside, although that could just as easily have been a symptom of my aversion to hides. I discovered how much colder it was about to get when I opened the window slots that face out over the Marshes and a breeze drifted in bearing greetings from what's left of the Arctic sea ice. The window opened on a startling and panoramic sprawl of the Insh Marshes, the mountains beyond and the raw wildness of Strathspey at its most unfettered. The only problem was that I could see none of it because the fog had the place by the throat and appeared to have wrung the life out of it. Nothing moved. Nothing made a sound, at least nothing wild made a sound. The A9 made a sound, a distant and incongruous bass grumble, which at that moment in that situation was as a voice from another world. An hour frittered itself away into the blue-grey oblivion. My coffee flask, which was supposed to sustain me through elevenses and lunch, became my one defence against the nothingness of that hour. Then quite suddenly, and piece by piece, the nothing began to crack open, and a new Earth was born right in front of my eyes.

Mallards appeared, swimming. I have never been so pleased to see mallards, ever. Their pool appeared, then grew and grew until it became an acre of open water. I heard greylag goose voices (but saw no geese), a lapwing sighed (but I saw no lapwing). Then sunlight burst apart the mist to the north and revealed two roe deer a hundred yards apart between tall banks of reeds which dwarfed them. They looked grey in their winter garb, white scarves at their throats.

One pond after another, the intrinsic character of the Marshes began to reveal itself, and most ponds wore skins of ice. But the pace of the unveiling was surreally slow. It is in such situations that you realise how the idea of the slow-motion film was born. Then far above the Marshes a mountaintop appeared ... a mountaintop without a mountain to support it in the sky. It would take another half hour before the entire mountain had coloured itself in. It began to feel as if anything could happen.

Then one of the ponds loudly emptied itself of all its mallards, most of which I had not seen until that moment when twenty of them hurtled into the air, their flight unnaturally fast and their alarm cries unnaturally loud in the slow, soft context of the morning. Back on the water, something long and dark and blunt-nosed trailed a vee-shaped wake. It edged ashore, shook itself and stood in the sun watching the retreating, curving flight of the mallards. It was a big dog otter, and my guess was that it had been stalking the ducks and that the mist had cloaked its presence. I had never considered the possibility before of an otter using a ground mist to conceal itself as it hunted.

Sunlight had now reached to within about thirty yards of the hide, although the shadow of the hill behind would keep it from warming up the hide itself. Just beyond the edge of the shadow, a screen of reddish-looking scrubby birches was partially hiding another roe deer. It caught my eye only when it turned its back and the white blaze of its rump struck a jarring note, which blew its cover. It turned its head to look back along its spine and gave the hide a long, hard stare. I daresay the hide produced a lot of human noise from time to time, but this morning there had just been me, and making human noise is something I take pains to avoid when I'm alone in a situation like this. Then it stared hard left and its ears went forward. I looked where it was looking and there were two more roe deer, and these advanced soundlessly to where it stood, and for a moment all three had gathered in a tight bunch, the red of the birches in front of them and the sunlight full on them, and from their different angles they all turned their heads towards the hide, and presented me with one of my better roe deer photographs ("damned with faint praise" is the phrase you are looking for here). The smallest of the three, last year's young, was a markedly different shade of grey-brown from the others, a kind of olive shade. Olive, the other roe deer ...

For a long while they became the entire focus of my attention. It was clear they were feeding, but not at all clear what they were eating. The vegetation had that fag-end-of-winter look that promised no nutrition whatever, and the land where they stood was as much water and peaty mud as it was solid ground. Yet they fed constantly, but whatever they were eating was hidden from me by the long, pale, straw-coloured grass. Finally they emerged into a more open spot, and I realised how deep they were digging with forefeet and with muzzles, and that there was a great deal of tugging to free their food source. Roots. That's where there was new growth and nourishment, underground. It was turning into a surprising morning. I looked at my watch. It had been four hours.

I retraced my steps back up through the woods, the lower part of which was quite unaffected by sunlight. But as I climbed I could feel the air warm and the trees began to glitter and drip, hundreds of trees at a time, an extraordinary percussive symphony.

Back at the top of the wood, the sun suddenly poured through, and after my long shift in the frigid zone I stepped out into something that was properly warm. I guessed that the temperature had got a dozen degrees warmer in those few hundred uphill yards.

*

It occurs to me as this exploration of winter advances that buzzards keep cropping up. There are good reasons why that should be so, not the least of which is their new-found abundance. One of the consequences of that is that many more people who are not instinctively drawn towards nature think they are seeing eagles, which brings the following conversation to mind.

So I met this man in a bar and he said:

"I know you. You're the nature guy."

I've been called worse. I nodded.

"Just saw a thing: it was a golden eagle sitting on a fence post."

And my head groaned inside itself and I thought, "Why me, God?" but I smiled instead and said:

"You sure? Buzzard, maybe?"

He shook his head.

"Eagle. It was huge."

And it was warm and comfortable in the bar and the fire was on and I had been reading the paper, so I really hadn't wanted conversation right then, right there, and I particularly didn't want the over-familiar buzzard-on-a-fence-post conversation. But I didn't want to appear rude either so I laid aside the paper, fixed the stranger with a tell-me-about-it kind of look and said:

"Tell me about it."

"Tell you what about it?"

"Where was your fence post?"

"At the side of the main road, a mile back."

"Now tell me what you saw."

His beer arrived. He drank the top third without pausing, sighed theatrically and nodded his appreciation.

"Long drive," he explained, then: "What did I see? It came up out of the grass verge as I drove past, almost hit the windscreen; carrying something furry in its legs – they were hanging down. And there was something white I couldn't see properly at first. But the road was empty so I pulled over on the verge and had a good look back. The furry thing had blood on it. It was under the eagle's feet."

Another swallow accounted for the second third of his pint. I said:

"Three things: one, did it perch upright or with its tail horizontal? Two, were its legs yellow or feathered? Three, was the white thing by any chance a plastic wing-tag?"

"Okay then. One, it perched upright. Two, the legs were bright yellow. Three, aye, it was a white disc stuck to one of the wings with a big … "

"With a big letter C on it?"

"Aye. How'd you know?"

"Okay, you saw a buzzard, and a buzzard in your windscreen IS huge!"

"Ach, is that all? I thought it was an eagle."

"Don't be disappointed. You saw an almost-eagle. A buzzard is a fabulous bird. After all, yours was impressive enough to make you think you'd seen an eagle. Don't think any less of it just because it wasn't what you thought, or wasn't what you wanted it to be. And that particular buzzard, with the white wing-tag with the big letter C on it, spends half its life walking about in the fields pretty much where you saw it, and most of the rest in the woods across the road."

"Why does it have the wing-tag? What's the C for?"

"Good questions. And I don't know, and I don't know anyone who does. I also don't know why anyone would want to tag a buzzard. But then I don't much care for wing-tagging birds at all. It's a device to satisfy the nosiness of people, and if you were to ask the bird, it would tell you it would rather not have wing-tags. No one has ever convinced me that the powers of flight of a bird with wing-tags are not hampered. The design of birds' wings has evolved for a few million years now and they've always used feathers. The addition of plastic makes a perfect design imperfect. And no one has ever convinced me that birds have not been killed when a tag snagged on a tree or a fence, or ... "

He hadn't bargained for this stuff and he had already lost interest. He downed the rest of his drink, announced his departure and his last words were these:

"Ah well, maybe you're right. I still think it was an eagle."

I mention the story because the buzzard must be the most misidentified bird in the Highlands, especially among people who are new to the Highlands or very occasional visitors and the one thing they want to see before they leave is a golden eagle, and the notion must have come into my mind at least partly because I was back in the Insh Marshes, and there are few better places in the land to put the two species into some kind of perspective. My simple rule of thumb is this: if you are in any doubt, it's not a golden eagle. But that is of limited use to someone who is in no doubt at all because they don't know what an eagle looks like in relation to a buzzard, or what a buzzard looks like in relation to an eagle. You can refine that idea by considering the bird's environment. You don't get golden eagles sitting at the side of the B970, so the chances are that if you see something eagle-shaped and magnified by an early morning fog sitting on a telegraph pole at the roadside and watching you as you drive slowly past, with the best will in the world that's not a golden eagle, that's a buzzard. On the other hand, you don't get buzzards at 5,000 feet and still climbing. So if you see what looks like a small golden eagle high overhead when you're on the Cairngorms plateau and you think it's small enough to be a buzzard, it's just that the scale of the place has defeated your eyes and it's an eagle a thousand feet higher and still climbing. And on yet another hand, the Insh Marshes some 3,000 feet lower than the plateau, and a landscape flat enough to command the River Spey to dawdle in the western lee of the Cairngorms for a few miles ... that is buzzard territory *par excellence*, and buzzard territory *par excellence* sometimes produces extraordinary results.

When I am not refrigerating myself in one of the RSPB's hides at the Marshes, my favourite viewpoint there is a blunt headland of heather and rock and birch trees. It shoulders out from the mountain massif to invade the edge of the Marshes, a low outpost with miles-wide views. I go often in autumn, winter and earliest spring, mostly to prospect for whooper swans, but also for all the swans' fellow travellers that find reason to linger there, and for the place itself, for its hard-nosed mountain landscape setting. The word "landscape" is slightly misleading, for mostly, and especially in winter, it's more water than land, and it's that combination of shallow water lying over grass that endears it to the swans, to all wildfowl and to the nature writer. There was a day when I washed up there a few winters ago and the swans were half a mile away and scattered widely, and I wouldn't be able get any closer to them without getting back into the car and driving all the way round, and I was done with driving for the moment. I filed the idea away as a possibility for the end of the day if they were still there, but as it was, there were geese and lapwings in a field of grudgingly rough grazing on the very mountain edge of the marshes. The sharp, querulous staccatos of the greylags were shrapnel for the ears, flung by a north wind with an unforgiving edge, whereas the thin, woozy sighs of the lapwings rather drifted up on it, a sound that bathed the landscape like a gentle wave of newly melted ice. Yet there was a satisfyingly yin-yang-ish harmonious aspect to the resulting blend, which somehow amounted to rather more than the sum of its parts.

Enter from directly overhead that old familiar contralto down-curve, that bluesy minor-third, that haunted voice, and I leaned back and looked up to forage among the purple tracery of winter birch branches until, in a clear patch of cold blue, I found the thickly patterned spreadeagle of buzzard wings. The bird was moving sideways into the wind as if it were being towed along by the primary feathers of its starboard wing. For all my determined stillness, I was being watched, assessed, dismissed, and the bird cruised on towards the lapwing field, still going sideways … and followed at once by its own mirror image crossing the same patch of sky, and it too was flying sideways against the wind but leading with the port wing. Because I was looking at the underside of the second bird's wings from below and behind, as opposed to below and in front with the first bird, I saw their rich patterns in a quite different light. And the patterns themselves differed from bird to bird, because, as I have suggested elsewhere, there is no standard buzzard uniform.

So there were two birds out over the lapwing-and-goose field, and for a moment it had seemed like a good idea to change position so that I had a view of the field and its airspace unencumbered by branches. Memo to self – don't. At least not yet. I have found that when you are in buzzard country *par excellence*, there are often more pairs of buzzard eyes watching you than you know about, which is why I have developed this slightly odd-looking technique (I'm guessing here, I've never watched myself) of standing with my back against a birch trunk, and slowly inching all the way round the tree looking up and keeping my back in contact with the trunk. Although I knew there were two buzzards out there to the north, which was the direction I was facing, and although I also knew that two buzzards over a field full of lapwings and geese can sometimes put on quite a show if they're in the mood, I began my slow circumnavigation of the birch by turning away from the buzzards and towards the east.

I was a degree or two beyond east-north-east when the third and then the fourth buzzards cruised over the trees, one looking down at me looking up, the other looking side-headed at the sky. The third called from no more than thirty feet up and directly overhead, a cry so sharp-edged and (as I fancied it) so specifically aimed that I felt it nail me to the tree. Tingling scalp and startled shoulder blades jerked back against the bark in a tiny but perfectly co-ordinated spasm of response. It was an ice-cold voice the bird directed straight at me.

It is absurd, of course. The buzzard and I both know I don't speak buzzard. It was calling the attention of the fourth buzzard to my presence. And I had been so convinced I would be indistinguishable from the birch trunk where I leaned to any third and fourth buzzard eyes, thanks to my inch-perfect, slow-motion manoeuvre around the trunk. The fourth buzzard called back and immediately appeared in that portion of the sky where the third still lingered. The two birds shared that space for a moment and called there just once, but the call of the fourth bird began just before the call of the third bird, so that their voices overlapped, and as one was more or less a tone above the other and curved in a steeper glissando arc to a deeper denouement, the effect was of a kind of menacing harmony unique in all my days and nights in wild places. I imagined a duet of wolfsong dwindling to its last deepening and discordant bars.

The two buzzards veered towards the north as the first two had done, flying sideways, the starboard wingtip of one almost touching the port wingtip of the other, so that it was a single creature with a double wingspan that crossed the clear sky directly overhead, and I thought that if the thirsty traveller in the bar had seen this, he would have held the almost-eagle in formidable respect forever more, for I have done just that myself.

It was time to give up trying to be a birch tree, time to walk slowly to that space on the headland where the trees relented and offered up a wide view over the lapwings' field. The original buzzards were still there, circling at more or less my eye level and about a hundred yards away, and so were buzzards five and six; and buzzards three and four cruised over the birches that surrounded me on three sides, and now the buzzards had become a throng. Six buzzards at eye-level and in the sunlight, and loitering without any apparent intent at all, but – also apparently – enjoying the company of the others less than a month before the nesting season begins with all guns blazing, all hackles raised ... it was a moment to weigh up every ounce of that compact, power-packed profile, to garner tiny flight details for future use (one bird paused on stiffly held wings to lift a foot towards its beak and nibble it for several seconds; one half-folded its wings and surged forward in level flight as if a turbocharger had just kicked in; one hovered on slowly beating wings, tail held vertically below its head). And then, from behind and above, the seventh buzzard called, and then from the low ground beyond the geese, I heard another, so I turned and re-focussed the glasses, and through a blur of mobilising greylag geese there were three more buzzards, and these abandoned what had been a leisurely northwards procession and made a pointed beeline for the throng.

Ten buzzards.

So let's see. I had come here to watch the swans, but I had come here too knowing the place from old seasons and its capacity to surprise me with its wildlife riches. I had come to this side of the headland in the first place because I had heard geese, then their lapwing companions, and decided I would drop in on their field to see what was unfolding there. Then, buzzard by buzzard, the whole mood of the hour transformed, and when the last three panicked the goose hordes, the sky was as full of big beating wings as any single pair of human eyes could possibly take in. And then I felt as if – finally – I had achieved something of the birch's stillness, for I was still and the sky seethed and the air resounded with the clatter of several hundred geese and the eerie tumult of ten buzzard voices that wheeled and dived and soared and spiralled as they cried and … hey, what happened to the lapwings?

There is a school of thought, to be found exclusively in the minds of a section of the country's gamekeepers, that there are too many buzzards, and that it should be made easier to get a licence to shoot them. This is why, because sometimes buzzards turn up ten at a time, because their range is spreading, because they constitute that rarest phenomenon in the 21st-century landscape of Scotland, a prospering species of raptor. It is almost unheard of in our recent past, thanks in no small measure to the activities of that certain section of gamekeepers. Two things have happened to assist the buzzards' cause. One is that pro-wildlife legislation has got tougher and is better policed, and the other is wildlife crimes are much more widely publicised in the media. So those keepers who cannot tolerate the improving fortunes of a wild creature if it causes them the slightest inconvenience have raised the cry again with Scottish Government ministers:

"Too many buzzards!"

But there is no such thing. There can be no such thing. It is one of the most basic principles of nature that an abundance of predators is only possible when there is a superabundance of prey, and if that prey includes literally millions of gamekeepers' pheasants released into our countryside every year so that clients pay handsomely to shoot them, it also includes rabbits, rats, voles, stoats and weasels, and various other forms of what they are pleased to call vermin.

Not all keepers feel this way. I have had invigorating conversations with those who like to work with nature rather than against it; who know that when the population of a raptor like a buzzard soars from a troubling low point to a spectacular high, that high is false and soon enough the population will relax back to a stable level. Besides, you don't remove protection from a protected species just because it has recently achieved a position of strength. But all that presupposes that no one takes the law into their own hands; the landscape *is* still pock-marked with poisoned carcases. Strange how public opinion never comes down on the side of the poisoners.

Hopefully this time the buzzard is here to stay.

Rejoice.

And no one should worry that it's not an eagle.

ALMOST EAGLE

Buzzard is almost eagle,
more than hawk,
opens tins of cold air
with cutting edges
of sunwise spirals.
Blue's the background sky
best suited to such languid copper,
not golden enough for eagle
which prefers thundercloud grey.

Twenty-one
I Went Out to the Hazel Wood

THEY CLING TO THE OUTERMOST EDGES of the western fringes of Gaeldom like the frayed hem of an ancient kilt. They are rags and tatters of woodland, remnants of remnants. They are among the last souvenirs of the original wildwood, the most primitive and least tampered-with of its direct ancestors. The Atlantic hazel woods of our western seaboard – and a handful more on Ireland's west coast – constitute a habitat unique in the world. Perhaps they are the oldest of all the native habitats of post-Ice-Age Scotland. They hold the great ice in their memory, and in their DNA. Perhaps they have something to say to me about the nature of what winter has become. It is a nature writer's mission rather than a climatologist's, but then this book is a nature writer's mission. Winter has become so unstable, so unsure of itself, so erratic; winter has lost its sense of purpose; winter has lost its way; winter is just plain lost. I was looking for something stable and eternal to cling to myself. And nothing clings to eternity more tenaciously than an Atlantic hazel wood.

From the west coasts of Sutherland and Ross to Skye to Ardnamurchan to Mull to Knapdale and the island of Seil in Argyll, these dense and low-slung woods curve uphill from the ocean's high-tide line to a distinctive pattern dictated by the wind. They will never grow taller, and for as long as they have held the final frontier of the land against the onslaught of ocean winds, they never have. The ocean has never overwhelmed them but ocean winds limit them. Tree and ocean have reached an amicable pact, a peace treaty that has lasted 10,000 years.

Step inside such a wood, on the west coast of Mull. Feel the millennia tumble away. Immerse yourself in its embrace and the press of trees abruptly reduces your awareness of the world to the next few yards, sometimes the next few feet. Again and again the architecture of such a wood commands you to turn aside, bend double, unpin yourself from brambles, wade bogs ... any combination of these and more or less all the time.

And the trees are eerie.

They writhe their trunks and limbs. Many of them are effectively self-coppicing, that is, they produce dozens of stems instead of a single trunk. Our own distant ancestors learned from nature how to coppice trees, and especially hazels, so that they might create endless supplies of firewood and of straight poles for building. Often in the Atlantic hazel woods, the trees just do it themselves. If you walk there in a certain mindset and if the day is soft grey and calm, the effect can seem curiously aggressive, nervy, edgy; and if the sun shines, they throw such a web of shadows on the woodland floor that it adds to the untranquil aura of such places. When Yeats went out to the hazel wood in *The Song of Wandering Aengus* "because a fire was in my head", it was not to cool the fire that he went there, but rather to cut a hazel wand so that he might catch a trout. The uneasiness of hazel woods is not the environment you would choose to cool a fiery head. If, on the other hand, what you want is an instant fishing rod, it's perfect.

Hazel woods are also vocal. The trees rasp and rustle in a good-going wind (and on Scotland's Atlantic seaboard the wind is good-going more often than not), and groan and creak when the wind gets excited, and these are notes of protest that ocean winds have heard for almost as long as there have been hazel woods on an Atlantic shore.

Everything here is apparently ageless, or at least it evokes those imponderable times ensnared within the implicit vagueness of the word "Mesolithic". It means, since you asked, relating to a transitional period of the Stone Age between the Palaeolithic and the Neolithic, so somewhere between 12000 and 3000 BC. Further back than that, we're guessing beyond the level of our competence, but there is ample evidence to suggest that at least some of our Mesolithic ancestors knew how to burn and cut, both to improve grass for the animals they hunted and to create more prolific hazel woods that produced more wood for building, more firewood and more nuts. The profusion of hazelnut shells unearthed by archaeologists at some of our oldest known human settlements is emphatic confirmation of their importance as a food source and, crucially, a food source that could be harvested and stored for winter.

It occurred to me too, walking this Mull wood, that probably then as now, hazel woods were also a preferred habitat of brambles, and that too would enhance their value to early wanderers and settlers. And the more inclined to settle our ancestors became, the more valuable were their hazel woods. The mysterious crannog builders, for example, used hazel and alder posts, and both are trees that thrive in wetlands. The earliest farmers in the West Highlands laid claim to hazel thickets or planted their own, and found endless uses for the flexible slim branches: Yeats's Wandering Aengus was not the first man who ever caught a little silver trout by hooking a berry to a thread on the end of a hazel wand. They also make good fences, creels, any shape or size of basket you care to imagine, hoops for barrels. There were creel houses and outbuildings like barns made from hazel. In a daft moment, I wondered how I would begin to make a creel house if I had been a wandering Mesolithic chiel 5,000 years ago and made landfall hereabouts. I decided I would make two circles first, a small one which would let the smoke out from a central fire, and a large one that would define the floor area, and which could be pinned into the ground like a tent. Then all you have to do is join the two together with curving hazel wands to make a dome, then cross-hatch them with horizontal hazel wands. Nature has always approved of its tribes – and we are one of these, remember – living in something so organic, something so characteristic of the landscape where it stands. And sometimes, when we do still take the time and the trouble to listen to nature, we surprise ourselves. In some parts of England, for example, where hazels can reach fifty feet high (they achieve nowhere near half that on this blasted shore), they are conservationists. They are being planted and coppiced beneath oak trees right now to assist the cause of English bluebells and nightingales, and who would not want to assist the cause of both?

Meanwhile, on Mull at the end of a weary winter, it seems they assist the cause of brown hares. I walked in on two of them resting in dappled sunlight, ears flat along their backs, both reluctant to move despite my blundering intrusion. When eventually they lost their nerve and decided to make a run for it, they effected a half-hearted retreat across the woodland floor and stopped again not twenty yards away, and still well inside the trees, sitting up and looking back, ears tall. It seemed to my eyes that a hazel wood was a confining kind of habitat for a hare, but then I wondered if perhaps it was an extra defensive measure these hares had adopted in recognition of Mull's steadily growing population of sea eagles. This coast in particular is increasingly accustomed to that huge eagle shadow rippling across shoreline and cliff face; across its hazel woods. I pulled back, chose a different route, stopped out of sight and downwind and waited. In ten minutes, the hares had ambled back to the very glade where I had found them.

The moment put in mind an old September in this very wood, the shoreline air thick with young swallows and martins cashing in on the insect hordes above and around the hazel wood. I had one eye on a bruise-coloured storm that was powering its way across the sea towards this Mull shore from Tiree and Coll, both of which had vanished in the last few minutes. I heard it coming, for it packed its own wind and arrived with a salvo of hailstones that sizzled off the sea, off the shoreline rocks, then off the trees. By that time, the swallows, the martins and I had come to the same snap decision – head for the hazel wood. I had stepped into the lee of one of the bulkier non-hazels of the wood, a silver birch, and almost at once the skinniest twigs of the surrounding hazels were invaded by birds. They perched upright, chattering, dozens of them in a few square yards. I had seen this happen before in reed beds, but not in a wood. There again, a hazel wood a yard above the high-tide line probably doesn't look so different from a reed bed, when all you want to do is get your head down in a storm, when your solitary need is met by something thin and upright to cling to.

The storm crashed by, the sun rushed out, and the birds, as if on a signal, exploded in a whispered cacophony of rasping wings back up into the insect-rich air and resumed the slaughter. One moment there were swallows and martins all around as thick on the hazel trees as catkins in February. The next, there were only leaves for company, and in the stillness that followed the storm's gusto, the trees' voices were the whispers of skeletons couched in an antique tongue.

It is curious how some landscapes draw you in and reach you with at least a sense of their formative years. Some achieve the trick by baring the rock bones of the landscape corpus. Some – glaciers or the aftermath of glaciers, for example – demonstrate at a glance the convulsive nature of the hand that devised the architecture of their landscape. Others – like volcanoes, like sea, like polar ice – use perpetual restlessness to challenge our own transience. A Scots pine wood uses the deep, dark green primitiveness of jungles, a realm so all-consuming that you cannot imagine that the landscape ever wore any other garb. They have in common with the hazel woods that they trace their ancestors directly back to the great ice, and they contemplated no other guise from that day to this. Such a pedigree communicates itself effortlessly.

But an Atlantic hazel wood has a different technique from any of these. It lies along the westmost edge of the land as if it has just waded ashore, or as if a mighty breaking wave had petrified as it unfurled, then fossilised over millennia into a chaotic tsunami of trees. I know, I know, I'm taking liberties with the evolution of the raw stuff of the planet, but these are trees unlike any other. If your idea of the kind of tree that makes you happy is a trunk from which branches and a canopy spring forth, you are in the wrong wood here. Rather, this is a half-caste wood, biologically rooted between a tree and a shrub. From inland and above, or from the sea homing in on the land, the thing looks neat, ordered, corralled and curved by the ocean and its winds into something compliant and obedient. But inside, it seethes. There is a crackling, spindly, electric energy about a tree with thirty trunks, each of which rocks and swithers independently of all the rest and at the wind's bidding; each of which throws a shadow on the woodland floor. And every dancing shadow is interlaced with the dancing shadows of the next tree and the next, for it is in the nature of hazels in an Atlantic wood not to leave more space between trees than what is strictly necessary to get the job done. The whole thing has the effect of a dance to the music of time.

So might it then have been a woodland like this one, but on Skye rather than Mull, that determined the outcome of an epic fight between the Ulster hero Cuchullin and the Skye warrior-goddess Skiach, for it was known even then (and whenever "then" may have been) that hazelnuts possessed a magic that conferred knowledge on those who ate them? One of many versions of the legend has it that when Cuchullin heard that Skiach was operating a school for heroes in the Cuillin of Skye, he crossed the sea in three strides to land at Talisker Bay, for he was already a true hero and he was intent on wiping out the opposition. Skiach enrolled him in her school and he proceeded to defeat every pupil in hand-to-hand combat. This impressed Skiach enough to permit him to fight her daughter, whom he also defeated. This in turn infuriated Skiach to the extent that she deigned to descend from the mountains to fight Cuchullin herself. They fought inconclusively for days, until finally Skiach's daughter persuaded them to pause long enough to eat a deer roast that had been stuffed with hazelnuts. The two combatants reckoned privately that the hazel wisdom would give them the knowledge to defeat the other. Instead, it gave them the knowledge to realise that neither could overcome the other, so they made peace instead. They also made this pact: that if either should ever need the assistance of the other, it would be given unconditionally "though the sky fall and crush us". Cuchullin returned to Ulster. Skiach called the mountains after him – Cuillin.

It is more than just a wood you enter when you step into the edgy embrace of an Atlantic hazel wood, more than just food you acquire when you eat the nuts of an Atlantic hazel, and it was ever thus. The legend imitates nature, imitates the pact the hazel wood made with the ocean, that both might thrive and accommodate each other.

The thing is, it works. At the end of a winter in which the dominant characteristic was a climate in chaos, a chaos contrived by our confrontation with nature, the moral of the story was never more obvious. We are Cuchullin and Skiach before they ate the hazelnuts; if we are to pull back from an abyss of unknown depths and disasters, we have to stop the fight. It can be done, a way can be found, we can be the hazel wood to nature's ocean.

Nature tells us that every day. But first, we need to take heed. We need to listen.

Part Three

SPRING

Harbingers

Whiles, the jackies hud their wheesht,
an eerie cortege abune the birks, conversin wi' nocht
but the saft creak o' fower-hunner weengs,
the land's loudest whisper.
In its unchancy wake the hale Highland Edge
shiddered and stilled
wi' a whoosh o' silence.
That was winter breathed its last.
Then, at a signal frae the yorlin on the wire,
the first moon o' spring heaved up i' the east,
a thissell-cok skirled i' the gloamin,
while deep i' the Mediterranean sooth
far, far past France,
a gowk atop an olive tree
checked in wi' its biological clock
and thocht: "Aye, it maun be time".

Twenty-two

First Syllables

I like to go outside and paint pictures in the early spring. I suppose it's my way of trying to be a tulip, pushing my way out of the tight white bulb of winter and opening a little color against the drabness.

Ted Kooser, *Seasons in the Bohemian Alps*
(University of Nebraska Press, 2002)

THE LAND IS PATCHED with frozen and slowly thawing snow, depending on whether it lies in shadow or sunlight. Ben Ledi, this Stirlingshire landscape's symbolic pyramid, seen through a waving screen of bare birches, has been whitened and softened and curved and blunted by masses of snow that fleeced the mountains in the night. Far below, Loch Venachar lies in a *contre-jour* dwam, its surface mimicking sky colours – iciest blue, various greys, white and gold – and contriving to hurl fragments of all of these up the hillside, so that it looks as if sky and loch and land have been daubed by the same brush, that this portion of the Earth has been unified by nature in colour and texture and purpose. Paul Cézanne would do just that in his later years, flooding his canvasses of Mont Sainte-Victoire with daring bravado, and from foreground to middle ground to mountaintop and on into the sky, the whole patched with the same few shades of greens, yellows and blues, and leaving just enough canvas unpainted to insinuate flecks of brightness on mountaintop and cloud. He wrote then:

I become more lucid in front of nature…but I cannot attain the intensity which unfolds to my senses. I don't have the magnificent richness of colouration which animates nature.

And:

Art is a harmony parallel to nature.

And his biographer, Alex Danchev (*Cézanne – A Life*, Profile Books, 2012), wrote:

Harmony, like beauty, was being redefined.

So, on a February afternoon of can't-possibly-be-spring-yet, the ghost of Cézanne bestrides this living hillside between Loch Venachar and Ben Ledi, animating nature, redefining its harmony and beauty by flooding its canvas with a limited palette that does not discriminate from foreground to loch to mountaintop and on into the sky. The result is a landscape fizzing with energy. But is it spring?

A bare, half-folded-fan-shaped rowan tree cuts through a low hill skyline so that its many-branched crown arcs against the sky and reveals the neat and placid silhouette of a vertically perched kestrel clasped to the topmost inch of the topmost twig. For the next five minutes it is utterly motionless (and for how long before I first saw it?), while the sky behind and above jigs and reels where wind and sun and cloud and blue and unpainted scraps of canvas conspire to create the appropriate setting to show it off. But the kestrel's preoccupation is the land below the tree, and that land is all pale gold and straw-shaded grasses, liberally patched with snow that gleams with hints of all those sky shades.

The bird throws its wings wide, raises its tail, and a shudder goes through it, and when that subsides it has realigned its stance from vertical to horizontal, and in the process it has revealed itself as a female kestrel, and now she too has redefined harmony and beauty. She will fly any moment.

She flies west. West is my direction, too, but more slowly now, for she is ahead of me, and I would like to encounter her again as we trace our parallel contours across the hillside.

She is not hard to find. She's there beyond the next small rise in the land. She perches on air now. Every feather and nerve-end is a-flicker,

apart from her head, which is the still centre of her world. She steps
down a yard from her perch, she banks, chooses a new course, urges
forward into the west wind. I never saw a raptor that did not prefer
to hunt into the wind. It is as true of thrush-sized merlins as it is of
eagles, as it is of kestrels. Facing the wind achieves control. A tail wind
brings chaos, unless the bird's ambition is to cover a lot of ground
without the need for control. A hunting kestrel is precise. She will
wheel onto a tail wind only when she reaches her own idea of the edge
of her territory or her comfort zone, and then she may well surge all
the way back to where she started, and there, if she's still hungry, she
may turn and start again.

She keeps pace with me for about a mile. Several times I will over-
take her because she is head-down in mid-hover, but sooner or later
she reappears going west, going past me, always below me, always
rising somewhere beyond to hold up against the sky again, intimately
coupled to the wind. Finally, fruitlessly, she whips round in not much
more than her own length and barges away east, downwind.

The path is comparatively new and has made a neat, deliberate
breach in a drystane dyke that crosses it at right angles. It is not the
first breach, and they are not all this neat, for the dyke wears the forlorn expression of the redundant and disregarded. But it inclines away
uphill towards a wooded little crag down which shivers a muttering
burn, and it reads like an invitation: "This way." The snow patches
lie thicker there, ensnared by tussocks, a neatly stitched seam all the
way up the shadowed side of the dyke. The burn's voice grows louder,
blends into the fractured, percussive rhythms of a half-hearted waterfall hidden somewhere up there in the trees that crowd the crag and
the low ground beneath. This hillside is full of these little dens, the
gorges of their burns steep enough to discourage the grazing tribes
throughout the centuries of careless farming that held sway hereabouts. But this land is in the hands of Woodland Trust Scotland
now, and evidence of new native woodland planting is everywhere. A
long, slow process of healing has begun, which is why I come often.
So much of our relationship with nature is conducted in an atmosphere of battlefield; I greet these reprieved and resurrecting acres with
over-emotional regard. The forgiveness of nature always moves me. It

rises to accept this extended helping hand, and its response swarms all over this land, a freewheeling generosity.

Up near the crag, the dyke is taller and more intact. A level square yard of hillside at its base offers a seat, a backrest and a windbreak. My backpack offers coffee and biscuits. The sound of the unseen waterfall rushes into the void left by silenced footsteps and stillness. Settle for a while. The view faces east. A tall, slender birch of singular elegance distinguishes the middle distance. It leans away from its hillside, but then ten feet above the ground it begins to curve gently back until it achieves something slightly past vertical and (to my un-birch-like eye) perfect balance. My eye lingers there not just because of the beauty of the solitary tree, but also because the sun alights fitfully on a distant hill called Uam Mhor, and quite by chance my choice of a seat has put the birch and the hill on precisely the same sightline. But the sun is on the hill, and not the birch, so the vivid snow gleam of the hill appears from behind and therefore apparently from *within* the birch. The tree is lit from within.

What was it you said, M. Cézanne?

I become more lucid in front of nature...but I cannot attain the intensity which unfolds before my senses.

I think perhaps I know how you feel.

Then, quite unannounced, the unambiguous voice of spring: it creeps into the edges of consciousness as if from far off, but it cannot be far off. It infiltrates the predominance of the waterfall, even though it is much quieter, yet because its pitch is much higher and occasionally strident, it finds ways through the sound-screen of the fall, through the gaps in its acoustic limitations. Somewhere above the fall, high in the crag's highest trees, a mistle thrush sings. Has it just begun, or has it been singing all along and it has taken time for me to tune in to the changed circumstances created by the angle of the dyke and the crag? The song reaches me in short, staccato phrases, often tapering away to silence, one diminuendo after another, and further fragmented because from time to time the fall drowns it out. But listen. If you like your harbingers well-toned, jazzily inventive and far-carrying, accompanied by coffee *al fresco* and a birch tree performing passable impressions of the burning bush, and if you are willing to turn a blind eye or two to the snow-patched land...then here on this Cézanne-animated February late afternoon, these are the first syllables of spring.

The singer is an un-mated male. And while it's true that you can sometimes hear him on a fine afternoon of late December, and at any time in January, these are moments of overture. But this, this is song for the sake of song, an advertisement, yes, but also an outpouring of intent, a declaration that winter is lost and irretrievable now. It is the first day of mistle thrush spring.

My mood suffuses. It permeates hillside and drystane dyke (which moulders day by day at nature's prodding and urging, regressing back into hillside). It permeates tree, crag, waterfall, thrush, song. The process of grafting on to nature's late afternoon hour slowly creeps beyond mind, beyond senses, becomes physical, becomes bodily. The thing is to be *of the land*, to breathe in unison, to keep its peace.

On and on the thrush.

On and on the waterfall.

On and on the solitary birch, silvering the air.

These are the golden moments. They let me in, and briefly, I belong.

*

Something about the birch.

What?

What changed?

Why does it suddenly snap into sharp focus as if it has just wandered up the hill this moment, to stand there and adopt that leaning, curving pose? It has not moved, of course. It has not become more silvery. Its shadow has not deepened. But where its many-branched crown arcs against the sky, it reveals the neatly folded silhouette (clasped to the topmost inch of the topmost twig) of the very same vertically perched kestrel. And I never saw her arrive. How long has she been there?

On and on the fall.

On and on the thrush.

But the kestrel's reappearance unsettles me. It concludes a circle. And the knowledge creeps in with the thickening dusk that I belong beyond it.

Twenty-three

Falcons of the Yellow Hill

There is a curious relationship between peregrines and kestrels that is difficult to define. The two species are often seen in the same place, especially in autumn and spring. I rarely saw one of them without finding the other close by. They may share the same bathing places, the peregrine may occasionally rob the kestrel of its prey, the kestrel may feed on kills the peregrine has left, the peregrine may attack birds the kestrel unwittingly puts up for him. In September and October some peregrines seem to copy the kestrel's way of hunting, and I have seen the two species hover together over the same field. In a similar way, I have seen a peregrine hunting near a short-eared owl, and apparently mimicking its style of flight. By March the relationship between kestrel and peregrine has changed; the peregrine has become hostile, and will stoop at, and probably kill, any kestrel hovering near him.

J.A. Baker, The Peregrine, (Collins, 1967)

THERE IS AN OLD SCOTTISH BALLAD in which the young man professes his love for the young woman thus: he will never stop loving her until the whins stop flowering. You like to think the woman was botanically savvy enough to know that whins flower to one extent or another every month of the year. Otherwise, the singer is out of luck and there is no ballad. I mention it because on the last day of February, and from half a mile away, the whins still looked furled. They sprawled, impenetrable and dark green as stoorie old beer bottles, all the way from the roots of the big trees that fringed the bottom of the hill to the big crag that fringed the top. That sprawl was only stymied where buttress and scree intruded, where even whins fail to draw sustenance. But that view of the whins on their hillside from half a mile away was, like so much of these winter-into-spring days, something of a deception. Shrink the distance to a handful of yards and you would have found whin flowers star-bursting open in vivid yellow clusters all over the lower slopes, and that only the sheer dark mass of the still-unflowering bushes had masked the reality at a distance.

It was cold that day, the last day of meteorological winter; it snowed lightly, dustily, prettily, and every few minutes. And the coldness of the air brought to mind Margiad Evans, who wrote one of my favourite winter-wind images in all literature: "the wind is a tooth in the breast." Besides, there had been some very sinister weather forecasts, couched in a language (the "Beast from the East" – the Met Office had started talking like the *Daily Mail*, which was vaguely disconcerting) designed to attract the attention of the media so that no one should be in any doubt about what was coming our way from Siberia. Sadly, it worked, and weather-hysteria broke out. Cue panic-buying in the supermarkets. But for once, the reality more or less lived up to the hype. An impressive snowstorm was about to set in and last for several days, and unless you were a nature writer writing a book about the nature of spring, life would pretty well come to a standstill.

For the moment though, and before that freakish storm broke, I made a little hay while the sun shone between charmingly feathery snow showers, safe in the knowledge that whatever the nature of the Beast that lay in wait, come April the hillside would be a yellow blaze you could see for miles, as it was every April. Walking there, I would be able to get agreeably drunk on the smell of coconut, which is the whins' gift to the world. At least that was the theory, but more than thirty years of writing about nature in Scotland has taught me that it is a restless creature, that it thrives on variety, and that what I once thought of as reasonably settled patterns are being dismantled by an increasing tendency towards random and restless weather, itself a microcosmic symptom of an infinitely greater global climate chaos. Even keeping half an eye open for the vagaries of climate change teaches you that that very restlessness is on a quickening downhill trajectory at the end of which lies mayhem. The "Beast from the East" made crazy headlines while it lasted (it dumped eighteen inches of snow in my garden in thirty-six hours, which was exactly eighteen inches more than in the whole of the previous winter), but it was over and done with in a week, and in one week more the wind had returned to the west and temperatures were in double figures. But then it got cold again when spring should have sprung, and in my workaday landscape, everything stopped again, and that troubled this watcher of nature.

★

From the foot of that whin-clad hillside, the skyline is a crag. It is half a mile long, broken only by a gully that splits almost the entire hillside, and that same entire hillside brims with birds in spring. These can drink and bathe in safety and with discretion in the gully's steep-tumbling burn, for it burrows deep once it escapes the gully, and whins and the hardiest of trees crowd round its lower reaches. The birds include not just the crag dwellers (peregrine falcon, kestrel, jackdaw, raven), but also the whin dwellers (robin, wren, dunnock, finch, warbler, chat, yellowhammer), and the woodland dwellers from the band of tall conifers and huge beeches that shields the foot of the hill from the road (sparrowhawk, owl, woodpecker, wood pigeon, blackbird, thrush, magpie, jay: it's a vociferous wood). Nature is profligate with its birds here, which in turn ensures the presence of a diversity of raptors – nesting kestrels, buzzards, ravens, those woodland sparrowhawks, and occasional red kites whose nest I have yet to pin down. And I would love to know how many foxes thread the whins and the skinny paths up through the rocky heights. They show themselves in sunlit pauses between whinbushes or tiptoeing across screes, glimpses of fiery red to complement the pervasive yellow. But the roost-rulers, high in the penthouse of the crag, have long been the peregrine falcons, or so it has always seemed to me, but this perverse spring was about to challenge one or two of my most painstakingly composed theories.

The hillside is two miles away from my writing table, so I wander that way often and never return empty-handed. And I have wondered from time to time if the peregrine that occasionally speculates above the gardens and woodland near where I live is one of that crag's pair.

My inclination thinks that it is. My reasoning is that if it were from a different and nearer nest, its raucous nesting-season voice would have betrayed the place by now. Besides, the crag-nesters could fly from there to here in less than five minutes, and I think that sometimes that's exactly what happens.

One of the fascinations of this particular pair of peregrines is that they have those nesting kestrels for near neighbours. They are separated by no more than 300 yards, which seems to be very near-neighbourly for two such virtuosic raptor-fliers. They can both hover, and they can both sprint, but the kestrel does hovering master-classes that are beyond the skills of any peregrines I ever saw, while the power-diving peregrine is the fastest creature in this sky or any other. When they hunt, mostly they rely on their own specialisms.

Even more intriguing is that their territories overlap, so you might think that their explorations of the hunting possibilities of the same hillside and beyond are bound to get on each other's nerves a bit. With that in mind, I invite you to reconsider that passage from J.A. Baker's *The Peregrine* quoted above, because as I sat making hay while the sun shone between snow showers that last February afternoon, something very unusual was about to happen. Bear in mind that I have watched peregrines on this hillside many, many times over quite a few years now, and while I have witnessed occasional tetchy spats with kestrels (a consequence of which was inevitably some spectacular flying, but never physical injury to either party – a kind of gesture politics), I have never seen anything like the behaviour Mr Baker describes. If you are unfamiliar with *The Peregrine*, it is, by any standards, an extraordinary book. The edition in my bookshelves was published in 2011 (the original in 1967), and features an introduction by Mark Cocker, an accomplished nature writer, naturalist and environmental tutor. He enthuses thus:

Today, it is viewed by many as the gold standard for all nature writing, and in many ways it transcends even this species of praise. A case could be made for its greatness by the standards of any literary genre.

Hmm. In the rarefied world of nature writing in particular, the reputation of Mr Baker's book is almost legendary, so much so that I tend to wonder if many of those who cite it have actually read it or just swallowed the legend. But anyone (especially another nature writer) with contrary opinions would do well to think twice before committing them to print... There, I've thought twice. I believe the reputation is inflated. In places, the writing is undeniably vivid, isolated pools of beautiful prose. But in other places, it's just plain unbelievable, and many people accustomed to witnessing the lives of peregrines have let it be known that they suspect there is an element of fantasy at work. I sail with the doubters in this.

The insinuation that the peregrine consciously mimics the hovering flight of kestrels and the low, slow ground-quartering of a short-eared owl takes some swallowing. Just because the peregrine is famed for its speed does not mean that it is incapable of resorting to one of the many tricks of flight when circumstance calls for something other than speed. It does not need to be shown how to do these things by other species.

And the end of the book, in which Mr Baker disturbs a sleeping peregrine and it doesn't fly away, is surely a dream the author had, and nothing to do with ornithology. I have no problem with an imaginative approach to nature writing. I do have a problem with rendering the imaginative as if it were nature itself. But waiting in the wings, a bird of a very different feather was about to challenge some of my reservations about Mr Baker and his book.

*

So it was the last day of February 2018, the snow fell in frail fragments of showers that brought to mind the blown seed of rosebay willow-herb – nothing more robust than that – and I had gone out to the hill to see how far advanced the nesting season preparations of falcon and hawk might be, or if they had even begun at all.

My favourite approach is to walk in the shade of the big trees along the base of the hill until I have reached a point from which I can see the peregrine crag, the gully (the ravens' home) and a certain whin-shrouded rock above a hefty buttress where the kestrels nest. There I like to pause and scan the lie of the land. Between the buttress in the west and the edge of the high crag in the east – about half a mile of hillside – nature contrives a stage set on which it improvises an unending production that never fails its one-man audience and occasionally enthrals. It's like *The Mousetrap* – it just goes on and on. The buzzards routinely drift in from both east and west, not exactly natives of the crag, but they live within sight and sound, and they exploit its potential of lesser birds, rabbits, mice and voles. This is my wide-angle view, where I take the temperature of the hour. Settle and still. This is the best part of the job, re-examining that which is familiar – known landscapes, knowing what to expect, having expectations first confirmed then confounded by something new.

So a male kestrel stepped up and out from an old ash tree rooted in a scree slope, side-slipped across the air and flew parallel to the face of the hill, leading with the open primary feathers of its left wing, then eased to a hovering standstill above a small clearing of steep, grassy hillside between advancing jaws of whin bushes. One sunlit moment, wings high, tail fanned wide almost vertically below his head, a glowing triangle of pale and dark tawny wings and breast, grey skullcap, black edging to pale silvery-grey tail, sleek in his breeding prime.

Head down. What does he see with his supremely evolved falcon eyes that can differentiate, from fifty feet above, between a blade of grass moving in the wind and the whiskers of a crouching vole a-twitch with fear? It's easy to decide he has eyes for only voles, mice, shrews, small packages of food wrapped in fur. Or – if necessary – beetles, insects, worms. His birding preferences – skylark, meadow pipit, for example – are elsewhere, on the far grassy, heathery flank of the hill.

But might he read the land too? Might he ponder its changing face? Every spring the whins advance, consume more open ground, meaning less room for voles and mice and worms, less hunting terrain for the kestrel tribe. Arguably it also means more nesting cover for small birds, but that suits the peregrine and sparrowhawk better than the kestrel, for the kestrel is a mouser by instinct, a birder only by necessity, so every spring this hillside becomes a little less kestrel-friendly. Was that, I wondered, in his mind too, forby the need to find the next vole?

I don't have a falcon's eyes, or a falcon's brain, so I see things differently, reason things differently, and I am ever wary of second-guessing what goes on in the animal mind. But from where I sit on the stone wall in the lee of the big trees at the bottom of the hill, and looking up at the kestrel looking down, the bird's dilemma as I see it is this. The kestrel pair has a good nest site on a flat rock atop a small rock-face and overhung (and therefore shaded and mostly hidden) by one more whin bush. It has served them well, proved fruitful. But how much longer before it becomes a nest site on a flat rock atop a small rock face in a dark green and bright yellow desert? So do the birds stay put, and if so, must they change their instinctive behaviour to accommodate the changed circumstances? Must they become birders for a living, become more efficient at catching prey in the air rather than on the ground? Or, must they accept that their preferences mean hunting further from the nest and having to carry prey further back to the nest, which means in turn (if Mr Baker is right and the per-egrines become as intolerant of nesting season kestrels as he says they are) that they become more vulnerable for longer to falcon-on-falcon predation?

Or do the kestrels pull out?

Do they abandon the safe nest where generations of their tribe have prospered (thirty years' worth to my certain knowledge), take their chances further along the hillside beyond the orbit of this pair of per-egrines at least, and beyond the whins, or on the far side of the hill where there is plenty of open grassland but where nest sites could be a problem (for there are no crags and precious few trees)? And will they reason all that out and make a decision, or will instinct simply kick in and evict them? Will nature cry "Enough!" and urge them on their way?

With my questions still poised – kestrel-like – on the hill air, the hovering bird fell thirty feet to a few inches above the whins and sped in level flight towards the blunt bulk of the buttress, a manoeuvre so sudden and low-slung and flat-out that it had the air of drastic evasion. The source of its discomfort was not hard to pin down. The courtship flight of a pair of peregrine falcons is a berserk chase through the heart of the home territory, and as remarkable for its control and its preci-sion as for its raw speed. God knows what it does to the hearts and minds of the lesser fowl of that hillside. Its objective may be nothing more than pair-bonding, but when it free-falls from several hundred feet above the summit, then crackles along the face of the crag from end to end in a blur, many a small furred or feathered heart must skip a beat, many a small beast or bird must freeze in fear or dive for the deepest cover it knows. Given that one of those flimsiest of snow showers was falling and lent a further frisson of subtle beauty to the spectacle, the whole event was simply a thing of wonder.

The kestrel, unimpressed as far as I know with the concept of a silk-screen of falling snow as a thing of beauty, and given that it knows it can hold its own in the peregrine's company more often than not, nei-ther froze nor dived for cover but rather flew in the opposite direction on a lower contour, and I found him perched in another tree below the buttress, having effected that temporary discretion which is the better part of valour. The choice of perch was interesting. It was in the topmost branches, so not taking cover, not deferring, but knowingly seeking out a particularly wide and unobstructed view of the entire crag. A bit of an object lesson slipped into place: sometimes the sheer spectacle of a predatory presence is a weapon in itself, even when the behaviour is essentially domestic rather than intentionally threaten-ing. The kestrel will be well enough versed in the wiles of peregrine flight to know that when it hunts, it hunts alone, and when two of them cross the territory in tandem in the run-up to nesting time, it is typical nesting behaviour, not typical hunting behaviour. Yet still the kestrel flew, and flew to a more useful vantage point.

So he would have a keen eye for what the peregrines did next, for they segued seamlessly into a long and more dignified oval-shaped circuit across the entire hillside at the level of the base of the crag, a circuit that passed (coincidence or intention – who knows?) a few feet above the kestrels' hidden nest ledge. But this time the perched kestrel did not flinch. As the peregrines completed their circuit, they split apart: the female rose to perch near the eyrie ledge, the male drifted slowly up at an angle and back across the face of the crag to a perch in the big gully, no more than three or four yards from the scruffy, twiggy mound of the ravens' nest. So it had buzzed the kestrel rock and door-stepped the sitting ravens in the same manoeuvre; surely a point was being made about dominance of the airspace over the other predator tribes. It did occur to me, however, that it had happened while the backs of the local buzzards were turned, and if any of the neighbours were built to out-muscle a peregrine...

The thought remained uncompleted, for I still had the glasses on the perched peregrine in the gully when it took off in a manner that suggested urgency, almost a vertical leap, then a steep climb up the cramped confines of the gully's airspace until it cleared the hillside and emerged against the sky. There it began circling slowly, crying out a shrill and repetitive three-syllable note with more than a hint of alarm to it. A second bird crept into the glasses much higher than the peregrine. There followed a few seconds of confusion while I tried to rationalise scale and distance and decided that I was seeing something much larger and much further away. Then it banked, unfurled the full scale of its vast acreage of wingspan and its tail blazed vivid white in the sunlight, and these are the unmistakable emblems of a sea eagle. That frail snow still fell on a light but ice-edged wind from the east, sunlight illuminated it from the south-west so that it glittered as it fell, but the eagle descended from a clear blue northern sky towards the south, towards the peregrine, towards me. I thought (and I may have said it out loud to no one): "This should be good."

*

These are Lowland hills, grassy and plateau-topped, barely reaching 2,000 feet. The crag is at the south-west corner of the range and is an untypical feature. To the south, low-lying flat fields sprawl away to the unspooling River Forth as it heads for its estuary. If you think of the sea eagle as a bird of the Hebridean West, with all of that land-and-seascape's grand gestures (the sheer scope of that repertoire of islands, the illimitable ocean and sky, the surf-washed phenomenon of the Skye Cuillin), the sight of such a bird transported into this comparatively domestic place can be stupefying. It just looks plain wrong, like a whale in a pond.

The eagle descended slowly above the peregrine, which in turn descended slowly above the gully, apparently keeping a healthy 100 feet between them, presumably backing himself to outsprint the eagle if it came to that. I acknowledge an uncharitable moment when I hoped that it might come to that, if only to see what it looked like. But when the peregrine drifted into the open throat of the gully and paused there to execute two level sunwise circles, awaiting developments, the sea eagle did not follow it down. Instead it banked again (another vivid flourish of that tail the shade of sunlit snow) and flew away east along the front of the hills just above the top of the crag and towards the peregrine eyrie ledge. The peregrine's response was to follow, fifty yards behind and fifty feet lower. Both birds flew slowly. The sea eagle's oversized wingspan flapped loosely, glided a few yards with the wings held still but in a shape rather like a wave, flapped again, the whole technique looking as if the bird was making heavy weather of the simplest of level flights. And then there was perhaps the most remarkable moment of the whole encounter between the two birds: the peregrine started to mimic the flight pattern of the eagle, down to the loose-limbed nature of the downstrokes, and although it clearly attempted the wavy-wing glides too, it was not quite so convincing.

"Some peregrines seem to copy the kestrel's way of hunting," wrote J.A. Baker. And: "...In a similar way, I have seen a peregrine hunting near a short-eared owl, and apparently mimicking its style of flight." Until now I was blithely associating myself with the doubters among Baker's readers, but here was what certainly looked like deliberate mimicry of a sea eagle. But to what end? What on earth is the point? Is it play? Is it a kind of flattery, an attempt at ingratiation? Is it deliberate and calculating or merely instinctive? Baker says "*some* peregrines" as though he thought it was not a universal trait in the species. It occurred to me, too, that if it had been a golden eagle rather than a sea eagle, it would have flown along the top of the crag in a stiff-winged glide without a wingbeat, a feat it can reproduce at almost zero knots, and I suspect that might not be in the peregrine's repertoire. But is that the point, a purposeful exploration of one more of the possibilities of flight beyond the peregrine's renowned capacity for flat-out speed, and perhaps guile is the end product in order to fool predator or prey species, the way a skylark or a dotterel feigns a broken wing? At the very least, I need to re-appraise some of Mr Baker's ideas.

I watched both birds until they vanished beyond the skyline that marks the end of the crag. I wondered how far falcon would shadow

eagle. I guessed until it was well beyond the margins of the home territory. I gave him another hour, but he did not reappear. I imagined him
sitting upright on a ledge or the top of a conspicuous tree, staring east
where the eagle had vanished, lost to even the phenomenal eyesight
of a peregrine falcon.

In the meantime, it had stopped snowing.

*

A long spell of wintry weather relented on April 9th, and something
recognisably spring-hued crept over the horizon and seeped along the
woodland at the foot of the hill. I could almost taste the difference on
the air. There were two buzzards and two kestrels above the west edge
of the crag. The unmistakable mewing buzzard voices drifted down
and rubbed shoulders with the hysterical, giggling falsetto of a green
woodpecker. The wind had veered from east to south, the temperature
had eased away from the frigid zone and nudged into double figures
– just. It was the first day I had seen flying insects, and no sooner had
the realisation lodged in my mind than I heard the first chiffchaff,
something like three weeks late. By the time I was back at the car four
hours later, I had heard six different calling chiffchaffs. Did they all
arrive at once? But the yellowing of the hillside, which is such a characteristic of spring here, had stalled halfway up, and even the whin
blossom on the lower half was nothing like the density of old springs.

I paused at my accustomed stance against the wall that edges the
wood, and the buzzards were pretending to be golden eagles, which is
always worth watching if you don't happen to be in golden eagle country. The female was locked into a horizontal spiral that travelled east
but seemed not to gain height at all, the opposite process to that which
is evident in most buzzard spirals, but if your purpose is to scan the
hillside at a leisurely pace for rabbit traffic across the small clearings in
the whins, then such a flight technique is perfect for the job in hand.
Her mate was much higher and almost stationary, holding up against
the wind, working his tail more than his wings, so that from time to
time the silhouette was almost kite-shaped, for no bird in these skies
leads more fluently with its tail than the red kite. Maybe Baker was

onto something and they all borrow from each other when living in such close proximity.

Suddenly the kestrel pair was charging down through the airspace between the stationary male and the sideways-spiralling female, apparently intent on heading off the female's eastward journey, which was now more or less directly over their own nest ledge. My long experience of this hillside concludes that kestrel–buzzard action is much more routine than that of the kestrel–peregrine variety highlighted by Mr Baker, but perhaps his corner of the Essex coast was devoid of buzzards in the 1960s. The male buzzard now tipped forward off his airy perch, half closed his wings, and fell into the fray, and for perhaps half a minute all four birds tore up and across the hillside and in and out of sunlight and shadow; the kestrels chattered and the buzzards mewed, and I was aware of nothing else on the face of the land. No blow was struck, and the whole thing had the air of ritual rather than outright aggression. Then the buzzards eased away round the west edge of the hill, where I have always assumed they nest out of sight from here, and the kestrels perched a few yards apart, one in a fine old ash, the other on a nondescript hillside rock, both perches within yards of their hidden ledge.

The whole encounter had been so blatant, so conspicuous, so demonstrative, that I was surprised that it had not attracted the attention of the peregrines. Or had it? I turned my glasses towards the peregrines' end of the crag, and there was the male on what I think of as his look-out rock, standing erect, and I wondered (a) how long he had been watching, and (b) whether all peregrines have regular look-out perches. There is a corroboration of that idea in James Macdonald Lockhart's book *Raptor* (Fourth Estate, 2016), in the unlikely setting of Coventry Cathedral:

> When I reach the bench I find them as I had left them the week before. Both birds are perched above me, the male on a ledge high on the spire of Holy Trinity, the female on the flèche of the new cathedral, directly opposite her mate. The bench sits in the ruins of Coventry's old cathedral. It is a contained space away from the noise of the city, not unlike the corrie on the side of the mountain

in Sutherland, a place of enclosed stillness, where the ruin's walls hold and amplify the sound of the falcons calling to each other... One June, whenever I had a spare morning, I hurried back to the cathedral ruins, arriving at the bench soon after dawn, the sun turning the cathedral's sandstone a deep chestnut red... The falcons were always there, at home, often perched in the same place where I had left them.

In the glasses he looked tall, taller than you would expect if you are familiar with the bird in every guise other than standing erect on a look-out rock. It is particularly marked with the larger female. They are not large birds, but they strive to create a larger-than-life presence whenever they perch near the eyrie. The notion disintegrated the instant the perched male flew and resumed his compact size and shape. That first handful of wingbeats always looks clumsy to my eyes, even chaotic, but after a few yards it smoothes itself out into supreme fluency. This one proved to be a short flight, a sharp turn back along the face of the crag and an arrow-straight climb into the rock face, disappearing in the instant of landing. That old trick! I knew exactly where he had perched, the rock was well lit; I have good binoculars, but I couldn't see him. The peregrine has that capacity to become rock if it chooses.

For the moment there was no bird in the sky, and I set off for my own favourite perch in all that landscape. An old rowan tree stands quite alone on the hillside, and for the moment at least it is beyond the reach of the whins. On its uphill side is a perfect grassy couch, and with the trunk for a backrest I can sit there in relative comfort for hours, facing uphill, watching the entire length of the crag, the entire height of the gully, the hillside sprawl below the crag (where a fox or a roe deer might materialise at any time) and a huge tract of sky. I settled, drank coffee, tuned in to the penetrating calls of chiffchaffs that filtered up through the wind from below, their sudden confirmation of spring's arrival.

I was thinking about birds of prey and their nests, or lack of them. If kestrels and peregrines can function perfectly well without building a nest (an occasional compromise is made by squatting in an old crow nest), why do buzzards, sparrowhawks, kites and ospreys need them, and why does a golden eagle build so massively on a mountain ledge or transform the size and shape of a Scots pine, always adding to the previous year's structure? Sea eagles also build massively. Golden eagles, in particular, constantly freshen the nest throughout the nesting season, bringing green sprigs of rowan and birch and weaving them into the structure. Why does a peregrine not do that? Why is it willing to settle for a bare crag like this one, a sea cliff, a window ledge on a city tower block? Or, for that matter, a ruined cathedral?

I spent two agreeable enough hours sitting by the tree, making notes, scanning the crag, the hillside, the sky, but it was as if a kind of torpor had taken possession of the landscape. I had seen no peregrine in all that time, and of all the conspicuous residents of the crag only the ravens had showed themselves. By late afternoon I was back at the foot of the hill, walking slowly by the edge of the wood, reluctant to take my leave of the place. That old familiar sense of unfinished business.

The buzzard pair from the east, beyond the peregrines' ledge, came spiralling across the hill, that other familiar sense of recognition that belongs uniquely (in my experience, at least) to this hillside, and by which they travel across the front of the hill while executing flat spirals, each circuit concluding a little further to the west. So I began exploring in my mind the extent to which any one set of landscape circumstances infiltrates and makes demands on the characteristic behaviour of individual species. These buzzards could traverse the hillside in straight lines and at different levels, and they do, but just as often they choose the flat spiral technique, and by constantly circling they can effectively see what's going on behind them as well as what lies ahead, and as the land falls away beneath them then rises again they scan the uphill and downhill of the view with the minimum of fuss. And if they too have a problem with peregrines, theirs is a technique of travelling that watches all the compass points all the time. It's clever. Is it rationalised, or is it instinct?

I have no way of knowing. No job requires a more open mind than mine.

The buzzards stopped abruptly. One flew into the big trees and perched high up. The other flew down to no more than a yard above the whins, picked up speed, drew in its wings very much in the style of a golden eagle. Over a hundred yards of hillside, it flew in and out of the whins, then suddenly rose at a shallow angle towards a big ash tree less than fifty yards directly uphill from where I stood. At once, a peregrine flew out of the tree with that ungainly shimmy while the wings co-ordinate, then a superbly sleek and low-slung burst of exquisite speed beneath the buzzard and away across the hill. The buzzard perched in the tree the peregrine had just vacated. What it looked like was an eviction, an assertion of a pecking order, of hierarchy. That's what it looked like. I have no idea if that's what it was. I know of peregrine enthusiasts whose observations include buzzards suffering under a peregrine regime. In *Raptor*, James Macdonald Lockhart writes:

Almost all birds are at risk from peregrines. There are records of geese, black-backed gulls, even buzzards being struck down.

Yes, there are. But are those anomalies that have been folded into the peregrine lexicon by those who have a vested interest in assembling a peregrine mythology? Again, I don't know, but I think there is a good chance that, as with Mr Baker's *The Peregrine*, the bird's role as a kind of superhero of nature is overstated. I had just seen a buzzard respond to the sight of a peregrine perched in a tree (a position from which it could just as easily have launched an attack on the buzzard if it had been in the mood) by taking a singularly aggressive initiative. Seconds later, the buzzard's mate arrived and perched in the ash, and after a few more seconds, they mated there. Thinking about it all now, I wonder if the outcome had been determined by a simple calculation that was self-evident to all parties: it was two against one.

I found the peregrine in my glasses again when it broke the skyline and dropped to a high, wide-open, level, grassy terrace, the grass still bleached to that fag-end-of-winter shade of no recognisable colour at all. It perched there, and as it did so, another bird I had simply not seen broke cover, flew the length of the terrace at almost ground level, and pointed straight at the perched falcon, which once again took flight. This new bird flashed an emblematic tribal badge no less conspicuous than the sea eagle's tail, a white blaze at the base of a long-straight tail. It was a female hen harrier. This just wasn't the peregrine's day, but it made mine.

But that day was not quite done with me yet. The peregrine vanished behind me but the harrier wheeled and retraced its journey along the terrace, then alighted on the ground. There, after fussing with something in the grass, she rose a yard above the ground, wheeled once more, and traversed the ledge for the third time, but this time her attitude was quite different. She travelled at the speed of a weary cart-horse after a long day between the shafts, and her sleek profile was troubled by a hefty morsel of prey bunched up, dark and bloodied, and stashed in her talons beneath her. I don't know what it was. I guessed that – wittingly or otherwise – the peregrine had disturbed the harrier feeding in the grass, and that the harrier had retreated rather than defend her prey, possibly as a matter of tactics rather than fear. But the peregrine did not attempt to steal the unguarded prey, so once again I was questioning Mr Baker's book. Ah, but just at that moment, as the harrier inched low and slow along the terrace, the peregrine returned, not to attack the harrier but to mimic its flight from about fifty yards behind it, keeping a distance, showing no aggression, but perhaps – just perhaps – escorting her off the premises.

So I am no closer to drawing reliable conclusions about Mr Baker's book, and as he died in 1986, it's too late to ask him about it now. I came to it very late. I came to all English nature writing late, for I was raised on the voices of my own land – Burns, of course, and perhaps he was the first nature writer of all of us, Seton Gordon, David Stephen, Tom Weir, Don and Bridget MacCaskill, Adam Watson, Nan Shepherd, Gavin Maxwell, Mike Tomkies, and a clutch of poets that included Norman MacCaig. With so many voices steeped in the landscapes in which I labour myself, what need did I have of England's scribes? Ah, but then, of course, I found the writing of Margiad Evans, whose soft-voiced and close-focused nature writing took my breath away, and I went from there, and it was on the journey of discovery which followed that I met J.A. Baker's radically different book about peregrine falcons.

The falcons of the yellow hill had to endure – like so much else in the spring of 2018 – some very untypical conditions, not least of which was that the yellow hill never did turn that brilliant top-to-toe yellow that is how I had come to think of it. A lot of things changed that spring, and one of the consequences of writing it down will be to remind myself to re-read and re-appraise *The Peregrine* by J.A. Baker.

Twenty-four

The Backward Spring

A BACKWARD SPRING

The trees are afraid to put forth buds,
And there is timidity in the grass;
The plots lie gray where gouged by spuds,
And whether next week will pass
Free of sly sour winds is the fret of each bush
Of barberry waiting to bloom.

Yet the snowdrop's face betrays no gloom,
And the primrose pants in its heedless push,
Though the myrtle asks if it's worth the fight
This year with frost and rime
To venture one more time
On delicate leaves and buttons of white
From the selfsame bough as at last year's prime,
And never to ruminate on or remember
What happened to it in mid-December.

Thomas Hardy, April 1917

ONE HUNDRED AND ONE YEARS after Thomas Hardy's pen shivered its way through those lines, having fun with rhyme schemes even while he was making a serious point about the jeopardies of facing nature when spring sleeps in, the spring of 2018 was posted missing. On the very day that the Met Office announced: "Tomorrow is the first day of meteorological spring," what would turn out to be a foot and a half of snow began to accumulate in the garden, changing its shape, obliterating its short flight of stone steps, blurring the distinctions between lawn and rockery and shrubbery, and cloaking everything in bloated silence.

Two things happened that gave me pause for thought. The first was that my one dependable symbol of the end of winter (an early-flowering dwarf rhododendron whose native airt is Himalayan) gave up the ghost. Every year for forty years, its flowers have preceded its new leaves, and it has illuminated February-into-March days with a low-lying cloud of pale pink flowers as cheerful as it is incongruous. Even after what had already been a cold winter, it began to bud in the accustomed manner in February of 2018, then the snow arrived on Siberian easterlies, and once the snow melted again after about five days, what was left was shrivelled brown. It took until mid-May for its new leaves to recover, but there were no flowers.

The second symbol was at the end of the street where an open area of grass and trees is bordered by a burn, an innocuous-looking thing that spends much of its life underground, but it played a decisive role in the Battle of Bannockburn (it is a tributary of the Bannock Burn and apparently helped to screw up any meaningful progress by the English cavalry, back in 1314; there are long memories hereabouts). A few years ago, on the 700th anniversary (a good excuse for a party, given those long memories), someone planted early-flowering daffodils along the top of the bank. But in the February of 2018, they abandoned their early-flowering tendency and gave up on the idea of being daffodils for a full month. I should explain, perhaps, that cultivated flowers are not my thing; I like wild orchids on Lismore, starry saxifrages on Highland mountains, twinflowers in pinewoods. Gardening and I hold each other at mutually agreed distance and regard each other with mutually agreed distrust. But those daffodils and that rhododendron – these two standard-bearers on the frontier between winter and spring – are exceptions to the rule for which I graciously concede my gratitude to horticulture.

Springlessness, then, was suddenly rife across the length and breadth of the land and making news and causing more or less wholly unnecessary chaos to society as we know it. Climate change deniers stirred themselves in their dinosaur lairs, dipped their pens in bile and gloated in the letters pages of complicit newspapers, braying variations on a theme of "whatever happened to global warming?" But, predictably, they resumed their stupors and their slumbers when the whole thing was over in five days, and within a couple of weeks London and the south-east recorded temperatures in the twenties, then within another couple of weeks, in single figures. Climate chaos is what we have, what we are responsible for and what we suffer from. And as the backward spring cowered in its chrysalis long past the moment when we might reasonably have expected the butterfly to flex its peacock wings, and even as Siberian winds whipped fallen powder snow into drifts the depth of breakers in a surfer's paradise, spring in the real Arctic was arriving two weeks early. Polar ecologists at the University of California, Davis, introduced newly published research in terms that gave me a third pause for thought:

Spring is arriving earlier, and the Arctic is experiencing greater advances of spring than lower latitudes. Over the past ten years, spring has come a day earlier, but two weeks earlier in the Arctic, where temperatures are rising twice as fast as the global average and ice fields are rapidly shrinking.

The report added that in April 2018 temperatures in the High Arctic (where there had been no sunlight since the previous October) had been above freezing level for a total of sixty-one hours. Then, as May dawned in Scotland with raw winds, and a dearth of both migrant birds and insect life for them to feed on, a team of British and American scientists drew the world's attention to the changing condition of the Thwaites Glacier in Antarctica, "a structure that drains an area the size of Britain". The change suggested potential for rapid melting or even complete collapse. So far, changes to the glacier have only been detected by satellites. The scientists were announcing the beginning of a five-year project to examine the glacier at close quarters, to find out exactly what is happening. If their worst fears are realised, the potential for global disaster is more or less limitless. The scientists encapsulated the difficulties ahead thus:

We do not know how quickly the glacier will contribute to sea level rises, and whether we have decades or centuries to prepare for it.

Not "to prevent it", please note, but "to prepare for it". One risk is global inundation of coasts – and therefore coastal cities, towns and villages – because if things are going horribly wrong with the Thwaites Glacier, one consequence could be a rise in sea levels of 1.5 metres. To put that into context, the Intergovernmental Panel on Climate Change (established in 1988 by the United Nations Environmental Programme and the World Meteorological Organisation, and with a membership of 195 countries) believes that if humankind embarked on radical and sustained action on greenhouse gases, we *could* limit sea level rises to something between twenty-five and forty centimetres, but that does not allow for an event like the collapse of the Thwaites Glacier. The bill for the Anglo-American Thwaites project is £20million. If it averts or even moderates global consequences, it will be cheap at twenty times the price. But meanwhile, be afraid.

One more symbol of the backwardness of spring 2018 came from the Woodland Trust. The trust runs a project called Nature's Calendar, in which members send in details of the dates when significant events in nature's year actually occur, in this case, the first records of bluebells – or wild hyacinths – in flower. In 2017, the first recorded date was in the south-west of England – February 9th. In 2018, the first recorded date was in the south-east of England – March 20th, or thirty-nine days later.

By April 20th 2017, the trust had received 716 records of flowering bluebells. By the same date in 2018, there were seventy-three.

*

March comes in like a lion and goes out like a lamb. It is one of those clichés with which the folklore of our seasons is carelessly strewn. The missing word is "sometimes". In the backward spring of 2018, March came in like a polar bear and went out like a flu victim, spluttering and out-of-sorts. For more than thirty years, my idea of spring was articulated by the return of sand martins to a certain bay on the north shore of a certain loch, because for more than thirty years I had followed the fortunes and misfortunes of a pair of mute swans that nested in a reed bed that rounded off the north edge of the bay. I would keep tabs on the swans throughout the winter, but once the spring set in, I settled into a more organised routine of watching them prepare for the nesting season, a process which, among many other characteristic events, involved clearing out any unwanted birds and beasts from a large area of the north end of the loch and a lochan beyond it.

And sooner or later, and more or less reliably in the last two weeks of March, I would arrive at the loch to find the first few feet of airspace above the surface aswarm with the dull brown charms of hundreds of sand martins. "More or less" because I was never one to keep records of such things; I own nothing remotely like an archive, and I have always been content with the knowledge that they have returned, and to acknowledge it with welcome and gratitude. Repeatedly, and over those decades, the sand martins slipped unobtrusively and on cue into nature's rolling scheme of things on the loch, the swans' scheme of things too. And always, within days of their arrival, the flock would fragment and a hard core would drift a mile upstream from the loch and settle in where a ten-feet-high bank of bare earth curved round the inside of a long bend in the short life of the River Balvaig.

The Balvaig flows east out of Balquhidder Glen, coils and uncoils lazily across a wide, flat-bottomed floodplain known locally (but not on any maps) as Loch Occasional, beyond which (still coiling and uncoiling) it heads more decisively south to Loch Lubnaig, where its long, tree-girt thrust into the loch creates two bays, one of which is the undisputed realm of the swans. And halfway between the two lochs the river heaves ponderously from east-making to south-making by way of one long bend, and it is there that the bank rises to ten feet above the water, there that the sand martins call home, and there that they begin with formidable industry to excavate old and new burrows in the bank's accommodating soil. The first sites to be claimed are always the highest, the ones sheltered by a grassy overhang, a green cornice. It is there, too, that the greatest concentration of nest burrows lies, for they are also safest from sudden spates and rising river levels, and the Balvaig is particularly accomplished when it comes to dismissing the strictures of its banks.

The backward spring produced headlines all across the country proclaiming that nature's migrating tribes were far behind schedule and, having confirmed notable absentees from within my own work-aday landscapes, it was the second half of April before I contemplated an expedition to check on the martins' progress. The path from road to riverbank runs along the top of a long, narrow strip of woodland that falls steeply to the "shore" of Loch Occasional. The wood is an open one of oak, birch and willow, with a lush, grassy and ferny under-storey. The river itself only comes into view when the path emerges beyond the end of the wood, and from there a short diversion between small fields of rough grazing leads to the bank directly opposite the martins' headquarters.

A morning's anticipation of reunion dissolved in about five seconds. Not only were there no sand martins, there was no river. The vast ton-nage of snow that had assembled on Balquhidder Glen's surrounding mountains and lesser hills was responding to the most grudging of thaws by pouring down mountainsides in avalanches and impromptu waterfalls. Loch Occasional was a square mile of shallow water cov-ering a treachery of grassland and bog, but also including much of the watercourse of the river itself. Its presence was only traceable by curving lines of trees in single file where they still clung tremulously to submerged riverbanks. To hosts of small birds, up to and including waders, and to mammals of any size, shape, or persuasion, up to and including me, the place was simply out of bounds, for nothing about it was reliable. On the other hand, if you were a swan, a goose, or a duck, Loch Occasional was a part-time paradise, for nothing suits the web-footed, long-necked tribes better than being able to feed on grassland through shallow water. A slow sweep of binoculars revealed mute swans and whooper swans, greylag and Canada geese, mallard, goldeneye, goosander, wigeon, teal, tufted ducks and little grebes. And alone among that host, a widely scattered presence of solitary herons tried to make sense of their temporarily redefined world.

The following day, I tried a little nearer home, where a much smaller but no less reliable sand martin colony on the Sheriffmuir edge of the western Ochil Hills was equally bereft. But an area of grassy mounds and grass-and-heather moorland nearby revealed prolific burrowing, not by martins but by short-tailed field voles, and there were thou-sands of new holes. Such profusion lures predators, and the droppings of fox and pine marten were equally profuse. Likewise, a flat-topped rock that I know to be a regular short-eared owl perch had pellets around its base like pebbles on a beach. And that day I heard the year's first skylarks and, laving their columns of song with jazzy woodwind licks, three curlew voices confirmed that nature had not completely forgotten its repertoire of spring anthems. A red kite inched uphill into the narrowing confines of a handsome little glen, the bird's rich colours deepened by the dourness of the day, the poor light, the imminence of rain, and it too was vole-hunting.

Then I turned away west to face where the mountains of the first of the Highlands were lost behind an advancing frontier of new rains. There was an extraordinary beauty in that sky that fell unbroken to the nearest edge of the moor, for it was horizontally bisected high up, and while all was dark and glowering beneath that line, above it was a much paler shade, just as uniform as the other, but somehow refreshing, even invigorating. I could imagine Mark Rothko standing where I stood, contemplating that sky and its possibilities. For in my mind was a painting from 1963 where two almost monochrome bands of such shades were kept apart only by the slimmest dead-straight horizontal line of white paint. It's in a copy of the catalogue for a memorial exhibition in Venice following his death in 1970, and which was given to me by my great friend George Garson. He had gone to Venice to see the exhibition. Just inside the front cover of the catalogue, on a page by itself, is the following:

Telegram received by one of the Executors of the Estate of Mark Rothko, deceased February 25th, 1970:

> "*Profoundly moved by Mark Rothko's tragic death. Remember in deep sorrow his voice, his gestures, his very secret and enlightening radiance.*
> *His painting is one of the most magnificent in this century and leads to a new wholeness of thought and vision.*
> *Franz Meyer, director, Kunstmuseum, Basel.*"

"A new wholeness of thought and vision"…now there's an epitaph worthy of the occasion. And a catalogue representation about four inches wide of a canvas that was ninety inches wide and painted fifty-five years before I stood that day on that moorland edge in the backward spring of 2018 looking for sand martins, had just stopped me in my tracks and made me appraise a grey sky in terms of great art, a sky that many standing in my shoes would have described as "dreich".

I shook my head in barely comprehending wonder and thanked the man silently for his art, for his new wholeness of thought and vision, and I thanked (for perhaps the thousandth time) my dear-departed friend for handing me the catalogue one day in 1991 and saying something like: "You're ready for this now." I'm not sure. Even now.

Then the moment transformed. The three curlews lifted unhurriedly from the moor and cruised into Rothko's sky, drenching it in guilt-edged threnody, then descended in silence and vanished below the skyline. It was just as well, perhaps, that I was on my own right then, for no one would have got a word of sense out of me for the next hour.

★

The martins came eventually, but in half-hearted numbers, and it was difficult to see how they could retrieve much from such a backward spring. Loch Occasional did what it always does and shrank back into the floodplain; the river did what it always does and adapted its girth and depth to fit snugly back within its banks, revealing that the sand martins' bank had survived one more inundation. I kept a discreet distance from the bank, watched just long enough from the cover of trees to confirm that those martins that had bothered to complete the journey were doing what they should be doing, then I turned back. Whatever the prospects for them now, my presence would not help. Instead, I lingered the morning away at the edge of the wood, where the high-water mark of Loch Occasional would have been less than a fortnight before.

There were two swans far out on the floodplain, feeding among its myriad pools. I thought at first they might have been the mute swan pair up from Loch Lubnaig, taking advantage of easy feeding. But once I settled binoculars on them I realised they were whooper swans, and in a more forward spring than this one, whooper swans would have been back in Iceland by now. I was attracted to the idea that they might stay, of course, and try and nest on one of the glen's two lochs or by the river. Such things do happen every now and again, the swans finding enough of an Icelandic atmosphere to persuade them to stay. It happens especially in the far north of the Scottish mainland and in both the Western Isles and the Northern Isles. But there are relatively recent precedents, too, in places like Loch Lomond, and in Highland Perthshire where a pair nested for three years but had their eggs stolen each time, and they finally departed, suitably discouraged, as well they might.

Ornithologist Mark Brazil's monograph, *The Whooper Swan* (Poyser, 2003), notes that "whoopers have a long and traceable history in the British Isles", that as glaciation ended and ice sheets shrank northwards, the tundra-like aftermath would have been perfect for them, and there is evidence to suggest they bred regularly during the Little Ice Age between the 15th and 19th centuries. Then, after a long absence in the 20th century, whoopers have been breeding again since 1970. In 2003, the bird was considered to be "a rare and erratic breeder". That still sounds about right, but if the climate continues to warm, and our winters grow generally milder, the birds may vanish from our shores once more, taking other Arctic migrants back with them.

Meanwhile, by early May, there were still those two birds scaring the resident Canada geese witless and adding their bright white grace to the landscape, and consoling this nature writer and unashamed fan of whooper swans on one more troubled morning of the backward spring. Occasionally a muted-brass syllable of their conversation drifted across to me and mingled agreeably with the year's first snipe voices. And on the hillside across Balquhidder Glen, I could see a handful of red deer out on the open hill feeding in pale sunlight. What began to unfold was one of those situations in which I delight: very slowly, my absorption in my surroundings and the small movements of nature across the low ground became a moment, a blink of time in the testimony of the mass of mountains beyond. I was of no more account than that snipe calling metronomically on a tussock, arguably of less account than that pair of Icelandic itinerants or the incomer Canada geese, or the ancient, seen-it-all-before heron up to its shins in tepid bog water. And for the purposes of all these creatures, I had become landscape. For a nature writer, it is in circumstances like these that anything can happen.

How long I sat on a moss-draped rock with my back to an alder trunk before I realised it was already happening above and behind and over my right shoulder, I have no idea. But I became aware, as if from a great distance, that a new sound was abroad on the land, not out on Loch Occasional, not on the hills or the river, but in the wood that surrounded me to north and south and east. I believe I had registered the sound and that it was getting closer before it began to make enough of an impact on my mind, my awareness, for me to respond to it. Such moments exist in a different kind of time to the one I use to measure my days and nights, and it passes more slowly and more meticulously, and more preciously, too, for it permits me to respond to nature's presence both as a whole and in its component parts. The eternal problem is that my response is never capable of holding on to it all, far less write it down, for I am constrained by the writer's limitations and my subject is limitlessness.

Finally, the sound came clearly into focus. I have been through situations like this many times now, and I have taught myself that if movement is necessary, then it should be very, very slow. I am, after all, trying to be a bit of the landscape. This much I decided at once: something was moving through the wood across its slope from my right to my left so that soon it would pass behind my back. It was moving slowly and stopping often, and when it stopped there was a strange rasping sound, with the rhythm of a handsaw being deployed in short bursts. It was that sound I had been hearing at the edge of my consciousness while my mind was elsewhere.

The mossy stone where I sat was only about a foot high. The tree trunk at my back would screen most of me. I slid forward off the rock as slowly as I could, lowered my upper body and rolled over in the same moment so that I was prone on the bottom of the slope and facing uphill. I had done it as gently and quietly and fluently as I knew how, but when I raised my eyes, it was to meet head-on the full-bore, double-barrelled stare of a roebuck at ten yards. He was thickly cloaked in his grey winter coat. He had wintered well, he looked solid and muscled and well-fed. His six-point antlers were newly cleaned of velvet and smeared in blood by the process. He lowered his head even as I watched and slashed them several times left and right among the grass, ferns and brambles, a gesture that merged elements of brute strength, bad temper and natural grace. Whether it eased the irritation in the new antlers or provided an outlet for pent-up breeding season energies, I could not say, but when he raised his head again and stared hard at me, it was hard to resist the notion that hostility lay behind the eyes. It could not have been helped by a broken length of bramble bush that had become snared in the tines and hung down in front of his eyes. He lowered his head again, raised a front foot to pin the bramble to the ground and jerked his head upwards to free the obstacle. It was so deftly done that it was surely a well-practised routine.

He turned his head sideways and barked twice, and I saw his breath hang in a cloud in the morning's cold air. An answering bark came from the trees not twenty yards away, and at once the buck and his unseen doe were running through the trees, their rhythmic barking underscored by the sound of their feet. The next time I saw them they were far out on the floodplain heading towards the river, and they took with them the shreds of the frail binding that had held together those moments of enchantment in which I had briefly lingered.

*

The careless volume at which everyday human life is pitched has become troublesome to me. Never has quietude seemed so elusive. If it were a species, it would be on the verge of extinction. And you cannot launch captive breeding programmes for quietude.

An estate agent's for sale ad described a neighbouring house as being in "a pleasurably peaceful edge-of-town cul-de-sac". Whoever wrote it, they were not here when the gas pipes were being renewed just after the tarmac had been re-laid, when the extensions were being built, and sundry domestic and local authority and builders' leaf blowers and power saws were singing along to the strains of two different radios tuned to two different stations. Every vehicle attending to such enterprises had to reverse the length of the street because the enterprises rendered the turning area not negotiable, and as they reversed they engaged the "I am reversing" bleeper, a species of noise pollution designed to communicate the bleeding obvious. "Scottish Gas – looking after your world" was emblazoned on several vans. Not my world, it isn't.

After one particularly worse-than-fruitless morning, I took evasive action, packed a water bottle, a couple of bananas and a notebook and pen into a small backpack that already had two cameras, a mat and a folded bivvy bag to sit on, as well as a compass and some chocolate as permanent fixtures. Forty minutes later I had parked my car in some trees, and fifteen minutes after that I stepped downhill from a well-walked path into the complicit depths of an oakwood. I squelched around the rim of a small bog, taking advantage of some rotting broken branches that reduced the impact of the glaur, emerged onto a sunlit rocky corner of riverbank, and there the healing balm of riversong was a mercy to my every sensibility. I sat. I breathed deeply. I looked round. This is my idea of home, not that otherness I had just walked out on. This is where my sense of belonging lives; not necessarily this particular river, but the embrace of nature symphonic in my ears and my heart and mind. I took out the notebook and pen and began my working day again in the middle of the afternoon.

If you travelled towards the first of the Highland mountains heading north-west from Edinburgh or Stirling, the first sight and sound and music of a proper Highland river would be right here. I perched on the rocks six feet above the river and the same distance from the edge. The river was deep and tranquil immediately below me, shallower at the far side. There were rocks enough to produce white water and gentle waterfalls fifty yards upstream and thirty yards downstream. The upstream white water glittered silver in full sunlight. It emerged from beyond a bend in the river and it was a band of fractured white from bank to bank. But the river grew calm almost at once, and by the time it had reached my rock it was all but silent, except that a tiny riffle half an inch high and a foot long bubbled a short thread of magic, a song pitched right on the very edge of my hearing. If I looked at it directly, though, that helped, and the tiny dancing of the thing laid a detectable vibrato on its essentially contralto whisper; sight exquisitely and minutely enhanced the sound.

Of the two waterfall voices, the upstream one was both louder and higher-pitched, and its rockier course was more percussive. The inside of the bend produced the throaty notes; an elegant little fall hard by the outside had a musically metallic, xylophonic edge; and the widest stretch of white water between these two had ordered its twenty-or-so mini-falls into a fluent blend from which the whole fashioned its essential, recognisable sound. The whole time I sat there – about three hours, at a guess – there were birds singing from the nearest trees (some overhanging, some whose roots waded into the river margins). At different times, these included wood warbler, willow warbler, chaffinch, dipper, blackbird, song thrush, goldfinch and one-wood-wind-note bullfinch, and I wondered after a while whether there was anything in the idea that riversong stimulated birdsong.

Mostly, I sat facing upstream, partly to have the sun on my face, partly because upstream was the more notable fall (yes, the prettier one), partly because the rock where I sat was more accommodating of an upstream-facing sitter, and partly for the view. That band of sun-silvered white water was backed by a row of ten tall conifer trees – Scots pines and Douglas firs – and a mass of birch and oak in vibrant spring greens, and beyond and above all that, the handsome blue-green bulk of the summit and north shoulder of Ben Ledi was draped across an all-but-cloudless sky. No mountain in this part of the world dignifies its landscape setting with more natural grace than that one. My eyes and my heart and everything within me that contributes to my nature writing instincts are gladdened by its presence more days of any one year than not; I celebrate it, I am gratified by it, and I greet and leave its presence with a glad hand, and my mind mutters to itself: "here's a hand my trusty fiere…" for you can sing that immortal slice of the genius of Robert Burns to greet an old landscape as well as a new year.

The downstream fall had no such backdrop and no singing birds. But from where I sat, it provided an agreeable termination of the downstream view of the river just before it rounded one more bend and vanished. And crucially for my state of well-being, for my immersion in that symphony of nature, that lesser fall contributed the perfect acoustic counterpoint to the song of its upstream kindred spirit.

All afternoon, a non-stop procession of mayflies flew by, sometimes in dense clusters thousands strong, sometimes strung out in mere hundreds. Fly-fishermen the world over emulate them with flies of their own devising, but then I never did understand fly-fishing. The flies themselves caught fire as they passed me and I turned my head to follow them into the sunlight, and they were yellow and gold sparks and they thronged the first dozen feet of airspace above the surface of the water. From time to time one would land on the bright rectangle of my open notebook and bask there for several seconds, only moving on when the nib of my pen approached too close, and it transformed again from something grey and black into one more gold and yellow spark. If you have never thought there could be beauty in a fly, you need only watch a newly hatched horde of mayflies trekking upstream into the afternoon sunlight above the course of a Highland river with a song in its step. Only once in the whole afternoon was there the hard slap of a splash, but my eyes were on my pen and the notebook page at that moment, and when I looked up there were only widening ripples, so I never saw the rise, the bite, the fish-glitter, the supple twist in the air and the splashdown.

I left the river when the wind strengthened and cooled and I began to hunger and thirst, and I was healed again until the next time. But no wild Highland river has ever failed me yet.

Twenty-five

The Mountaineering Badger

IF I WERE TO FOLLOW the river for a few upstream miles, as I have done by car, bike and on foot surely a thousand times by now, I would come to the base of a mountainside that clasps a secret world to its mutilated body, nothing less than a new wilderness. I have lost count of how many times I have threaded its chaotic slopes, almost always in April or May, how many times I have celebrated the eccentric beauties of a Highland mountain spring that hardly anyone sees. For although this mountainside is the same age as all the others in the glen, sculpted and steepened by the same glacial hand, in an extraordinary way it has been born again. And there, 2,000 feet up the mountain, shining in the sun like a ragged mainsail, is its birthmark – its re-birthmark.

What happened was that about thirty years ago, and for no known reason, the mountain burst apart. From the transient perspective of a single human life, we tend to think of mountains as symbols of permanence, of immovable stillness, all the more so in a country like mine whose geological history of the last 10,000 years since the great ice relented is devoid of volcanic twitches, added to which is the comparatively new knowledge that the mountains of Scotland are hewn out of the very oldest rocks in Europe. The cliché we reach for to represent great age is "as old as the hills". Yet mountains move. They shift, they shrink, they rise, they respond in innumerable ways to nature's irresistible, invisible forces.

The buttress had been triangular-shaped and dull grey and from far below it looked...as old as the hills. I knew there were cracks in it, some of them wide enough for my hand, one or two where I could get an arm and a shoulder inside. I knew, too, that just below the buttress, on a wide and level shelf, was a boulderfield that was a consequence of some old upheaval in the mountain's story. But when I heard that something of the mountain had burst apart, I climbed it again to see what had happened, and what I saw first was that something shone in the sunlight like a sheet of tinfoil. It was a wound. A huge wedge had fallen from the buttress, and the boulderfield on the level shelf began to move. A new rockfall began. But lying in its path was the one thing that prevented a much more epic landslide – a mountain oakwood, an oakwood that had already adjusted to at least one landslide, thwarted its descent at the cost of many broken trees, but which, in the manner of woods left to their own devices the world over, simply settled again to the new circumstances and grew more oaks, and these hemmed the boulders in.

So now there is a steep mountainside, an oakwood that climbs from the floor of the glen to somewhere around 1,500 feet and in which there is barely a square yard of level ground. The underfoot conditions are so treacherous, so fankled by rocks and boulders and great slabs of mountain rock, that very few grazing animals, specifically deer and sheep, care to venture within, and so the wood and its rich and varied understorey thrive unmolested. Yet there are paths. They are narrow and steep and they curve crazily, and some disappear under fallen tree trunks, others where two rocks have come to rest against each other. Following any of them for any distance is one of the chanciest pursuits in the length and breadth of what I think of as my nature writer's home territory. For although the paths climb the mountain, they were not made by people.

Somehow or other, sometime or other (the pursuit of biological truth on this of all mountainsides is an imperfect and inexact science), badgers established a sett here, and as you might imagine, the inhabitants don't always do things the way field guides say that badgers do things. Here, for example, is where I have seen a badger front-pointing up a rock face as near to vertical as would make very little difference to you or me, but fissured and splintered just enough for a badger with built-in crampons. The confidence of the climbing suggested two things to me: one, that this was an activity with which that particular badger was intimately familiar; the other, that she understood perfectly the wisdom of the first principle of rock climbing for humans – at least three points of contact at all times.

I was amazed because I had never seen it done before. I knew there were preposterous claims out there in some of the murkier depths of badger folklore and I have read a few that would make a saint curse in exasperation. But I had never heard of rock-climbing badgers, so the first time I saw it was through a vague haze of ever-so-slightly surreal disbelief in what my eyes were telling me. I was further amazed by the ease with which the feat was accomplished. Three times in my life I have been on good rock in the company of good rock climbers (I was never one of those and never aspired to be one) and what impressed me most each time was an apparently instinctive sense of perfect balance. I know it was not taught because I asked all three and none of them could account for it; when they started rock climbing, it was there already. If I could interview the badger, I imagine the answer would be the same.

There is also this: she didn't have to climb the rock face, she chose to. There was an easy alternative, a natural ramp that cut away at a gentle uphill angle from the ledge where she began to climb, and at the end of the ramp a clear narrow track angled back and up to the top of the rock face. I established over time that both the ramp and the track were worn smooth and devoid of vegetation by nothing more than the regular passage of badgers and the occasional fox, and I could walk effortlessly up the ramp and the track.

Spring was always my preferred badger-watching season, not least because of the arrival above ground of new cubs, mysterious little laugh-out-loud hovercraft-like creatures, with a miniature badger face at one end, that traverse their nursery terrain as if they are never quite in contact with the ground. And not least because of the badger's apparent love of bluebell woods. And not least because in my particular neck of the woods, badger-sett evenings and late nights were invariably sound-tracked by the roding riffs of woodcock flight as they patrolled their territories.

But the badgers of the broken mountain seemed to move to the beat of a different drum altogether, a lifestyle dictated by the landscape surroundings of the sett. Why they chose it at all used to baffle me, until one night it occurred to me that every time I went there – every time I still go there, for that matter – there was no human presence other than my own, and no sign of anyone having been near the place in my absence. Besides, my own presence is a thing of utmost discretion, silence and stillness (that and that alone explains why I have had a badger pee on my wellies while I was wearing them).

It was the third or fourth time I had watched this singular badger climb the rock face that I was struck by a peculiarity of her climbing technique. If you or I climb a rock face, we reach up for hand holds above our hands, sometimes to the very limits of our reach. A badger can't do that, can't reach far above its head, and this particular badger didn't even try. (It was always the same badger I saw rock climbing, easily recognisable by an irregularity in her left hind leg, perhaps an old wound.) With head close to the rock found holds with front feet right in front of her face – holds I could not see, incidentally. I never once saw her try to raise a foot above eye level. So instead of pulling with hands and arms and pushing with feet and legs as you and I would do, she was effectively pushing with all four limbs, always small movements but always quick and utterly flawless, so that the effect was of a seamless ascent that reminded me effortlessly of the way a cub crosses level ground. She climbed without a pause, and while she seemed to place her front feet with great care, the hind feet found grip and thrust instinctively – the balance thing again.

I came across the phenomenon for the first time one warm May evening when I had climbed up beyond the wood, almost to the source of the landslide, and borne on a warm wind from below, the delicious hyacinth scent of the bluebell wood in full bloom painted the air with every shade of perfect spring that I can ever imagine. I sat longer than I intended and the woodcock had already done a few laps of his idea of his own portion of airspace, and each time he passed, his croaky, squeaky voice sounded like the first few notes of Ellington's *C Jam Blues* so that I got the piano riff stuck in my head.

When I finally decided to descend, I picked a bouldery way down through the wood, for I knew by now there were badgers on the mountainside but I was short on details, like where. I had begun to suspect that the rock face with the ramp might have something to do with it, and headed for a distinctive larch that marked the point where a badger path crossed open ground between the rock-fall wood and the larch plantation (badgers in there too!). At the last moment, I decided to see if I could descend onto the top of the rock face and watch the ground in front of it from up there. I was within a few yards of the top edge when I heard unmistakable badger voices from below. I listened hard. Two badgers, and it sounded as if they were on the ramp, which could mean that any moment one of them, or both, might appear on the track up to the top of the rock face from the end of the ramp. I crawled the last yard and was about to peer over the edge when there was a yelp from below and the sound of badger feet scrabbling on the rock below. I was still pondering how that could possibly be when a badger face appeared from below the edge and stared at me from eight feet away. The animal dived downwards and sideways and disappeared into what I thought was unyielding rock, which gave me something else to ponder. I looked over, saw nothing, except that there was a second badger on the ramp, looking up. In an instant I saw its scut disappear, again apparently into unyielding rock.

I had caused enough mayhem. I left making it clear that I was going, but the next day I was back, and with the wind blowing my scent away from the rock face, I took a long hard look at it in good light from a flattish rock with a helpful screen of birch and hazel. Because in a badger haunt as untypical as this one, you just never know. There was a hole at the bottom of the rock face, and I now realised that the rock face was actually just one side of a house-sized boulder. Instead of excavating a tunnel and a series of chambers and with a huge spoil heap for a doormat, the badgers had simply dug into the space beneath the boulder; there was no spoil to speak of, and the hole they had dug was narrow from top to bottom and wide from side to side. Nothing about it looked like a badger sett. But it was in there that the second badger of the night before had disappeared. And I now saw how the first badger had disappeared, although I still had trouble believing that it could have climbed the entire rock face from the sett entrance to the top edge. There was an angle in the face, to the right of which there was a long crack several inches high, and the badger had made a scrambling descent into the crack. Later I would discover that it offered a kind of hidden fire escape onto the open hillside and the path to the larches.

The Mountaineering Badger

From then on, I simply watched from the birch and hazel screen, and from there I saw badgers emerge from the solitary entrance (at least it was the only one I ever found), and almost invariably turn right onto the ramp; *almost* invariably because every now and then the slender sow with the damaged left leg turned left and into the wall, and began to climb straight up. And it was then I saw how she climbed. I realised then that when it comes to the inner workings of life in a Highland badger sett, I didn't know the half of it.

Twenty-six

An Island Pilgrimage (1) – Mull and Iona

Almost at once we were in a heavy sea, and the wind blew with such force that all idea of crossing to Fionnphort was quickly abandoned, and, sailing before the gale, the course was set for the sheltered creek near the little fishing village of Kentra. Things looked serious...each person had perforce to lie at the bottom of the boat so that the ferryman might see the more easily to avoid the overfalls of the heaviest waves...But with April better weather would come to Iona and to its sound, and there would come an end to the gales from the west and the south-west - gales which on one occasion prevented the ferry-boat from crossing for a week or more, so that no intercommunication was possible between the island and the far side of the sound, though it is scarce a mile in width.

Seton Gordon,

The Land of the Hills and the Glens

(Cassell, 1920)

"A CUP OF TEA, please."

"Are you staying, or are you going on the ferry?"

"I'm going on the ferry."

She looked out to where the boat had just begun to nose into the pier from its offshore mooring, rocking slightly as it advanced. Her brow furrowed (despite herself, it seemed, for she had one of those clear and unlined Hebridean faces with a brow that looked as if it was not given to furrowing) and after a little consideration she said:

"I'll better give it to you in a paper cup."

I wrapped my hands around the cup and was briefly startled by the heat. It really was a paper cup. But what the Met Office like to call "the wind chill factor" (a pompous-sounding cliché instead of saying "it's going to be a damned sight colder than it looks") reduced the tea to tepid over a hundred yards, by which time it had stopped warming me, inside or out. I sipped as I walked, tea-drinking pilgrim. Standing at the rail of the upper deck, I sipped the cool dregs and remembered. It had been ten years.

I was staying up in the north of Mull for a few days. Ben More the day before had been in truculent mood. Gales and stinging, sleety snow had forced a retreat from near the summit. There was no view, and the view is the whole point of that particular mountain, and don't let any Munro-bagging fetishist tell you otherwise. There is nothing in all Scotland, all Britain, to compare with the view from Mull's Ben More. And it was May. I was alone, I decided to regroup the forces of endeavour behind a rock. Coffee. A dram (a small one, a taste, purely psychological), distilled just up the road. It is one of the miraculous properties of single malt whisky that it ensnares the essence of the landscape that gave it birth, and right then, right there, that whisky tasted like stinging, sleety snow had been distilled and bottled.

A window in the storm, a seductive blink of sun, I hung in there for a little longer. The window slammed shut. The sleety snow thickened and stung. Down then, cold and defeated. But in the evening, May in the woods at Salen was blissful, warm, saturated in birdsong. I decided Iona next day would be my respite. Go as a pilgrim, supplicating my God whose name I spell Nature. I have written before that I discarded churches years ago, found what I needed in Nature. But Iona Abbey was extraordinary, and if the appropriate word for the defining characteristic of the place is not "spirituality", then I don't know what else it could be.

Columba? Hardly. He had been dead six or seven hundred years when this abbey was built, and it has grown derelict and been restored since then. His had been a timber thing, modest as the coracle that ferried him from Ireland under the horizon. Yet perhaps it is his gift that endures, his granitic faith in peace. Wherever else in the world that most flawed of ideals has faltered, on Iona it never has in a thousand years. It never has because of all who came after. Pilgrims. Sipping sanctity and cooling tea.

From the ferry railing with an empty paper cup in my hand, then, I remembered crossing the waist of the island to white sands, white as the summit snows of yesterday's mountain. And I remembered The Blue. Our planet plays host to innumerable shades of blue, and I consider myself fortunate to have seen my share of them. But when I saw the Iona Blue that first time, I was numbed by colour. It was the particular blue that begins at your feet where the sea lies in a pool as still as ice over white sand. From there it flows seamlessly through deepening shades and deepening layers of ocean. It is blue beyond colour, blue as spiritual experience.

Now, ten years later, standing at the rail of the ferry, going back to Iona on a day somewhere between the last of winter and the first of one more spring, and with a now crumpled paper cup in my hand, it was the blue I remembered; and there was Rum, far past Mull and far past Coll, Rum off the starboard bow. I had forgotten about Rum. And how small Staffa is.

This time I walked past the abbey. I thought I might save it for last. I wanted to climb Dun I, the lowly summit of the lowly island whose old Gaelic name is just that single letter, I. It means island. I wanted to see white sands and to drink my fill of Iona Blue. And suddenly I realised that it was one year since my mother had died. She was a religious woman, she called her faith her "rock", and at least I could understand that analogy, and there is no worthier place to pay tribute to rock than Iona. It's Scotland's first rock. It is older than most other fragments of the planet that many of us will ever step on. It was nature's foundation stone. Having laid it, she stood on it and began to lay down the rest, and to throw up other volcanoes to play with for another billion years. So my tea-sipping pilgrimage suddenly found an edge of purpose. Mum liked Iona. She came here once on a bus tour. You could not pay me enough money to go on a bus tour, but after Dad died, Mum had eighteen more years and with those she travelled, as far as Florence twice, and sometimes she just took the bus to the Hebrides. Now, for no reason I could name, I associated the occasion and the islandscape with the date. I am no keeper of anniversaries, especially the anniversaries of deaths. I remember lives best, and I need no dates to celebrate and be grateful for the lives of both my parents. Suddenly, however, I thought that perhaps a quiet moment in the abbey at the end of the day might be appropriate. But Columba had something else in mind.

I climbed Dun I, bullied uphill by a westerly that would have shivered Seton Gordon's spine. I crossed the summit and sat in the lee of a west-facing rock. I could see white sand. I could see Iona Blue. I could see down the broad spine of the island. I could see up the island to Rum. And beyond that, identifiable by its ragged glimmer of snow, the Skye Cuillin. I waved, because that is how I greet friends-in-landscape. I descended to the shore where the wind filled my eyes and my hair with white sand and the Iona Blue was a song beyond music. I turned. I climbed back over Dun I. By then the summit was a wall of wind that took my breath away and rammed gallons of its own icy breath down my throat. I sat again. I sat this time because standing was too difficult. And sitting in that rage of winds, sand-smitten and colour-drenched, I found the utter calm which permitted the remembrance. Nature soothes the soul. A friend wrote that to me once.

I walked back to the ferry without entering the abbey. I wondered how many other pilgrims had ever done that. If any. My pilgrimage was honoured without it. Columba, presiding spirit of pilgrims, keeper of souls, or whatever, conjured the most vivid remembrance at Iona's disposal, not within the confines of a building but in the un-confines of nature. The abbey may be the focal point of what Columba's legacy has become. But it is I, the Island, which is the cathedral of this pilgrim.

"*So, did you get to Iona today then?*"

"*Yes.*"

"*What was it like?*"

"*Windy. Freezing.*"

It was too soon after the event to explain, too soon to think. I have since found this, its source quite unknown to me:

Part of the inheritance of the Celt is the sense of longing and striving after the unattainable and incomprehensible on Earth...Forlorn, he has the sense of fighting a losing battle for all his soul holds dear, for the simple life of old, for the beauty of the world threatened with utilitarian desecration, for outlived ideals.

That part of me which is Celt suffers from that part of the inheritance. But perhaps it must also take the credit for the eye that yearns towards the Iona Blue, and for a kinship with summit winds, for an idea that hit me between the eyes on the summit of Dun I, an idea of pilgrimage, an Island pilgrimage for nature and one of which Columba might have approved. And the next stepping stone should be Lismore. But Lismore lies on the far side of Mull, and no crossing of Mull should pass without quiet consideration, for unless you are an embryonic saint with a coracle at your disposal and you have voyaged from Ireland, it was ever a part of the pilgrim's journey to and from Iona. And for me, more often than not, Mull has been the journey's be-all-and-end-all, and among many, many souvenirs to which I fondly cling is this one, which was not without its own savour of pilgrimage.

High above the north shore of Loch na Keal, a six-miles-long gouge the Atlantic has torn from Mull's waist, a small clenched fist of ash trees bows perpetually eastwards, shaped and shaved by salted ocean winds. They are perhaps fifteen feet tall and they will grow no taller, but the wonder is that they survive at all. Nearby is the ghost of a blackhouse, dark-stoned and low to the ground, suffocating in bracken, drowning in its own dereliction, the usual deaths for Hebridean houses of a certain age, the ineradicable spoor of the Clearances. The blunt, low-lying island of Eorsa is moored out in the middle of the loch. Its profile climbs in flat tiers to a flat summit, like so much of Mull's landscape, the incline gentle from the east, abrupt as a staircase in the west, ending in a perfect right-angle and a 100-foot cliff. Its shape and dark mass look so implausible, as if has just been towed there and left for the night, so that every time I pause here after the inevitable absence of years, I half expect to find that Eorsa has been towed away.

I nurture a small ambition as far as Eorsa is concerned. As yet it is unfulfilled, but there's still time. It is to hitch a lift on a small boat some sublime day of late May or early June, or a canoe would be good if the day was sufficiently sublime, the weather forecast sufficiently unimpeachable, and if I ever learn to handle a canoe. The purpose would be to spend a day and a night and a dawn there, watching Ben

More respond to what Yeats called
The blue and the dim and the dark cloths
Of night and light and the half light
and in the manner of the pilgrim. For doesn't the small island's flat summit sit deferentially at the mountain's feet like a supplicant, an island within an island, a stance devised by the parent island for the considered contemplation of its own Everest, its own Chomolungma, its own Mother Goddess of the World?

I recall an old April: new snow enlivened the top 500 feet of Ben More, the water pale off-white at its feet but becoming blue and bluer up the coast so that it was a royal shade out by Treshnish. The wind was a north-westerly and all knife-edges, bombarding the Western Isles with fast squalls. But on the shore of Loch na Keal it was merely persistent. There were only two sounds. There was the twiggy jabber of the passage of the wind through the ash trees (black-budded and utterly bare) and there was the soft, penny-whistle monosyllable of golden plover. There were two of them on a heathery shelf, dark against the sunlit sea, calling to each other. The call of a golden plover holds a quality of threnody that tantalises a human ear. For something so high-pitched and thin, it penetrates inexplicably deep, reaches improbably far back. I know, I know, it does no such thing. It is simply a contact call between two birds, but it is a dull soul who stands on such a shore in the company of golden plovers and hears only a contact call between birds. The Gaels, who by and large are not dull souls, call the bird *feadag*, which is also the word for a flute. *Fead* is "whistle" (or a high-pitched wind noise) and *feadan* is the bagpipe chanter, and whether they named the chanter after the golden plover or the other way round would take the mind of a Gaelic scholar, which I am not. But a chanter in the hands of a great player is an elemental force and just as affecting on a human ear as the spring *piobaireachd* of the golden plover, whether you hear the call-note's enigmatic fade or the slow-winged aerial song (a golden smirr).

The sun was over the mountain's eastern shoulder. West of Eorsa, Loch na Keal crumpled like tinfoil where it dazzled. Then the wind stiffened and chilled. A glance to the north-west showed that Coll had vanished. A driven stormed thrashed down the sea, swallowed

Treshnish and Staffa, then bore down on Ben More itself. The thing sizzled over Ulva, crossed the mouth of Loch na Keal, as if a curtain the height of the mountains had just been closed. But on my side of the loch not a drop of water fell, though the temperature dropped and the rasp of the wind tormenting the ash trees drowned out the *feadagan* (at the last gasp their silhouettes flattened, beaks to the storm).

The mountain blurred.

But the sun still bored into the mass of mountain and storm, and for minutes more, the softened shape of Ben More remained intact.

The storm piled in.

The mountain faded.

The little island vanished, swallowed whole.

But the sun still bored into the mass and the mountain edges faded and brightened in and out of the edges of sight, until eventually it vanished and for ten minutes it stayed vanished.

But the sun still bored into the mass, pale and dim as clouded moonlight, and never did the storm snuff out completely its tinfoil patch on the water.

Then the wind eased. I turned and saw the fish shape of Coll resume its place in the sea.

The curtain peeled back, the mountain stood forward to resume its stance and its familiar shape, but it was brighter than before where the sun lit its topcoat of new snow.

The storm moved away east, less of a force to be reckoned with now that it had taken on the mountain and lost. In its path lay Lismore, but Lismore is moored in more sheltered waters than these.

Twenty-seven

An Island Pilgrimage (2) – Lismore, the Great Garden

LISMORE: AN LIOS-MÒR IN GAELIC, The Great Garden. It's the first thing you learn about the place. I once told that friend who said nature soothed the soul: "One thing you must do before you die – go to Lismore at orchid time." The explanation of Lismore's fertility and profusion is a geological fluke: it's a long, thin slice of limestone. The final act of glaciation (final in the sense that nothing comparable has happened in the last 10,000 years, but in the next 10,000 years, who knows?) contrived an ice cap on what we now call Rannoch Moor, from which glaciers flowed in every direction. As these melted and the sea rose, Lismore almost drowned. Rannoch's glaciers hurtled Etive granite westwards then south-west down the Great Glen, which explains why, now that the sea has finally settled down (final in the sense that nothing comparable has happened in the last ten millennia, but given the imponderables of global warming, who knows?), you find erratic boulders marooned on top of Lismore's narrow plateau. A hiatus in the sea-settling process that began something like 8,000 years ago and lasted something like 3,000 years, accounts for Lismore's collection of raised beaches, caves, sea stacks, peregrine-strafed cliffs. Lismore is both a geological showpiece and an idiot's guide to the godly art of making landscape where ocean and mountains meet. But for me, it was also a search for a glimmer of hope, a quest for confirmation that unlike, say, the winter of 2016–17, the spring of 2018 would actually turn up, however fleetingly, so that in the best tradition of pilgrimage I could raise my hands to the heavens, shout my hallelujahs and proclaim that mine eyes hath seen the glory of the coming of the swifts, or some other symbol of confirmation. When I set out from Stirling for Lismore, it was already April 23rd, and if you could have cut open a wedge of the wind it would have had "winter" lettered all the way through.

The reasons for choosing Lismore were twofold. Firstly, we are old friends given to occasional hail-fellow-well-met reunions at long intervals, mostly during old springs, and it has shown itself reliable enough in its capacity to harbour spring earlier and for longer than most of Scotland. Secondly, it feeds nicely into the notion of pilgrimage, especially once the decision had been taken to revisit that old Iona spring, Iona being something of an original source for pilgrims in Scotland, what with Columba and all that flowed from his endeavours there. So the writing mind followed the spoor of an admittedly selective thread of pilgrimage's history, so that a pilgrimage within a pilgrimage might unfurl, and that led directly to Lismore. From there, it would travel only slightly less directly to another island of particularly fond acquaintance, and in the process it would bind the west coast with the east, Scotland with England (or at least with that part of it that once thrust its northern border as far north as the Forth), and Columba with Cuthbert, the dove with the eider – Lindisfarne, one of the five parishes that once comprised the old Northumbrian fiefdom known as Islandshire. The idea germinated boldly, buoyed up by the considerable consolation that even if not so much a whiff of spring graced such a pilgrimage, there was always the renewing of auld acquaintance with friends-in-landscape.

★

These are the most familiar of roads. The car follows them instinctively. All it needs to be told is where to pause, where to turn off, where to stop. These are the arteries of my nature-writing territory. But I had never seen them look like this. I left Stirling in late April, crossed the Highland Edge at Callander, past Loch Lubnaig and the Balquhidder Glen road-end, over Glen Ogle, through Glen Dochart, past the Glen Orchy road-end, across the Black Mount and the edge of Rannoch Moor, then into Glen Etive under Bucahaille Etive Mor, where I stopped and stared. All that way, the entire landscape was only the palest shade of grey away from being utterly colourless. Buachaille Etive Mor, in my mind the handsomest of all mainland Argyll's mountains, was pallid and weary, wrapped in rags of cloud shaded from black to hodden grey, and looking as lethargic as an old stag that had just tholed one winter too many. The only vigour to be seen anywhere at all was in water – every mountain gully and every burn and river and waterfall seethed white, and every wind-and-rain-whipped loch and lochan was dowsed in the same forlorn mourning shades as the mountain. Near the layby where I had pulled off the road was a dead blackface ewe, the perfect metaphor for the landscape where it had died: one more heap of widely scattered grey and black, symbolic of the mood inflicted on the land by the overlong and predatory winter. It had its teeth and talons locked into the corpus of what should have been prime springtime, choking the very breath of life out of the land.

Glencoe, that most galvanising theatre of Highland geology, was likewise as moribund as an east-coast haar in January, a grey shrug. All along Loch Leven the mood held sway. Then I took the Oban road for the Appin coast, rounded a long bend where Loch Leven gave way to Loch Linnhe; the sea brightened as it broadened, and the Earth awoke. It was as simple and sudden as that. Along the Atlantic coast the force field of the Gulf Stream had taken winter by the scruff of the neck, smacked it around the head a few times and heaved it into the stinkpit of dead seasons. In its place were daffodils ablaze on the verges, fat-budded rhododendrons (a presence that twenty minutes back down the road seemed as unlikely as pixie dust) beginning to burst into violent red and purple (all colour looked violent at this point in the journey), clusters of larches and birches that greened as they clustered, and – ye Gods! – palm trees adorned cottage gardens.

One more layby, a path through a thicket, birdsong that included willow warbler (Africa meets Argyll, a recurring miracle), and there in the midst of a sea view were four great northern divers, and close enough and well-enough lit for binoculars to paint in the black head, beak and neck; the neck with a white incised tattoo of tree trunks, as if an Ansel Adams photograph had been miniaturised there. I know, it's an extravagant image, but being giddy on the sudden confirmation that spring is not yet wholly extinct is an excusable circumstance for extravagance. So, as well as the tree trunk tattoo, the binoculars also articulated the white breast with wavy zebra stripes, black back with white-on-black grid of crossword squares and a smothering of white spots as vivid as a starry night.

These waters – and all the way from Argyll to the Northern Isles – are sacred to the nomadic tribe of great northern divers as they drift north through the spring, before making the leap of faith that commits them to journey's end in Greenland. These April-into-May days have seen gatherings of rare spectacle, including 417 off Kintyre in 2001, and two years earlier, 781 at Scapa Flow in Orkney. When I read about that, I thought: "I hope it was a sunny day." Imagine that starry-night plumage, multiplied by 781, daylight constellations, a mobile Milky Way of birds adrift on Scapa Flow. What an antidote to the blockships, the barriers, the wrecks, the war graves, the gun emplacements, and all the other wretched souvenirs of World Wars I and II: suddenly a sea fog is split apart by the sun and there on the water is an ocean-going fleet of 781 great northern divers.

That's why nature always wins. Always.

The day's destination was Port Appin, with Lismore a ten-minute ferry ride away in the morning. There were two eiders on the pier. Eiders have a talismanic presence in my life. They have a happy habit of rescuing me on lonely shores. They make me smile. They nest in circumstances that make me realise how little I really know about the singularly specialised fieldcraft of becoming landscape oneself – something I preach to others and try to practise myself. But then I would stumble on an eider duck on her eggs, "stumble" because her nesting takes me by surprise, because it is so perfectly done, the surroundings so eider-brown and discreet, the stillness so utter; and I feel like bowing in deference, in flagrant admiration, and for the way she would stoically meet my gaze. The colour brown was never so deftly nor so beautifully utilised to make such a perfect blend of function and art.

As for the drake, I cannot do better than Gavin Maxwell, who thought its breeding plumage suggested "the full dress uniform of some unknown navy's admiral". Sometimes the descriptive power of Maxwell's writing is heightened to a pitch that reveals his painterly credentials (he was a portrait painter before he gave his creative life over to writing). In *Raven Seek Thy Brother* (Longmans, 1968), his admiral analogy was followed by this:

> *The first impression is of black and white, but at closer quarters the black-capped head that looked simply white from far off seems like the texture of white velvet and shows feathers of pale scintillating electric green on the rear half of the cheek and on the nape; the breast above the sharp dividing line from a black abdomen, is a pale gamboge, almost peach. From the white back the secondary wing feathers of the same colour sweep down in perfect scimitar curves over the black sides, adding immensely to the effect of a uniform designed for pomp and panache...*

And now there was a pair of eiders on the ferry pier at Port Appin, conferring their blessing on the 21st-century spring pilgrim's arrival. There was a time – the late 19th and early 20th centuries – when the eider population in Argyll waters blossomed to such an extent that it became known up and down the west coast as the "Colonsay duck". Why numbers increased from an admittedly low start is not clear, but inevitably, once it became a ubiquitous presence, the human population began to plunder its eggs and the sumptuous cushions of its own breast down with which it lines its nest. The female on the nest is the ultimate definition of a sitting duck, for it is so unwilling to leave its eggs even in the face of the most blatant of threats, that she can literally be lifted by human hands, her eggs and down cleared from the nest, and then she can be replaced where she sat, all without so much as a syllable of protest. One way and another, the bird's own natural vulnerability allied to our constant tampering with the naturalness of coastal waters mean that as the 21st century advances, each new spring reveals a sharp decrease in nesting eiders. From oil pollution to shooting (to protect mussel farms) to the myriad consequences of warming seas, our species is forever inventing new ways to trouble the duck once befriended by saints.

The first thing to be said of Lismore across the quiet sound that late April evening is that finally I found somewhere that looked like it was taking April seriously. It was green! And the crags of its north end were girt with trees: limestone and ash, how they love each other's company. In the hotel that evening, I reminded myself of Robert Hay's vivid evocation of the significance of where I was going in the morning. At the very beginning of Chapter One of *Lismore – The Great Garden* (Birlinn, 2009):

> *From the top of Cnoc Aingeal, the fire cairn of Lismore, you look northwards into the jaws of an Earth movement of unimaginable scale and age. Three blocks of crust, wandering over the surface of the planet, collided with such force that their edges crumpled upwards into mountains of Himalayan proportions. After many millions of years of erosion, only their roots survive as the modest mountains of the Scottish Highlands, Norway, Greenland and the Appalachians…Even now, 400–500 million years later, aftershocks of these events are still being recorded as earthquakes in the Great Glen, the most recent in October 2008 near Glenfinnan…This crumpling, squeezing, twisting and heating somehow combined to lift up, into the middle of the Fault, a slice of ancient limestone that eventually would form Lismore…*

The ten-minute ferry crossing from Port Appin eased alongside the slipway under Lismore's blunt and craggy northern pow with a gentle rumble, like an old lion. I had two destinations in mind. One was a quiet north-west corner of the coast where I could sit and watch a small cluster of islands and skerries that had "here be otters" written all over them. The other was Cnoc Aingeal, the fire cairn of Lismore, for the view "into the jaws of an Earth movement of unimaginable scale and age". There I thought I might stare into the 500 million-years-old birth throes from which – in its own good time – my own love for a mountain land drew succour. That was the plan, at least, but as with Iona, there were ambitions and expectations and then there were "events, dear boy, events".

At that pivotal moment in my journey into spring, the one for which my mind's eye had contrived a host of mountain landmarks that would befit the jaws of an Earth movement, the spectacle was not all that it might have been. Ben Nevis had presided over my vision, because that's what Ben Nevis does, for all that it is among my least favourite mountains. I have never climbed it and don't plan to, because it attracts hordes, and the hordes bring noise and rubbish and that was never the kind of company I care for in the mountains. But the Glencoe mountains and the lovely Beinn Bheithir of fond memories gathered in the east, and Ardgour (which has nothing to prove in that company) fringed the western shore. But for the moment, all was sunk deep in a singular shroud of thick, clinging, towering grey cloud.

Then there was a wheatear, pert on a rock, spotlit by a glint of sun, set against a blueing wedge of sea. The wheatear was widely known in Britain as "whitearse" until the name began to offend Victorian sensibilities and an absurd clean-up campaign resulted in one of the most thoughtless bird names in the history of ornithology. It's a bird of the hills and the wild open places. Ears of wheat have nothing to do with it, and it has nothing to do with them. But when it flies, and especially if it crosses a square yard of sunlight, its arse is unmistakably brilliantly white. This particular whitearse was the first I had seen that backward spring, which made it four or five weeks late. It would also prove to be the first of a series of spring firsts whose paths I crossed that day. Lismore yielded migrant birdsong, notably willow warbler and wood warbler. There were violets, primroses, wood anemones and milkworts.

On a cliff-edge, a mat of salt-wind-washed hawthorn clung to improbable life by sprawling over several square yards instead of attempting a trunk and limbs and branches, for which aeons of evolution had prepared it. Instead, it was nowhere more than seven or eight inches high. I looked for a central "trunk" or perhaps a root, but so dense was the flattened mass that I could not find one.

A kestrel held up against a considerable wind. Then, when it whipped away downwind, the lower slopes of Ardgour blurred agreeably through the binoculars. Then, looking down on the bird from a cliff-top, it was the sea that flowed beneath it. Strange to see land-lover windhover haunt the tide. This, I rebuked myself silently, is what is missing from your life: the intrusion of sea into the lives of everything in nature, from whitearses and windhovers to hawthorns and mountain ranges, to the geology of islands that can throw a limestone fluke into the heart of a sea loch and make it look as if it was planned all along, and to the way trees grow round a crag. That day on that island, pausing often to hug the spirit of spring close to me with longing and a sense of intimate kinship, I heard the words of one of my favourite jazz ballads drift through my head and linger there: "Spring can really hang you up the most".

Among the ashes were two whitebeams, and I have admired white-beams for many years – from a circular stand of ten of them I pass on my regular morning walk for coffee and newspapers, to a startling intrusion high on a slope of Glenorchy of all places. Here, they flour-ished a crop of exquisite grey-green, ready-to-burst buds, and rose darkly from cliff-face shadow to cliff-top sunlight, at which point they obeyed the law of the land that decrees that all cliff-top trees will bow to the prevailing wind so that they leaned away east. But whitebeams almost in leaf: now we were really getting somewhere.

A perch on a level shelf of raised beach provided limestone fur-niture for lunch, and an uninterrupted view of that ottery clutch of small islands and skerries. In such a situation, "lunch" can occupy a couple of idyllic hours, even otterless hours (for so they proved). There was first of all the situation itself, the perch on Lismore's northmost crags, the foreground of sea that continued to respond to the sun's sluggish emergence by changing and deepening colours in horizontal bands that darkened by degrees into distance, Ardgour's handsome mountain profile that also responded to the change in the weather by shrugging off cloud and baring hill shoulders. There were grey seals out among the skerries, more great northern divers on the water, and two kestrels came and went and soared above the crags or above the cliffs and stalled on the air there, and not for the first time in my life I envied a hovering bird its view of the world below its airy stance.

The rising tide finally eased the seals into the water as their couches (also limestone) flooded, and with that, as if the evicting influence of the high tide had climbed the cliffs to the raised beach left by that old Rannoch glacier, the galvanising company of spring announced the end of lunch. A rough path dipped towards the shore, where the evidence of otters was omnipresent – a litter of spraints stitched with fishbones, crab claws and broken shells, and ground-down grains of shell so densely packed they looked like rockpools.

Then, from the shore at Port Ramsay, just as sunlight began to enliven the visible world, a familiar shape emerged from a cursory scan of a wood across the water, an erect grey-brown slab that looked too big and too heavy for the comfort of the tree where it appeared to have been hung, like a sheet left out to dry. More careful consideration revealed that it was not hung but perched. Then it raised its head from its breast where it had been rearranging its feathers with an implement that looked like a cross between a sickle and a banana, and instantly became a sea eagle. And there it stood and there it stared and there it settled into prolonged stillness, looking as if it might spend the entire afternoon in that attitude. It was a telling example of one of the bird's character traits that distinguishes it from the golden eagle: it has no fear of humankind and its works, humankind's settlements and humankind's noise. This one was in full view of Port Ramsay's street of houses in the middle of the afternoon while the residents went about their business. The nearest house to the tree where the bird perched was about 200 yards. A collie barked. Two people worked on a boat. Three more chatted in a garden between house and shore, their voices carrying far over the quiet water. Two cars appeared from opposite directions at the one road junction, stopped there while the drivers conversed through open windows, engines running. The sea eagle feigned disinterest, but it is a safe bet that it took in everything.

Not one of the people I could see appeared to know that it was there; either that or its appearance in that tree was so familiar that it had become part of the furniture.

I mulled over the bird's changing fortunes. One hundred years ago, almost to the day, the last of its kind in Scotland, in all Britain, was shot, and it was not as if no one knew that it was the last of its kind. Its extinction had been achieved deliberately. Now this, where a small island community appeared to be quite indifferent to the presence of one of the most astonishing birds in the northern hemisphere, casually perched on its doorstep. Mull across the water has even turned it into a tourist symbol.

*

Lismore's small parish church is unexceptional. It was also turned back-to-front when the Victorians modernised the 14th-century cathedral. "Cathedral" is a confusing term: this was not Durham or Kirkwall or Lincoln. This was modesty, writ small. A reconstruction in John Hay's book shows a single-storey building like two semi-detached cottages with a tower at one end. But for all its modesty, it provides a 21st-century link that reaches back to Christianity's very first trade mission into Scotland. What connects Iona with Lismore and beyond is the same idea that underpins this entire endeavour of mine to beat a path through all four of nature's seasons. It is the idea of pilgrimage, a journey as a means to an end that binds destination to a particular quest for understanding.

The single name that leads the pilgrim and the historian from one island to the other is Moluag. Relatively speaking, he is the unsung hero of pilgrimage's saga that binds Iona to Islandshire, Columba to Cuthbert, dove to eider. Bear in mind that "relatively speaking" should not obscure the fact that we are talking about saints here, so by definition there is a degree of fame attached to Moluag in that there is sainthood. He was on Iona with Columba, and there is a tradition that they failed to extend saintliness towards each other. The handed down stories suggest at the very least that the two were competitive in their missionary zeal, that there was an unseemly power struggle over Lismore, and that Moluag won it by fair means or the other kind. It seems that even saints sin, albeit mildly.

But once he got his feet under the table on Lismore, his stewardship is unblemished. He chose the site of a long-established Pictish religious centre for his own abbey and education centre. It seems he was always in Columba's shadow as Lismore was in Iona's, and his abbey never rivalled Iona in grandeur or trappings. The present church is nearby, as is the Sanctuary Stone from who knows which of Lismore's religious eras, and quite possibly it pre-dates them all. It is also known as Clach na h-Ealamh, the Swan Stone. So perhaps the swan was to Moluag what the dove was to Columba and the eider to Cuthbert. Perhaps. Robert Hay notes that in the *Martyrology of Oengus* Moluag is given this accolade:

The pure, the bright, the pleasant
The sun of Lismore
That is Moluag of Lismore in Alba

Legends appear to overwhelm any glimpses of truth when it comes to the 1,500-year-old reputations of saints, but, given my own fascination for the tribe of wild swans, I like the idea that asylum seekers and other fugitives were immune to prosecution for a year and a day if they could touch the Swan Stone.

*

I took the high ground on the way back to the ferry, found the kestrels again. They were hunting over the summit above the ash tree crags, tilting the land and the sea and the whole island to their bidding at the whim of supremely articulate wings, or hanging from the spread fan of their tails, wings beating time to the song of the wind.

How does that feel? To hover? I know it's a means to an end for a hunting falcon, but I sometimes wonder if, occasionally, it hovers just to enjoy being there, high up and looking round. Sometimes it's as still as the North Star. Sometimes it's as fidgety as a sparrow. Sometimes it tires of its stance and stops moving everything – folds up its tail, stiffens its wings – and miraculously it moves forward doing nothing at all, and then it stands still again, finds the wind, and is either fidgety or still. James Macdonald Lockhart wrote in *Raptor* of that moment:

The bird is standing still, walking into the wind.

Perfect. But is it ever up there when it doesn't have to be, when it isn't hungry, when it doesn't have chicks to feed, when it isn't teaching fledglings the artistry of kestrel flight? I suppose what I mean is, does it ever come up here to admire the view, up here above Cnoc Aingeal, the fire cairn of Lismore? I thought that if I were a kestrel up here, I would want to do that, and then I would like to sail north into what John Hay called "the jaws of an Earth movement" and flirt with the wind where it is no longer an ocean wind or an island wind but a mountain wind on first-name terms with the mountains and their gods. Then wheel at the narrows of the loch and sail back to this very rock, drift down to a perfectly controlled landing then turn and look where I had just been, and admire it, recall the thrill of the flight, just ever-so-slightly out of breath.

It was not the best day for the view. The jaws were clamped shut by a great smother of cloud. It rained there, as it so often does whenever Ben Nevis and Glencoe are in the frame, but Ardgour and Mull had begun to stir themselves, to shake themselves and stretch like a waking fox. And the sea in among those ottery islands and skerries had deepened to the deepest, darkest blue of all the sapphire shades. The West in spring does this, transforms moment by moment, to form new shapes, new colours, new moods, new scenes and acts of wild theatre, and all of it achieved with kaleidoscopic sleights of hand and flights of fancy, as if a kestrel were tapping the kaleidoscope.

A strange bird call on the air.

I stopped whatever it was I was doing and gave everything over to listening. The sound came from behind and below. It was constant, and there was more than one voice at work – so, the contact calls of a flock on the move? It sounded like nothing I could put a name to. The sea was grey down there, down where the calls seemed to be coming from, and it was only after a speculative search with the binoculars that I found a skein of seven greyish birds flecked with brown and white and flying in a perfect vee. They flew at wave-top level and they might have been curlews except that they did not sound like curlews, did not fly like curlews, and were too small for curlews. I thought about plovers but that didn't work either. They were a hundred feet below and 200 yards offshore, and they swept round the north end of the island and vanished. I was still scratching my head when the answer raised a cautious head over the steep cliff edge. They had landed just beyond the point where they had disappeared. The head was that of a compact, striped curlew-ish bird, and the beak was that of a compact, straighter, blunter curlew beak. It was a whimbrel, last seen on Colonsay two years ago; and two years before that I had been overtaken by two as I drove north through Caithness en route to Orkney. A flock of seven was the most whimbrels I had ever seen at once, a rare event and getting rarer. Its Shetland stronghold is in dire decline, and if they cannot sustain a population there, Scotland may lose them altogether. Just like the choughs, like the wildcats.

A single hawthorn tree stood on the cliff edge. It was about five feet tall, but its limbs were so writhing and wizened that it might easily have been fifty years old. Its trunk was no more than six inches high, whence it despatched four skinny limbs more or less upwards, and the whole thing and its sparse foliage bore the shape of the wind. It was a cruel twist of fate that planted its seed there, on the very crown of the very rim of the cliff-top. It stood out against sea and sky, and hardly against the land at all. Its stance was as precarious as the tree was tenacious. Within its modest dimensions, it seemed to be flourishing, a mote of life in a vast land-and-sea-and-skyscape. I wished it a long life. I have thought of it many times since then, and I have envied its place on the map of the world. Lismore has always treated me well. This time, it treated me better than ever. I could understand, perhaps, how earthly competition had briefly overcome the saintlier instincts of Cuthbert and Moluag when they first saw the possibilities of the Great Garden.

Twenty-eight

An Island Pilgrimage (3) – Lindisfarne, Islandshire

South of Berwick-on-Tweed is Islandshire – that part of Northumbria in which lie Holy Island or Lindisfarne and the Farne Islands group. Islandshire is, even at the present day, a lonely district, and it is perhaps the only county of the east coast where is to be found what I may truly call the Hebridean atmosphere.

Seton Gordon

A Foot in Wild Places (Cassell, 1937)

FOR THE HEIRS TO Columba of Iona, Lindisfarne was a home from home, furnished with echoes of that Hebridean land-and-seascape. Among the earliest of pilgrims to Iona after Columba's death in 593 AD was a temporarily deposed Northumbrian king called Oswald. During his stay he was impressed enough by what he found there to nourish the hope that he might convert his own kingdom one day. That day arose in 634 when he was given his crown back. One way or another, that year was a turning point in the pilgrimage business. At Iona he had been impressed by a young monk called Aidan, and it was surely no coincidence that in that very year, Aidan founded an abbey on Lindisfarne. By then Aidan had already founded Melrose Abbey, so now the eastwards migration of Christianity had crossed the entire breadth of the land, and Columba would surely have approved of its final destination on Lindisfarne.

Meanwhile, in Dunbar (now in East Lothian but then a northern outpost of the Kingdom of Northumbria) a boy was born – also in 634 – in whom all of the above would coalesce, and who, all but 1,400 years later, would capture my imagination. His name was Cuthbert. One night when he was seventeen (and here it may be advisable to have some pinches of salt to hand) he saw a light fall to earth, pause there, then retrace its steps heavenwards. It was, he assumed, lighting the way for a human soul to ascend its way into heaven. It transpired subsequently that Aidan had died that night. Cuthbert did what any susceptible seventeen-year-old mortal who has heavenly visions would do – he went to Melrose. He became a monk. He was good at it. In time he became a prior, and the next step would have been abbot, were it not for the fact that at thirty, he moved. To Lindisfarne. For the next ten years his reputation grew. But then, he either got fed up of the celebrity business or he felt called to become a hermit. One way or the other, he became one, and established his hermitage on Inner Farne, and from then on, he got on extraordinarily well with eiders, which is why I rather liked him.

I first turned up on Lindisfarne as a teenage with a bike, and one way or another, and at irregular intervals, I have been doing it ever since. South-making does not come naturally to me. It never has. My roots are planted on the north shore of the Tay estuary and I have never made any secret of the fact that my landscape preferences lie between the compass points of north and west. Stir into the mix my innate Scottishness (I was born here and I have lived and worked here all my life), my trade as a nature writer, and the knowledge that if I travel south nature will be in better heart where I have been than where I am going and all my preferred landscapes will lie behind me rather than ahead of me...consider all that and you may understand that any crossing of the English border is an undertaking that teeters precariously on the outer edges of equanimity.

And be in no doubt: Scotland into England is not one region of Great Britain into another. That was never how I interpreted the lie of the land. Rather, this is international business, a border between nations. This is France into Spain, Austria into Italy, Denmark into Germany, Canada into the USA. It is not that I am blind to England's many natural charms, rather that I bring to bear on my appreciation of them something of Lord Byron's comparative assessment set against his childhood memories of Lochnagar:

Though Nature of verdure and flowers bereft you
Yet still art thou dearer than Albion's plain,

England! Thy beauties are tame and domestic
To one who has roved on the mountains afar –

Oh! for the crags that are wild and majestic,
The steep frowning glories of Dark Loch na Garr.

Such was the old familiar preoccupation of my state of mind as another mile of the A1 slipped by, another bend in the road was followed by a crest in the road, and then there it was, without warning or fanfare, ten miles away and thrusting palely out into the grey-green sprawl of the North Sea, there lay Lindisfarne. And after more than a hundred miles of grey and featureless sky, the island stirred in a halo of weak but brightening sunlight. And right then, right there, as the English border hurtled towards me at sixty miles per hour, I felt love and longing, for I have been there before and loved what I found there.

Besides, I trust Seton Gordon. I always have. So when he writes: "… the only county of the east coast where is to be found what I may call the Hebridean atmosphere…" I believe him. His assessment matters to me, partly because he knew more about the Hebridean atmosphere than most people and articulated it thoughtfully and sometimes unforgettably in many of his books, not least in *The Charm of Skye* (Cassell, 1929), which is my favourite of his books, and was his favourite too. Skye lured me into what is now a far-flung appreciation of the Hebrides that has endured for fifty years. And for more than thirty of these, as a writer, I have travelled a line of latitude coast-to-coast across Scotland from the Tay estuary to Mull and it has been a fertile seam for me. Among much else, it has produced this:

MULL FERRY
(Arrival)
Waves in fractured parallels
stacked seven shades of grey
among old rock familiarities

that jigsaw into place; See!

That piece is me,
fitting back into its empty space
in the geology of my islandness.
Not that this is my native shore,

and I'm no prodigal here,
yet whenever I return
nature kills me fatted calves
and broaches flagons.

(Departure)
My life's other shore,
the native mainland one I ply
far from island ferries
insists on this retreat. See!

There's my piece again,
fitting back into the empty space
it left behind to indulge
my temporary islandness,

and where I am frequently prodigal
(while behind my back the island
wishes me safe journey,
haste ye back). And so I return

to that native place in my life's puzzle
but it's a light anchor I drop.
I stare out at a grey sea
without islands.

Somehow, in past readings of Seton Gordon, I missed that mention of "Islandshire". It's strange that I was unaware of its old name, because one way or another, Lindisfarne and its Northumbrian hinterland had quietly got under my skin, and it's something I would like to have known about the place. It is immediately obvious that it suits the place well, and it has endearing overtones. So I greeted the Border with a wave, because had I not just crossed out of Berwickshire into Islandshire? And didn't that remove some of the unhelpful echoes of old animosities from the Scotland–England thing?

So Islandshire (as I shall address it for evermore) has recommended itself to me for fifty years, and Seton Gordon has been among its ambassadors, and several of his books have been a constant presence through all my adult years and others have ebbed and flowed through. And Seton Gordon, in turn, came recommended to me first of all by an old uncle whose love of wild Scotland, birds, books, photography and cycling were effortlessly communicated to me and found a willing disciple. His name was Stuart Illingworth, he was my mother's brother, and he gave me my first bird book and my first malt whisky, so he was a considerable and benevolent influence on my young life. But he also introduced me to Lindisfarne when I was that teenager with a bike, roped me in with two of his chums on a cycling trek from his Peebles home to Northumberland, without ever telling me that part of it – the parishes of Ancroft, Belford, Elwick, Holy Island, and Kyloe and Tweedmouth – was historically known as Islandshire. I now consider this to be remiss of him.

He did, however, fuel my burgeoning interest in Scottish independence by talking mischievously about how an independent Scotland could annex it, bring it back where (as he saw it) it still belonged. And he had been a captain in the Lovat Scouts in Burma during World War II, and seemed (as I saw it) to have a grasp on the essentials of how it might be done. When I suggested the natives might put up some resistance (given that when King Oswald was in charge there was a time when Northumbrians overran the south-east of Scotland as far north as Fife, and that they might see the natural order of things differently), he swotted away my concerns as schoolbook history. But when I saw the place, when I considered the possibilities of not having to cross the border to get there – a Hebridean atmosphere in our far south-east – I confess I rather liked the idea.

Today, I still cherish two memories of that first encounter with

Lindisfarne. The first was – of course – the causeway, for I had never seen anything quite like it. It was the speed with which the sea fell back, the road consolidating and shedding water like a surfacing submarine, before finally defining itself in a way that recalled an old movie in which Charlton Heston as Moses parted the Red Sea, the people surging towards the Promised Land along God's suddenly revealed causeway. Thinking about it now, what a way to end a pilgrimage.

My second souvenir was the first sight of the seagoing cluster of the Farne Islands.

Because we had come on it all from the west (not the north, as has been my habit in recent years, driving down the A1 rather than cycling from Peebles), and from high above, I saw how the land suddenly opened up and tilted all Islandshire towards that pod of islands; and hadn't there been something in schoolbook history about St Cuthbert?

Now the connections come thick and fast. A few years later, as I expanded my mountaineering horizons, I had become profoundly smitten by a passionate relationship with the Cairngorm Mountains, and my deepening awareness of the significance of Seton Gordon unearthed this in his book, *The Cairngorm Hills of Scotland* (Cassell, 1925):

> *In the immense silences of these wild corries and dark rocks, the spirit of the high and lonely places revealed herself, so that one felt the serene and benign influence that has from time to time caused men to leave the society of their fellows and live on some remote and surf-drenched isle – as St Cuthbert did on Farne – there to steep themselves in those spiritual influences that are hard to receive in the crowded hours of human life.*

This interweaving of the 4,000-foot high mountain plateau and the sea-level island into a single philosophical strand took my breath away when I first read it. The idea that one writer could be so confident in his own knowledge of his native landscape and 1,500 years of its human history and make of them such a singular and striking image was new to me. When, in time, I wrote my own book about the

Cairngorms, not only did I quote the passage (twice), and not only did I borrow from it (the book is called *A High and Lonely Place*), but when I elaborated on my own idea of what constitutes "the spirit of the high and lonely places", I reached for the example of St Cuthbert too:

> *The spirit is, I think, a collaboration of landscape forces, of light, of weather, of space, the mingled chemistry of which creates a tangible presence of nature that demands a response in those who encounter it. Respect for the spirit is the first commandment of the wilderness... The spirit lingers most blatantly on the plateau. There is no mountain sensation to compare with its sweeping plain, its corner-to-corner skies...the restlessness of its air that can wash great freedoms through a receptive human mind in the manner of St Cuthbert's surf...*

So this land of Islandshire tilts towards the islands, and if you happen to come upon it from the west, your eyes reach down and out to them, and the chances are that you have just had your first glimpse of journey's end. For 1,500 years now, from Columba's Iona to Moluag's Lismore to Aidan's Melrose to Cuthbert's Lindisfarne (the "daughter monastery" of Iona), that way lies journey's end for pilgrims culled from every strand of humanity. For some of us, following in our own time and for our own motives (and perhaps especially the nature writers among us), there is arguably a sense of rightness about following in the spoor of a saint who befriended eider ducks; and given that in my own case others who had gone before also included my uncle and the man whose work he introduced me to – Seton Gordon – why would I not warm to the symbolism of it all and have it embrace the love-in-landscape that I cling to?

On a March day, then, that faltering backward spring of 2018, I arrived at the mainland end of the causeway to be greeted by a low-flying welcoming party of brent geese and their guttural benediction, which I chose to translate roughly as "hail fellow, well met". And this being the 21st century, there was also an impatient queue of half a dozen cars gnashing its teeth, drumming its fingers on its steering wheel and running its engine, as if collective irritation was a force to be reckoned with that might annihilate the gravitational pull of the moon and get the job done so that the sea would ebb away from the causeway that much quicker, and my carefully constructed illusion about the rightness of pilgrimage cracked and splintered and dematerialised before my eyes. What price a quest for those "spiritual influences that are hard to receive in the crowded hours of human life"?

A vast and bright red four-wheel-drive pick-up truck the size of a tug boat overtook the queue at speed, plunged into the retreating sea water, blasted a bow-wave that would not have disgraced the QEII in her pomp, bullied its way across. And the more timid drivers in that tetchy queue looked longingly at its dwindling tailgate and muttered in unison:

"I'm gonna get me one of those."

The brent geese, which have more sense (as well as wings, admittedly), flew over again no more than a dozen feet above the queue's throbbing roofscape, for it is nothing more than a fluctuating part of their landscape, that landscape which is always fluctuating in any case, always restless. Lindisfarne constantly tampers with its sea, and the sea constantly tampers with Lindisfarne, rearranging its dunes, and cutting it off from the rest of the world twice a day, then reconnecting it and baring tracts of puddled sand in the process, to which wildfowl and waders and seabirds flock in their many thousands and from all across the northern hemisphere. The brent geese, which are among the most restless of Lindisfarne's tribes, forby the fidgeters on four wheels, drifted a little further from the queue with its fumes and its engine rumble, landed again a hundred yards away, causing a certain amount of readjustment among curlews, shelduck and godwits. I get impatient with impatient queues and idling engines so I retreated half a mile up the road to while away the wait in a café. I saw that it was almost noon. What was it about noon and godwits? Then I remembered. It was Seton Gordon:

The godwits decided at last that the wide estuary was unsafe for them, and rising to a great height they made for the open sea.

Delicately pencilled against the blue of the noonday sky they constantly changed their position. Now flying in a close bunch, now in V-shape formation, they sped towards the friendly sea, their narrow, slender wings, fast-driven, recalling the flight of the peregrine. For a moment the flock turned as one bird and hung poised on the breeze. A second flock joined them, and the great multitude of birds which had temporarily become confused, changed into an orderly gathering that wheeled, glided and dipped as though directed by a single mind...

It was from *Afoot in Wild Places*. There is a page marker in my copy, a small feather, and beside the passage in faint pencil and in my own handwriting it says: "Masterly."

So I sat with good coffee and a quiet contentment that spoke of journey's end. The sea wore a calm and muted sheen. But again and again and far offshore, a single wave would rise out of apparent calm, travel at speed over perhaps 200 yards, then break with a kind of controlled grace. Moments later the next wave would rise up from nothing and follow it in. It became mesmerising. The small huddle of the Farne Islands crouched before them.

It was time. Lindisfarne, the Holy Island, and its Hebridean atmosphere awaited. As I eased my car onto the causeway a pair of eiders made way. I have never been indifferent to that crossing, never taken it for granted. Few pilgrims ever are, whatever their motives. Sheila Mackay, an Edinburgh writer who has a long association with the island offered this, in a book called Lindisfarne Landscapes (Saint Andrew Press, 1996):

The shining tidal pools of the Slakes, which bear the Pilgrims' Way, will mirror blue skies and scudding clouds. But even if the day should chance to be grey and wet, soaking the hundreds of folk descending the hill from Beal towards the Pilgrims' Way, in spirit they will remain undaunted. For they are pilgrims and the day is Good Friday. They walk barefoot, some share the burden of huge wooden crosses on their shoulders. They sing that their faith will remain constant, "come wind, come weather".

An Island Pilgrimage (3) - Lindisfarne, Islandshire

They congregate from all over England and from Scotland. They represent several denominations and have come to Lindisfarne, one of the holiest places in Britain, to re-commit their faith in this spectacular annual act of worship. They are joined by a few others, of no particular persuasion, but who sense, perhaps, that something missing from their lives might be retrieved, like a jewel in the sand, by walking the Pilgrims' Way to the edge of Holy Island at Easter.

I have looked from both ends, and at both low and high tide, along the line of tall poles that marks the route of the Pilgrims' Way across the low-tide sands between Lindisfarne and the English mainland. It is a more or less reliable way to effect a crossing on foot more or less dryshod and – crucially – avoiding quicksands. I have to admit at this point that I am completely unmoved by it, unpersuaded by the need for the ritual, and for three reasons. Firstly, I am not *that* kind of pilgrim; secondly, I don't subscribe to that kind of faith (far less the urge to carry a huge wooden cross to prove…what exactly?); and thirdly, while it is unarguable that I can think of something missing from my life – that "jewel in the sand" I may or may not be able to retrieve hereabouts – it certainly wouldn't be retrieved on a public holiday in the company of hundreds of others. It is nature I seek an audience with, so if I were not to go alone, I would need the company of one singularly attuned to the notion that what is truly sacred is the land itself, and that nature is best met where the vast spaces of sea and sky conspire and collide with the edge of the island in the silence of low tide or the sound and fury of the cry of birds and the beat of breakers. I've written before of how much I like edges, and whatever else, Lindisfarne is an edgy kind of place, and its shores, especially its northern and eastern shores, constitute the edge of an edge.

Here is a tract of the shore where a half-beaten path the width of one pair of boots threads an uncertain trail through marram grass round the base of the dunes, and at low tide the sheer sprawl of dark sand looks as if the sea has been replaced by a flowing tide of tea-coloured beauty, the illusion of liquid assisted by wide tidal pools that declined temporary abdication when the rest of the sea took leave of its senses and vanished an hour ago. They have no colour at all, but they gleam, and crowds of crabs and shoals of other shell-thirled creatures flock to them or perish in the attempt.

A close inspection of the shore revealed tideline caches of feathers (eider, for sure, possibly short-eared owl), a handful of which now decorate my bookshelves so that every now and then I pick one up, run a daydreaming finger along one edge, and remember.

The day.

The hour.

The moment.

The atmosphere.

Or a draught from the window or the door lifts one from its temporary berth in front of the George Mackay Browns (I thought he of all the writers gathered there might enjoy their islandness) and drifts in an unhurried spiral towards the floor, just possibly brushing a guitar string on the way down, and I stop what I'm doing while I watch and let my thoughts rummage around the idea of a second spring for the feathers, so that however briefly, they fly again and delight the eye of the watcher.

Atmosphere.

That word again, in Seton Gordon's thoughtful observation of eighty years ago: "…the only county of the east coast where is to be found what I may call the Hebridean atmosphere…". And if your particular pilgrimage can accommodate the time to tune in to such an elusive consideration rather than, say, a preoccupation with trying to save your soul, you may find that there *is* an atmosphere. I think I know what he was getting at, and I think it may have been truer then than it is now, for he had long conversations with natives who worked from small boats, and their preoccupations would have been very similar then to what he might have found on any small, inhabited, low-lying Hebridean island. Benbecula, say, or Gigha. Or – yes – Iona.

*

There came a moonlit evening then, a spring tide of boisterous breakers, and the relative sanctuary offered by the uncrossable causeway, a shoreline more in thrall to the sea itself than most, is when you might expect nature to beguile you from the sea too. Instead, the natives emerged from the eerily moonlit and heaped-up landscape of the dunes. The shadows between the heaps coughed up perhaps the last thing you might expect to go hunting here – a family of foxes. With the low-tide flats out of reach for the moment, the beach was thick with birds, standing, sitting, dozing, waiting.

It makes no difference to the eyesight of a fox whether high tide is sunlit or moonlit or neither, but darkness tilts the odds inexorably towards predator and away from prey. It became clear almost at once there was a strategy, that it had to do with one adult fox making a conspicuous presence of itself while the other lay as flattened and stretched and still as a length of beached driftwood. Two leggy cubs sat at the base of the dunes, engrossed, watching, learning. I stood in a shadow, engrossed, watching and learning myself.

The conspicuous fox trotted towards the waves as if it had not noticed the birds at all. Then it stopped, sat, looked around and did nothing whatsoever. A few minutes of this unnerved the birds. Finally, they snapped and panicked and flew, only to find as they took flight that the other fox was among them. I have seen this or something like it happen three times now, and on only one of the three was the tactic successful. The surprise is that the birds fall for it at all; you would think that evolution, race memory, whatever, would teach them that when the fox appears they vacate the premises. On the other hand, they work on the safety-in-numbers principle. There are hundreds in the flock, the worst that can happen is that two of their number succumb. So the odds of survival of any one individual bird are high.

Lindisfarne calls itself Holy Island, and has done for a long, long time. But really, it's no holier than any other. First and last, it is nature's island. The creatures of nature massively outnumber the human population, even when it is swollen by the unholy summer processions across the causeway and the holy ones across the sands. The oldest pilgrimages here are all nature's. We call it migration.

Twenty-nine
May in June

THE COUNTY OF FIFE is no one's idea of wilderness. Much of it is quietly agricultural. There are small, Lowland hills and planted woods, a handful of bird-rich lochs enlivened by the occasional spellbinding intervention of a sea eagle. The south-west is still trying to recover from its long-dead coal-mining past. But its long coast, which binds the Firth of Tay in the north to the Firth of Forth in the south, is a simple, blunt-edged, wide-open collision between the rock of the land and the North Sea. There is no Hebridean atmosphere here. You look out on a sea without islands.

Except one.

Five miles out into the North Sea, off a bonnie thrust of land called the East Neuk, lies a scrap of singularly uncompromising terrain, the basalt love-child of the east coast sea haar and the east wind, just over a mile long and less than half as wide, and on an early June late morning it was drenched in sunlight, seabirds and the white blossom of sea campion as dense and deep as snowdrifts. The Isle of May in June is quite something.

From the mainland shore at Anstruther, where they have succeeded in elevating fish and chips to a high art and failed utterly to stop day trippers from tossing bits of fish and bits of chips to the gulls, the day was what you might call beautiful, the harbour tranquil, the sea as blue as alpine gentians on a postcard from the Alps. But when I called at the office of the *May Princess* to collect my ticket, the skipper's brow was furrowed. It was possible, he said, that we might not be able to land because of the swell out there. And because the entrance into the Isle of May's slipway is tight on a good day, there was a degree of concern. A phrase I learned on the Hebridean island of Mingulay came into my mind then – "not so much a slipway, more occasionally negotiable rocks". It hardly seemed appropriate to mention it at that moment. So passengers were being offered a refund, just in case they didn't fancy it. The skipper said he was sailing in expectation of landing, it was an improving picture, and it was simply a question of how much improvement and how quickly it improved. But this would be my fourth crossing to the May, the first three had been truly memorable, and the island-addicted acquire a feeling about skippers and crews, and these guys were good. I took the ticket.

The boat was full, about eighty passengers, and no one seemed to want a refund. Later, one of the crew explained that out there, "that bloody east wind" that brought us the Met Office's greatest hit of 2018, the "Beast from the East", had simply never stopped blowing more than two months later, and that explained the swell. So the skipper plotted a course that would enable us to turn straight into the swell, "which will be more comfortable for you". We all liked the sound of that word, "comfortable". We were not all sure we believed it was appropriate, but when it comes to small ferries in the North Sea, "comfort" is a relative commodity.

Puffins in ones and twos and fifties and sixties, and gannets in wave-top fives and tens, streamed across our bows almost as soon as we were clear of Anstruther harbour. Cormorants and shags, guillemots and razorbills, sat on the swell (looking smug, mocking our caution), and grey seals eyed us uncertainly and stroked their whiskers. On board, we amounted to a motley ballast. This was the place and this was the season for an impressive array of "mine's bigger than yours" telephoto lenses, the biggest of them like steroid-enhanced baseball bats. There was a certain amount of ostentation going on, a surprising number of passengers were wearing a surprising number of thousands of pounds worth of gear around their necks. And a certain amount of good-natured geek-photography conversation drifted across the deck. Others pointed their phones. The accents were multi-national, multi-lingual. But "puffin" is easy in any language. And everyone laughs and smiles at puffins. And the sun bore down on us and all was well in our world, and the island advanced down the sea towards us and its cliffs grew tall and acquired detail and shouted "kittiwake, kittiwake" at us. The

May Princess danced to the sea's tune and our spirits were high, until it came to...

The tricky part.

The skipper homed us in on the entrance between occasionally negotiable rocks. That entrance seethed with white water. The undulations of that troublesome swell were, admittedly, well-spaced, which also meant we had time to see them coming. They looked muscle-bound and, well...big. In fact, BIG. One by one they toyed with the *May Princess*, had their fun, and moved on, then they thudded into the island with a percussive roar, and the waters of the entrance became temporarily not-negotiable again. And again, and again, and again. We bounced, slewed, waited, held on to something, waited. The skipper in the wheelhouse watched the entrance, turned to look over his shoulder, while one of the crew appraised each wave from outside the wheelhouse, called out the possibilities or lack of them. Finally, there was a moment, collectively and individually we girded our loins, and we went in. Suddenly the water was calm, glassy, the waves elsewhere. We, the passengers, burst into spontaneous applause that was part admiration, part gratitude.

At once, a hundred Arctic terns swarmed into the air above the inlet, and the rocks amplified and threw their voices at us. It was never the most musical of bird voices, but in the same way as unexceptional human voices can sound sensational in a choir, the effect was of both a glorious anthem of nature and a spectacle of extraordinary beauty.

And this was why we came. This was what we were here for. We stepped ashore to make our own accommodation with the Isle of May. We would worry about getting out again when the time came. From first moment to last, and throughout the island, this glorious ritual of the terns and its soundtrack rose spontaneously, as if it were the voice of the island itself and that it might have some message to communicate to us. Every time it happened, it stopped me in my tracks. I listened hard. I stared. I was, frankly, thrilled by it. It struck tremors of who-knows-what between my shoulder blades. I felt grateful, almost worshipful.

The backward spring had held the terns back. They were late in arriving, like so much else, and their nesting overtures had just begun. Once the birds are sitting tight, you don't get these extraordinary flypasts. Walking on the path through the nesting grounds is not like this. Instead, they pick you off one at a time and fly at your head. If you are lucky, they brush your hair with a wingtip; unlucky, and they draw blood. If you have been here before and know the ropes, you raise a hand high above your head with a camera in it and you press the shutter button and keep pressing as the terns take aim. There is always the chance of a good photograph (in my case, one in about 200 attempts among the tern colonies of my life), and they won't draw blood because they aim for the highest point of any one human inter- loper. And if you are on the Isle of May at nesting time and you enjoy free entertainment, it's worth getting back to the boat twenty minutes before sailing time, finding a good spot on the upper deck, and watch- ing your fellow passengers take evasive action as they run the gauntlet. You will laugh yourself sore.

My particular comeuppance on that score was two years ago when, being well schooled in the ways of Arctic terns, I deployed my usual high-camera-hand technique and escaped unscathed, only to be ambushed moments later by a greater black-backed gull, which is about the size of a Lancaster bomber to the tern's Spitfire. I still bear the scar. There is a moral in there somewhere, and I am still trying to work out what it is.

Ah, but then there are the eider ducks.

By comparison with the terns, there is no more stoical, immovable, silent nester than the eider duck. She looks you in the eye and just sits there on her sumptuous couch plucked from the down of her own breast, the living, breathing definition of "dead still". She is a yard from the path. She has felt the earth move beneath her as she has watched the footwear of a boatful of us pass by, some stopping right beside her to point cameras and phones, others inexplicably unaware that she is there, just a yard from their footfalls, fooled by stillness and the best natural camouflage on the face of the island.

A curious truth falls into place here. It is that although these must be among the most visited – and therefore the most disturbed – seabird acres anywhere in Scotland, they are also among the most successful. The island is a National Nature Reserve, access is by ferry only, and from Easter until the first of October. And because visitors know this, and because they come to see the birds, they also come in an attitude of respect, and their behaviour is almost universally predictable. Despite their blatant scrutiny and the chatter and general craziness that emanates from around eighty widely scattered humans constantly on the move, the birds thrive. Because of the peculiar circumstances of the Isle of May, and a regime that insists that everything is secondary to the well-being of the birds, this benevolent ritual of people walking only the network of paths actually appears to function like an extra protective membrane. The birds are safe from everything but each other. (A black-back swallowing an eider chick whole is as commonplace and as distressing for a human observer on the Isle of May as it is anywhere else.)

The eider colonies are a case in point. All around the country their numbers are in free-fall, but here they nest and they hatch and they fledge in record numbers. A survey in May 2018 revealed 1,183 nests, an increase of four per cent since the previous survey in 2016. Consider the nature of spring 2018, and be very, very impressed.

Up in the centre of the island there was a pool with a ditch. Just where the ditch enters the pool, two eider ducks were escorting six newly hatched ducklings on what is the defining rite of passage of every eider ever born: wherever the nest, they have to get to the sea, for there, and only there, lies relative safety. That means running the gauntlet of predators, and on the Isle of May, that usually means the big gulls. The sea means the safety of crèches, amalgamations of broods well marshalled by several females. I watched the six blackish-brown chicks plod up a short patch of mud and disappear into the ditch with one duck in front and the other behind, riding shotgun. She kept looking back, but the direction of travel was resolute. I wished them safe passage. It's a tricky and imperfect art, raising a brood of eiders once the nest is abandoned, but they work on the basis of safety in numbers, and on the Isle of May in particular, they get the job done.

*

That island day of birds in never-ending raucous splurges set against a huge, blue east-coast sky, or against breeze-bowed, meadow-like drifts of sea campion, finally distilled down to two individuals, one eider duck and one puffin. These caught my admiring glance and held it, and kept returning it again and again, so that the memory of them has become indelible. I have been studying two photographs I took, remembering, reconstructing their extraordinary moments.

The eider duck was sitting on a nest, I think. The doubt stems from the lie of the land, for it masked the entire bird apart from the head, which appeared to me as a left-facing profile. Sunlight lit the top of the head, the forehead, and the upper mandible of the bill, the top of one eyelid, the top of one cheek. The back of the head, the whole of its neck and the lower mandible were in deep shadow and looked black. Every square centimetre of the picture was crammed with swarming sea campion. The head of the bird was perfectly positioned at the base of a shallow vee in the land that extended from one side of the picture to the other. The edge of the vee was also where the sea campion flowers were in sharp focus. A tiny cluster of seven flower heads was particularly striking because its immediate background was the black-looking mass of the eider's neck. The bird must have been sitting on a ledge, just beyond the vee and hidden by it, which was why only the head was visible. The top half of the picture was the high bank that rose some distance behind the bird and beyond the vee, and it was an abstracted, out-of-focus mass of green and white. From top to bottom and edge to edge of the picture, the only thing not sea campion in various states of sharpness was the head of the eider duck, and even that had lost the tip of its bill because it was masked by flowers. The stillness was somehow unnerving. So was the unshakable confidence of the bird in the sureness of its place on the map, its place in the island's scheme of things. It impressed me. Not least because such a sensibility is quite absent from my own life. My long-standing admiration for eider ducks just deepened perceptibly.

The puffin was also on an edge. But unlike the eider's fragment of the island, it was a cliff edge, and I could see the whole bird. It stood, presenting a right-facing profile, and it looked at me looking at it, and we were about thirty yards apart. After a couple of minutes of this, it flew, and I assumed my audience was over. But it was back a minute later and came into land with orange webs thrust forward and whirring wings held high, to land in precisely the same spot, to assume precisely the same attitude as before. This happened five or six times over quarter of an hour. Each time it flew, it couldn't have travelled any distance worth speaking of, did not land on the sea or dive beneath for food. I wondered if it was a game, or if it was unpaired and looking for a mate and that my presence and stillness was completely incidental to the ritual.

But on the sixth or seventh occasion I noticed something I had never seen in puffins before – and from Shetland to St Kilda, the Treshnish Islands to the Farne Islands, and from Auchmithie on the Angus coast to St Abbs on the Berwickshire coast and the Farnes off the Islandshire coast, I have seen a *lot* of puffins. So when this Isle of May puffin returned yet again just after I saw what I had never seen before, then stood facing right and hung around for a while, I was ready for when it took off again, to see if it repeated the manoeuvre. As soon as it turned its back to face the cliff edge, I focussed my camera lens and pressed the shutter button as the bird prepared to launch into space and kept pressing. I took one useful photograph. It showed the bird the instant before it left the cliff edge. The head was forward, the back was almost horizontal, almost parallel with the ground. The wings extended horizontally from the "shoulders", but only as far as the outer end of the "forearms", where both wings were angled down well past ninety degrees so that the wingtips pointed back *inwards* towards the bird's feet. It was in that attitude that it became airborne.

Then the bird was gone, the cliff edge was empty apart from a frieze of sea campion, and I was scratching my head. What was that manoeuvre designed to achieve? Air brakes? A tight bit of precise steering round the back of an inland-facing cliff and through a gap beyond before it could reach the open sea? Or extra speed? Eagles accelerate by half-folding their wings, but not like that. I consulted the one book I own that analyses bird flight and explains why certain birds deploy certain techniques to meet different circumstances. None of them approximated to what I had just seen. My dilemma was compounded by the fact that the puffin had vanished over the edge the instant it took flight, so I had no idea what followed. Perhaps I could pin down an expert in the sophistication of bird flight, and all would be prosaically explained. In the meantime, the extraordinary stillness of the eider, the restlessness of the puffin, and my constant interaction with the raw stuff of the island and its sea (and the mainland shore that set both off to such good advantage), have left me with a very persuasive sense of wilderness ensnared in a scrap of basalt anchored five miles off the coast of Lowland Fife.

Thirty
The Poetry of Mountain Flowers

EVERY APRIL, I MAKE the same promise to myself: I must become more fluent in the poetry of mountain flowers. I don't mean flower poetry ("Wee, modest, crimson-tipped flower"…"I wandered lonely as a cloud"…"Cwa' een like milk-wort and bog-cotton hair"…that kind of thing), but rather the almost invariably accidental poetry that characterises the language of the names of mountain flowers, whether composed by scientists or by real people.

This annual rekindling of good intentions is mostly occasioned by my first encounter with the mountains' idea of spring, with purple saxifrage. "*Saxifraga oppositifolia*," purrs the botanist, mysteriously scorning the bunched fists of startling purple flowers in favour of the plant's prosaic (some would say boring) character trait of leaves in opposite pairs, hence *oppositifolia*. Such dimwit tendencies make me wonder if science sometimes mislays its brains, yet no one with an ear for rhythm and cadence can deny the buoyant, flowing surge of *Saxifraga oppositifolia* when you roll it around your tongue.

The Gaelic, however, is something else: *clach-bhriseach purpaidh* – "purple stone-breaker". What genius came up with that one? What inspired mountain wanderer first examined an eye-level cluster of purple saxifrage under a dripping-wet rock overhang that far-off spring day, noticed that it was rooted in the very rock itself, and reached for the image of a stone-breaker, as if the plant had prised the rock apart by virtue of its own muscle-power, rather than parasitically exploiting an existing fissure? Whoever it was, a poet's sensibilities were at work. Anyone who believes that you cannot get blood out of a stone has never seen the *clach-bhriseach purpaidh* flex its tiny muscles on a wall of old granite. Likewise the sceptic who thinks faith cannot move mountains.

The poetry of saxifrages is even better served in the case of the starry saxifrage. In truth, it is no starrier than any of our other native saxifrages, but the sound of its Latin classification, *Saxifraga stellaris*, glitters like the nebula of Orion. And the Gael's *clach-bhriseach reul-tach*, the starry stone-breaker, is surely worthy of a constellation all of its own. The starry saxifrage and I go back a long way. I first met one face-to-face high on Beinn a'Bheithir above Ballachulish, and so long ago that it cost me a shilling (I was *very* young at the time). I had pulled a hanky (another artefact from a bygone age) from my pocket and the coin tumbled out with it, bounced once and disappeared into a crack a few inches wide. I fancied I could still see it glinting palely there, and I crouched down and peered into the gap. But all was black beneath except for the upturned star of a single white flower. It was starlight I had seen, not a shilling. Not long before this encounter, I had acquired the invaluable knowledge of inverting my binoculars to turn them into a microscope. This was its first practical application, and I discovered that the starry stone-breaker is much more than a five-pointed white star. Firstly, there are twice as many tiny red stamens as there are petals, and secondly, there are two vivid yellow spots on every petal. I know now that this discovery has the kind of impact on the botanic community that pointing out the red breast of robins has on ornithology, but then and there I was on my knees in wonderland.

And what really moved me was the tiny daring of the thing. The crack opened into a black underworld two or three feet deep and about as wide. There was space there for a whole Milky Way of starry saxifrages, but apparently sustenance enough for only one. That single stem with its single flower head aglow in that chamber of gloom is surely the most primitive – and the most poetic – thing I have ever seen. I have tried several times over the years to make a poem of it, and I will probably try again, but so far the thing has proved too elusive for me, as elusive as a shilling lost in a hole in the ground.

If none of that impresses you, perhaps I can interest you in the case of the mountain avens. The late glacial period of our last ice age, about 10,000–15,000 years ago, is known among people who worry about such things as the Dryas period. "Dryas" may not be the most lyrical-sounding of names, and *Dryas octopetala* is more percussive than lyrical, but there is a kind of poetic rightness about its unique significance. It is better known as the alpine flower, mountain avens. *Octopetala* is fairly straightforward – eight petals – but why *Dryas*? I'm glad you asked. Such was the profusion of mountain avens fossils datable from the late glacial period that the people who make decisions about how to christen swathes of time lasting 5,000 years drew their inspiration from arguably the loveliest of alpine flowers. No flower was ever better designed to make its mark on an ice age, or, for that matter, to thrive in 21st-century Scotland. From the north coast to Kintyre, and from Angus to the Hebrides, it turns the white star of its fair face to follow the sun through the day, likes cool and humid exposed places and has a contemptuous attitude to frost. So it is right at home on the Atlantic coast at sea level and on the flanks and broad ridges of our Highland and Border hills.

Alas for the mountain avens, poetry has rather let it down, which is strange and a touch unjust considering its beauty. Even the choice of *octopetala* is as suspect as it is prosaic, because out there in the wild world it can have anything between seven and ten petals. Perhaps science took its cue from the Gaels, whose *machall monaidh* means something like "large-flowered mountain plant", whereas any self-respecting poet would have mustered something like "yellow-hearted star of the mountain snows".

The older books of Seton Gordon offer intriguing glimpses into that inches-high world of alpines. Here he is on the subject of dwarf cornel, also known as *Cornus suecica*, a favourite of many a Cairngorms walker:

...At first glance, four white or pale yellow petals tinged with purple appear to grow on each flower stalk, but a closer inspection reveals that these "petals" are in reality "bracts" and their function is to attract by their conspicuous appearance the attention of the insects that fertilize the plant. The bracts surround a large number of minute purple flowers with yellow stamens. The fruit is a red berry. It was said by the Highlanders to create appetite, and the plant was called by them lus a' chraois – the herb of gluttony...

Poetic or what?

It is strange, now that I think about it, that I haven't tried to write more flower poems (two, actually), especially given the amount of time I spend on shores and mountains in thrall to those tiny species that seem to be able to move effortlessly between such extremes of habitat, but shun the in-between zones; something like sea pinks, for example, also known as thrift, or even sea thrift. They dance on the edge of the high tide, blasted by ocean winds and half drowned by salt spray, yet they also have the extraordinary capacity to smother the highest plateau thrusts of the Cairngorms at almost 4,000 feet in fleeting magic carpets of pink. Sometimes in its mountain guise it flowers for no more than a midsummer week or two before it is plagued by the Cairngorms' appetite for midsummer frosts or blizzards, or both, and shrivels to blackened husks.

Seton Gordon also wrote this little aside about it:

...Most botanists believe the thrift of the Cairngorms to be the sea thrift (Armeria maritima). An article by Mr Harold Stuart Thompson, F.L.S., on the thrift of the Scottish hills appeared in The Journal of Botany in 1910. This writer thought that the thrift of the hills was a form of Armeria maritima, but Mr F.N. Williams has suggested that it is really Armeria alpina, the thrift which grows on the western Alps from 7,000 to 9,000 feet above the sea.

Posterity seems to agree with Mr Thompson, and so do the Gaels, who call it *neomean cladaich* – "daisy of the shore" – wherever it happens to grow. Anyway, in the spirit of the poetry of mountain flowers, whether rooted on the Cairngorms plateau or on an island shore 4,000 feet lower, here is one of my two flower poems because it happens to be about thrift and because it's April again and I have just renewed my promise to myself.

PINK

Pink, you might think,
is a shade that ill-becomes
a Presbyterian sense of place

until a self-sown sea of thrift,
a drift of glowing snow,
invades the tidal space.

One Sunday-savvy otter,
respectful in Sabbatarian gray,
contemplative as a monk at Lent,
forgot herself that day,
and half-drunk on the scent,
squirmed wantonly, singing,
then trotted guiltlessly home
chasing butterflies and bees,
the tell-tale petals still clinging
to the fur above her knees.

I mentioned above that I have only written two flower poems. This is the second one (strange that they should both feature monks, but in case you are not well versed in jazz, the Monk referred to in this poem is Thelonious of that ilk, jazz pianist of distinction):

THE SOFTLY BLUES

The softly blues of speedwell
by a shadow-and-sunlight mountain tree
are pianissimo, man,
Monk in a minor key.

Easy now
with only height to lose,
I got those low-on-the-mountain
softly speedwell blues

Thirty-one
The Sanctuary

THE TREES I HOLD DEAREST are those that remember wolves. You will find them, for example, among the Scots pines of the Black Wood of Rannoch. Some have great girth and vast reach, having demanded their own space sometime in the first fifty years of their youth, and more than 200 years ago. Some are older, but dead. After 300 years of life, one of these has already stood for a hundred years of death – leafless, barkless, broken, bare, a tree of bones. But death for such trees does not impair their remembrance of wolves, any more than it impairs their capacity to sustain uncountable generations of uncountable numbers of lesser lives, lesser than Scots pines, lesser than wolves.

Wolves are not so long gone as you might think. Sometimes, here and there amid heartland tracts of Highland Scotland, like the Black Wood or the Black Mount hills and woods around Loch Tulla, I have become aware of an absence, and I put it down to wolves. That sounds finicky, I know, but such landscapes have a way of dislocating time. There is a harder-edged wildness at work there, and the sense of it reaches you almost like a scent, or the sound of it is in your ears like a threnody, for it laments its own incompleteness. For thousands of years, this was a land shaped almost as much by wolves as by ice, and the wolves were shaped by the forest.

Wolves have been gone from Rannoch for more than 200 years, but perhaps not much more. It is a perfectly plausible proposition that they held out in Rannoch's twin fastnesses, the Moor and the Black Wood, for decades after they had been rendered extinct in much of the rest of the land by the people because...because they were wolves. Tomorrow, some sweet tomorrow of our own choosing (and the decision is ours to make and the process is simple and the difficulties more or less non-existent and ecological benefits immense and permanent), we will declare the place a Sanctuary, and they will return to Rannoch, and the remembrance of both tribes, wolf and Scots pine, will renew and refresh.

Why Rannoch? Practicality and symbolism; the required beauty, the required grandeur, the required scale; and yes, if I am honest, for a stage that befits the dreaming and daring of such an enterprise of wild theatre. But mostly, it's the natural choice for the practicality and the symbolism, for Rannoch is at the centre of the land, and (as we have seen from the Lismore chapter) the forge that fashioned the shape and the nature of our post ice-age land, radiating glaciers from its towering ice cap in every direction, furrowing the land with glens and flooding them with lochs and sea lochs and firths. Besides, travel is in the nature of wolves, and over subsequent decades, new generations can radiate outwards from the centre in whatever directions they choose, following the natural spoor laid down by the Rannoch ice cap and its glaciers. It is the most organic process imaginable. And as they radiate, they will spread the lifeblood of ecological renewal, for theirs is essentially a benevolent, reinvigorating regime, and a healing regime for nature.

Aldo Leopold wrote in *A Sand County Almanac* (Oxford University Press, 1949):

> *The practices we now call conservation are, to a large extent, local alleviations of biotic pain. They are necessary, but they must not be confused with cures.*

Scotland's landscape requires cures, nature requires us to allow it to flourish unimpeded and on a scale it has not enjoyed in a thousand years. It sounds complicated and daunting. It is neither. One ferociously simple idea can go a long way towards achieving it.

Restore the treeline.

The treeline is the upper limit of altitude at which native trees grow naturally. In Scotland, that limit should be at a little over 2,000 feet; "should be" because although the treeline is still there, there are no trees anywhere near it. Actually, that's not quite true – there is Creag

Fhiaclach. If you were to clamber up through the Scots pines that still throng the flanks of Coire Buidhe above Loch an Eilean in the northern Cairngorms, you will eventually arrive at that melting point in landscape evolution where the corrie gives way to the plateau's almost limitless repertoire of winds. Now watch what happens. All the way up through the corrie, the pines have been growing in the normal way, and – naturally – they have thinned out and their stature has diminished towards the upper reaches. But then, and with a suddenness that startles, the trees shrink to waist height and then to knee height, and they have taken to growing horizontally. You wade among treetops. Welcome to Creag Fhiaclach, and welcome to what's left of Scotland's natural treeline. It's about 400 yards. That's it. That's all there is. But consider how many hundreds of miles of the 2,000-feet contour there must be in Scotland, then consider the astounding potential which would flow from a restored treeline. The only limit on that potential is our imagination, for once such an undertaking begins, nature's imagination would be literally limitless. "Rewilding" then, if it is to have lasting significance at all, depends on scale. Scale is everything. "Local alleviations of biotic pain" won't do. So why don't we consider restoring the treeline? All of it.

Of course, it cannot be restored in isolation, for a naturally occurring treeline must be fed and sustained from below. Essentially, what should be planted is a skeleton forest, within which nature will reassert its own priorities, its own diversity, its own densities of trees. And with our already steadily growing beaver workforce, wetland will reassert a crucial presence, crucial to the well-being of the forest, crucial to the flourishing of biodiversity. With the wolf to spearhead nature's reworking of the old order – the human order – the very land will begin to recover its health, and everything in nature will be better off and so will we. In a chapter called "The Land Ethic", Aldo Leopold had this to say on the subject of our relationship with nature:

> *The land ethic simply exchanges the boundaries of the community to include soils, water, plants, animals, or collectively: the land…a land ethic changes the role of Homo sapiens from conqueror of the land community to plain member and citizen of it. It implies respect for his fellow members…*

Spring

So that's why, wandering alone among the quiet places of the land, especially somewhere like Rannoch and the hills of the Black Mount beyond, I sense an absence that I put down to wolves, and that's why the trees I hold dearest are those that remember wolves.

★

The Black Mount is a western outpost of Rannoch if you approach from the east, or an eastern outpost of the historic realm of Glenorchy and Inishail if you approach from the west. In my mind's eye as I see it, and nature's mind's eye as she sees it, the Sanctuary extends from Rannoch in the north and east to Loch Tay / Loch Dochart / Loch Awe / Loch Etive in the south and west. If you follow that progression from Rannoch, east to west, sooner or later you will part the screen of a sudden pinewood and find Loch Tulla there, as wild as it is beautiful, robed in trees, besotted by mountains.

A tiny island not far from the shore harbours a clutch of larch trees. The sea eagles that used to nest there every year were blasted to oblivion in the 19th century. Their near neighbours on a birch-clad island at the western edge of the Moor met with the same fate. But this was always eagle country, and it did not stop being eagle country just because its eagles were (what's the word?)…euthanised. Besides, if I think I can sense the land's mournful remembrance of wolves, surely this century's generations of wandering young sea eagles raised on both coasts can surely sense (and mourn) the absence of their ancestors as they drift this way with increasing frequency, for what they see is a land fit for sea eagles and ready to be re-colonised. They also see that golden eagles still live here, for they somehow clung on despite the slaughter. They were always warier of man and his guns, always presented more elusive targets, and today the presence of golden eagles is a good omen for the sea eagles. The old island nesters of Loch Tulla and Rannoch Moor could both see the comings and goings of the golden eagles that nested at a certain crag not far away, and when the new sea eagle generations reoccupy the same sites they, too, will see the comings and goings of the new golden eagle generations at that same certain crag.

As for the eagles of the crag and the air and the water, so for the wolves of the mountain, moor and forest. This was wolf country, too, and for the same reasons: the wildness, the space, the food supply, and the more or less limitless opportunities to reach out to new territories in every direction and so extend their presence, to lay claim to the Sanctuary. And those other great manipulators of wild country in nature's cause, Scotland's reintroduced beavers, are already nibbling around its edges. Serious inroads are a matter of time. The world-famous reintroduction of wolves into Yellowstone in the northern United States has demonstrated that wolves and beavers work in tandem to transform biodiversity. This land, this Sanctuary, is where nature can begin again to effect cures.

I stepped this way one early May day of that backward spring, and I went first in search of its ospreys. In the story of the osprey's return to Scotland of its own volition, which began in the 1950s, the ospreys of Loch Tulla were comparative latecomers. If you know where to look, there is a sightline through trees to an osprey eyrie. Further south and east they had bucked that season's trend of migrating birds by turning up right on time, but it became obvious at first glance through the pinewood to where the nest tree stands on the loch shore that here they had not turned up at all. The nest, what was left of it from the previous year after a winter's mauling by wet gales and snow winds, slumped at an angle that suggested one more healthy gust could tip the whole edifice onto the beach. It was a forlorn ruin with a tuft of grass growing in what had once been redoubtable timbered walls. That grass was the nest's only sign of life. It was possible, of course, that the ospreys had abandoned the site and moved further up the shore or across the loch, but that day and a return visit ten days later would reveal no glimpse of them, no sign of a new nest.

It was a troubling omen, for I had shown to my own satisfaction that waters where ospreys thrived were also likely to suit wandering sea eagles looking for territories as their recovery spreads across the face of the land. Seton Gordon wrote very specifically about both sea eagles and golden eagles right here, and as evidence grows of sea eagles returning to historic sites, sites where they once thrived more than a century ago, I have high hopes for this one. It seems perfect in every way. But as I write this, I am no nearer to knowing why the osprey nest was not rebuilt. I am consoled, however, by personal observation of young sea eagles moving in both directions between Scotland's east and west coasts, and more often than not their line of travel is along a swathe of latitude roughly between the Tay estuary and Mull, so Loch Tulla is perfectly placed and it is surely nothing more than a question of time.

Meanwhile, early May around Loch Tulla was not looking like itself. The larches wore only the mistiest, palest of green tinges; a square yard of wood anemones at the foot of a pine tree was the only flower in sight; the hill grasses simply looked defeated; the mountain overlord of Stob Gobhar across the loch was still scarfed and banded with deep snow, and a new powdery fleece had gathered around the summit in the night. I headed for the shore. There are often signs of otters along the banks where a quiet river uncoils from the west, so I would start there.

It was the very last few inches above the shore where spring suddenly stirred: a pair of common sandpipers I had simply not seen sped out from a hidden patch of muddy ooze, inches above the water, inches above their own reflections; these are birds that deal in inches. They piped in high-pitched triplets and quadruplets, curved in a surface-skimming arc to a new shoreline ooze where they landed, flared their wings inches-high above their heads, and fell silent, tails working like silent metronomes. It was a start.

Then the cuckoos.

Out of profound silence two birds began a precisely executed call-and-response routine, so precise that the second bird sounded like a perfect echo of the first, so perfect that I wondered if it *was* an echo. But then the second bird moved closer to me and the first one stayed put, and still they called without a break, on and on and on, cuckoos on a loop. What finally stopped them was the intervention of a third bird, a third call, a wrecking ball for the rhythmically perfect call-and-response of the first two birds. They stopped calling at once. But now the third bird went on alone, and to add to the chaos it had already caused, its call was "wrong". The standard, production-line cuckoo call is a minor third. This one was a major fifth. But the high note was imperfectly formed, for it emerged as something like a corvid squawk, as if the bird was determined to hit the note right in the middle but lacked the range and had to reach for it, and never quite got there.

It is still the only time I have heard such a thing, but once, up in the golden eagle glen I know best among the mountains of Balquhidder, a jazz cuckoo turned up and lingered for weeks. Instead of the two-note, minor third production-line call, it had a third note. But the three notes were not equally spaced. The third note had a slight delay built in, so that the rhythm it produced was that of a jazz waltz. As a part-time jazz guitar player myself, and as one who has composed a jazz waltz (mysteriously titled "A Wee Jazz Waltz"), this particular cuckoo was a particular delight. On days when the eagles failed to show, it would brighten the mood with its jazzy voice. What I wonder is whether the distinctive voice passes down the generations or whether (as I suspect) it dies with the singer, in much the same way that Frank Sinatra Junior ain't no Frank Sinatra.

Eventually, all three Loch Tulla cuckoos fell silent. I wondered how they would fare in such a spring. Because the insects were drastically depleted by the overlong winter, so were the insect-eating birds – like the pipits that cuckoos rely on to bring up their monstrous chicks, with their perverse instincts and built-in egg-eviction scoops on their backs, which clear pipit eggs from pipit nests. Sometimes nature works in mysterious ways. I don't believe for a moment that there is such a thing as "the balance of nature", and whenever I hear anyone extolling the virtue of such a phantom concept I offer up the same response: it's cuckoo.

★

"*Tiu-tiu-tiu, tiu-tiu-tiu…*"

Ah, that new voice is no cuckoo. And in this corner of the Highlands it is as rare an utterance in the conversation of spring as the cuckoo is ubiquitous. I had expected to find ospreys and found none; in my wildest dreams I did not expect greenshanks, and I found two. They came towards me as low over the water as sandpipers, wingtips almost touching, then split to two different scraps of shoreline fifty yards apart. As each bird landed, one three or four seconds after the other, it also displayed the sandpiper habit, the habit of many waders: it raised elegantly angled and pointed wings high over its back, and these were silvery white in the still reluctant sunlight.

Greenshanks dress to blend in. They wear the shades of summer peat bogs and bog cotton; or, on the wrong kind of sluggishly cold May day, the shades of peat bogs and snow. The shades in question are dark grey and light grey and white and green and greyish-brown and greyish-white and greyish-green. On the nest, which is typically a half-hearted scrape in the surface matter of Sutherland and Caithness or Lewis and Harris (so cool, wet, rocky, peaty, watery, windy), the brooding bird sits in the lee of a small rock or a piece of ancient bog-wood, and the chances are you won't see it at ten paces, which is why the greenshank dresses to blend in.

But greenshanks are also the most contradictory creatures in the Northlands. They are waders that don't flock. And while they may wear the shades of peat bogs and bog cotton in order to be more or less invisible, they will insist on opening their mouths and giving the game away. Even the bog-standard contact call of the greenshank (never mind their high-up and handsome pre-nuptial, pair-bonding carol) can water the eyes and gladden the heart of ornithologists. It says "*cheep*", but it does so with a silence-stabbing potency and a hint of impending pibroch that are the stuff of birder eulogies. If you are fortunate enough or skilful enough (usually both qualities are required) to be present within sight of a nest when the birds change over on the eggs, the approaching bird announces its arrival, and then its presence, with an outburst of extrovert cheeping that can last for ten or fifteen minutes, and if you don't know what you are listening to by that time, then you need to get out more.

And to further undermine its low-key presence in solitary, wild places, when it flies away from you it flashes a white blaze of feathers in the sunlight that tightens your throat and confirms your diagnosis, and you mutter under your breath to no one at all: "Ah, greenshank!"

The best conditions in which to view a "drab" bird like a green-shank are not to be found in days of blue-skied sunlight, but on days like that one of thick, fat clouds welded together to smother every square mile of open sky, when the sand dunes are as dulled as cold tea, and late winter is drawing its blinds down to meet the advent of dusk. Then, that solitary greenshank, that haunter of lonely shores and wild, unpeopled tracts of the north of the land, is suddenly and mysteriously aglow, a creature of some finery. Every dark-greyish feather on its back and upper wings is edged in white, which imparts to the bird an air of stained-glass delicacy quite at odds with the kind of life it leads. The white of its underparts rises up towards its neck and throat where it is striped with black, stripes that break up into orderly lines of tiny patches. The bird zipped around the shallowest stretches of the pool, sifting it with lowered and ever so slightly upturned bill. It moved in mazy, unpredictable courses, and in the flat white light that bounced back from the water and the snow, this single greenshank glowed like a fragment of one of the windows of Chartres.

These new arrivals at Loch Tulla were no winter refugees, but a pair that showed every indication of nesting. And even though they were a long way south of what one might think of as their breeding heartlands, there is something about this loch and its immediate surroundings that reeks of wildness, that beckons to what a nature writer is apt to think of as symbols of wildness, and the greenshank is certainly one of those. If you come on the place having crossed Rannoch Moor, or (as is almost invariably the case in my travels) from the southmost edge of the Highlands through Balquhidder and Glen Dochart, or even from the north – from, say, Glencoe or the Ben Nevis range – there is a sudden sense of an oasis, of a harder-edged, thicker-skinned landscape that seems to belong directly to none of its surrounding lands and watersheets.

The pinewoods have something to do with that. Native woodland invariably adds a wild edge to a mountain landscape that is missing where the trees have been wiped out by the dead hand of deer forest and grouse moor management. Rannoch Moor was a woodland, the souvenirs are everywhere buried in its peat, bits of trees that – if you could ask them – would tell you all you ever needed to know about wolves in the Sanctuary. Where the woodland is still present, to one extent or another, nature tries harder, and those wilderness-thirled species that find it so hard to find a home in Scotland are drawn to the Loch Tullas of the land. Witness the frequent encounters with pine marten droppings in the woods, along the tracks and even on the road. And now, having been troubled by the desolation of the osprey nest, I was reassured to some extent by the discovery of a pair of greenshanks.

One of the birds had perched by the mouth of the river and began walking the shore of the loch towards me. The second bird called twice then flew across the bay to land right beside the other. They came on together, stabbing the mud, sifting the water's edge, reaching into the nearest tussocks. Everything about their behaviour suggested they were newly arrived, that they had yet to contemplate a nest site (the male doesn't so much build a nest as scrape a choice of three or four token depressions in the land; the female chooses one of them, apparently on the basis of it being somewhere to sit and better than nothing, but not much). For the moment, they were flying and feeding companionably. Abruptly, they turned back along the shore then flew into the mouth of the river and vanished among its high-banked bends. I set off slowly and quietly in their wake, with the secondary intention to check for otters. A leisurely exploration of the mouth of the river revealed some old otter spraints, no new tracks, an astonished pair of greylag geese that burst up from the quiet river in an explosion of big wings and far too many decibels for the good of my intentions, for their explosive flight away across the loch had alerted my presence to every other tribe of nature within half a mile. I quietly withdrew and promised myself to return in around two weeks to check on the greenshanks.

Late in the afternoon, driving out along the single-track road to Bridge of Orchy and the road east, there was a last glimpse through the pinewoods to the loch. I was driving slowly, the road was empty, and I was happily rewinding the day through my mind while keeping one eye on the road and the other on the land as it drifted by. There was a small flash on a last corner of the loch but vivid enough to be eye-catching. It was a fragmentary thing, a tiny flaring of bright white, but a thing that struck the corner of an eye in a way that roused that instinct which I trust so utterly. I pulled off the road to investigate but already I thought I knew what I had just seen, for it was another of my native land's ambassadors for wildness, and I had glimpsed it occasionally on Loch Tulla over the years. There it was again, in the glasses this time, the same heaving movement and just a few yards out from the shore. It was a movement like a boat rolling, baring the hull all the way to the keel, then righting itself, the whiteness diminishing then vanishing as the motion restored to its proper place a superstructure immaculately patterned in black and white and marbled grey. Behold the black-throated diver preening as it swims.

Then I realised there was a second bird just ahead of the first, swimming slowly towards a small and thickly wooded island just offshore, the perfect setting for a black-throat nest. They would like the cover, and as long as there was a short and easy route from the water to a flat nesting area that involved no more than two or three yards of walking, it looked ideal. The walking distance would be crucial, however, for although the black-throat is a supreme swimmer both on the surface and underwater, and a powerful flier, its legs are set so far back in its body that it walks with all the aplomb of a fencepost. That second bird, which I took to be the female, vanished behind the island and did not reappear, but its mate remained in full view, and going nowhere fast. Crouching by a broken old pine trunk, and with my head already full of the day's events and an atmosphere that had led me to pursue a train of thought about the particular species of wildness I always sensed when I came here, I suddenly had a strange moment of déjà vu.

It involved a different diver on a different loch, and for that matter a different pair of binoculars, for it was more than thirty years ago. I had gone to visit an old friend, the late Mike Tomkies, at the isolated Loch Shiel cottage he called Wildernesse. Mike was the most uncompromising nature writer I ever met, and in the early days of a friendship that sadly did not go the distance, he was incredibly generous and encouraging to me. He had done some groundbreaking work on his local black-throats, and he was raving quietly to me about them and what they meant to him while we watched a pair joust with the waves that could suddenly tear across that loch with the breath of an Atlantic storm about them. I can do the moment no better service than to quote a passage about them in his best book, *A Last Wild Place* (Cape, 1984):

For me they embody as no other creature does the wild spirit of the loch...when flying high on their short but powerful wings they look like arrows of twanging steel...Their magnificent summer plumage, with its rich blend of slate greys, blue greys, purples, blacks, creamy underparts and sooty throat patches must be the sleekest of all water birds', and their array of intricate white neck stripes and snowy wing bars, if you're lucky enough to get close, dazzle the human eye...

He also described it in purposeful swimming mode as "steaming along like a small barge".

On Loch Tulla that cold day at the beginning of May 2018, the "barge" in my binoculars was idling, and there were the stripes and there were the dazzling, snowy wing bars. I was as sure as I could be that these two divers were not yet nesting, that they somehow epitomised the particular aura of wildness that I always sensed on this high, mountain-and-pinewood loch, that they functioned almost as an ecological barometer of the place, and that – like the greenshanks – they were waiting for that backward spring to catch up, and that if it did not catch up soon, they might simply not nest at all. My mind drifted from there to those other rarities of nature in the Scottish Highlands that inhabited the place – the greenshanks, the wandering sea eagles, the native golden eagles, the otters, the pine martens and the ospreys that had so mysteriously failed to appear; and how I would love to know if somewhere in the wildest fastnesses of the loch's mountains and pinewoods there might not also be a surviving pocket of wildcats. If such an isolated survival can happen anywhere, it can happen here. Two weeks later, the very middle of May, I was back, and I was looking for all of the above, but more than anything else, seeking reassurance about the greenshanks and the divers.

The day was warm, the first really warm day of the year, as long as you kept something solid between yourself and an edgy east wind that had barely paused for breath since it ushered in the "Beast from the East" at the beginning of March. There were new pine marten droppings right at my feet as soon as I stepped in among the trees. I headed straight for the mouth of the river with the intention of working back from there as far along the loch shore as inclination led me. I noticed as I walked that there was no hint of new grass anywhere, that the mountains were still ridged and heftily corniced with snow. The river revealed nothing at all, absolutely nothing: no living mite, no tracks in the mud, no otter spraint, no greenshank call, no sandpiper piping. It was as if the season had gone backwards, despite all the new warmth and the sunlight. I turned and walked the loch shore, a narrow strip of bog and tussock between the water's edge and the birch and pine-woods that climb steeply there. The big larches out on the headland looked marginally greener, and as I scanned the woodland I admired alder, willow, rowan, holly in small cliques, but only the holly was green.

I reached the osprey tree in a mood that was tumbling towards something uncharacteristically morose. Then a greenshank flew from the very edge of the shore and only seven or eight feet in front of me. I had not seen it; it had been sitting tight until it lost its nerve. I thought for a moment I might have disturbed a nesting bird, but it flew in complete silence, and a thorough search revealed nothing at all. Its footprints were everywhere in the mud, however, so it was reasonable to conclude that it had simply been feeding. It flew about 200 yards to a spit of land that jutted into the loch, and there it vanished, and I saw no sign of it thereafter, no sign of its mate. The osprey nest appeared to have tilted a little more. I pored over the loch, found some wigeon and teal by the far shore, the two greylags, and nothing else at all, certainly nothing that looked like a black-throated diver.

I turned the glasses on the mountains. I know one golden eagle eyrie just a watershed away, and sometimes on previous visits I have seen the birds cross it in both directions from the lochside. I watched for over an hour – the sky, the ridges, and that elusive middle distance as Mike had taught me. The snow on a long stretch of ridge had melted from a series of buttresses just below the ridge, creating the impression of a system of arches, a sort of viaduct of solid snow, an extraordinary illusion that blazed in the sunlight. But no eagle shadow crossed the viaduct. I had come that day with two ideas in mind: one, to catch up on the greenshanks and the divers; the other, to check on the progress of spring. Now I decided to move to a high wedge of pinewood so that I could sit and watch the island where I had seen the divers. I found a broad pine trunk with a flat ledge among the roots and a cushion of pine needles, out of the wind and in the sun. My job does not get much better than this.

I had a long, lingering look at the island in the glasses. The two sides of it that I could see were thickly wooded right to the very edge, a few old and tall birches, the rest of it crammed with alder. I could make out nothing that confirmed either the presence of a diver nest or the complete absence. It was always possible that on the first visit the birds were simply prospecting, exploring various possibilities before they felt ready to nest, or perhaps before they felt that the laggard spring was ready for them.

I settled in for a lengthy stay, ate lunch about 3p.m. (it's the sort of thing that happens on such occasions, suddenly I think: "Oh, food. I should eat.").

There was a wide view over the bay beyond the island towards the south-east corner of the loch and to the mountains beyond. As the afternoon advanced, the sun warmed and the wind that roughened the surface all day fell away and the loch grew calm. It also changed colour over an hour or so from serried greys to almost colourless white to sky blue and then to an ever-deepening blue as the sun shrugged off the last of the clouds. Every few minutes I quartered the loch and island with the binoculars. In between these searches I watched the trees, the sky, or just let my eyes wander, scanning the middle distance. Sometimes, when you just sit, effectively become pine tree or mountainside, or in this case, both, nature sends out an emissary to check you out. Not today. Nothing moved. I opened a notebook, laid a pen across its open pages. Sometimes you have your most original thoughts when you are out there and nature drops something priceless into the lap of your stillness. An hour later, the pen still lay where I had put it, the white paper unbesmirched.

I looked at my watch finally. It had been five hours in all, three of them sitting right here. These are the days when you learn a little about the pace at which nature sometimes moves; these are the days when you learn a little more about yourself in nature's company – how you respond when she makes unusual demands of you. Then somewhere between 300 and 400 yards out from the island, a moment of bright white amid the deep blue. A breaking wave stirred up by a stray gust? Or…even in the binoculars I was unconvinced, for it vanished as soon as it brightened. Then it stood on its tail, opened and flexed short wings and the bright white flared again. Then I saw it dive, and it was grey and black as it dived. And that was it.

One glimpse of a greenshank, one of a diver. Nothing more, but oddly, it was reassurance enough. I have never needed to know where the nests are, I was never that kind of nature writer. Nests are places where people should not be. Nests are what the wildlife needs to get by, to maintain their toehold on a scrap of land. We should be no part of that. What matters to me is that they are here. That they take their place in the biodiversity of this extraordinarily beautiful loch. Of all places, I learned that lesson most vividly right here.

Mike Tomkies' last word on the black-throated divers was this:

Here, like the eagle or the wildcat, is a creature beyond man, rare because it is beautiful, rare because its needs are sensitive, rare because it requires solitude and has for centuries survived in true wildness. It is the true spirit of the magical loch…The loch will out-live me and possibly all human life and all I can do is seek a little longer to know its heart.

Thirty-two
Renaissance

THE HOPEFUL OAK

Salome she isn't
(she dances without veils)

she's quite dead
but still dances

naked and skeletally elegant
trunk straight (dead straight)

three limbs six branches
upraised broken-ended

yet lovingly tended
flimsily screened

scantily greened
by three birch saplings

Salome she isn't
but even naked and dead

she reaches hopefully
for the stars

GLEN FINGLAS HAS BECOME CENTRAL to my writing life. In the landscape I think of as my nature writer's territory, it lies on the first upslope

of the Highland mountains as you enter them from the south. Behind you lies Loch Venachar, whence the local ospreys will fly across the last of the Lowland hills to their south, two miles to a low-lying, shallow and conspicuously well-stocked loch, in search of easy pickings among the anglers in their boats. Then, of course, they must gain a thousand feet of height again, this time carrying two pounds or so of rainbow trout, re-cross the hills, then glide back down to the nest tree. All of this is a much more fruitful technique than peering into the unguessable depths of the loch at the base of their nesting tree, the tree where a sitting bird facing north looks out across the loch to a mountainside that is in the throes of changing colour, of transforming the fortunes of everything that lives there; it is, truly, a landscape in the throes of renaissance.

I walk here regularly in every season, often following the same paths and the same routes through the higher pathless tracts, because the walking offers the opportunity to watch the renaissance of a landscape in real time. This is how you bring a lost landscape back to life. It may not change visibly from day to day (other than those endless variables wrought by conspiracies of light and weather and season), but if you continue returning over the months and years you develop a sense of nature at work in a primitive, imaginative and benevolent way. Nature's secrets are uncovered by reworking the familiar, by trying to write what I think of as the portraiture of place, and by going back again and again over years, decades, understanding it better each time.

And when you tread an unfamiliar landscape for the first time, you take the familiar with you, in your head, in your fingertips (because you have touched the trees and the old rocks, and because your pen hand has written them down) and in your heart because you have learned to love that confiding familiarity; and when you look at any unfamiliar land through the prism of that familiarity with nature and how it works, you find that – of course – the unfamiliar land works in very much the same way.

I had stepped aside from the path up through the oakwood because the slant of ice-cold spring sunlight had illuminated a tree in a certain way so that its shape had caught my eye, and I thought I might photograph it or draw it or simply sit beside it for a while and try to write it down. It was fostering a rowan in its fork; where the trunk divided into three mighty limbs, a bowl had formed and a hundred years or so of bits and pieces of the parent tree had accumulated there, broken down into a kind of compost fuelled by a hundred years of rain water and, I suppose, the occasional accumulation of snow. Somewhere along the line a bird or a squirrel or a pine marten had disposed of an undigested rowan seed there, and it took root. I sat and scribbled, and one way or another I looked into my idea of the mind of the oakwood and tried to fathom out its sense of itself. Put like that, it sounds faintly preposterous, a fool's errand at best, yet such approaches to nature in pursuit of a kind of intimacy have been at the heart of nature writing for 200 years. Here is Henry David Thoreau writing in *Walden*:

One old man, who has been a close observer of Nature, and seems as thoroughly wise in regard to all her operations as if she had been put upon the stocks when he was a boy and he had helped to lay her keel...

I thought of the beginning of this very book, of the arrival of autumn geese above my boyhood home when I was a four-year-old, and what was that but nature "put upon the stocks", and had I not been helping to lay the keel ever since? And what was this with the oakwood but another plank in the keel?

The point of the endeavour is twofold: to enhance the relationship between the writer and his subject, and to foster a climate in which the eternal possibility exists of the miraculous, the unpredictable moment of revelation. The American Barry Lopez wrote in *Arctic Dreams* (Scribner, 1986):

Whatever evaluation we finally make of a stretch of land, no matter how profound or accurate, we will find it inadequate. The land retains an identity of its own, still deeper and more subtle than we can know. Our obligation toward it then becomes simple: to approach with an uncalculating mind, with an attitude of regard. To try to sense the range and variety of its expression – its weather and colour and animals. To intend from the beginning to preserve some of the mystery within it as a kind of wisdom to be experienced, not questioned. And to be alert for its openings, for that moment when something sacred reveals itself within the mundane, and you know the land knows you are there.

Fat trunks rippled with inches-deep moss, fooled the eye with too-early-in-the-spring foliage of ferns, not oak leaves. An ambience of age pervades the innards of a mature oakwood, assisted by stillness. I could hear wind, but it was high up and elsewhere, and the woodland floor was breathless. I followed the edge of a kind of terrace where self-sown birch saplings crowded into the space vacated by felled spruce plantations from the bad old days. In the damp and eager hillsides of the Highland Edge, birch trees are the most enthusiastic of colonists, and everywhere in their wake come the willows, the alders, the rowans, the hollies, the occasional splash-and-tremble of aspens. Beyond this incursion, the oaks resumed, and I met one leviathan tree that had insisted on – and now defended – a vast tract of land and airspace. Beneath it there flourished another level terrace of short, emerald grass, and that moment of that March afternoon of the backward spring, something suddenly yielded and sunlight flooded the terrace. That was the oak's gift to me. I sat, spread out lunch, notebook, sketchbook, camera; I basked in nature's company, "…and the land knows you are there…"

The nearest oak tree to the leviathan was about twenty yards away. It was a runt, impossible to age (without a saw), just as it was impossible to assess how long it had stood like that, for it was quite dead. But I was captivated by its form, its pose that suggested dance. The trunk was slender and straight for no more than a dozen feet, split into three skinny limbs and six skinnier branches, all of them broken and not a single twig among them. But from where I sat, and as if to disguise or otherwise mitigate its many fatal wounds, three birch saplings cast a net of twigs before it, and as the first of the spring buds were beginning to open, the effect was of a see-through, soft-focus screen behind which the dead tree was frozen in an attitude of dance. I made the poem that begins this chapter for it.

★

The steep path changes character once it emerges from the oakwood. The oak trees had been hemmed in on the lowest slopes for so long by commercial plantation above, the thoughtlessness of the forestry industry. But once the regime changed, once Woodland Trust Scotland replaced Forest Enterprise, once the spruces were felled for good (very much for good) and the mission to re-establish a native Highland woodland ecology was in place, a combination of nature at its most opportunistic and thoughtful hand-planting has been transformative: a mountain birchwood has materialised in less than twenty years. Birds, butterflies, flowers, and a vastly populated new world of invertebrate life have nailed their colours to the mast of the enterprise – their colours, their voices, their eagerness to participate in the born-again mountain. So have a few mammals, notably fox, pine marten, red squirrel, roe deer, stoats and weasels, and I would love to discover that wildcats had found their way back here too, but the fates are stacked against the wildcat in Scotland and the stars are not well aligned, so I am not holding my breath. But all these mammal tribes use the paths to travel, and you find their inches-wide trails through the undergrowth again and again, especially around places they regularly anoint with their droppings. Walk softly, especially in the quietest hours of the quietest days and nights, and sooner or later you will meet them all.

The path responds to this new world variously. Firstly, its verges are freed from the deep shade of the oakwood canopy and eager colonisers have moved in to the sunnier, rainier, snowier, windier world of life beyond the oaks, from Scottish bluebells to eyebright and tormentil, to thistles and inches-high hollies, Scots pine, willow, broom, rowans and alders, among much else. Secondly, if you study the path from time to time (as well as the near and far trees, the skyline, the sky, and that so-critical middle distance – it's a complicated and imprecise trade being a nature writer), you can sometimes read about some of the inmates, especially the mammals. And if you go often enough, occasionally you get very, very lucky.

April was already a week old, and I imagine the weather forecasters were looking for high cliffs to jump from, for it was becoming increasingly hit-or-miss. The temperature in the south of England was fifteen-to-eighteen degrees, and here it was three-to-four. On the question of the icy rain moving through Scotland consolidating into snow, the Met Office seemed to have acquired an approach wondrously articulated by an old hill man I used to know as: "Maybe aye, maybe hooch-aye". Driving across the Highland Edge to Glen Finglas, it became increasingly clear to me that I had unwillingly embarked on an exercise in catching up with a weather front, and by the time I had walked up the path to the point where it cleared the oakwoods I was already deep in that twilight zone between rain and snow and walking steeply uphill...

I stopped to examine a skinny black hieroglyph in the short grass at the edge of the path, and I recognised it as the signature of a pine marten. Then I noticed there was another one on the far side, and just where one of those trails of bent-over undergrowth shimmied away deep into a swarm of birches so dense that the prospects of easing myself through it were not good. This second marten dropping was markedly fresher than the first. How long gone, I wondered. So I listened hard to the wood, and apart from the soft hiss of the hybrid snow-rain and the mutter of a hill burn, there was nothing at all to listen to. Not so much as a syllable of birdsong. This upside-down and back-to-front spring, which had shown up in February with the mistle thrush, had been bludgeoned into submission by the turbulence of March and vanished off the face of the Earth. Not a shred of new green clung to a single tree. In the tussocks beneath the trees, where the trail burrowed into the understorey of the wood, there were puddles of melted snow, and here and there were pockets of unmelted snow where the overhead cover was thickest. Everything about these thousands and thousands of birch saplings and the thickly grown grass-and-heather-and-fern-and-berry-plant hillside they grew out of was utterly cold and utterly sodden.

I walked on but I had taken no more than four or five steps when something stirred a couple of yards from my left boot and just inside the trees, something that had been there all the time and only its stillness had prevented me from seeing it. It was broad and brown and blurred, and my immediate first impression was that it had jumped a vertical yard into the air from a standing start, or even a lying one. My immediate first impression was quite wrong. It had *flown* a vertical yard into the air from a standing start, or a lying one. Then it snapped into focus and it was a woodcock. First of all, how do they do that? How do they generate the lift for that vertical take-off out of such cloying surroundings? Second of all, how do they learn the exquisitely articulate horizontal flight that followed? I had crouched again to watch it go, and I saw perhaps the first dozen yards of its flight. The gaps between the twiggy extremities of so many close-huddled birches varied between narrow and non-existent. So the flight dodged left and right, and first one wingtip dipped and then the other, and in addition the woodcock had to rise and fall every yard of the way, yet the flight was fluent and unfaltering.

It left a wake, for its wingtips (and I daresay its head and beak and breast, but especially its wingtips) flicked countless twigs as it flew, and every twig unleashed a shower or a cloud of brilliant droplets backlit by a low and wan and appropriately watery sun. For seconds after the woodcock vanished, the trees and their shed cargo of icy water hissed and shivered and shimmered. It was over and done with almost at once. It was and it remains simply one of the most beautiful things I have ever seen.

As the cloud slipped lower and I climbed higher, the rain yielded to steadily falling snow, so I spent more time watching the path, and there were more pine marten scats and more fox scats than I had ever seen there before, and quite a few of them looked fresh. It was reasonable enough, for if the dense undergrowth of the birch saplings was truly saturated – and it was – it made travel for such as a fox and a pine marten pretty uncomfortable, whereas the wide, rough-surfaced path designed for humans (their boots and their mountain bikes) was easy going for both fox and marten, and on such a day as this, mine was the only car in the car park and I was the only human in that part of the wood. All this I registered, and so I took extra care to move quietly and slowly, for who knows what might be round the next corner?

But first I turned aside for the waterfall. The fall is bridged now, or rather the mountain burn that feeds it is, and some distance above, carrying the new path. But for much of its life, there was just the fall. The crag the fall dignifies with its voices (for it has many voices) is still as well-wooded as ever – oak, rowan, birch, a few shapely pines and shapeless hollies, for the foresters and the grazing tribes kept their distance from its gorge – but I imagine all of that once yielded above the crag to the frumpy tenacity of junipers: stumble across these as you descended from the heights, floundering for your bearings in mountain cloud and snow like this, and it would have been as if you had blundered into an encampment of ghostly dwarfs to add to your troubles.

So the fall was ever a turned-aside kind of place, although now there is a signpost proclaiming a "viewpoint" (as if the whole wondrous mountainside is anything less than a natural festival of viewpoints, hundreds of them, if you have seeing eyes, constantly changing, constantly redefining), beyond which an admittedly discreet made-up path curls enticingly out of sight, although it ends fifty yards later at a railed-off stance carved out of the rock. Behold the viewpoint. Behold the waterfall.

The fall is split in two right at the top by a central pillar of rock. The left-hand fall is narrow and contained by a cleft at first but begins to widen as it emerges, then after about twenty feet it hits a ledge and explodes. The right-hand fall is three or four times wider, but it too is briefly constrained by a second cleft before it hits the same ledge, the falls unite and drape a single white curtain eighty feet down the rock face as if magnetised to it. The beauty of the thing is never less than haunting. When the burn is at its most boisterous, the effect is somehow emotional as well as beautiful. I know many waterfalls, and I like to linger beside them, but none moves me the way this one does, and perhaps it is simply because I visit it so often, although I think there may be more to it than I am willing to concede. I'm still working on it.

Gavin Maxwell wrote in *Ring of Bright Water* (Penguin, 1960) that the waterfall near his house was "the soul of Camusfearna". Another of my favourite writers, Ernest Hemingway, was thinking out loud about the soul in *True at First Light* (Arrow, 1999). He was in Africa and had been unable to sleep, and remembered a line of Scott Fitzgerald:

In a real dark night of the soul it is always three o'clock in the morning.

That got my attention because although I have no concept of what a soul might be or whether it exists, I have my share of three-in-the-morning darknesses. Hemingway was casting about for what the concept might be "in the terms that I believed" and came up with this:

Probably a spring of clear fresh water that never diminished in the drought and never froze in the winter was closest to what we had instead of the soul they all talked about.

And there was that line of Mike Tomkies about the black-throated divers being "the true wild spirits of the magical loch".

It seems to me that, in this context at least, this reaching for a soul/spirit is a way of literally coming to terms with a quality of beauty or primitiveness or wildness in nature that we struggle to put into words. Considering the accumulated skills of the writers I have just summoned in the matter of putting things into words, and considering that none of them is convincing in the use of the words "soul" or "spirit" (and they all assert or imply that religion has nothing to do with it), is it not just symptomatic of an acknowledgement that there are moments in our dealings with nature that we are unable to articulate because, as a species, we have distanced ourselves too much from nature, and the animal bonds which would once have bound us into nature's family have loosened and frayed to the point where we occasionally glimpse the ultimate fear, which is that there may be no way back? Or there is this from Barry Lopez in *Arctic Dreams*:

The land is like poetry: it is inexplicably coherent, it is transcendent in its meaning, and it has the power to elevate the consideration of human life.

I like that thought very much.

I don't live within earshot of the Glen Finglas fall, although I do sometimes dream about it, and I treasure moments I've spent there. I have also thought a lot about the kind of place it must have been when the land was wholly wild, before the forestry industry, before the overgrazing of the landowning regimes that preceded that, before hunting kings offered bounties on wolves…and perhaps 5,000 years ago when the native woodland was at its height and that country was at its most biologically replete, and that fall still fell. Something of that continuity inhabits the ambience of waterfalls perhaps to a greater extent than any other landscape feature. We are drawn to them in the first place because of their aesthetics, but we linger because they command us to with their inexplicably poetic coherence.

At the Glen Finglas waterfall, a rock wall near the viewpoint accommodates an alder. It grows horizontally from a crack in the rock. How deep within the rock's fissured and fractured innards this perverse tree has propelled its roots is a question to which I would love to know the answer, but unless an act of God or geology were to burst the rock apart, I never will. Its very existence astounds me. It has no trunk, but grows horizontally into space in two thrusts, apparently seamlessly joined at the root, one above the other. The upper one curves slightly upwards as it reaches into the void, the lower one's downward curve is almost a mirror image. A fragile tracery of a handful of slender branches and twigs sprouts from the end of each, and you must look at much of the fall through that tracery.

Sometimes the survival instincts of nature in the most unpromising of circumstances is a humbling thing to witness. As I watched, the snow thickened and began to lie on the topsides of the two pincer-like limbs. It was April, it was cold, it was snowing, but at the end of the skinniest twigs, little cones awaited, with patience that would shame a saint, the day that would finally dawn that permitted cone to become bud to become leaf. Cones? As if it didn't have enough to put up with, the alder is the only deciduous hardwood in the land to bear cones.

I took my leave of the waterfall and its heartstring-tug of a setting, stepped away uphill among Scots pines. These were, mostly, survivors from the forestry era. When the spruces were clear-felled to make way for nature, these upstart pines, wind-and-bird-borne from higher outposts above the old plantation, danced for joy in unaccustomed sunlight, bowed and bent themselves to the tune of winds they had never previously known. As they had grown from seedlings, they were quickly outpaced by the surrounding spruces in their vertical race for sunlight, so at their own pace they abandoned all notions of limbs, of girth, and grew branchless, straight and tall, hemmed in on every airt other than up. Then one day the clear-fellers moved in and at a stroke (at many, many strokes) freed them from their imprisoned youth. They would never be the handsomest of Scots pines (their only foliage is still just a meagre crown), but they are sources of seeds, and sources of seeds are the lifeblood and the diversity of nature's renaissance.

And there, where the viewpoint footpath rejoined the main path up through the reserve, one more pine marten scat gleamed dully among newly fallen wet spring snowflakes. That scat had not been there when I arrived. I had an idea and suddenly my day had a purpose. I turned back downhill to where I had seen the little trail that fed back into the trees, the trail whose entrance was marked by two scats on the main path. If I was right about increased marten activity on the main path because of the cloying saturation of the understorey, perhaps a little stillness at a known crossroads might produce results.

The trail took some finding, mainly because I had not taken enough trouble to pinpoint it on the way up and because close examination revealed a dozen such trails, all of them crossing or ending at the main path. Finally, I found what I thought was the right place and earmarked a pine sapling about twenty yards further down the path which could screen me while I watched. It was the longest of long shots and conditions were not conducive to a long vigil. As it happened, I didn't need one.

I reached the pine, turned to check the view, and I was still in the middle of the path when an adult vixen appeared from the trees on the left of the path and stopped, facing the trees on the opposite side. Seconds later, and from the trees on the right of the path, a pine marten appeared, paused half-hidden on the verge, then stepped forward towards the fox. It is no exaggeration to say that they met nose to nose. There was no sound, no contact; they simply met, scented each other, then moved on. The marten crossed the path and vanished into the trees on the left. The fox looked – for the first time – down the path to where I still stood. Then it looked back over its shoulder in the direction from which it had appeared and into which the pine marten had disappeared, looked back at me, turned uphill and walked away up the path. Ten seconds later there was nothing on the path but two pine marten scats and snowflakes.

Did they know each other? Almost certainly. Neither had a good reason to pick a fight with the other. So they recognised each other by scent, as in a greeting, established that all was well and moved on.

I have seen a lot of foxes. I have seen quite a few pine martens. I have met people who see both regularly. I have never heard of anything quite like what I had just seen. I turned and walked quietly back downhill. At my back, the snow drifted lightly across reincarnating forest. I looked back once to watch it, and as I watched I told myself that there is very little we can do that is more worthwhile in terms of repaying our debt to nature than bringing a half-dead forest back to life.

Thirty-three

Swan Song for a Backward Spring

THE PAGE IS PATCHED WITH SHADOW AND SUN, a small wind moves the shadows around the paper. Distant voices flow nearer, ebb further, none of their words and shouts has meaning except when a child cries.

Be still.

Permit only the writing hand to move.

Feel the late May warmth distil down to the here-and-now writing of the hand, the shadow dance. The distant voices have become a kind of soft focus that helps to sharpen me; they go further back but not quite out of earshot, while my eyes track the words that imprint the page beyond the pen, my own inky spoor. The voices are replaced by the one in my head, the one that articulates my own personal first commandment in the matter of doing this nature writing job:

Write in the very now where you find yourself. There is no substitute even in divine inspiration for the touch of the moment, the touch of daylight on the dream.

They are the words of Margiad Evans, and I never tire of quoting them to myself and to other people who are interested in nature writing and how it works. That's how.

The in-and-out sun is back. Just before it lit the top of the page I felt it warm my bare foot. Sometimes I think this is the very best time to write, if there is a small wind to take the edge off the sun's true heat. All I ever need then is somewhere to sit, something to write on, something to write with, something to say. An hour passes, leaves no sign it has ever been. Hours do that when I write this way.

A bird's chirrup sounds nearby.

I think "greenfinch" without looking up.

I know birds. Some birds.

Curious: the sounds of nature infiltrate the writing mind long after I have ceased to notice the many far-off human voices and the few that occasionally wander nearby, chattering. These, I noticed before, veer away self-consciously at the sight of the figure on the sun-and-shadow seat, writing. I lean closer to nature, and she to me, so that our heads touch, and I keep the people voices at meaningless distance. Except when a child cries.

A blackbird has begun. I don't remember him beginning, but now he is making something out of layers of song, using long pauses between fragments of his repertoire, making his music make sense. In its way, it is the same thing I do myself, so my writing listens to the blackbird, admires how he does it.

A crow brays four times and is silent.

What was that all about? Was that his idea of music? Did he make it make sense?

And did the still-singing blackbird notice, acknowledge, comprehend? Probably.

And does the blackbird now sing more blackly as a result of the crow? Probably not. The crow does not sing more tunefully as a result of the blackbird.

A child – a boy of about six – leads his own small tribe out of the bushes, two older sisters and a mother follow, too close for my comfort but not his. He sees me and shouts: "Hiya!" from ten feet away. He shouts with a big, open smile. He reminds me at once of my six-year-old self. I was a cheery, hail-fellow-well-met six-year-old too, eyes the uncluttered blue of the North Sea, hair of fine grass bleached fair by the east-coast sun and its compatriot winds, browning skin of freckles. My first friend was the wind. My first enemy was the haar that hove to beyond the cliffs in the evening, swept ashore in the night, silently stole the known world, stole even the voice of the sea. My favourite among first words was "Kittiwake!"

My parents were no one you ever heard of. He moved through the world straight as a ploughing horse, she moved through it singing.

When they linked arms and walked, she sang at his tempo. They are long dead now, but when I think of them it is in the springtime when the sun set on them in my eyes and the sun rose over the sea. Oh, have you never seen the sun rise out of the sea? It really is quite fine.

So my own smile warms my shadowed face and says to a smiling six-year-old boy:

"Hiya, yourself!"

I must look harmless enough, for although his sisters ignore me his mother smiles wordlessly but directly at me then herds her small, happy brood ahead of her like a good collie, quietly, no fuss, then out of sight. They looked good together. Her smile lingers where she vanished, like a scent. Likewise my six-year-old self.

They are replaced by a squirrel, a grey one – incomer, infidel, too tame, too cocky, too in-my-face for its own good. It leaps onto a tree and adheres there where it lands, halfway up the trunk. Good trick. Then it spins through 180 degrees from facing vertically upwards to facing vertically downwards. Better trick. But even in that position it contrives to look up, staring at me, begging for food with its eyes. I have advice for such a squirrel.

"The whole garden is food for you. Bugger off."

Off it buggers – still nature though.

The blackbird (I have just noticed him again suddenly, as if at a great distance) sings on and on from pause to pause, still trowelling layers of song onto what it is he makes, still making sense.

My resolve to stop writing for a while, to close my eyes and listen to him to the exclusion of all else, is confounded by the squirrel. It didn't bugger off at all. It canters across the grass towards me. When it stops, it is eyeing me up from a yard away. I resent its scrutiny. It doesn't smile and say: "Hiya." Its stare is not a greeting but an unspoken demand: "Gimme."

It stands two-footed for endearing effect. It won't work.

"Bugger off."

It steps nearer, eyeing up my feet. It seems not to know that these kick. At my first foot-flicking gesture it jumps back a yard, spins in its own length, four-footed spin, stands, feels in a waistcoat pocket with one hand, then buggers off, this time as requested.

My eyes return to the hand, the pen, the page, the shadows, the sun; my mind to the writing while the sunlight still illuminates the dream.

Suddenly, the swan.

Wingbeats up there in the eye of the sun, so heard rather than seen. That sound of wonder, that exquisite throb, four in the bar like a Freddie Green guitar, crescendo then diminuendo then gone. Where do you fly, swan? Why do you always gatecrash my quietest hours with such grace, such certainty, such timing?

Who's Freddie Green?

Played guitar in the Count Basie Orchestra for forty years, the truest pulse in jazz. I heard him on the radio last night, just before the news. I only listened to the news because there was more jazz after the bulletin.

In the bulletin, a girl aged eleven, in Alsace, France, hit by a car then thrown into a lake by its driver while she was not yet dead. She died of drowning and she died of her injuries. Eleven years old and she died twice. So the voices reach me again only when a child cries, or a six-year-old boy shouts: "Hiya!" and grins.

The bulletin finished with the sport and the weather, then the jazz kicked back in, Bessie Smith, "St. Louis Blues", 1920-something. The voice is crying out of its time like a child who died twice. Oh, but the cornet fill-ins make me smile; they shine like a sun rising up out of the sea.

What did they make of you, Louis, when you first stepped out of the shadow of King Oliver and began to play like that?

Sometimes I think it would have been good to have been in at the beginning of jazz, to feel all the tentative stirrings coalesce at last in a Louis Armstrong cornet solo, to see and hear all jazz gather behind its one true Messiah, confident for the first time of its direction. Sometimes, though, it's enough to let it lift me from the depths of the news bulletin, so that I think:

Yes, we're capable of that with the eleven-year-old girl, but also capable of a Louis Armstrong solo, of a Freddie Green that plays rhythm guitar with the pure certainty and the natural grace of a swan's wings. I wonder if Louis ever played with Freddie? I would like to have heard that gig.

Louis, in my ears, you make your music make sense. You and that blackbird.

The radio last night had followed Louis and Bessie with Billie Holiday, "Lover, Come Back To Me", Lester Young's tenor her foil, as Louis's cornet was to Bessie. It was too much then, tears through the music for an eleven-year-old girl who died twice in a lake in Alsace, France. After I pressed the off-switch, a blackbird beyond the window had brimmed the silence. We all try – blackbird, Bessie, Louis, Billie, Lester, Freddie, swan, even me on my good days – we all try to make our music make sense. And a six-year-old boy bursts from a thicket of bushes towing his preoccupied sisters, his attentive mother.

"Hiya!"

"Hiya, yourself!"

Then the wordless music of her smile, the swan song for a backward spring.

Part Four

SUMMER

Thirty-four

The Goddess of Small Things

Simmer's a pleasant time
Flowers of every colour
Water rins o'er the heugh
And I long for my true lover

Robert Burns

CONSIDER THE MOUNTAIN SORREL by your left boot. If you failed to spot it don't worry, you wouldn't be the first. At 4,000 feet on the Cairngorms plateau, there is bigger and more handsome stuff to look at. But summer is the Goddess of Small Things. So now that I have drawn your attention to it, why not give the mountain sorrel the time of day? I know, I know, it looks like nothing at all; it's basically a high-altitude dock leaf. What's this one…four inches tall? Yet up here, things have a habit of not quite looking like what they really are. That sparse cluster of kidney-shaped leaves at ground level is what botanists call a basal rosette, which is arguably too grandiose for what actually meets your eye. And those things at the other end of a skinny stem that morphs from red at the bottom to green halfway up, those are what pass for flowers, and it is true that they are on the nondescript side of insignificant. But let me show you something. Look closer, look deeper, look *inside* the flower. See the whole plant. The way to see what's there is to get down on your knees. Peel the petals apart. Do you see it? This is the fruit of the mountain sorrel, not a berry but a nut. I told you we were dealing with small things. It's about an eighth of an inch long. Three millimetres, if you don't do fractions. Turn your binoculars upside down, put the eyepiece almost against the nut and look in the wrong end, for now you have a microscope in your hand. And now that you can see it larger than life, what do you think that is, that green canopy to which the nut clings? Can you see how beautifully formed it is, like an open book; and can you see that it is exquisitely edged in red, the way the finest book pages are edged in gold? It's a wing. So when plateau winds blow (and the wind has a considerable repertoire up here, from the easiest of breezes like this July morning to an all-Britain all-time record of 176 miles per hour in January 1993), the nut flies until it eventually touches down and – in time, in time – it pushes a root into the tough plateau soil and a new mountain sorrel plant begins to come to terms with high living.

Now consider its neighbour. Notice that unlike the mountain sorrel's erect stem and spike of flowers and winged nuts, its neighbour is a horizontal, ground-level straggle of shining leaves. Such is the nature of summer in the high Cairngorms that ten days ago this strange growth showed not so much as a leaf bud. Plants of all kinds bloom late and wither early here. The growing season, such as it is, is fast and brief. These leaves are fully open. And if you care to lift up one or two, you may find a yellowish non-leaf growing among them, and if you have the capacity to set aside the evidence of your eyes and think outside the box, it may occur to you that it looks like a tiny catkin – because that is what it is. What you are looking at is a tree, an inch-high tree with its "branches" underground, a dwarf willow. And this is its Scottish homeland, the highest, pared-to-the-bone upthrusts of the Cairngorms, and what passes for summer up here is a short, sharp shock of a season (in the forty-something years I have known these mountains, I have acquired a complete snow calendar: that is, I have been snowed on in every month of the year, so including June, July and August). So short and so sharp that the leaves of some specimens have turned yellow in July, while others just a few hundred yards away are still in bud or have yet to bud at all.

The law of unintended consequences comes into play at this point, for the dwarf willow shares its homeland and its version of summer with ground-nesting dotterels. Ground-nesting, because up here there is nowhere else to nest. Commonplace words acquire a different meaning. "Nest" in the dotterel's case is the shallowest of shallow scrapes, a hint of a depression in the raw surface of the mountain; and "soil" is really not an appropriate word at all. The only possible explanation for the dotterel's choice of nest site is that its true heartland is the Arctic tundra, and the broad, bare plateau of the high Cairngorms is the nearest thing we have to an Arctic landscape.

Seton Gordon is still the supreme bard of this landscape almost a hundred years after he wrote its masterwork, *The Cairngorm Hills of Scotland* (Cassell, 1925), and his account of his life-changing 1921 Oxford University expedition to Spitzbergen, *Amid Snowy Wastes* (Cassell, 1923). Forever after, he would draw direct comparison between the two landscapes and point out the similarities between the Cairngorms above 3,500 feet and Spitzbergen at sea level. Thus, much of the dotterel's fragile Scottish population of around 400 breeding males centres around the Cairngorms, and most nests are at or above 4,000 feet, whereas in the Arctic it finds what it is looking for at about 100 feet above sea level. In the high Cairngorms, it likes to line its nest with moss, lichen and (if it can find them) leaves. The easiest leaves to pluck from any hardwood tree are always the withering ones that have changed colour, and in the case of all willows that means from whitish green to yellow. So the yellow leaves of some of the autumn-minded dwarf willows even in July are not just the easiest to pick, they are also the easiest to see. As Seton Gordon wrote in 1925:

The old withered yellow leaves are used by the dotterel for lining her nest.

I think it is quite possible that he was the first person to observe such a thing, certainly the first to think it was worth writing down.

*

A trackside bank in Balquhidder, at an altitude 3,500 feet less than a Cairngorms dotterel nest, is where I found my first fragrant orchids. I like orchids, the little wild ones that gladden a Scottish summer, not the haute couture monsters beloved by interior designers. There are 7,500 species in the world, around fifty of which are found in Britain, and no more than a dozen in Scotland (not including a bewilderment of sub-species and hybrids which I choose not to care about). An orchid that smells of carnations is a little special – hence, fragrant orchid. In the sparsely populated landscape of Scottish orchids, then, fragrant orchids are particularly thin on the ground. But when you do find them, they are worth lingering over: they are small and discreet, the colour is soft, subtle, pale and pink, and the mild but distinct carnation scent is sensational. In the glitzy world of orchids, this is the one that gives understatement a good name, the less-is-more orchid. Ah, but if you look close enough, and if you are willing to linger long enough and get your eye in – *see the whole plant* – you will unearth the fragrant orchid's scintillating, shimmering secret. Take a flower spike very gently in your fingers, get your own shadow out of the way, and turn the spike a millimetre at a time in the sunlight. Keep turning and staring and refocussing until, finally, the miracle is revealed: every petal is covered in tiny glistening scales. As nature's light shows go, it is not outshone by either aurora or supermoon. The effect simply astounds, and so does the tiny nature of the spectacle. So when I suggest that summer is the Goddess of Small Things, these are what I have in mind, among other things.

Which other things? Oh, you know...

Goldcrest eggs. Especially second and third broods, around ten eggs at a time and about the size of the fingernail on my pinkie, or about half an inch, fledging well into the summer in a nest the size of a toddler's bunched fist – a nest fashioned from moss and lichen and bits of spider's webs and slung from the fronds at the outer edge of a Sitka spruce. In sunlight after rain it looks more like a silk purse than a nest. Unlike the human population of Scotland, the goldcrest loves Sitka spruce and thrives in it from Galloway to Sutherland. I am with the goldcrest; I like Sitka spruce. I don't like how we grow it and what we do with it, but I have seen it in the Alaskan Panhandle, where it grows with grace and elegance in the company of western hemlock, aspen, birch, willow, wolf, grizzly bear and even humpback whale (for the Pacific thrusts long, narrow, questing fingers into that forest so apparently land-locked that you think you are walking along the shore of a lake until a whale the size of a small island heaves out of the water and you remember where you are). Two other things you should know about Sitka spruce: when it is left to its own devices and grows wild, it produces timber of such quality that it is the choice of some of the finest luthiers in the world to make some of the finest guitars in the world, and even in the atrociously contemptuous way it is treated by contemporary forestry practice here, the goldcrest still can't get enough of it.

It is the unmistakable scent of red fox that stops me, that blend of spice and peat and something stuck to your boot. Just there, the forest track emerges from the old-established plantation into a high and open heather moor under a suddenly wide sky, the moor newly planted with more spruce but also studded with heather and rock and pine outcrops, where self-seeded spruce and a scatter of small rowans thicken an agreeable mix with a hint of Scandinavia. Ben Ledi is suddenly there, as Ben Ledi so often is in this part of the world, and dark green and gold in the summer evening. At the base of the first of the outcrops, a hefty old pine had fallen years ago across a natural depression in the hillside. Time had homed in on the decomposing trunk and furred the walls and the floor of what had become a kind of accidental cave roofed in by the trunk and walled on one side by the massive, upended root. It was there that the foxes had denned, and in some comfort with very little effort on their part. It is a deep and dark and turned-aside place, and the only clue to the possibility of their presence is that cask-strength pungency. So you could say I have followed my nose. But just as I crouch towards the carefully discreet entrance, a Sitka spruce a few feet away unleashes a salvo of fluffy shrapnel. Never, I suspect, has a fresh-from-the-nest brood of goldcrests had such a startling impact on a six-feet-tall, thirteen-and-a-half stone mortal. A fledgling goldcrest is all of three inches from stem to stern, and as fluent in flight as a Kleenex tissue screwed up loosely into a ball. None of them flies more than a yard, a few have trouble perching, two try to get back into the nest, immediately betraying its presence within touching distance the moment I recover my balance and stand up. I would do better to stay crouched but the moment is unique in my long experience of keeping nature's company and I respond inelegantly. For perhaps ten seconds the air rocks with the whirring pulse of very small wings and there seem to be goldcrests everywhere. Then the noise stops and they vanish back into the spruce tree and are silent and still. I step quietly away from their tree. From the respectable distance of the forest track I apologise quietly for the intrusion. But now I know where they live, where the small miracle of them unfolds.

What other small things?

Dragonflies. Flanders Moss, a raised bog and national nature reserve a few miles west of Stirling, so more or less equidistant from east and west coasts, yet for all that, it lies at as near to sea level as makes very little difference. In early summer it transforms under the spectacular influence of an unbroken square mile of bog cotton, so dense and so level and so white that it effortlessly invokes snow. Summer snow is far from unknown in Scotland, and especially at 4,000 feet in the Cairngorms, but summer snow at sea level and the temperature at 20 degrees probably is pretty well unknown these last 10,000 years. No one notices the flowers of bog cotton. But after the flowers come the seed-heads, and each one of those is as the snowflake to the snowdrift. And it is this sea-level summer snow that is the setting for the dragonfly's finest hour, for both bog cotton and dragonfly need wet ground, preferably bogs, to thrive. Dragonfly: it is a confusing word, for it means both the species itself and the collective name for both dragonflies and damselflies. They inhabit the same landscape, and you will see them in sunlight. Page one of the Idiot's Guide will tell you that the main difference is how they perch: dragonflies perch with their wings open like an old bi-plane, and damselflies fold theirs neatly together along their bodies.

This is the story of one damselfly, or rather four. One species – the large red damselfly (which is large only in relation to the small red, two inches max) – but four members of that one species: two male and two female. How do I know? Because they are two mating pairs, and they are actually mating. I have a photograph. There is one pair, beautifully lit full-length, one behind the other on a bent-over blade of grass and low over a pond half-clothed in a species of moss with a Latin name I have no intention of learning. It makes a lovely backdrop to show off the banded red of the damselflies. And that is my shot.

Having admired the photo several times (by my standards it is a good shot, which, admittedly, is to damn with faint praise), I have noticed that the female has only one of her six feet in contact with the grass, the rest are in the air. This could mean that she has been lifted bodily from the blade of grass, got carried away you might say; or it could mean that she was just touching down when I took the picture. I can't remember. But more noticeable by far now – although not at the time – is that the pair have been photo-bombed by a second pair, which I didn't notice as I pressed the shutter button because they are head-on rather than side-on, and a head-on pair of mating damselflies looks like nothing on earth you or I have ever seen before, and I am content to leave it at that.

I became interested in dragonflies/damselflies for two reasons. One is that I go to Flanders Moss often because it is close at hand, and it is at least four different places at different seasons of the year: nature plays many cards there. The other is that I met a man called Ruary Mackenzie Dodds, a relentless champion of the dragonfly/damselfly cause and the author of two books on the subject that are also published by Saraband. We shared a book festival gig at Wimborne in Dorset, as well as the flight from Edinburgh to Southampton and back and an agreeably boozy dinner. This kind of thing doesn't happen often, at least not to me, but we have become friends and I have become a dragonfly enthusiast by osmosis, as opposed to by incredibly hard work, which is how he did it.

Here is Ruary, writing in *The Dragonfly Diaries* (Saraband, 2014) on the subject of blue-tailed dragonflies:

>*...such lovely delicate things, with those powder blue blobs on the ends of their slim black abdomens...most have blue thoraxes but some have other colours – red, green, purple...these are females, refucens, infuscens and violacea respectively. Apparently the thorax colours can change with age...*

And here he writes on his wife Kari's obsession with dragonfly larvae rather than the flying beasties they become:

...they just don't have the same magic as the adults: no stunning flying, no stunning speed, no flashing beauty. There's that ferocious labial mask, though, and the way they breathe through their backside...

Watching and listening to Ruary in full book festival flow is something of a roller-coaster ride, at the end of which you have been hugely entertained as well as informed, and you are just a little giddy and unsteady on your feet, and wondering how quickly you can get back to Flanders Moss and go and look for dragonflies again.

★

Lizards, as well. Flanders Moss in summer is strewn with common lizards, and the chances are that you would never see one were it not for the boardwalk that allows you to watch the myriad life-forms of a raised bog at close quarters without getting your feet wet or floundering up to your waist in glaur, which is what nature uses to make peatbogs. The raised rim of the boardwalk is no more than three inches wide, and an inch higher than the main path. But the lizards home in on it to sunbathe. The star attractions are the newborn ones, perfect miniatures of the adults and an inch-and-a-half long, including the tail, but meticulously curved into half that length; two together look like parentheses. But move too suddenly and they dive headlong into the bog.

Flanders Moss, at first glance, is all about space and light and spectacle all the way to its rim of birchwoods and its arc of mountains beyond. But stop and stay still and look close, and it is the small things you will remember.

When I chose the title for this chapter, and having written it on a notebook page with a fountain pen (my preferred way of writing), I thought I would begin with a list. This was it:

Goldcrest eggs and nests and chicks, wild strawberries, wild raspberries, blueberries, brambles, cloudberries, cloudberry flowers, small blue butterflies, small coppers, small tortoiseshells, small whites, small pearl-bordered fritillaries, small skippers, dingy skippers, chequered skippers, orange-tips, northern-brown argus, Rannoch brindled beauty moth, sea pink, sea spurry, sea holly, newborn lizards, scales on the petals of fragrant orchids, small white orchids, seventeen species of speedwell, wild mountain thyme, mountain avens, mountain sorrel (and nuts), alpine lady's-mantle, dwarf cornel, eyebright, bedstraw, house martins, sand martins, sandpipers, wrens, merlins, little-ringed plovers, little auk, little tern, azure damselflies, all damselflies and dragonflies apart from those ones that look and sound like Sopwith Camels, spotted flycatchers, headdress of redpolls and reed buntings...

Then I ran out of ink, and I thought better of the idea and that perhaps you might just like to make your own list, now that I've shown you how to get the hang of it.

Thirty-five

St Kilda Summer, 1988

BEHIND BORERAY

It is black behind Boreray and small.
All suns dance darkly here,
throw no shadows on rock this black.
Stac Lee is a black berg
its sunk seven-eighths beyond
the scope of suns and me.
We who sail our puny daring
under Stac an Armin
creep tinily by.

IT ALL STARTED IN THE EARLY SUMMER of 1988. I handed in my notice at the *Edinburgh Evening News*, where I had been working for eight years on the features desk, and at the invitation of publisher and landscape photographer Colin Baxter, I went to St Kilda, forty miles west of the Outer Hebrides, to write what would become my first book. Ian Nimmo, the editor of the *Evening News* at that time, and who had done much to encourage me to flex my writing muscles in his newspaper, gave me his blessing with the words "you must follow your star". So began an adventure that changed my life utterly. I had been a journalist from the age of sixteen. At the age of forty, I became a full-time nature writer literally overnight (and halved my income at a stroke). It was a fast transition: the book was published three months later, on the day after I left the paper. The only copy of it I still possess is the one I gave to my mother, and which I had inscribed:

For Mum with much love from the author!
Jim, October 1988

She had been very critical of my decision to leave the *Evening News* (she was not the only one among my family and friends and ex-colleagues). But seeing that book and holding it in her hands and reading the inscription…all that changed everything: her opinion of the enterprise swung through 180 degrees from a headwind to a tail-wind, and for the last five years of her life until her death in 1993, she became the champion of my cause.

My first book? I can no longer remember how it felt. Probably I walked on air for a few days, then I looked around, thought, "What's next?" and started writing my second book. I thought that was how it was supposed to happen, and as no one has advised me differently, I have just kept on doing it ever since. Still following my star, Ian. And thanks.

That life-redefining summer of 1988 seemed like a natural place to begin, as it was the first of all my nature-writing summers, for all that it had been temporarily thwarted at the very first hurdle. On the day I was supposed to travel to Oban to join Colin Baxter for the sail to St Kilda aboard a two-masted schooner, I was floored by a violent gastric bug. So I went alone three weeks later by the rather less glamorous route of a flight to Benbecula, in the Outer Hebrides, and then the Army's flat-bottomed landing-craft (the Army maintained a small base there at the time to service a cliff-top radar station). As one seasoned St Kilda veteran had counselled me: "She wallows like a drunken pig, that bitch."

As it happened, she declined to wallow. The evening ocean was as benign as the Crinan Canal. HMS *The Drunken Pig* was sober and demure. I stared at the ocean, at its raft of islands astern and its absence of islands ahead. I slept. Then a voice gatecrashed a dream: "Anybody want to see St Kilda? It's worth a look."

Oh, yes please. I wanted to see St Kilda very much indeed, for was it not to be the passport to the rest of my life? My watch said 5a.m. I went up on deck and the Atlantic was barely astir and the sky was pink and St Kilda was purple. And the voice was right: it *was* worth a look.

It is that first look that I remember, the one utterly indelible souvenir that has survived intact. It was a cardboard cut-out, as two-dimensional as a stage set, and it floated upright among leisurely waves. And it was purple. Or rather it was purples. The nearest island, a dour little tea-cosy-shaped rock lump called Levenish, was the darkest purple. My particular sightline set it against the much larger island of Boreray, and Boreray not only stood more than 1,200 feet straight up out of the ocean, it was the silhouette of a sea monster, and it was paler purple, borderline lilac. Over the next two weeks of camping alone, I would see Borerary from many angles in many weathers and every hour of the day and the dusk and dawn, and including the view through a gauze of gannets from the unhorizontal deck of a yacht at very close quarters indeed; but not once did that extravagant portfolio I would amass ever threaten to dislodge from my mind's eye that first of all my St Kildas on that first morning of all my nature-writing summers.

And Stac Lee was there too, a mere 600 feet high, but quite high enough for a lopsided parallelogram with no visible means of support, and that too was the paler shade of Boreray purple.

Then the boat dipped and I realised that parts of the superstructure were concealing parts of St Kilda, so I ran to the bow where wider oceanic miles lay unobscured. And there was Hirta, the main island, and there was the untidy sprawl of Dùn, Village Bay's eccentric, wafer-thin breakwater, looking like a bar of Toblerone that had gone horribly wrong in the baking.

These set pieces of the St Kilda archipelago, so familiar to me (in outline, at least) from a few books, from other people's photographs, from maps and film and drawings and paintings and word-of-mouth (it is astounding how many St Kilda veterans emerged like woodlice from under stones once the word of what I was doing leaked out) now made smithereens of my every preconception. While I stared and tried to respond in what I thought might be a suitably nature-writerly way to where I was and what I was seeing and what-the-hell-did-I-think-I-was-doing, by the way, something utterly new stole over me in the face of so much incomprehensible, volcanically tarnished age, and it was this:

Though I turned very slowly through 360 degrees, I could not see any other land, in any direction, none at all. And these first moments became my all-purpose visual definition of St Kilda, the one I have carried in my mind ever since. And so primitive was the encounter, so elementally simple – one sea, one sky, one scatter of improbable rocks – that I might have been the first of all St Kilda voyagers, one of a tribe of nomadic herdsmen coming curiously up the margins of Europe, exchanging bemused glances and agreeing among themselves that surely here was nature's last limit. For they would be accustomed to sailing where land was in sight, and on St Kilda, the only land very occasionally in sight (I would have one glimpse of a white-sanded Hebridean beach – Harris – in two weeks) is the land that you left forty miles behind to get here.

Time filters out the scents, the sounds, the touch and the taste of St Kilda on the air, and leaves only the sights (or the memory of some of them, at least), for every one of my fourteen days there was crammed with them. The freedom I was permitted to wander at will and alone meant that I crowded the days and some of the nights with everything all the time, occasionally retreating to my tent and my small portable typewriter to spill out the chaos of St Kilda into the manuscript of my first book. There was no time between the two, and no distance. And now, so much time has intervened, and so much distance; although I have returned often in my mind I have never returned in person. When I consider those first days of that first nature-writing summer (what a place and what astounding good fortune in which to begin), how could I ever improve on all that or add to or embellish it by going back? The simple passage of time, aided by memory's tendency to edit selectively so that only the essential remnants stand forward in any kind of clarity from such a head-on collision with natural forces: all that has distilled down to a single time and place, the indispensable pure gold that sustains one traveller's idea of that time, that place, my own personal St Kilda.

*

The north coast of Hirta is gouged by the sea loch of Loch a' Ghlinne, whose east shore ends in an inconspicuous little headland, Gob na h-Airde. *Aird* is "a promontory (not necessarily high)", according to Malcolm MacLennan's *Gaelic Dictionary*, which is the perfect definition. By the standards of St Kilda headlands it is not necessarily high, nor is it wide and nor is it handsome. In truth, the place looks like nothing at all to write home about, and it would have no place at all in the roll call of St Kilda's natural wonders were it not for what lies under your feet. "Arch", says the map, which is to say "hill" when what you mean is Everest.

There is a bit of a clue in the name of the level ground (and level ground itself is a rare phenomenon on St Kilda) that paves the headland – Leacan an t-Sluic Mhòir – which, like so many Gaelic phrases loses all its intrinsic poetic flourish in the glare of literal translation; but for what it's worth, *leacan* is flagstones, *sluic* is a hole and what you end up with is the "flagstones of the big hole". On these flagstones you can walk across the roof of what is arguably St Kilda's greatest natural wonder without knowing that it's there. To find the "arch" you must go to the edge of a 200-feet cliff and begin to scramble *down*. An easy natural ramp that limpets against the cliff face eases the process. The incredulous stares of razorbills and guillemots at very close quarters do the reverse, for they will imbue your tentative progress with a sense of the absurd. They stand erect like overdressed waiters with their hands behind their backs, waiting, waiting, intimidating, black eyes staring right at you, while all the while they mutter variations on a theme of "aaarrr", with intonations of surprise at the ungainliness of a six-feet-tall intruder; they perch on the outermost edge of the outermost rocks on the outermost edge of the cliff, while the human they mock insists on the innermost, apparently deriving some comfort from the sudden and very welcome presence of a rope handrail fixed to the rock. You cling, you descend, the ocean rises towards you, then the ramp runs out.

Behold the big hole. The very big hole indeed.

But the map did not say "hole" or "cave", it said "arch" and while I am familiar enough with those Hebridean arches that can barely accommodate the passage of a crouching canoeist, it takes a moment to realise that the very big hole is but one end of the "arch". This is "arch" but not as you know it. Welcome to *The Tunnel*.

I once wrote of this place that "memory in such a landscape is not to be trusted", and from this distance in both time and miles, I agree with myself; but here and now, sitting at an oak table in a house in the middle of the country (in other words, just about as far from either North Sea or Atlantic Ocean as you can get in Scotland), memory is all I have to work with. I think I believed then that my nature-writing life would always be like that (I was about halfway through the first week in the job), whereas it would never, ever be like that again. For once I got deep enough into The Tunnel to see its far end, where light and ocean poured in from the west, once I came to terms with the fact that the sloping, slippery, rock-fankled floor wanted to pitch me at every step into that unlikeliest of ocean furrows, once I grasped the raw dimensions of the place (imagine an aircraft hangar, the kind where they used to store Lancaster bombers half a dozen at a time), and once I realised that the Atlantic Ocean charged in from both ends and met itself in the middle with the most primitive *noise* I have ever heard before or since (it gives voice to itself in a natural echo chamber the size of a headland)...once I accommodated all that in one brain, one pair of eyes, one pair of ears, the significance of where I was and why I was there and what I was trying to do, and that it was only last Friday I had written the leader column for the *Edinburgh Evening News*, it was then that the otherworldliness of that new life hit home. My response to that overwhelming encounter with nature's company has since become something of a ritual whenever I struggle to cope with the evidence of my own eyes: I sat down. That was when I discovered how wet the rock floor of The Tunnel is, and how cold, but I sat anyway, and I stared, and I sat and stared and sat and stared.

And then The Tunnel sang.

Have you ever watched and listened to a wren singing from a perch on, say, a garden rosebush or the back of a park bench, and marvelled not just at the inventiveness and purity of the song but also the sheer volume from a creature the size of a table tennis ball? Surely the inside of a wren is just a hollow, nothing but a soundbox clad in skin and feathers, and a tiny aperture to let the sound out? The St Kilda wren (for it has its own sub-species: *Troglodytes troglodytes hirtensis*, since you asked) is a little chunkier than its mainland kin – "chunkier" being a relative term given that we're talking about wrens – and because it has a consequently chunkier soundbox its song is a little chunkier too. But that assumes that the song is being delivered – as it almost always is – from a conspicuous perch in the open air. The St Kilda wren that sang (and oh, how it sang, and sang and sang and sang) from somewhere deep in that gaunt auditorium, that colossal echo chamber... that wren became choral, became symphonic, for it sounded like a thousand wrens. And here, finally, was the only justification I have ever encountered for the overworked metaphor of nature as cathedral, for it is unarguable at least that The Tunnel is everything in nature that the cathedral is in humankind. It is huge and cool and dim within. And if you carry deep within you the sense of pilgrim in search of sacred ground, try The Tunnel before you give up the search. The light from its vast glassless and unstained windows may blaze beyond its 200-feet-thick walls, but inside it diffuses and darkens. The erratically vaulted roof is of the same mysterious cast that fuses the arts of sculptor and architect. There is also the same sense of atheistic sanctity that appears to dignify ancient stones manipulated into grand gesture wherever you find them. In The Tunnel, a single St Kilda wren was all the anthem nature required.

You can get too much of such a place, or at least I did. I began to feel overpowered, bordering on overburdened. Maybe daylight would help. Then The Tunnel started to moan in a discord of voices, woozy and dizzy-making. There, where the Atlantic meets itself in a vast, head-butting bruise, a dozen grey seals had ridden the surf to caterwaul at the very meeting place of the two Atlantics. They failed, utterly, to drown out the wren and its thousand echoes.

There was still the eastern entrance of the cartographer's "arch" to confront, but by now I had moved so far through The Tunnel that perspectives and sightlines had transformed. Now that colossal yawn doubled as a lop-sided picture frame for Boreray. Boreray never just appears, it seems, but rather it always has to make an entrance, and from The Tunnel it presents one more variation on that theme of sea monster with which I first beheld it at 5a.m. days before, days that felt like years. It would be no surprise at all to hear it roar. But when Borerary materialised in the mouth of The Tunnel, it had finally met its match, the one thunder it could not steal. There are the two most astounding fragments of Scotland's western seaboard, one framed within the other, but that is only possible because Borerary is four miles distant. Grand gesture within grand gesture.

Nothing comes back to me of the walk back through The Tunnel, back up its steeply-sloping floor above the two Atlantics, back out into the daylight of the overworld, back to the rope, the ramp. Were there still guillemots? Still razorbills? What I remember next is sitting on a rock out on the floor of the headland and trying to come to terms with the new knowledge that it is also the roof of The Tunnel, and all *that* was still going on beneath my feet. There was an eerie time of complete thoughtlessness. When it abated (a few minutes…half an hour… an hour?) I was still sitting on the same rock, and I was stupefied by landscape. Eventually, I simply stood and began walking the shore of Loch a' Ghlinne, having resolved nothing, having come to terms with nothing. It would take – and it has taken – the passage of years.

"Shore" is an almost alien concept on St Kilda. Usually, it is another word for clifftop. Other than in Village Bay, you don't walk along shores but along cliff edges. At Loch a' Ghlinne these vary between 100 feet and 600 feet. At its utmost, the western shore culminates in a headland called the Cambir, Hirta's most north-westerly thrust, and when it halts abruptly at one more clifftop the ocean is 650 feet below your feet. Halfway there, where the headland briefly narrows through a wind-bedevilled chicane, the map intones "Settlement" in that bizarre Gothic script it reserves for sites of antiquity. If there is a more un-settlement-like place on the map of my native land, I have never seen it. Yet it was there, on these flanks of Gleann Mor above Loch a'Ghlinne – and not to Village Bay – that the first St Kildans came and settled, planted roots of a kind 4,000 years ago. What were they thinking?

From the summit of the Cambir then, I began to think about where I was, what I had seen, where I had been; about the extraordinary reach of this uneasy coalition of rocks that can still burn a deep unease into the mind of strangers from boats, even after 4,000 years of occupation, even now so long after the final evacuation of the native population in 1930. The rocks still summon the curious, hypnotise them, and yes, stupefy them. From up here, The Tunnel's headland is lowly, the mouth of The Tunnel is nothing more than the mouth of one more cave. Loch a' Ghlinne, from up here, has – apparently

– many such mouths. By now, I knew it was a deception, and at that moment, the wind faltered, the afternoon was suddenly warm.

I sat on and on, sun high, the sea slack, and I set myself the task of trying to revisit The Tunnel's introverted underworld in my mind from this high and airy pedestal, to fuse those extremes in such a singular landscape into a single strand of thought. That way, whenever the landscape is recalled or revisited, I see not the surface of the land in one particular mood, but something bonded and deeper. I find it hard work, and it is perhaps only the particular preserve of the nature writer to go looking for such insight (for there is nothing remotely scientific about it), and it is as elusive as a flat calm on St Kilda. But in the unlikely setting of that aloof fragment of rock – an outpost of an outpost, poised halfway between the sea and the island summit – St Kilda suddenly achieved exactly that, a flat calm, and I urged my mind far back down into that tumultuous airspace, giddy with seabirds, and not a breath of wind. Far below, the sun lit up a small flock of kittiwakes, glittering white against the blackest of blacks where The Tunnel gaped, and then they dived inside.

In my mind I went with them. I was that outrider bird on the outermost edge of the right wing of the flock, the unaccustomed heat on my back. If there is happiness among birds, surely it is to be found in a flock of St Kildan kittiwakes riding the easy rise of thermals on splayed and gliding wings. The flock's entry into The Tunnel was as different from mine as it is possible to imagine. No tentative creep across wet rock in a state of primitive awe at the abnormal nature of the surroundings. Rather, the flock gatecrashed its sanctity with raucous self-confidence, oblivious when the sun on their backs yielded and the world grew dim and walled-in and roofed and cool. They cleaved the heart of its airspace, an undisciplined squadron of wavering, white and black-tipped wings, and the walls and the vaulted roof reverberated to twenty kittiwake throats chanting their own names.

I extricated my train of thought from the edge of the flock and tried to imagine instead how it would have looked if they had flown in while I was inside: *See how luminous the birds are in the gloom. Hear how the individual voices of the flock separate from each other, each responding to the unique acoustics. I can put a voice to an individual bird and every voice spills upwards – as elemental and elusive as spindrift and wind – into the vaults of The Tunnel, drifts back down again and again and again through chains of limitless echoes. "Kitt-ay-wake! Kitt-ay-wake!"*

High on the Cambir, I felt the wind return, saw the ocean stir itself with sudden soft, slow breakers of kittiwake-white. I wondered why the birds would take to The Tunnel at all. I have always associated them with those rocks where the water is whitest, flying eagerly into the exhilaration of storm, relishing the charging air, the booming surf, the ocean's highest, whitest surge. It occurred to me then that they had entered The Tunnel during that uncanny lull, that brief spell of windlessness, of sea idleness. Where, in all St Kilda, would there still be white water, one restless pool of turbulence? Where else but in the heart of The Tunnel, where sea flowed in from each end and the two Atlantics collided.

*

A few months later, at a book event in Fort William, I met one of the last surviving St Kildans. He was in his eighties and he had just been back, just once more.

"We all go back," he said, "just once more, just as long as we are able."

I thought how frail he looked, but how strong within. Like St Kilda.

I talked to him about The Tunnel. I tried to tell him how moved I had been by it. He looked up from his clasped hands on the table then, looked me in the eye, nodded once, gave me a half-smile, and turned his head away. He couldn't speak for a few moments.

*

That, then, was the summer when my nature-writing life began. Before I started writing this, I took that very first book down from my bookshelves and looked at it for the first time in years. The prose reads as if it was written by someone else, and in many ways I am a different person from the one who cast off confidently from the safe haven of the newspaper business on a journey to who-knows-where.

But what surprised me was the poetry. Colin Baxter had asked me to write set-piece passages of poetry or prose-poetry to sit opposite a few individual photographs. Bearing in mind that all I had had written up to that point was journalism, I rather wonder now where I found the nerve to write seven poems. Yet it seems to me now these few lines engaged more daringly with the landscape, with their brevity and their sparseness. So in the end I dusted down two of them, "The Old Song", which was at the very end of the book, and "Behind Boreray", chosen because of a remarkable coincidence that occurred while I was writing this chapter. It came in the form of an email from Beauly. It was from a landscape painter called Kirstie Cohen whom I had never met and whose work I had never seen. She was preparing a catalogue for her new exhibition at the Kilmorack Gallery near Beauly. It was called *St Kilda, An Atlantic Journey*, and she wondered if she could print one of my poems beside one of her pictures. The poem was "Behind Boreray".

The Boreray poem was the only one I had written on St Kilda, the only one that came home with me. I was offered a trip round Borerary and the stacks by the skipper of a yacht that had just put into Village Bay. I was helplessly seasick for about three hours, but the seasickness was a small price to pay for the chance to spend time with nature at its utmost, beneath trembling towers of rock and gannets. As soon as I was back on land (the land that still trembled whenever I stood still for hours after), I put the form of words down in a notebook, exactly as they appeared in the book, exactly as they appeared in the catalogue, exactly as they appear at the head of this chapter.

It feels as if the poems have been rescued, allowed out into the daylight again after a long exile in the twilight zone that all books inhabit when they are out of print once and for all.

THE OLD SONG

To have lived here,
a hovel on Hirta
for your only hearth
(not nomads of science or soldiery
nor passing prowlers with pens

St Kilda Summer, 1988

like me or Dr Johnson),
to bide all your times here
knowing no other's march,
was to look wilderness in the eye
and dare it to deny
your daily bread.
To have lived here,
content with all the world
in your embrace, at ease
with all its ways,
then hear compatriots whisper
"Evacuate!" was to feel
the soul's anchor drag,
to know that whatever the voyage,
wherever the final haven,
the journey was done,
the old song sung.

Thirty-six

You Have Not Seen Her
With My Eyes

THE RUSH. THE HOARSE ROAR. The rush is dead ahead. There is a scar like a furrow on the surface of the water. No, just beneath the surface. But, unlike a scar or a furrow, it advances – in a rush. The hoarse roar is slightly stage right. Ears try to drag eyes that way. The eyes think about it but not for long. This, the rush, this whatever it is that rushes and scars and furrows the surface from just beneath it, this is better. The eyes will not be distracted. The sheer speed, but also the control... they insist on it.

The eyes see silver. Not breaking the surface, not quite, not yet, although at every moment the tension quivers and surely the surface will burst apart now.

The eyes think, "Torpedo". Then they start to anticipate "Explosion". But not yet.

Instead, the speed increases. But the control remains precise. It all looks impossible. At least, it does to me. But I don't fish.

I don't fish and all I know of torpedoes came from war films a long time ago. And that rush – dead ahead, not quite breaking the surface, that silver, that shapeliness – that is the prototype. Someone with a scientist's mind stood on a riverbank like this one and saw this and thought, "Torpedo" and then "Explosion". I don't have a scientist's mind any more than I fish, which is not at all, ever. But my father was a soldier for ten years before and then all the way through the Second World War, and although he never talked about it (and there was a lot to talk about, what with Dunkirk, El Alamein, his admiration of Montgomery, Sicily, Berlin at the end; and I have his Victory Parade programme and photographs of him with a half-track truck he had driven in the desert), he relived something of it with his family: we were taken to see any number of war films, and as my maternal grandfather managed three local cinemas in the Lochee area of Dundee, it was easy. So there were films of the Army's war, the RAF's war and the Navy's war, and every now and then there would be a submarine in the film and then there would be torpedoes. So to that extent (and no further), I knew what a torpedo looked like just below the surface – the rush, the shape, the speed, the control, the explosion. And this that I could see now with enthralled eyes, this was the prototype. Dad never dreamed that a legacy of his soldiering would bear such strange fruit.

And then my eyes began to think, "When? When?" The explosion. Any second, the explosion. But still it came on, the rush, and the water caved in before it as its momentum cleaved the surface from beneath. Still it picked up speed, yet its torpedo shapeliness was pitted against the spate-fuelled charge of the river, against the press of tons of fast water still turbulent from the upstream chaos that generated the hoarse roar. I had a sudden intuition: an unlikely symbol, a new metaphor (new to me, at least, though maybe it's in the back catalogue of, say, Neil Gunn!) – the golden eagle of the river, because am I not forever writing how the golden eagle achieves control and speed when it fires itself upwind? This is the golden eagle's way, too. Golden eagle, Atlantic salmon; who would have thought they would summon the same techniques?

Then it turned. I never saw a torpedo turn before. No World War II movie torpedo ever turned, and those films were the beginning and end of my knowledge of torpedoes until this, this cleaver of the upstream summer river, the morning after days of rain ended and sunlight poured onto the river and the water was black except where it was dazzling white, the dazzling white in the river that was the source of the hoarse roar. So the Atlantic salmon opened a long curve that cut into the quieter waters of the near bank, and by that curve the hoarse roar came into play, for it was the roaring, dazzling, white water that had to be overcome, the roaring water that challenged the salmon's very right to exist, to return far into the upper river that spawned it. Unlike the torpedo, the salmon's explosion was designed to overcome the hoarse roar, not to sink it but to silence it, by leaving it behind. The curve widened then tightened. The furrow, that scar that was the salmon's torpedo spoor, lengthened and burst apart more of the surface as the speed increased, then the curve was done and the rush straightened and headed for the very heart of the maelstrom, that hoarse roar that was nothing less than the massed voices, pipes and drums of ten waterfalls stretched across the breadth of the river, and these pooled their thunderstorm resources in such an upheaval of white water and sunlight and sound.

Then the salmon dived and was gone.

★

There is a hole in the river, an ice-gouged hollow that has since become a broken, rock-walled sink. Just as the eagle glen has a headwall (the analogies between the two tribes do seem to line up to be inspected), so the salmon's river presents a landmark headwall that rears above the known landscape, and it is that which the salmon must negotiate. The river, even in this mood of bloated tumult, could not overwhelm the wall, but rather divided around it to left and right. So, crammed between the broken ends of the wall and its own alder-lined banks, it tumbled sideways into the sink by way of ten separate falls that collided and co-mingled in joyous reunion moments later in the deepest depths of the sink beneath the headwall, and the colour of that reunited river was sunlit snowdrifts, so that the whole spectacle almost dared you to look it in the eye.

The river's problem now was how to get out again. Almost all of it was forced (under what kind of forces and at what speed?) into a narrow channel of imponderable depth where the downstream-curved wall of the sink had long-since burst apart. That channel, just a few yards wide, was suddenly commanded to bear the burden of almost the entire river which was twenty times as wide before it hit the headwall, and the resultant volume, speed and power would reduce you and me to ruins, broken in many pieces. Yet it was this channel the salmon must swim through – upstream – in order to effect the explosion from the innermost depths of the sink that will carry it to quiet waters above. That explosion was the only thing that could silence the hoarse roar.

Deep beneath the ferment of the sink, the Atlantic salmon powered forward with utter certainty. He knows, too, that even here, the deeper he goes the less frenetic the water. How deep is that hole? I have no idea. The salmon knows, of course, just as it knows that the line it held through the channel is also the line that it must hold across the sink, because it will angle him directly towards the widest of the falls, the one immediately to the right of the headwall, the one nature has chosen for this singular fish. I am guessing this part because I can't see it, because nothing else can explain what happened next. I am guessing, too, that the salmon's self-confidence in its ability to hold to that line without the slightest deviation is justified; that although the water pressure is at its utmost down there, it is vertical rather than upstream or downstream, and the salmon has the power and shape and that faith that moves mountains and silences river roars, and these fuse into unstoppable energy. And from the bottom of the sink it builds a new momentum and tilts upwards until it is all-but-vertical then bursts the water apart and heads for the daylight. It knows (it remembers!) there is a shelf two-thirds of the way up the fall to the right of the headwall, and that is its only chance. The explosion when it comes is calculated to thrust him up and out of the throat of the roaring water to reach the ledge where he might just hold still long enough to gather new momentum and go again.

That, at least, is how it looked to me, but I don't fish. The salmon's mind is mysterious to me. Its destination seems never to be in doubt, nor is its ability to find its way. Consider this particular salmon up to the moment that it dived from my sight, deep into the channel, for its journey had begun the moment it decided it was time to go home, and thousands of miles out in the Atlantic from here. In due course, which covers innumerable hazards both natural and man-made – contrary currents, warming seas, predators, ships, nets, plastic in all its grotesque forms – it must find the island-strewn west coast of Scotland, then from out of that strewment it must select Mull. Having found it, it must decide how to bypass it, the north coast through the Sound of Mull or the south coast and the Firth of Lorn. A good map or a natural vantage point like the high ground of Lismore would seem to suggest that the Firth of Lorn is the obvious choice because it leads more naturally to what follows. But is there anything at all obvious about the return of the Atlantic salmon from mid-ocean to the fragment of moving water where it was born? I have thought about this quite hard, and I can think of nothing about the process that I can point to and say, there, that bit's obvious. Except that only by arriving at that same fragment of water far up some tributary of the upper River Orchy can that fish perform the single task for which it is hard-wired by nature: to be part of the process of producing the next generation of Atlantic salmon. It either dies in the attempt, or it succeeds precisely because it is an Atlantic salmon, and the demands of its whole life's journey are dedicated to this here and now. Nature asks a lot of this fish.

So say it chooses the south coast option then swings north up Mull's east coast. Why would it then resist the wide-open jaws and the tidal pull of the Lynn of Lorn and Loch Linnhe beyond? Why instead seek out the narrows of Connel, the Falls of Lora beyond and the first sinuous miles of Loch Etive? And then, with all the wild world at its disposal, how does it identify the unremarkable entrance into the skinny little River Awe?

The River Awe is a minnow of a river amongst the kind of water-courses to which this salmon is thirled. It is about five miles long and serves only to allow the waters of the mighty Loch Awe to make their way to Loch Etive and the ocean. So now, and having survived the man-made indignity of the barrage at the Pass of Brander (as grim a place as the Highlands ever devised, deep in the shadow of Cruachan), how tempted do you suppose the salmon is to turn south and explore the waters of the longest freshwater loch in the land, the twenty-five miles of Loch Awe, one of the natural jewels of mainland Argyll? Of course, the salmon knows better, because it knows where it is going and that, literally, it has no choice. So, in pursuit of its allotted task, it crosses the very top of the loch from west to east, then leaves it again by its north-east corner. It has found the River Orchy. There are a handful of relatively low-lying, relatively douce miles of Strath Orchy before the salmon finally veers north-east into the instantly turbu-lent and pulse-quickening river of Glen Orchy. From here it will have alders for company every mile of the glen, for they line and shade both banks in single file with more than a hint of a guard of honour about them. It is nothing less than a prodigal Atlantic salmon deserves on the last leg of the final homecoming. Welcome home to Glen Orchy of the Falls!

In the midst of the ten falls then, a torpedo is on the move. The prelude is only guessable, and anyone's guess is as good as mine. But, at last, the fish is there and all but vertical, canted a few degrees forward, the tail winding up the momentum even as it finally explodes from water into sunlight and spray, and oh how it glitters in those few seconds of something like flight. And then it seems to reach forward, its bodily attitude lowers towards the horizontal and it strains its every phenomenal resource into a last thrust of forward motion and the waterfall seems to rise to meet it and it hits the wide ledge squarely in the middle and, with who-knows-what manner of gymnastics, it holds on where it lands, and it does not slide back.

The lull is breathless. The waterfall might have the good grace to hold its fire for a few heartbeats in recognition of the leap, the landing, the tenacity to cling. But good grace is not in the nature of waterfalls. It batters on down, and it roars on and on. But now, suddenly, in the world of the Atlantic salmon, the roaring and boiling and water-furies of the sink are behind it. From here, from the ledge two-thirds of the way to sanctuary, it knows the way. In its own time, it will find the second momentous thrust, the lesser explosion, and it will cruise upstream and away from the tug of the last great obstacle in its path. There are other waterfalls on the Orchy, and the power of the river in this mood is fierce along its entire length. But this is what the salmon is good at, and the golden-eagle-like control that comes with swimming upstream reasserts itself. A deep pool lies in an eddy of the bank. Alders cast their shadows along every yard of it. Perhaps there is where the salmon slides into the gloom. Draws breath. Rests.

★

"The least sympathetic of humans must admit a touch of awe," wrote Marion Campbell in her exquisitely pitched portrayal of her native land, *Argyll – The Enduring Heartland* (Turnstone, 1977). I freely admit to that touch of awe.

"Even 'the wisest fool in Christendom', King James VI and I, could write of the 'salmon-like instinct to see the place of his birth and breeding' in planning his one journey northward after his ascension to the English throne."

James, having thus ascended, moved his entire court from Edinburgh to London in 1603 and only returned once before his death in 1625. The surprise is that he invoked the salmon, that its way of life and compulsion to return to its native airt was well understood even then, compared to, say, the wilful lies and ignorance that attended the lifestyle of the wolf.

Marion Campbell lived at Kilberry on the Knapdale shore, as did her family for 400 years. She was also my friend. My conversations and correspondence with her over the last decade of her life offered me rare insights into Argyll's – and Scotland's – past, present and future that would have been quite out of reach to me otherwise. She had wanted to call her book *My Argyll*, which is nothing less than the Argyll of 5,000 years of its story, and the undateable years of legend. She defended the notion in her introduction with a Gaelic phrase from "our poet" Donnchaidh Ban MacIntyre: *Chan fhaca tusa i leis na suilean agamsa* – "You have not seen her with my eyes". That was her so-generous gift to me: that she let me see something of Argyll with her eyes. "Heartland" as she referred to it, is simply one of my very favourite books. I have been reading it for more than forty years. It is among the most elegant books that anyone ever wrote about any aspect of Scotland.

She was writing about Glen Orchy when she invoked James VI and the salmon, and in a curious way that at least has echoes of my own tendency to home in on Glen Orchy, its river, its falls, its alders, its pine-wood remnants, its otters and golden eagles, and one in particular of its mountains. I have been doing that for almost fifty years. Marion died in her eightieth summer; 2019 was her centenary year, 2020 would have been her one hundredth summer. It was a good moment to go back to Glen Orchy, to make a pause of gratitude there, to watch a salmon confront a meeting of waterfalls (for these are always portentous places).

In truth, the Marion Campbells of this world are beyond time. She was writer, poet, historian, archaeologist, and a living, breathing fragment of the land where she was born, lived and died; her family lived there in an unbroken line for four centuries, and they live there still. And the themes of *Heartland* endure. The River Orchy still "roars with the voice of an angry ghost in a long-severed Celtic head". The Atlantic salmon still homes in on Etive, Awe, Orchy. The Atlantic itself still laves Kilberry's shore, tide after tide. Tides are a recurring symbol. She planned an autobiography, called it *Tidemarks,* wrote one page – about the tide beyond her window – and abandoned it. But you could argue that *Heartland* is her autobiography; or, at least, a lyrically real-ised self-portrait for her voice is everywhere in its pages. Just as the river *is* Glen Orchy, so Marion Campbell *is* Argyll. She was Marion Campbell *of* Kilberry: she was of that place.

"Yesterday Was Summer" is her title for a chapter on childhood, but no sooner has it established the timescale of her lifetime than it extends its reach, because "…my grandfather, born in 1844, kept a diary from boyhood to death…he knew a man brought up by an old woman who remembered 1745". *Heartland* set sail with the first currach and the hunter-gatherers, but its final chapter is called "Tomorrow" and is an unambiguous endorsement for Scottish independence. And "…the long sigh of tide-turn is heard already".

The consuming project of that sphere of her life where historian and writer united in common purpose was a biography of Alexander III. It took her forty years, on and off, before *Alexander III – King of Scots* was published in October 1999, appropriately by The House of Lochar on the Argyll island of Colonsay. She died the following June, her work done. I miss her still.

*

If you are an Atlantic salmon in the River Orchy, mostly all you will see of the world beyond the banks is alder trees. Yet if you are walk-ing or cycling by the river, it may be that you don't notice the alders at all. They line both banks in single file, leaving only enough space between trees to accommodate each other's unimpressive canopies. Behind them, the aspens, the oaks, the birches, the Scots pines, the willows and the hollies compete for the level ground of the flood plain, and crowd down towards the alders; and behind these, millions of spruces and larches clothe hillsides most of the way to mountain tops. The forestry industry has been none too gentle with Glen Orchy. But set against so much swarming summer greenery, the alders are so inconspicuous they practically vanish. Most of the time, wherever they grow in any kind of profusion, vanishing is what they do best.

But what they lack in spectacle they compensate for in tenacity. They hold all the other trees back and for two reasons. One is that they are thirled utterly to water, to damp places, wet places, waterlogged places, and yes, to the outermost edges of riverbanks. The other is that they have evolved a technique to safeguard their right to the role of guard of honour for the epic marchpast of the Atlantic salmon. The tree produces two kinds of catkins: long dangly ones, which are male (sounds about right), and little cones, which are female. The cones hold the seeds and the tree drops them in its own roots. The result is that either they seed there and guarantee the next generation of alders on the parent tree's stance, or the river washes them off and carries them to a new landfall further downstream. So the continuity of alders is fed from the water, and no other tree species gets closer to the riverbank than that. The alders of Glen Orchy, then, line the riverbank in perpetuity. Wouldn't it be nice to know when they first moved in, for the alder is a pioneer species? It would have been at the head of the queue when the last ice age ended around 10,000 years ago, and given that Glen Orchy would have been an early landscape feature as the glaciers from the icecap that was Rannoch Moor began to reconfigure the central and west Highlands into something we might recognise today, the alders of today's river may well be the direct descendants of some of the earliest trees to re-establish in the wake of the ice. So surely they are worth a second glance. There is one in particular that I have in mind.

For all the inherent modesty with which nature has imbued alders like these, the most beautiful tree in all of Glen Orchy is an alder, and a small tree at that, even by riverbank alder standards. It is so edge-of-the-bank in its stance that, with the river in this extravagant mood so that it roars a tenfold waterfall at an Atlantic salmon, the alder wades. Here is where the roots splay neatly then steepen down over rock into the river's peaty embrace. But many alders wade. What makes this one beautiful is its compact and balletic pose, which its water's-edge stance only enhances. The trunk rises straight for only about six feet, at which point it bends at forty-five degrees and reaches up and out over the shallowest water. But only four feet up from the roots, the trunk also throws a limb out towards the water and almost at right angles, and that limb begins at once to bend upwards. The result is a sinuous profile formed by the two limbs, the first staying close to the shore, the second reaching for the mainstream. The alchemy they achieve derives from the shapes of the two spaces enclosed by the two limbs as they curve towards each other and then apart from each other. One is a perfect oval, the other an elongated triangle. Change the angle of your viewpoint slowly and watch the shapes of the spaces change too, widening or narrowing, shortening or lengthening. The hypnotic effect is enhanced by the fact that the spaces enclose nothing but brightly sunlit and vigorously mobile river water. A gleeful wind shivers the leaves and lesser branches of the tree, yet their modest spread has a controlling effect on all movement. So the whole tree is anchored by the trunk but the limbs and the branches and leaves shift subtly against the background of the river's liveliness, and that liveliness is there in the spaces within the tree. I could watch this for hours. With a guitar in my hands I might have coaxed the tree's dance to make music. (I must go back with a guitar sometime and see what I can make of it.) As it was, all I had in my hand was a pen and a note-book to write it down.

I had brought my bike. When I rode on, relishing the midsummer quiet of the glen's delectable single-track road, I lingered over the sense of the tree, its swaying image gently seducing the memory as I tried to keep it bright in my mind, the zest of it, "the touch of the daylight on the dream". If you think that an extravagant response to a smallish alder tree on the bank of an Argyll river, you have not seen her with my eyes.

Thirty-seven

She Is of the Woods and I Am Not

THE PLACE OF TREES in the landscape is never far from my mind. I revere, I cherish well-wooded places. I stow away among them often. Sometimes, especially in summer, I feel the need to seek out cool places beneath old trees – oaks or Scots pines, for preference. And because it is summer and because I live in Scotland, and because summer and Scotland and trees are the component parts of an equation that equals midges, I like my cool places beneath old trees to be open spaces, and high rather than low-lying, and near enough to the edge of the wood to permit access for the wind, the better to keep me cool and move the midges along.

Here is one such open space, in a pine-and-oak wood that reaches a thousand feet uphill on both sides of a mountain river to a trinity of waterfalls, so water voices carry to me on an easy wind, and that adds to the allure. But right now, I just want the good Highland summer green that dresses the space beneath the trees. I know from many years of practice that this here-and-now with my back to an old oak trunk, sitting as still as I know how with the wind in my face...this open invitation to nature to drop in and spend the time of day with me is as likely to bear fruit as absolutely anything else I can think of.

THE WIND IN MY FACE

The wind at my back,
my scent and sound
blown before me
and nature a locked door.
The wind in my face,
my scent and sound

a shredded wake
and nature an open gate.
Enter, ask for owl eyes,
tree stillness,
now make what you can
of her secrets.

Then the roe deer. The doe. She walked from tree shadows, where dusk had begun to gather, into the one patch of that small clearing where the last of the sunlight caught her, and there she stopped and there she stood and there she glowed. But the reddening sun was only on her head and neck and spine and the top half of her left flank. The rest of her was dark. She presented an almost eerie illusion, as if the top half of a deer was swimming through the trees and the woodland understorey. When she stopped, she floated.

How long before she would see me?

She was still then, apart from her ears, and these flickered with a restlessness that belied her outward calm. The ears looked too big for the size of her head and they were pale grey, almost white, when they turned towards me, and trimmed with a sharp lace of black. With these she tested every airt of the woodland and far beyond. But I knew the wind worked in my favour. So did my stillness and my woodland-shaded clothes, yet *something* gave me away and her head swung round and I was pinned to the oak tree by her black-eyed stare. So I had the answer to my own question – how long before she would see me? – and that answer was about twenty seconds. The fact is that despite all the care I routinely take in such a situation, the deer is better attuned. She is of the woods and I am not. Each time I come back here, or somewhere like it, I have to re-acclimatise, shed influences from beyond the woods that – inevitably – I bring with me. And I am willing to bet that she will have known that I was here long before she trusted my stillness enough to cross the clearing and pause in that last scrap of evening sunlight.

A lesson falls into place here, a kind of first commandment and it cannot be repeated too often. It is that in all our dealings with wildlife, from watching a roe deer cross a clearing on a summer evening to reintroducing lost species (say wolf, beaver, sea eagle) with consequences that will endure for hundreds of years, it always takes time. And mostly giving the required time to watch and learn and understand – letting nature take its course – is where our side of the bargain falls short.

The doe turned from side-on to head-on, and as she did so that low and intense sunlight travelled across her as she realigned head and neck and chest and back, until only her face and chest were brightly lit, lending her a faintly ghostly air. I wondered why she had turned like that. What I expected was that she would turn to face away from me then turn her head back to look at me down the length of her spine, ready for flight. But this had the air of something more confrontational, or perhaps just more contemplative, weighing up my threat, or absence of threat. Then she stamped one forefoot. A soft thud like a muffled drumbeat. Was that for my benefit, an invitation to leave the premises? Or else, a signal…?

A juniper bush shivered and her fawn materialised from its dark-green fleece and came to stand alongside her, a perfect miniature mirror image except that it lacked the sunlit patches, being completely in shadow. The fawn could have been no more than two months old, yet she had obviously acquired from her mother the art of the disconcerting stare.

Then, without a sound, they both turned to their right as if it was a well-rehearsed manoeuvre, walked beyond the sunlight to a more open patch of ground, a distance of no more than twenty yards. Then, without another glance they both started to browse. The doe constantly raised her head to look back but I gave her nothing, no cause for alarm. I was oak-tree still. I hoped that the warmth and the admiration I felt for her and her offspring in that place at that moment would transmit, that she would catch the sense of it and relax.

I watched them for a few minutes more and, if I am honest, I envied them their place on this wooded hillside, for they had an involvement with it, an intimacy with that land and everything else that lived and breathed there, an intimacy that is light years beyond anything I might ever hope to achieve. Then they moved off silently into the trees. With their disappearance, I considered what I had just seen and the dilemma that it had just dropped in my lap. And this is part of the nature writer's condition, for in my head were the words of an old friend called Don MacCaskill. Don was a forester, the Forestry Commission's chief forester for the Strathyre Forest, and a very untypical one at that. He was a brilliant naturalist, an award-winning wildlife photographer, he hand-reared foxes, his dark-room walls were lined with photographs of wolves. The words that made me realise, quite early on in our friendship, that he did not quite fit the mould of a Forestry Commission chief forester, were these:

"A forest is not a forest without deer."

And of course he was right. The corollary of that is also true: a deer is not a deer without forest.

*

I have always loved that hour when daylight turns to dark, especially high-summer dark, which, on the Highland Edge means a bluish grey half-light. Eventually, just as I was about to leave, the unmistakable voice of the roebuck boomed into the clearing and hung on the air, deep and throaty, two harsh syllables designed to put the fear of death into any other roebuck within earshot. Fear of death is only a slight exaggeration. Few creatures the length and breadth of wild Scotland defend their territory as uncompromisingly as a mature roebuck in high summer, for that is also the roe mating season. I watched his silhouette follow precisely the line taken by the doe a few minutes before. She was somewhere out there just ahead of him in the gloom, but he knew precisely where. There is a dead oak tree, a runt, not far away, and stamped into the grass around that tree is a perfect circle, the ring of the roe mating season where buck follows doe in a ritualised merry-go-round of salacious intent. I had seen him earlier in the day as he crossed a patch of brilliantly sunlit bracken and he was a beast in his prime and lord of his manor. There are places in the Lowlands where roe deer numbers are a problem, but on the edge of the mountains and in woodlands like this you do well to get a view like that. But the glimpse of his silhouette as the gloaming gathered around the edge of the clearing (for he had paused where she paused, scenting her progress), *that* was the prize, that was the glorious moment of confirmation of Don's words, and what a photograph he would have made of the moment. I simply kept it in my head until it was time to write it down.

A forest is not a forest without deer.

And the deer is not a deer without the forest.

Never was. Never will be.

Thirty-eight
Solstice

THREE IN THE MORNING. It doesn't take much to waken me at such an hour. I am not the most efficient of sleepers. An unaccustomed bed in an unaccustomed house is as likely a circumstance as any. The unaccustomed window with its unaccustomed view is open. There is light through a gap in the curtains. It is the week of the summer solstice. Cross the room to the window: the sea is across the street (the high tide will pause at slack water a few yards from the pavement). Its colour is a phenomenal shade, the palest turquoise I ever saw, a shade surely unique to a pre-sunrise east coast sea. But the sky in the north-east looks ready to burst into flames. By 4.30, the sea will dazzle. In the course of such a day it will scatter shades from that turquoise to mid-grey to pink to colour-free dazzle to slate blue to royal blue to a late afternoon tapestry of blues that will drape navy along the horizon, then to slate and lilac and through paling greys to white at about 10p.m. And in twenty-four hours' time it will work its way up to dazzle again and repeat for seven unbroken days.

It was to be that kind of week.

*

I find that the years pull me east more often. Something about the pared-to-the-bone simplicity of that coast and the lure of a quiet country: land a curve of dark red sandstone cliff, sea a slab of smooth and blue-grey unpolished marble untrammelled by islands and undaunted by mountains. The sun will rise out of such a sea and so will the moon. Have you never seen the sun rise out of the sea? The moon? Oh, it really is quite fine. Uniquely among all the landscapes of Scotland, summer is the east coast's finest hour. And compared to the west and the north, tourism is sparse; its shore is unsung. I speak, I sing, as a native. The east is my native shore.

On the west coast, that sliver of my inheritance that is Celt lays claim to me; I succumb to a thraldom of Hebridean islands and their complicit mountains. I stir to the summons of the Skye Cuillin, the subtler seductions of Cìr Mhòr on Arran, Ben More on Mull, lowly Dun I on Iona, Beinn na Gudairean on Colonsay, the Sgurr on Eigg, Dun Caan on Raasay, Clisham on Harris. On the north coast, Orkney's pod of whale-shaped islands speaks to me in calmer tongues, more George Mackay Brown than Sorley MacLean, whereas Shetland and Fair Isle are where (it seems to me) the north of the world begins and I thrill to that benevolent shiver of Norse-tongued names for island, hill, rock and bird (dunter, not eider; shaldur, not oystercatcher, swaabie, not black-backed gull; tirrick, not tern). An exquisite northern other-worldliness begins there and sometimes I have aspired to that... Alaska, Iceland, Norway, beyond where the Arctic increasingly lurks just within reach of my idea of what may yet be possible.

All of that began aged about twenty. But when I look on the east coast, something else happens, something that laid claim to those first twenty years before islands and West and North knew anything about me, and all I knew of them was in books by other people, glimpses on family holidays. And, of course, the first twenty years of anyone's life lay down the bedrock on which whatever follows must stand or fall, for good or ill. And I was lucky with my bedrock. Dundee, on the north shore of the firth of the finest river in the land, sculpted from two hills of its own, was more surely bedded in the county of Angus then; "Dundee, Angus" was its postal address. And forby the hills and mountains that crowd the north of that county, forby the beaches and the bird hordes of the firth, there was the tantalising coast of my young years that reached from Montrose in the north by way of Auchmithie, the Bell Rock, Tentsmuir and Fife Ness to the East Neuk and the Isle of May. That was the seagoing inheritance into which I was born, and its light is all the shades of gold.

And if you are sufficiently well attuned, oh how it sings! It is Scotland's skylark coast, for the fields and moors roll down to the clifftops along much of its length, and the larks spring from the grasses and clusters of wild poppies and ox-eye daisies, and by the time they are a yard off the ground they are singing, full-throated from the first note, as self-confident as Beethoven's *Fifth* or Louis Armstrong's *West End Blues*. And in places they cling to their slender columns of song held aloft on warm summer winds a dozen to an acre. And the east coast throbs with the croon of eider drakes, and wherever those grasses and poppies and scrubby bushes and small trees spill over the edge to thicken the sea cliffs, summer is further adorned by carolling whitethroats and the grin-inducing och-aye of puffins.

Such is the land into which I was born, where summer announced itself in shades of red sandstone and tawny sand, seas the width of the known world and skies that went on forever. I astounded my parents at the age of two or three when I said "kittiwake" without any prompting: I heard it, I said it. Whenever I revisit the east coast now, I feel something akin to what the writer and mountaineer David Craig (sitting content-edly on a rock ledge) called "the sense of rightness regained", and there is nothing the finest views in all the sung shores of the world can do about that. It means, in my case, regaining the native rightness, the landscape whence all the others sprung, the original understanding of my place in nature's scheme of things (tiny, lowly, watchful, wonder-filled). There is also a revised sense of belonging, which seems to matter to me more at least some of the time, and more often than it used to.

And there is, of course, much more to the east coast than the portion that accommodated my boyhood and youth. Much of it is essentially Lowland in character, but a Caithness coast, for example, is a very different place with a very different sensibility. More often than not, until fairly recently, questing travels on that coast were inclined towards north, and it was Neil Gunn's eyes I looked through. But then this book's journey took me to Berwickshire and the cliff-hunkered village of Burnmouth, and there, over the course of a single week, I learned to imbue the east coast with a music that I had only heard dimly until then. For the Berwickshire coast itself was also something of an unsung shore in my own mind, a portion of my native shore that mostly lay beyond my accustomed horizons. It seemed to me then that I would benefit from immersing myself in a comparatively unfamiliar tract of my native shore to sit alongside the more familiar. Then I stumbled across a cottage a handful of miles from the Border and with the sea on the other side of the street. And the first thing I heard when I parked and opened the car door was the ever-so-slightly eerie, atonally beautiful, curiously wolf-like chorale of grey seals.

At that moment, even before I had unpacked the car, I thought that perhaps I had found a defining song for my unsung shore. A simple principle fell into place that first afternoon and evening, and it grew on me far into the night. It was that the ebb and flow of the tide coincided with the wax and wane of the sealsong. The ebbing tide uncovered acres and acres of flat rock carved into long, parallel north–south furrows, and as soon as the furthest-out rocks began to appear above the waves, so did the heads of the seals. It is pushing it to suggest that they formed an orderly queue to step ashore, but the effect was something similar, for they gathered on the seaward side and swam around until they found what they were looking for. And once they settled (a relative term for a grey seal colony on haul-out rocks, for theirs is a restless way of life), and from time to time and at any time of the day and night, and in concert and solo…they sang.

All week they sang and they sang, but their song was intermittent and so unpredictable that it surprised me every time it resumed. And after a couple of days and nights it did begin to feel like a resumption, as if it had just retreated beyond earshot and I never heard it go or realised it had gone until it drifted back hours later; and in much the same way I would stop hearing the sea for a while (the weather was a midsummer idyll and the sea responded in character so that it lay much of the time like that slab of sunshine-polished blue-grey marble I had grown up with decades before, smoky pale grey unpolished marble after sunset), and at low tide when it had retreated beyond the rocks it was little more than a conspiratorial murmur.

The great joy of that potently harmonised sequence of days and nights was to awaken in the wee small hours with a hint of dawn in the eastern sky beyond the open window and perhaps it was a single seal voice that crept in under the old stone lintel, and I would imbue a single voice with an added edge of wildness for no other reason than the serene mood of the time and place and atmosphere and moment.

Then an answering voice would be joined all at once by half a dozen others, and once again it had struck me that they seemed to avoid harmony deliberately, and again I thought of wolves, for that is the way with wolfsong, too.

The view of the land across the bay in front of the cottage ended in a little headland, which, in a certain light, had the appearance of the head of Hollywood's idea of an Apache brave in profile. After a few days it became apparent that the rocks beyond the cliff he embellished were the source of much of the sealsong. The last full day of my stay turned out to be the summer solstice, and the tide table suggested that a couple of hours of late morning and early afternoon sitting on the clifftop directly above the Apache would offer prime seal viewing.

It did. As the sea fell back and back, the water was studded with the heads of approaching seals, and it seemed to my inexpert eyes that they waited for the sea to clear from a particular long and almost level rock before they emerged. Eventually, there were about sixty grey seals, arranged along four rocks, and as it happened the rocks were aligned largest to smallest from right-to-left, south to north.

The inland side of the big rock's platform accommodated two small pools, each about the size of a single adult seal, and a kind of natural waterslide over seaweed. In the course of two hours, these were in almost constant use. I hesitate to say the seals bathed in the pools given that they spend so much time in the water anyway, but it looked that way, or perhaps they liked the feel of the seaweed; and there was a suspicion of glee at the way they used the slide to move from rock back into water, but that too could have been human imagination rather than seal biology.

The singing was more sporadic than ever in the middle of the day, and most of it came from the smallest rocks. I wondered about its purpose. It's not a contact call, for most of the time they are literally within touching distance of their kin. But it is a far-carrying sound (wolves again, and whales!) so perhaps it is designed to send information up or down the coast to other haul-out rocks. Or out to sea.

Those clifftop hours were as agreeable as any of the entire wild year. But then, just when I thought that it couldn't get much better, there were dolphins.

They breezed across the wide entrance to the bay in speeding, gleaming curves with dorsal fins curved like breaking waves. Sporadically they galvanised into steeplechasing leaps. The sun bore down on them. The seals watched them, or ignored them (they are no slouches at the art of porpoising themselves when the mood is on them). I suddenly realised I was gasping out loud and smiling. Seven or eight dolphins, perhaps more, putting on a show for the landlubbers on seal rock and clifftop.

Then the perfect dive. The last of them soared from the water, steepened its descent, and as it re-entered the sea it was perfectly vertical. In my mind's eye its spread tail flukes hung for a moment and suspended the weight of the entire dolphin directly below it, then followed the most graceful torso of that inshore water back into the sea. That was the image that endured, that became the shape of the midsummer solstice, just as the seals became its song.

But the moment would produce the most extraordinary encore. Later that evening, I was sitting in the cottage living room listening to music and staring out of the window at that sea across the street. By then I was beguiled by it, for it was both constant and constantly transforming, changeless and constantly changing its mind, its voice, the very process by which it came ashore. If your imagination runs to the notion of a slow-motion kaleidoscope, this was it. Wave patterns became virtuosic, colour became relentless diffusion. No matter that the sun was setting 200 miles over my shoulder in the Atlantic Ocean somewhere west of the Mull of Galloway, within the symphonic scope of the North Sea were tiny tone poems of every colour I could think of and some I could never have imagined. A wave a few inches high curved lusciously around folds of black, mahogany brown and egg-yolk yellow before it collapsed and vanished as if it had never been. In its place another arose, ice-blue, purple, crimson, gone. These lights flickered and faded in the shallows and among the few still bared rocks.

Diffusion.

I looked at the word on the page where I had just written it down. Then on a whim I reached for a dictionary and found that in the context I had ascribed to it, it suddenly amounted to something rather more than the sum of the parts.

1. to spread (something) out freely in all directions; 2. to break up and distribute (incident light) by reflection; 3. the process whereby particles of liquids, gases or solids intermingle as the result of their spontaneous movement; 4. reflection of light by a rough reflecting surface; 5. the spread of a cultural characteristic.

I never thought to encounter something like poetry in a dictionary. I read the compiler's take on my word and congratulated myself on my choice of noun. Then I thought better of it and instead I congratulated the compiler and the English language on its capacity to invent such a word with so many strings to its elegant bow.

Diffusion. Nice job.

I drifted into a kind of deep sea reverie of surfacing whales with phosphorescence breaking about their flanks, and falling in dripping sheets from the long upraised pectoral fins (they were humpbacks I fantasised, they always are), curtains of folded points of fire. For a few moments the walls of the room faded and the sea had made of me a wholly consenting prisoner. And then in the real sea world beyond the real window in the real wall in front of me, my attention was drawn back to where there was a dark curve and another, and another, and another…the dolphins had come back. I was watching dolphins from the sofa.

Mostly, you work hard to come close to nature, hours of travel and patience and stillness (that above all things) to win a handful of moments' reward. That is as it should be. Your species and mine has engendered in nature a profound mistrust of our doings in wild places, such has been our wholesale and increasingly aggressive abuse of our place in the world for centuries. But if you are inclined to come close to nature, to win a degree of intimacy there so that nature confides some of her secrets in your presence, then that mistrust must be overcome by a dedicated deference and by setting out to encounter nature *on nature's terms*. And as Nan Shepherd put it in her unsurpassed (and probably unsurpassable) little masterpiece, *The Living Mountain* (Aberdeen University Press, 1977): "This is not done easily nor in an hour. It is a tale too slow for the impatience of our age." But if you listen to the land, listen to what nature is trying to tell you, then once in a while nature will reach out to you when you least expect it, and sometimes the results are extraordinary. These are the blue moon moments. Watching dolphins from the sofa was one such.

Of course, then there was the undignified scramble for binoculars, the rush to the door and across the street to the edge of the sea, there to stand and stare at the quiet miracle that is the unhurried grace and ease of a pod of dolphins with somewhere to go. The swimming is matter-of-fact, flirting in equal measure with surface and underwater, devouring distance. It is quite different from the playing-to-the-gallery high jinks they deploy when they ride the bow wave of a ferry or one of those specialist dolphin boats, such as the one I was briefly permitted to steer out in the Firth of Tay a few summers ago. When we came back into harbour at Broughty Ferry I thought briefly that nothing could be finer than to skipper a boat like that. But after a while, once I had re-lived the process a few times, once the adrenaline rush of the moment had dissolved, I thought better of the notion, I decided I would prefer to be a dolphin.

But it was Burnmouth that redefined the dolphin in my mind, when nature reached out a hand to me, and I reached out in return and took it and held on. I choose to believe that nature's purpose at that moment was to fasten into place that connection established earlier in the day, a connection that had been growing and strengthening throughout the week, so that it was secure for all time, so that it honoured in the most remarkable way a sense of time and place in nature's relentless pageant.

*

The tide hauls itself away from slack water just beyond the cottage door. The seals feel the change far out in their deep-sea wherevers, respond to its summons, and home in on their low-tide couches, those narrow parallels of grey rock, straight as harbour walls. From the top of the headland above the Apache's head-dress, looking north up the coast at the full extent of those sprawling parallel rows of rock, the effect is of a bird's eye-view of a ploughed field, albeit it one that was ploughed long enough ago for the furrows to have fallen in here and there. To the east is the sea. To the west is the single street of Burnmouth at the base of its cliff. The rest of the world either lives beyond the sea or beyond the clifftop. "The rest of the world" includes the village that the road maps and the road signs proclaim as Upper Burnmouth, and it is as utterly of that land of fields and woods as Lower Burnmouth is utterly of the sea and the cliffs. I sensed that here was a landscape with a story to tell. I looked back to the seals. The reason the seals home in on the place is surely the nature of the place itself. The seaward edge of the low-tide rocks is a perfect refuge to while away the low-tide hours. Eventually it will be raised just above sea level and because it is long and straight and level it can accommodate all the hauled-out seals that linger along this corner of the coast, and offer them a fast and simultaneous retreat into the sea if danger threatens from the land.

I wondered how long the ancestors of this group of seals were accustomed to hauling out here, and if today's generation had inherited any awareness of the pedigree of the rocks. What I looked down on from the top of the headland was the aftermath of nothing less than the original collision between Scotland and England. This coast from the Border north through Burnmouth and as far north as the edge of Eyemouth is officially the Burnmouth Site of Special Scientific Interest, although in truth, the interest extends a little further than the limits of geological science. To the west of the fault, the rocks are Silurian and somewhere between 420 million and 430 million years old; to the east the rocks are Carboniferous, a youthful 335 million to 355 million years old. Non-geologists might struggle to grasp the significance of this. I only mention it because I am one such and I did – struggle.

So, deep breath, and here goes: the two continents started to drift towards each other. First of all, what causes a continent to "drift" and why are two drifting at the same time? One consequence was that the ocean between them was squeezed. Another was that the ocean floor was pushed *underneath* Scotland. Oh, wouldn't you love to have seen that happening from a safe vantage point, just to see how it works? And I know this is basic stuff for geologists, but bear in mind that I, non-geologist that I am, had just found this out and here I was sitting on top of the Apache's head-dress on a beautiful midsummer morning, scrutinising what even to my eye was an unusually formal looking arrangement of rocks, and I had only come here in the first place because of the seals. And suddenly, I was having to contend with the question: how does an ocean floor get pushed? What manner of forces does it take to achieve that, having first squeezed the ocean itself?

Now for the bit you might begin to understand and then recognise. While it was still joined to its old continent, perhaps an outpost of western Denmark or southern Norway, sediments from Scotland's rivers poured onto the ocean floor to form "fans", but as the ocean floor slid beneath the Scottish landmass, those sediments were scraped off, and instead of lying on the ocean floor they were heaped up into substantial mountains. But then, as the geologists might say, "erosion dominated over deposition", and the mountains wore down, and the result is what twenty-first-century Scots call the Southern Uplands.

Then Scotland and England collided. And again, wouldn't you have loved to be there and witness that first forging of two restless neighbours that would become one restless land? Unfortunately, as always with geology, it was just before our time.

The new Scotland's new mountains poured new sediments from its newly reconfigured rivers, and these flowed into what is now southeast Scotland and formed a coastal plain, and finally, this corner of Scotland began to look like itself.

Finally (finally for the moment, for in reality there is no end to the story of the land and its uneasy neighbour, the ocean), when grazing animals finally got here, they found the sea cliffs too steep for them, and a counter-conspiracy of coastal grassland and landslips on the cliffs created a mosaic of vegetation and bare soils ripe for colonising by adventurous plants. Among these is kidney-vetch, a modest yellow cluster-flowered member of the pea family.

All of which explains why, on a warm June morning of 2019 this Scottish nature writer crouched by one such yellow cluster admiring not the flower itself but the small blue butterfly, which rather dotes on kidney vetch. The small blue is a bit of a watercolour butterfly, and it helps if you are looking at the underside of the wings where pale grey predominates and graduates with exquisite subtlety into sky blue. The cliffs are also something of a stronghold for the northern brown argus, which is as boldly handsome as the small blue is demurely pretty. Chocolate brown with orange and white accessories, animated by full-on June sunlight, you never tire of the male's fast flight around its territory. If you do find one on patrol, remember where you found it, because the chances are that you might find it there again when you come back. And be sceptical when your field guide preaches at you that they are difficult to approach. Sometimes, if you are willing to sit dead still, they approach you. Every time I come across this kind of thoughtless field-guide speak I cite the example of the Scotch argus in Glen Orchy a few summers ago, a moment of startling and unfettered joy in nature's company, which, after a few retellings, resulted in this:

ANOTHER OF THE REASONS WHY I'M SUSPICIOUS OF FIELD GUIDES

Scotch Argus (a butterfly not a drink)
lives in Glen Orchy, or more accurately,
I never saw one anywhere else.
Whenever I'm in Glen Orchy (damp,
peaty, sweet-watered, flower-drenched,
Argyll in a nutshell)
and it's the butterfly time,
I expect to see them.
A field guide I own intones:
"...restless and difficult to approach..."
yet they keep bumping into me. And here,
where I sit half drunk on bog-myrtled air,
are five of them, one on every fingertip
of my left hand. All of which offers up
another of the reasons why
I'm suspicious of field guides.

With the butterflies drifting a few feet away across the cliff face rich in its summer gladrags of flowers and grasses and shrubs, I was permitted to bear witness to a moment that concluded a circle of events that had taken hundreds of millions of years to arrive here. It is no small thing, such a moment.

And if I might return for a moment to the notion voiced by John Muir – "When we try to pick out anything by itself, we find it hitched to everything else in the universe" – one of the things I like about my day job is how moments echo each other across time and landscape. And thanks to the butterflies at Burnmouth that emerged from a 350 million-years-old geology lesson, I forged a link within my own idea of my own country between its Lowland east and its Highland west, Berwickshire with Argyll.

And then there was a still more startling echo.

A few days after I returned from Burnmouth, I was driving back towards Stirling from Flanders Moss, so as land-locked as mainland Scotland permits. It was a still, early evening, the fields of the Carse of Stirling quiet under their arc of mountains. I was alone, I had my window down, the car CD player was playing Yo-Yo Ma's newly released reinterpretation of the Bach Cello Suites, which to my mind is a perfect pinnacle in the art of making music. Then I saw a red kite hunting low over a field.

The road was deserted. I stopped, cut the engine, and with it, the music. The car flooded with the warmth of that late-June evening and a profound quiet, and the two fused into a stillness of rare quality. The red kite in hunting mode is both slow and silent, often stopping on the air, head down, fork-tail splayed, sunset-shaded. In this manner it drifted sideways across the field, then back again, a pattern of shallow zigs and zags as elegant as it was purposeful. Then it changed tack and came towards me, so that now I saw it head-on and slowly filling more and more of the binoculars. It was no more than thirty yards away, not ten feet off the ground, when it stopped, held still, raised half-folded wings high above its head, pulled both legs and feet together and stretched them vertically below its body, and in that attitude it fell, and the soft thud of its landing was the only thing I could hear. But the point is this: in the instant before it began to descend, wings high, legs and feet together so that the realigned shape of the bird was widest at the top where its half-shut wings created a pair of matching wedges, and narrowest at the bottom where the closed legs and feet brought the whole thing to an elegant point. What came in to my mind in an instant in that Stirlingshire field was the perfect dive of the Burnmouth dolphin, for the shape of the kite echoed the shape of the other.

Sometimes I think that summer is my least favourite season. Then something like that happens, and what Muir said of everything being hitched to everything else in the universe…it is every bit as true of the seasons, and the reality is that just as there is really only one ocean and we have given different bits of it different names, so there is only one season and we have given different bits of it different names too, and there is just as much chance of glimpsing eternity in midsummer. And when you do, you will find that that glimpse is hitched to everything else in the universe of the seasons. The red kite rose and flew off (it missed), resumed its zigzag pattern away across the field, passed some big trees and vanished into the next field.

Meanwhile, back in Burnmouth, I was still left with one unanswered question. It nagged me all that week. It nags at me still. What happened to the ocean that got squeezed? And then a second question as unanswerable as the first: is that ocean bed still underneath Scotland, quietly awaiting the advent of one more geological upheaval, perhaps to be rescued from sub-sea ignominy and become mountain, its new rivers glittering in unaccustomed sunlight? In the process, will we regain our long lost land bridge to continental Europe? The wolves would be pleased, at least. All we lack now for wolves to reintroduce themselves is a land bridge, for as I write this they are in every country in mainland Europe again, and no one has been eaten alive because of it. In the meantime, we have the kidney vetch, the small blue and the northern brown argus as a legacy from the last time we heaped up new mountains hereabouts, that and an unsung coast that has found its voice, and I have heard it sing.

Thirty-nine
Bass Notes

My Burnmouth week had a boat trip built in from the outset. For years I had wanted to sail out to the Bass Rock. Being in the company of 150,000 gannets was only one of the reasons why. The other, the more pressing in my mind, was to examine at close quarters the Bass itself. The Rock.

I really only knew it from the far side of the Forth, from the upper jaw of the Firth, from Fife, specifically that stretch of coast between Fife Ness and St Monans, twelve miles away from the out-on-a-limb headland of the Ness, and still ten miles of open water away from St Monans. From such distances the Bass rather settles into its East Lothian hinterland and the blunt silhouette of the Lammermuir Hills, spired and spiked along their skyline with wind turbines as tightly packed as spruce trees in a spruce plantation. The Bass suffers a bit by association, identifiable more by its pallor than its essentially monumental nature. In midsummer noontides, it wears an indistinct shade of bluish-off-white, the product not just of the backlighting of a south-making sun, but also the restlessness of gannets in epic numbers blurring its contours and thickening its immediate airspace, not to mention the colossal spread of their essential byproduct, also known as guano, also known as bird shit.

Then, in the evening, as midsummer suns dawdle and dip down towards the north-west, the Bass explodes with light and stands forward from the Lothian shore, its islandness restored. That low-to-the-horizon brilliance that sizzles across the miles of open water reinvents the rock, picks out every fissure and gully and cave and also illuminates the smooth deep grey places of the north face where even gannets cannot find a toehold, far less a nesting place.

Such is the Bass from the Forth's northern coastline, but now as I drove towards the Scottish Seabird Centre and veered west at Tantallon's glorious fourteenth-century red sandstone clifftop castle, the Bass materialised in some majesty on its moorings no more than two miles offshore. I understood then that from every angle and in every light and whatever the distance, the Bass at peak gannet season is both irresistible force and immovable object fused into a landmark of nature as great and compelling in its landscape as any mountain.

But its show was about to be stolen. By puffins.

No one had told me about Craigleith, an inauspicious little island half a mile offshore, and which turned out to be on the boat's itinerary, too. It is everything the Bass is not: low-lying, inconspicuous, grassy, supporting a vigorous plant community, and where the Bass is virtually a gannet monoculture, Craigleith is biodiverse. As the boat approached, the water was suddenly awash with puffins, and then so was the island. I could have stood up and punched the air, except that I am not a particularly demonstrative creature, and the boat was so well-filled that if I had punched the air, I might have taken out two fellow passengers with my follow-through. And there were also eider ducks, fulmars, grey seals, razorbills, great black-backed gulls, cormorants and shags. Oh, and rabbits. And Craigleith has a bit of a story to tell, for it is at the heart of the Scottish Seabird Centre's SOS Puffin project.

Of all the reasons I have heard for the decline in puffins all across the North Atlantic, the one that accounted for a population crash on Craigleith was in a class of its own: an invasion of tree mallow. This native of mainland Europe's western shores is a favourite garden plant, but given the chance, it can grow in dense thickets up to nine feet tall. Its arrival on Craigleith was disastrous for the island's substantial puffin colony (28,000 pairs in 1999, down to 1,000 in 2007) because it colonised their nesting areas and made impenetrable barriers between bird and nest burrows. The SOS Puffin project recruited a squad of volunteers to attack the tree mallow every October, once the puffins had gone, and slowly, the numbers began to recover.

The mean twist to the story is that the seeds of tree mallow float, and that once they had got into the water around the East Lothian coast, the floating seeds could have been delivered onto the island unwittingly by swimming birds – like puffins, for example. The project goes on, for tree mallow is a tenacious beast, but at least, as I write this, and for the moment, the puffins are ahead of the game.

But there was still the matter of this:

"If the puffin becomes extinct, they will never forgive us."

It had been just a random thought, and I have many such random thoughts in the course of a day and mostly dismiss them. This one rankled. It niggled. It squirmed its way into a different corner of my brain and went to work there. So I stopped and looked at it for a while, and now, what I think is this.

First, you must buy into the proposition that you and I are nature and not a superior creature outwith and above nature's laws. Otherwise, there is simply no hope, all is lost, and it won't be just puffins you will mourn, because sooner rather than later, and most likely sooner, ecosystems will cease to function because we will have ruined all their resources, and without natural resources our species is doomed, just because you didn't buy into that simple proposition. We *are* nature's creatures.

Nature has put the plight of the Atlantic puffin before our eyes for two reasons. One is that what is happening to it is simple to understand: the behaviour of our species is ruining its essential habitat and food supply. The other is that at an unthinking, aesthetic level, we love puffins and we still go to great lengths to watch them just being puffins. Two summers ago, on a visit to the Isle of May, I eavesdropped on a small group of fellow-passengers as the boat headed back for the mainland. It became clear that they were regular travellers to puffin colonies all around the coast of Britain. They agreed among themselves that Isle of May was nothing like as good as the Farne Islands off the Northumberland coast, because there you could see more birds and get much closer, and you didn't have to walk so far. (The May that summer had 40,000 pairs.) They talked of nothing but puffins. There were nesting eiders right beside the path that eyed you from the depths of one of nature's most perfect stillnesses: nothing. There were waltzing clouds of Arctic terns that flared up from a standing start into the afternoon sun and simply dazzled the beholder's eye: but they were unbeheld by the puffineers. In a slightly troubling way, they were puffin crazy. They are far from alone. And perhaps nature is suggesting that there is something to work with here, that the puffineers are themselves a resource that can be redirected to champion nature's cause through puffins.

Listen to the land.

What it says is this: the Atlantic puffin is doomed.

In its greatest stronghold – Iceland – its natural defences are down. The experts say so, the professional scientists, even while they are still surrounded by 5 million puffins. It is a deception. It is not sustainable. Among those who are not listening to the land in Iceland are hunters, trophy-hunting for puffins. And the hunters, too, are fooled by the deception...look, there are millions of them, plenty for us!

The land is also saying this. Consider the relative demands the two species make on the planet: *Fractercula arctica* and *Homo sapiens*. The Atlantic puffin eats sand eels, and no more than they need. The idea of overfishing is incomprehensible to them. They make burrows in grassy clifftops for their nests. That's it. In winter they head out to sea and look after themselves. What they ask of nature is just enough fish and a clean ocean. That and a climate in which extreme weather events are rare enough to be manageable. They are scarcely more demanding of the planet than fresh air.

On the other hand, the demands our species makes on the planet include this one: we want it all and we want it to do our bidding. One of many consequences is that we deny puffins a reliable supply of its life's essentials, this bird that we profess to love so ardently that year after year, summer after summer, we fill boats and sail to offshore islands to feed our two-faced puffin love. "Two-faced" because at the same time, the species to which we belong is also sealing the puffin's fate. Unless we listen to the land, then, unless we pay heed to what it asks of us, the puffin *will* go extinct. The case is so unambiguous. That random thought that provoked this wee polemic – "If the puffin becomes extinct, they will never forgive us" – is clearer to me now. "Us" means the entire human species wherever we impinge on the North Atlantic. "They" is nothing less than every other tribe of nature with which we share our portion of the planet; it will finally be clear to them that if we reveal ourselves to be incapable of accommodating puffins in our twenty-first-century world order when their demands are so modest and simple, what chance is there for complex ecosystems?

Perhaps nature is banking on our love of puffins, that it may yet persuade us to pull back, to remind us that for all our worst excesses we remain nature ourselves. That we cannot live beyond nature because nature is all there is, and we will use up all the resources that keep us alive. But before that happens, we will have killed off the puffins and our species will spend its declining years on a planet devoid of puffins.

This is the passenger pigeon's story all over again, only this time we cannot say that we never knew, that we were unaware of the consequences of our actions. Yet the land is telling us what to do. All we have to do is to rediscover the lost art of listening to the land. Otherwise, how long do you suppose it will be before the last time you saw a puffin turns out to be the last time you saw a puffin?

*

Craigleith slipped astern, and for the moment at least, so did the disquiet about the place of puffins in the landscape. The Bass Rock makes the instant impact of an eclipse: you can't take your eyes off it. And the passengers on this boat are not puffineers. An island of 6,000 puffins is not enough for the puffineers, and as you don't get to land on Craigleith, not close enough either. And as the prime object of the exercise of this boat trip is the Bass Rock and its top-to-toe fleece of gannets, and 150,000 gannets on a lump of rock is perhaps just too raucous and reeking, they will have gone to Farne or Lundy, Skomer or Lunga, wherever the odyssey leads them. While they still can.

The appeal of the Bass is twofold: one is the stupendously in-your-face architecture of the rock itself, its heave up from great flat breadth of the firth, its uncanny presence; the other is the mind-liberating spectacle of the gannets that assaults four of your five senses at once. (You do not want to be in a situation of having to touch a gannet. Once, about thirty years ago now, I was confronted by just such a situation; the scar took a long time to heal, of which more later.) So here, as the boat closes in, is a wedge of all-but vertical rock and sky, two thirds rock, one third sky. The rock is grey, not the red sandstone of the coastal cliffs and the castle. It is the 320 million-years-old core of a volcano, so was in its prime back when Scotland and England were colliding with each other. Think of it, the core of a volcano where nothing at all can live…becoming this. It has evolved into 75,000 gannet-sized nest sites, hacked and splintered and shattered into tiny cliffs and ledges. The rock is much more white than grey: the bright white of gannet plumage and the dull white of their droppings. The sky, a pale white, is turbulent with the flight of wide wings. These are six feet from tip to tip and pointed at the ends, the hallmark of ocean wanderers, the apotheosis of which is the albatross. It is not so surprising then, that one turned up right here on the Bass Rock in the summer of 1967, a black-browed albatross. According to the Scottish Ornithologists' Club's two-volume *The Birds of Scotland* (SOC, 2007):

It consorted with Northern Gannets and tolerated the close approach of humans. While the Gannets appeared to accept it and it was seen to indulge in partial display to disinterested gannets, it was frequently mobbed by gulls. It returned to the Bass Rock for about four months in 1968 and once again in 1969 for one month.

Almost inevitably, it became known as Albert and newspapers and TV crews homed in on the Bass to enhance his celebrity. It was revived when he appeared again periodically between the early 1970s and the early 1990s at Hermaness on Unst in northmost Shetland, where he built several nests (though they remained empty) and where, strangely enough, I finally saw him. It was 1991, and I was researching a book called *Shetland: Land of the Ocean* (Baxter, 1992).

Shetland, I was discovering after visits in all four seasons, is forever dipping into a reservoir of magic tricks to play on those who go to scrutinise its landscape. At the northmost point of the northmost point of the land in April I expected big winds, maybe a flavour of something Arctic – not icebergs exactly, but something to plug me into the northness of the place. Instead, halfway across my walk out to Muckle Flugga I had stripped to the waist, and when I got to the coast opposite the lighthouse on its unforgettable rock, the ocean was almost lagoonish and gannets sat panting away the heat. I sat among puffins, burdened only by sunlight, staring in disbelief at the lighthouse, for its upended self was perfectly reflected in the water, as were hundreds of swimming puffins. I thought: "So, this is Thule?"

The gannetry was at its most aesthetically pure, no downy, scruffy chicks yet and no immatures with their weird piebald plumages, just a drifting whitewash of mature adults in pristine breeding plumage. Except...*what's that?*

It took a few moments to characterise it as a bird at all. It sat in the midst of the largest mass of birds on the rock. Any way I moved the binoculars at all, whether horizontally, vertically, diagonally or randomly, the image in the lenses simply looked like this...

gannet, gannet. gannet, gannet

...and it was repeated on and on wherever the glasses roamed across the rock, except that suddenly there was a patch of birds that looked like this...

gannet, gannet, gannet, gannet, gannet, gannet, gannet, gannet, gannet, gannet, gannet, gannet, gannet, gannet **GIANT** gannet, gannet, gannet, gannet, gannet, gannet, gannet, gannet, gannet, gannet, gannet, gannet, gannet, gannet

It takes a lot of bird to make a gannet look small. In the context of a Scottish island landscape in 1991, the only thing I could think of that I had ever seen achieve something of that effect was a white-tailed eagle, but the only one of those that had been heard of in Shetland back then was almost certainly a young bird from the Norwegian gene pool that supplied all our sea eagle reintroductions and which in pursuit of some facet of racial memory we simply do not understand was trying to get back to Norway. Besides, the slumped and folded ogre at Muckle Flugga looked nothing like a sea eagle. The initial complication was while every gannet I could see was facing the same way and side-on to me, this creature was facing me head-on, and all that I could make out was a vivid yellow bill and some markings above its eyes that looked as if they were the result of some over-strenuous strokes of an eyebrow pencil. The preposterous image messing with my troubled mind perhaps could be explained by a mild case of heatstroke (I was clutching at straws again), but then the suddenly blindingly obvious illuminated the moment: a black-browed albatross. And only then did I remember all the stories and newsreels and newspaper column inches about Albert.

It stood then, towering above the heads of the sitting gannets, and as it did so, it began to unfold its wings, and these were not gannet-white but shearwater-sooty. They unfolded forever and ever. One of the most impressive aspects of gannet flight is its wingspan, all six feet of it. This wingspan was twice that length. To my intense frustration, the muckle monster of Muckle Flugga furled its wings again, sat back and resumed its patient scrutiny of the wingless creature on the mainland clifftop. That would be me, surrounded by puffins blissfully whiling away the midday sun. I suspect that's what Albert was doing, too. In the next two hours, I didn't see him move. Nor did I see a single hostile gesture towards him from the gannets. There was a vague awareness that I was witnessing a moment of some significance, at least in ornithological history.

I think the last known sighting of Albert the albatross, better known as Alby, was out on Sula Sgeir, halfway between Lewis in the Western Isles and the Faroes. But it was strange, that afternoon on a boat out of North Berwick and hard in under the cliffs of the Bass Rock, filling the glasses with that "mind-liberating spectacle of the gannets that assaults four of your five senses at once" – strange that I should think of the albatross, and my liberated mind went off on its own on voyage of memory that washed up on Muckle Flugga.

★

As the boat neared a tall wedge of rock, the sheer number of birds washed over my mind like surf, and trying to estimate just how many occupied even this wedge of the total island was in the more hopeless realms of the fool's errand. The census is done every couple of years with an aircraft, some computers and lot of aerial photographs. Yet the restlessness of a gannetry this size and at such close quarters is positively energising. It looks chaotic at first, but the more you look, the more you see.

From a nature writer's point of view, the good thing about being on a boat that does not set passengers ashore, is that everyone on the boat is compelled to sit still and watch, and sitting still and watching is my preferred way of spending my working days. I judge the landscapes where I want to work over-time and I try to find situations within them where I sit down and grow still and watch, and try and write it down. It is very, very unusual, or at least it has been in my experience, to find another human being who is willing to share the vigil with the required degree of stillness and immersion in the land. And yet here, because the landscape has been predetermined and the only means of getting here has been taken out of the passengers' hands by the boat operators, they simply sit, face the rock, and watch. Stillness is hardly necessary: it's not like the gannets didn't see us coming. But there is a kind of agreeable camaraderie because we are all united by the common purpose of the trip. The seriousness of the photographic equipment and binoculars on display always intrigues me, and most people didn't wear binoculars and simply pointed mobile phones. Others wore back-bending rucksacks stuffed with very expensive telephoto lenses. There is – always – on birdwatching boats, an element of stuff-strutting variations on a theme of "mine's bigger than yours", but here it was minimal and relatively unintrusive. It is always hard to read how intently and analytically the other passengers are looking, but all I can do is try to memorise what strikes me, so that I can write it down in a notebook later.

In any one wedge of rock where my eye alighted, all the birds almost invariably sat facing the same way. It saves space and reduces conflicts with the neighbours. Not that there are no conflicts – there are dozens, hundreds, probably thousands of them every day, but they tend to be ritualised, a territorial defence of a sitting bird's territory of perhaps one square yard. Think about it: so many birds in such a finite and unforgiving lump of rock – there has to be a degree of organisation. Every bird must find the right square yard of rock every time it comes into land. Even when you scan the airspace above and alongside the rock, where there are flying birds in blizzard proportions, you find yourself picking out patterns.

For example: here is a piece of sky with 100 birds in it (it is a very small piece of sky). I only know this because I have a photograph of it, and I have just counted them meticulously. Firstly, all the birds except four are flying in the same direction. Secondly, all the birds except four (the same four) are flying with their wings held in a loose "W" shape. The four with a different agenda have their wings held straight and wide. All the birds nearest the edge of the rock appear to be in tight little squadrons of between six and a dozen, suggesting to me that they had all just taken off together, underpinned by collective decision. It is not far-fetched. Think how organised are their long-distance flights to and from the feeding grounds: wavetop skeins from a dozen to a hundred, regimented and efficient. Studies at the Bass Rock in around 2000–2001 found that feeding flights can be anything up to 335 miles. This capacity to extend its food searches far beyond local waters is one reason why gannets seem to be prospering while birds like puffins, fulmars and kittiwakes are struggling. There is some evidence to suggest that in addition to the essential knowledge of good fishing areas over a large area of open sea, they also follow fishing boats and work where they work. That, too, suggests a sophisticated degree of organisation.

The boat heels away from the Bass and heads back for North Berwick. The conversation level rises, variations on a theme of the day's edited highlights. All eyes now are astern. For the first time, the best view of the Bass is bathed in the best light. "Wow!" and "Look at that!" reverberate around the boat. The Bass catches fire as it subsides into the distance. The lighthouse and its adjacent long black wall (an old souvenir of garrison and prison) are as a buckle and belt across the waist of the Bass and they clasp the three essential thirds of the rock together. To the right of the lighthouse is the great vertical grey wall of the tallest cliffs, ledgeless and therefore birdless. Below the light and its wall, the bottom third is the rock's ground floor accommodation, a long and tapering wedge of wrap-round rock that reaches right to the waterline, and that is simply smothered in birds. It is a crazy paving of ledges and tiers, small fissures and buttresses. At its left-hand edge it rises past the end of the wall and connects to the Bass's most distinctive feature: its colossal dome of birds the entire width of the rock and rising to a shallow summit, a tilted snowfield of birds.

A great fan of dark clouds right across the sky is breaking up, blue fragments begin to burst through. The airborne hordes of gannets are the first to catch the sun, then the light spreads across the crown then down over the bright white of the lighthouse buildings, then the ground floor begins to glow. The sun chases down the boat's wake and finally that ribbon of dazzle is all that binds us to the receding gannet realm that can so liberate a human mind.

*

I mentioned having once been confronted by a situation where physical contact with a gannet appeared to be inevitable. It was a Bass Rock gannet. The situation arose about thirty years ago when I went for a walk out from Aberlady Bay along the beach towards Gullane, just a few miles to the west of North Berwick. I came over the dunes that lie on the landward side of the sandy beach and my eye alighted on something white at the edge of the tide. It moved awkwardly. In the binoculars it resolved into a gannet. Gannets don't walk along sandy beaches. They have no reason to. Other than an occasional step to resolve a nesting season spat on the Bass, I can't imagine them walking anywhere at all. They deal in the realms of water and air, and they have no reason for land other than to lay an egg on it every year. So it is an unaccustomed and unwilling walker at the best of times. This turned out to be not one of the best of times.

It was a weekday and the beach was empty. I was on my own. One of the gannet's wings was half open and something pale green was caught there. I walked slowly in a wide semi-circle to try and make my approach as unthreatening as possible. I was thinking it might some-how avoid stressing the bird but it would prove rather too late for that. The pale green thing streaming out from the apparently damaged wing was a piece of fishing net. As soon as I realised that my heart sank. The piece of net was not just caught around its left wing, its left foot was ensnared too, with the result that every time it moved its foot the net tightened and bit deeper into the leading edge of the wing. I could see now where the blood seeped.

I sat down on the sand and had a good look through the glasses. It seemed just possible that if I could get hold of the trailing piece of net, I might be able to free the bird's foot. Then, it also seemed just possible that the bird itself might be able to manoeuvre the net from the cut in its wing and out towards the narrowing wingtips, and finally be free of it. Whether or not it would then be able to fly was a completely different question. The chances of the gannet sitting still and docile while I tried to get the net off were not high. Now, a quick call on a mobile phone would have brought a swift response from an SSPCA worker in a boat or a 4x4. Thirty years ago, I didn't walk with a phone in my pocket.

Get this over with. A bold approach produced a predictable flap-ping and painful retreat from the gannet, but I persisted, talking in a hopefully reassuring voice, until I got hold of the net. For a few moments I walked behind and slightly to one side of the gannet as it tried to get back to the water. It occurred to me that from a distance it would have looked like I was taking a gannet for a walk on a kind of leash. Its struggles had succeeded only in looping the net round its huge webbed foot twice. Improbably, by flicking the loose end of the net as it moved its foot, I freed up one of the loops but the other was tighter.

The bird stopped. I crouched by its tail and eased a hand towards the still-trapped foot. I was within an inch or two of getting hold of the square of mesh that held its foot when the bird turned its head towards me and that beak that crushes the life out of fish for a living grabbed my bare wrist and let go again a couple of seconds later. The pain was extraordinary.

Three things happened at once.

One – I let go of the net involuntarily.

Two – the gannet made for the water still towing the net, uselessly flapping its wings, and contriving quite by accident to free its own foot as it fled, but not the net from its wing.

Three – a neat bracelet fashioned entirely from beads of my own blood appeared magically on my left wrist.

I watched the bird as it beat the water with its wings and travelled about fifty yards offshore. I reasoned that at least it was safer there than on the beach, where sooner or later it would lose a fight with someone's pet dog. If it did manage to extricate the net from the cut in the wing, then extricate the entire wing from the net, perhaps it would heal out on the water.

When I examined my own wound I saw that the bird had punctured the skin in twelve places round my wrist. They were all shallow, but they all bled and the cumulative effect was really quite impressive. The following day I was in a shop and when I handed over the money, I did so with my left hand, and too late, realised that the assistant was staring in some horror at what looked like an unsuccessful attempt at slashing my own wrist. I thought about trying to explain, something beginning: "I was bitten by a gannet when I tried to help it along the beach..." and then I thought better of the idea. I wore the bracelet for weeks before it faded.

Forty

The Land of Havørn (1) –
Under the Blue Mountain

A WARM WIND OF OPPORTUNITY blew my way in the summer of 2018. Four years before, I had written a book called *The Eagle's Way*, which, among other things, highlighted the role of Norway's west coast in providing the birds which permitted Scotland to reintroduce the sea eagle. In the course of writing it, I made a contact who offered to help me to see that eagle-rich land-and-sea-scape for myself. The time and the space in my writing life turned up in due course and I headed for a land that will stay In my heart and mind forever: Lofoten. Lofoten is Norway's Hebrides, a chain of islands of the north-west coast, but with two distinct differences from the Hebrides. One is that every island looks like the Skye Cuillin, it's airspace so crammed with mountains that at first glance you wonder where they put the towns. The other is that they lie inside the Arctic Circle. The trip promised to slake my lifelong thirst for islands and northness. It also taught me a priceless lesson at first hand, that I had misinterpreted what the word "Arctic" means in the 21st century.

★

THE WORD IS *havørn*. Literally, "sea eagle", when the sea in question is Norwegian and it quivers with islands tumultuous with mountains. And now I travel back there in my mind, oh…so often. And in my mind, in my mind's eye, and for that matter in my mind's heart, there constantly reappears a particular mountain. It is just one of hundreds by which Lofoten stamps its identity, its temperament of storms, its uncategorisable beauty, upon the consciousness of the susceptible travelling mind. Mine was one of the susceptible ones. That singular mountain made something of a habit of rising before me again and again throughout my time there. It seems to me now that whatever my direction of travel, there it was, casting its shadow, barring my way or staring down at me as I sidestepped it deferentially, imposing its aura, impressing itself upon on me.

What was special about it? It wasn't tall or pointed or razor-edged as so many of Lofoten's summits are. But if you have an imagination like mine, it takes the shape of an eagle, a huge eagle head thrust forward from a pair of mantled wings (these are mountain ridges that rise slightly at the "elbow" then bend almost at right angles, as mantled wings do, then droop almost vertically in folds and gullies that suggest illimitable depths of feathers such as are revealed if you ever see the chest and belly of a perched sea eagle tormented by big winds). The chances are you go to Norway with preconceptions about the natives' taste for mythology (and come back with them, too: trolls glower at you from every tourist shop window) and a particularly vigorous tribe of Norse gods. If your imagination ever strays – as mine occasionally does – back to that long-lost era of worship that placed its gods on mountaintops all across the northern hemisphere, then surely here was an apotheosis among mountain gods. So here was a mountain that was surely primed to haunt a susceptible mortal like me. So the mountain and the bird that in a roundabout way had lured me here have become emblematic of that astounding landscape.

The connecting flight north up the Norwegian mainland from Oslo to Narvik was the part of the journey that moved from one planet to another. Looking down on glacier-strewn summer snowfields and mountain summits from 30,000 feet, two thoughts occurred to me. One was that somewhere down there, the invisible line we call the Arctic Circle had just been consigned to my south, and that had never happened before. By the time the aeroplane reached Narvik, it would be 120 miles to my south.

The other thought drifted back to the whole question of flight – of the vexing human addiction to air travel despite everything we now know about its consequences for the planet, and, because of the nature of the enterprise at hand, sea eagle flight. Without having to climb to

30,000 feet or anything like it, without having to seek permission to take off and land, without consuming so much as a single millilitre of aviation fuel, and in complete silence, a sea eagle could make the same journey this plane was making, enjoy the same view of the mountains and their glaciers, except that it would be unconstrained by the frame of a cabin window. It would take much longer, of course, but as a result of its flight the air through which it passed would be utterly unimpaired. A sea eagle wingspan is large, at least by bird standards: a big female can nudge up towards eight feet, or 252 feet and nine inches less than an Airbus, not that I was flying in an Airbus to Narvik, but you get the gist. Flight as designed by nature is an exquisite phenomenon. Flight as reinvented by humankind is more or less grotesque. Such was the conflict that troubled me.

It's not that I do this very often: my carbon footprint is a light one. But somehow it all felt so much more intrusive in somewhere like Arctic Norway. It is impossible, of course, not to be seduced by the view of glaciers and summer snowfields from 30,000 feet, but just in case there was the slightest chance of slipping into a complacent frame of mind that assumed all was well with the Arctic world, the captain of the aeroplane started talking to us as he prepared to land in Narvik. He spoke first in Norwegian, but it was obvious at once even to non-Norwegian speakers that he had just said something remarkable, such was the immediate and animated response all through the cabin. Then he spoke in English, concluding the standard landing script with the non-standard bit: "…and the temperature on the ground is…ooh, thirty-four degrees Celsius".

"Did he say twenty-four degrees?"

"No, I think he said thirty-four degrees."

He *did* say thirty-four degrees. I did some quick mental arithmetic: ninety-two degrees in old money, 120 miles inside the Arctic Circle. Oh yes, the system is well and truly broken. On the tarmac, the heat was like a wall. In the airport, the man from the car hire firm said:

"Hi, welcome to Spain."

That week, Norway and Sweden would record their hottest ever temperatures. A climatologist talked on the radio about "a dome of heat stationary over northern Europe". The nature of summer in the far north of the world had just lurched into uncharted territory.

The drive from the airport deep into the islands was bridge after bridge, causeway upon causeway, mountains that leapt from seas and fjords and lakes and other mountains. When the car finally stopped I wasn't so much travel-sick as sick of travelling, but then I discovered that I had come to rest in a magic land, a tiny village that clung to a mountain-rimmed fjord.

I was having trouble coping with the day's hoard of sensations, and just when I thought there could be nothing left but troubled sleep, I remembered our small party hadn't eaten for quite a long time, and we ate smoked salmon and French bread and drank wine on a tiny terrace outside a timber cabin. It was 11-o'clock-going-on-midnight and the sun shone. It was somewhere about then that I learned the working definition of the phrase "Arctic Circle". It has nothing whatever to do with land or cold, and everything to do with light. It is a mathematical line drawn at latitude sixty-six degrees and thirty minutes North. Its purpose is to mark on a map of the north of the world the southern limit of that zone wherein there is at least one period of twenty-four hours every year during which the sun does not set, and another during which it does not rise, and it is as simple as that. That knowledge made things a little easier to understand as the evening stretched on and on into the wee small hours and the light scarcely dimmed. The day finally came to an end when I simply let my heart and mind and travel-weary body find what felt instantly like the most natural of homecomings, wreathed in beauty of a particularly rare order, and in unaccustomed warmth.

*

The first morning after the night before began at a tiny nowhere on the map called Eggum, which, mysteriously, seemed to infiltrate my mind with a Yorkshire accent. It is an end-of-the-road place on the seaward edge of the island of Vestvågøy, and beyond the end of the road there was a track that threaded a narrow shelf of land between a wall of mountains and the Norwegian Sea. Might that, I wondered, be a fair description of almost every other road in Lofoten?

We parked under a mountain at the end of the road. Always, it seemed, as that week unfolded, we parked under a mountain. Always with mountains like these, not high but as sharply defined as the Skye Cuillin, they demand that you look up first. Clouds had crept in during what passes for night at these rarefied latitudes of summer, and as yet they still clung to summits, although such a sun and such a heat was about to burst them apart, annihilate them. Where the ridge disappeared into the cloud for the moment, there was the expedition's first sea eagle. I hadn't even had time to put my boots on. A small cluster of ravens clamoured around it, voices softened by distance, adrift among the thermals, falsetto, throaty, harsh and sweet, deadly serious and comic.

Did they think they might embarrass a sea eagle? Or did they even think? Is this just ritual, the clamour for the sake of the clamour, with all the effectiveness of farting against thunder? She (the sea eagle, hugely female) contrived a back flip to present talons upside down at the posse of irritants. I don't know exactly how that must have looked from a yard away, nor how unsettling it must have been for raven flight given the air currents that must have flowed from such wings as they executed such a manoeuvre. Almost at once she righted herself again by completing a barrel roll and suddenly she was alone in the sky and in possession of precisely the same piece of mountainside as she had been when the ravens turned up. It was as if she had simply assessed the opposition, called up the one gesture she calculated would be necessary to deal with it and executed the gesture while apparently resting on a cushion of warm air. The ravens' instant, scattered departure suggested they knew they were outclassed, but there again, they almost certainly knew that before they moved in. Perhaps it is simply that in the evolution of the relationship between sea eagle and raven, they have come to the conclusion that to irritate is better than doing nothing at all, that they must fulfil a stipulated principle of the natural order. Ravens are spectacular fliers in their own right, but inevitably, they lack the grand gesture and the raw power of an eagle.

By any standards, the sea eagle's manoeuvre was very impressive – any standards that is except one. I have watched my fair share of meetings between sea eagles and golden eagles in Scotland's island west, and while it is true that a sea eagle will usually out-muscle a golden eagle on the ground and drive it away from a kill, if the confrontation is in the air I have yet to see the sea eagle that can match the golden eagle's apparently limitless repertoire of the art of flight. They are out-flown and out-thought every time. In any other company other than golden eagles, the sea eagle excels against all-comers, and it can certainly afford to be contemptuous of ravens.

I tried out a couple of mountain names in my head: the mountain where the sea eagle held sway was called Mustaren, an outcrop of a ridge at 400 metres on the way up to Jellvollstinden at 746 metres. This gave me an immediate yardstick to work with, for the mountains, all of which rose from the sea, *looked* much higher. The midwinter imagery beloved of Norwegian tourist brochures and climbing guides reassert their essential Arctic-ness of which this preposterous heat-dome had stripped them. In that midwinter guise they looked as imposing and shapely as the Swiss Alps. With new landscapes, especially landscapes rooted in seas and flooded with twenty-four hours of daylight, you have to make adjustments of scale, and it takes a while.

Something else fell into place as I watched the sea eagle cruise the ridge. Throughout the length and breadth of the Lofoten archipelago there must be hundreds of such mountain ridges, their cliffs wide open to seas and fjords and lakes, hundreds of suitable nest sites for sea eagles, hundreds of places to fish and catch seabirds, and as a result, surely hundreds of sea eagles. Norway harbours more than 2,000 pairs, more than ten times as many as Scotland. I hazarded a hasty guess, which more considered deliberation has reinforced, that Lofoten alone surely exceeds the Scottish population. So what fell into place that first morning under a modest mountain called Mustaren was a clear understanding of why a sea eagle raised on Scotland's east coast might seek to reclaim its west coast Norwegian ancestry by crossing the breadth of mainland Scotland: in pursuit of some instinctive quest for a land of mountainous islands that eagle would naturally end up on Mull, the Small Isles, Skye (perhaps especially Skye with the Lofoten-esque Cuillin mountains at its heart).

A second essential truth I had previously only guessed at was now confirmed for me, too. In Lofoten, and for that matter throughout

Norway, sea eagles comfortably outnumber golden eagles, a situation that was the historical norm in Scotland until the Victorians embarked on a campaign to blast the sea eagle from the face of the land, a campaign that was all too successful. But the growth of the sea eagle population in Scotland is now such that sometime in the next twenty years the historical norm will reassert itself and the sea eagle will once again outnumber the golden eagle in Scotland, too. The situation should trouble no one, for the two species thrived side by side for many millennia, as they do today in Norway, and they resolve their differences effectively; and as we have seen and are seeing increasingly, the young of both species are happy to share the same airspace as they criss-cross the land, all its coasts and all its heartlands.

Having relished the company of eagles of both species for many years now and watched the sea eagle reintroduction project with eager fascination throughout all its phases, it was the sea eagle tribe that put Lofoten on my personal map of the world in the first place, and here was the best of all omens for my time in Lofoten in the first hour of the first morning on the first day. The eagle veered below the ridge and was lost to me, but I sensed that I had just found a new relationship in nature that was utterly true and life-enhancing, and that would never leave me. I hugged the knowledge close, for its quality was as rare as it was precious to me. I turned and headed south down the coast towards Utdalen, south down the outermost edge of outermost Arctic Norway.

*

A lake lay in the lap of two curving mountain ridges, each of which climbed to cliff-girt, cloud-nudging summits before swooping a thousand feet to collide beautifully at a low mountain pass that I would call a *beallach* at home. It is the Gaels' word. The landscape of north-west Scotland, and especially the Hebrides, is named by two languages, Gaelic and Norse, for the Vikings made their presence felt there, too, and left their fingerprints all over the map of the land. Again and again, the landscapes of Lofoten would stop me in my tracks with echoes of the Hebrides.

The heatwave held, slowing the pace; the morning was still, the lake lay as flat as a sheet of newly forged steel, dark greyish blue that evolved into dark bluish grey, and only paling where a band across the middle of the water caught a hint of a matching band of white cloud high above the summits. The grassy shore was thronged with tall buttercups and orchids. All that moved at that moment were slow clouds, and on the water, a slower and apparently solitary black-throated diver.

So that first walking mile inside the Arctic Circle was lathered in sun cream, graced by eagle and diver and wildflowers and what felt at first glance like a gasp-out-loud, out-of-this-world landscape, except that in this particular corner of the northern world it would be replicated again and again and again. The combination of lakes, fjords and open sea strewn with apparently endless variations on a theme of near and far mountainous islands and lined to the east with the higher, bulkier mountains of mainland Norway...that would recur relentlessly and become the signature-in-landscape of the whole adventure. That, and for the moment at least, a climate that appeared to have migrated from the Med. The black-throated diver was so indolent that it was tempting to believe it was sunbathing. Such conditions were as unfamiliar to Arctic-born birds as they were to Arctic-born humans, and neither species appeared to have had any more idea about what to do with them than the other.

I tried running the name of the lake around in my head, Nedre Heimredalsvatnet, and the *vatnet* suffix occurred often enough for me to conclude that it means "lake". The particularly striking mountain that rose from the south-east corner of the lake and soared from the *beallach* was the north face of Blåtinden. We were destined to meet again and in equally alluring circumstances later in the day. For the moment, I was close enough for a black-throated diver to fill my binoculars, the bird idling and utterly indifferent to my blatant presence on the shore. From sooty-black stem to bright white stern, the most exquisite bird plumage in the north of the world blazed in sunlight.

Seton Gordon was deeper into the Norwegian Arctic when he recorded a historic encounter with a black-throated diver on Prins Karls Forland (which he rendered as the very un-Norwegian-sounding

Prince Charles Foreland), Spitzbergen, in July 1921:

Flying at great speed, and slanting towards the water, there came a dark, diver-like bird which settled on the lagoon near us. Through a powerful glass, and after careful watching, it was identified as a black-throated diver...the first definite recording for Spitzbergen. It probably nested later by one of the hill tarns, as yet ice-bound, in the interior of the Foreland.

He was writing in his book *Amid Snowy Wastes* one hundred years ago, and decades before the concept of global warming had reared its troublesome spectre. He described an utterly different Arctic world from the one where I walked. The tarns were ice-bound, it was still snowing, and "the snow on the Foreland was still almost continuous...Winter often descends on Spitzbergen before September arrives, so Prince Charles Foreland must be under almost eternal snow." Ah, but that was then. Now, whatever happened to the concept of eternal snow, even in Arctic Norway?

It occurred to me suddenly that he was making his first trip to the Arctic, as the photographer on an Oxford University research trip to Spitzbergen. He was a student, passionately interested in the wildlife and landscape of the nearest thing Scotland has to the Arctic, the plateau lands of the high Cairngorms. And the black-throated diver would have been as a bond to the other landscape love of his life, the Hebrides. Now, I was making my own first trip to the Arctic, and in our different ways we had both seen and responded keenly to a single black-throated diver. I never tire of Seton Gordon's books, and I am always delighted to feel some kind of connection, however vigorous or tenuous, to his trail-blazing nature writing. For a moment I was amazed that it should happen north of the Arctic Circle. Then I thought:

"But of course it would happen here. Why wouldn't it?"

It was an extravagant setting to frame a single black-throated diver: the tranquil lake, the two mountains beyond its far shore, each dipping a mighty shoulder towards the other, a fraternal clasp, the warmth, the tranquillity, the verdant green that smothered the lower half of the mountains and reached high up into gullies and surrounded buttresses. This was not the Arctic I had believed in. Seton Gordon's iced tarns and eternal snow were what I had expected, even though I am well read about the crisis in Arctic ice and Greenland's disappearing glaciers, with the extent of the melting transmitted in billions, even trillions of tons of water. It took this moment of bearing witness to drive the message home. And do you know what was the most sinister aspect of the evidence confronting my own eyes? It was so utterly beautiful. It had never occurred to me that climate's cataclysm was so two-faced.

In my head I heard again the voices that had introduced me to this new reality, voices both incredulous and uncomprehending...the two passengers as the plane prepared to land:

"Did he say twenty-four degrees?"

"No, I think he said thirty-four degrees."

And the car hire man:

"Hi, welcome to Spain."

The heat on the tarmac that was like a wall.

If it was any cooler out on these islands, it was a matter of a couple of degrees. And a black-throated diver looked like it was wearing too many clothes. Behind my back, the Norwegian Sea sprawled, flat and silent and blue, every shade of blue you could think of, and every other island and all their mountains paled into the distance from almost navy blue for the closest ones to a kind of bluish off-white for the most distant. It was an extraordinary vision, and it was the most disquieting mask I have ever seen.

A pair of red-throated divers with two young were calling on a small fjord. In Scotland the red-throats nest in small lochans near the coast and fly down to the sea to feed. Black-throats nest on bigger lochs inland and fish where they nest. But here in Lofoten there is no "inland". The islands are long and narrow and stuffed with mountains and ragged-edged with fiords. In my mind's eye, red-throated divers are Shetland, Orkney, south Skye, Raasay; black-throated divers are the Trossachs, Highland Perthshire, Loch Tulla in the Black Mount mountains at the edge of Rannoch Moor, Loch Shiel...and it is only in winter when the twain shall meet in the firths of the east coast like

Forth and Tay, and in drab winter plumage at that.

For me, and thanks mainly to Shetland and one unforgettable night sleeping out on Raasay, it is the red-throated diver that is the embodiment of a particular strain of wildness, and while it does not "dazzle the eye" (to borrow the phrase from Mike Tomkies) there is a sleek silkiness to the red-throat, and the fact that the colour of that exquisite throat patch is matched in its neck stripes and in its extraordinary red eyes, lends it an almost unearthly distinction. And when the down-curving, far-carrying calls of the two adult birds synchronise in unbroken rhythmic call-and-response for minutes on end, it sounds like the very breath of the wildest of landscapes, like nature breathing. My first Lofoten day was piling one wilderness sensation upon another. It was dizzying, bewildering, overwhelming, and unrelentingly beautiful. And still the day was far from done with me. I was about to be reacquainted with Blåtinden, whose north face accommodated the black-throat's lake.

Its south-east face not only embraced a wide corrie with a high, hidden lochan, but it also towered over a roadside lake called Keilvatnet. For more than half my life now I have greeted the autumn arrival in Scotland of wild whooper swans from Iceland and Scandinavia as a presence that hones the most cherished wildnesses of my country with a keen Arctic edge. And of all those manifestations of wildness, of all those tribes of nature that define all nature's seasons, there is nothing – no wild presence of any kind – that has got so deeply under my skin and defined more truly my relationship with nature for fifty years. To my mind, whooper swans embody like nothing else my sense of wildness, of flight, and of northness. And there, on a roadside lake called Keilvatnet under a mountain called Blåtinden, which also gives succour to black-throated diver and sea eagle, there were two adult whooper swans and a very young brood of six cygnets, and that was a thing I had never seen before, and my heart turned over.

I had been to whooper swan nesting grounds before – in Iceland, where I watched them on the black-sand shores of a lake with the mighty volcano of Hecla for a backdrop. I was making a television programme about swans for the BBC, and one sequence appeared to show me getting quietly emotional at what I called "the missing piece falling into place", watching newly hatched whooper swan cygnets appear from beneath the feathers of the pen for the first time. The truth is that only the cameraman was permitted to stay on for as long as it took for the eggs to hatch, and my part in the sequence was faked. By the time they hatched I was about a thousand miles away, for I had been back in Scotland for several days. The experience put me off wildlife documentary television for life.

Later in the film, there is a sequence in which the fully fledged cygnets take their first flight. But it was filmed in Scotland using hand-reared birds. I was asked if there was "anywhere near Stirling that could pass for Iceland". I took the crew to a small, peaty lochan on a high moor just a few miles from where I live. The subsequent sequence was beautiful (it was filmed by Simon King, no less) and would have deceived every viewer. But the deception rankled with me, as deceptions always do, and it still does; witness the fact that here I am reliving the event twenty-five years later. I had never lost sleep about it, and at the time I was hopelessly naïve about television film-making. But from time to time, usually while watching a small group of north-making whooper swans on a small lochan of south Skye or north Mull some April or other, knowing they were preparing for the long haul back up the north Atlantic to nesting grounds in Iceland or Norway, I have thought how much I would like to lay those irritating demons to rest, to see wild cygnets on their native waters, and to be in a position to write it down. And suddenly, while my mind was on something else altogether, there they were, one late afternoon of midsummer on an island off the north-west coast of Norway. They looked to be about three weeks old, and they would have a lot of growing to do before late September or early October, when they would follow their parents back down the Atlantic or the North Sea, but twenty-four hours of daylight assists the process, with the possibility for twenty-four hours of feeding. Nature rarely leaves such things to chance.

The swans were at ease. The adults would never have known such weather before. The cygnets were born into an extraordinary season. But that demure image the family presented to the world was another deception. The very coupling of the words "swan lake" is a deception.

For these were as much birds of that mountain as they were birds of that lake. The adults would know the mountain as well as they knew the lake, how to fly over it and navigate through its upper slopes, how to find a way through the contours and spaces between its cliffs and buttresses, the upthrusts and gullies of its ridges; they would know its high lochan hidden in the embrace of its south-east facing corrie, the walls still flecked with the last of the snow. Swans like these have no fear of mountains, no reason to shun them, for they are among the strongest of fliers and their migration routes vary from wavetop level to the edge of the jet stream. Navigating mountain ranges and archipelagos is second nature to them, arguably first nature.

Often, when I encounter a family group of whooper swans newly arrived in Scotland from Iceland or Norway, I think about the younger birds, in particular – no more than three or four months old, their first 1,000-mile migration behind them already, still grey and improbably slim compared to the adults, still lacking the yellow blaze of the adult bill and the mellow muted brass voice – and I wonder what the landscape is like where they have come from. Now I can answer my own questions, now the final piece *is* in place.

Throughout the autumn and winter and early spring that followed that extraordinary Lofoten summer, I scanned all the whooper swans I saw: I seek them out on the reliable watersheets where they turn up year after year. These would include Loch Leven in Kinross, a national nature reserve and a gathering place for wildfowl and waders, and where whooper swan numbers often build up to over 200 before they scatter more widely across the land; Balquhidder Glen in the Loch Lomond and the Trossachs National Park, where the watersheets are hemmed in by steep mountainsides; its near neighbour Loch Lubnaig, where for more than thirty years now I have watched truly wild mute swans dish out a harsh welcome to whooper swans that pause there; Loch Dochart, a watershed further north from the Balquhidder lochs and with a harder-edged Highland feel; the Lowland fields of the Carse of Stirling just to the south of the first and last mountains of the Highland Edge.

Then there is Caerlaverock on the Solway coast, Scotland's most southerly shore, where they gather at a Wildfowl & Wetlands Trust reserve and are fed daily by reserve staff; the whoopers join the expectant throng of mute swans and geese and ducks in response to carefully timed calls and whistles from the staff before food is thrown to them from a wheelbarrow while human visitors come to watch the spectacle from a purpose-built hide. I don't much care for that part, for it makes wild Arctic swans behave abnormally and turns them into performers to gratify something that strikes me as less than admirable (the trust does all kinds of admirable work but making wild birds put on a show is not part of it).

When I first wrote about swans in a book called *Waters of the Wild Swan* (Cape, 1992), I attempted to articulate my fascination for whooper swans, in particular:

> *I see in whooper swans a kind of kindred spirit in nature, a restless haunter of lonely places, an inclination to the northlands of the world and a marked determination to preserve its wilderness instincts and keep a wary distance from man and his works...*

What happens at Caerlaverock is a betrayal of that idea, at the very least.

In all those landscapes, I looked for a family group with six cygnets. It was frankly daft, because even if I found one (I didn't – several of four, one of five), there was no way of knowing whence they had flown, but I rationalised it by convincing myself that it was just because I was there in Lofoten that week, when summer in the Arctic took leave of its senses, and I saw what I saw and my heart turned over.

*

I stopped working after I had been watching the Lofoten swans for a while. That is, I stopped consciously noticing details, the actions and shapes of the birds as they swam and fed and lazed and preened, the light on the water as the sun moved round above the mountain, the varying shades of green surrounding the lake and climbing high into mountain gullies, the way the mountain's aura seemed to cover the lake in a kind of protective haze of diffused light that had the effect of binding mountain and lake closer together so that the lake was more obviously a part of the mountain rather than a part of the island beyond the mountain.

In a way, then, the watching became disengaged from swan and water and mountain and sky and was replaced by an over-arching absorption in the complete landscape, almost as if I had *become* landscape. I have met the feeling before from time to time, but always in landscapes with which I have a long and intimate connection. Yet this was still my first day exploring Lofoten, and as such the connection was unique. Whatever I may or may not take away from the moment and from my scrutiny of the landscape and its creatures, the quality of *seeing* becomes extraordinary and utterly memorable. It permits, for example, an imaginary exploration not just of what I had seen the diver do, or the sea eagle and ravens or the swan family on their lake, but all their flights and everyday movements and events throughout their relationship with the mountain, and all the mountain's moods outwith this extraordinary heatwave.

*

A year later, looking at a map of the Lofoten island of Vestvågøya, retracing travels with my finger and lingering over some of the names scattered through the landscape (I speak no Norwegian at all but I am always curious about how a landscape is named and why) I paused at Keilvatnet, the lake under Blåtinden where I had seen the swans. By this time I knew that *vatnet* was simply "lake", but what was *keil*? Bear in mind that I had imagined the sense of a protective screen of diffused light during the time I watched the swans and their lake. I made a rudimentary inquiry about the meaning and the nearest thing I could come up with was *kell* and was astounded by the definition of "that which is covered over". It's a long shot, of course, but perhaps two of us had paused here in similar conditions several hundred years apart: someone who lived here or at least paused long enough to want to name the lake, and I coming curiously and in a spirit of openness towards what to me is a new land, and we had both seen or felt the presence of a kind of protecting veil by which mountain and lake and swans and travellers were bound. I felt strangely involved, mysteriously drawn to the place, although I was a thousand miles away again.

There was to be one more resonance, and that too would happen a year after the event, when I was recalling to mind that mountain, that lake, those swans, those divers. I was refreshing my memory about the mountain itself, reading notes I had made and looking at photographs I had taken, then a vast array of online images. And all the time, it was reminding me of somewhere else. I had been vaguely aware of it at the time, but now the awareness had become acute, so that it started to bother me. It was not just a degree of familiarity about the mountain profile, it was everything – the location on an island shore, the lake that seemed to belong to it, and the specific birds. I looked at the name of the mountain on the page: Blåtinden. Again I looked up the meaning of its component parts. *Tinde* is common enough and just means "mountain peak"; *Blå* is easy, too – "blue". My train of thought had been freighted with the possibilities of two mountains with a strong physical resemblance that were both central to encounters with those specific birds. And then it all clicked into place. It clicked into place because they also have the same name.

In Lofoten, the name is pure Norse: Blue Mountain Peak. On the Isle of Skye, off Scotland's west coast, an island to which I have travelled addictively for more than forty years, the mountain name is only part Norse, a relic from the Viking occupation like so many Hebridean names; the other part is Gaelic: Blà Bheinn. Blue Mountain. And if pressed to compile a shortlist of the mountains that have endeared themselves to me most powerfully, Blà Bheinn would be as near to the top of such a list as makes no difference. I have known it for more than half my life. Blåtinden I have known for that single summer encounter, and never set foot on it. But it burns its image and its name and its birds and its lake into my mind with such intensity that it can summon Blà Bheinn, and that is just one of many reasons why the tenacity of Lofoten's embrace has claimed a unique hold on my life.

Forty-one

The Land of Havørn (2) –
Islands of Dreams

My first thought about the unprepossessing little hill called Palheia was that this could have been what Scotland looked like 500 years ago. It is not, strictly speaking, Lofoten, but on the island of Hadseløya in the Vesterålen archipelago a little to the north. From its all-but-sea-level mountain birchwood to its 1,400-feet summit carpeted with alpine lady's-mantle, Palheia is rooted in my mind as a kind of wilderness garden of my dreams. It was also a startling manifestation – to my eyes, at least – of what a hillside in the Arctic can look like in high summer.

It wasn't just that I love mountain birchwoods, or that this one clambered uphill looking airily light-footed, it was also that it reached a natural treeline where it thinned and diminished and evolved into montane scrub. In Scotland, thanks to a combination of over-zealously manicured grouse moor and over-zealously neglected deer forest, a natural treeline and montane scrub are as thin on the ground as dodos. On Palheia, juniper thickened the spaces between and beneath the birches with shrubby, knee-high-to-waist-high deep green clouds.

The shelter offered by the combination of birch and juniper, a mild, wet spring and early summer followed by this blast of unearthly, un-Arctic heat, flung unprecedented growths of flowers all across the hillside, so eye-catching and unexpected that I scribbled them down, not so much to make a list (which would be singularly uncharacteristic of me), more in the spirit of a visual poem: clover, buttercup, bluebell, Arctic harebell, lupin, cranesbill, dwarf cornel, cloudberry, twinflower (purely a pinewood specialist in Highland Scotland and never this profuse), heath-spotted orchid, small white orchid, moss campion and alpine lady's-mantle. Lower down the hill many of these overlapped gleefully, creating the kind of interloping, seeping patchwork you can contrive with watercolours, but higher up, a few established their own zones. In ascending order these were the dwarf cornel zone, the cloudberry zone, the heather zone then finally the summit with its cap of alpine lady's-mantle, so dense it that it could only be avoided by stepping on protruding patches of bare rock. The flower of the alpine lady's-mantle is indifferent to the point of boring, like something withered on a stick, but a light mountain breeze riffling through such a thicket of it reveals the undersides and the rims of the leaves and these are silver, gloriously so in such oceanic sunlight.

A peregrine called from a crag, that hacking, back-of-the-throat cough of a cry. The peregrine is blessed by nature with special gifts, notably a beauty of design, grace and speed of flight, but it is tempting to think that nature was having a laugh when it gave the falcon that voice. My second Norwegian sea eagle in two days emerged from nowhere at all in the middle of the sky just above the last of the trees (how does it do that, appear in such acres of space and waving its great banner of wingspan at you, and yet you never saw it arrive?).

Beyond the trees, climbing beyond the cloudberry zone onto the sudden familiarity of a hillside clothed in short, wind-scoured heather, I had an idle thought: is it possible that there are golden plover in a place like this, a landscape that suddenly so resembled their nesting habitat in Scotland? With the thought unresolved, the summit arrived with a view north to sharp-pointed, sharp-ridged mountains and unbroken slopes that fell steeply to the sea, or rather to the skinny strip of flat and marginally cultivable land where the human natives lived. The built communities throughout these islands give the impression of having been washed ashore along such coastal strips or at the heads of voes, first shipwrecked then tidied up and painted and made orderly and presentable, often beautifully so, but everywhere the mountains leave the people very little room for manoeuvre.

That northwards view looked like an old film from the early days of technicolour: the sky the bluest of blues, the sea only a marginally darker shade of the same, the mountainside that rose with crafted elegance to its peak was vivid green to the very edge of the ridge, the very point of the summit, and only screes interrupted the astounding flow of flowers and grasses. If you had asked me what I had expected of the Arctic Circle archipelago on the edge of the Norwegian Sea before I got here, this would not have been close to my answer.

Something was happening on that distant peak, for it seemed suddenly to have splintered. The glasses revealed three sea eagles that had clearly been perched together around the summit, and now they lifted close together and in unison. What had caught my eye was the chaotic overlapping of six giant wings, hugely flexing high and low, hugely curving and straightening as the three birds heaved into the air and headed for the ridge. Two white-tailed, grey-headed adults were easy to identify in such sunlight, and the darker third bird was presumably the newly flown eaglet. Some chick. Five sea eagles in two days, and not one of the sightings dependent on a sea eagle safari boat loaded with fish to lure them close, although Norway also offers many of those. But really, all you need to do is go for a walk and look up. The three birds from the summit soon fell into their giant stride, taking the line of the ridge, buoyed by thermals, taking it easy, the young bird noticeably less fluent in flight than the adults, falling behind, driving forward to catch up, then all three side-slipped off the ridge out of sight beyond its far side.

These encounters would become the norm. There would be sea eagles every day of the week, binding into place my sense of these islands as the idealised source of Scotland's sea eagles, and nourishing my hopes that one day soon, Scotland's island west will be a sea-eagles-every-day kind of landscape, too, and that from that stronghold they reach out to every corner of my country, island and mainland, Highland and Lowland, for that has been their way in Norway.

Retracing my steps down this idyllic little mountain, slowing the pace, lingering, drinking in the place, writing it down, stopping to stand and stare, to sit and stare, finally pausing for a drink and a protracted seat on a warm granite slab, I was filling my head and my heart with the wonders of the place and the cup-runneth-over day, when the mountain spoke softly to me. Twice. The voice it spoke with has all the tonal quality of a penny whistle. If you know the instrument, you will know that you can increase the pitch by a semitone – or any fraction of a tone – by lifting your finger partially from a closed hole. The effect more or less perfectly mimics the call of a golden plover. There were two birds about five yards apart and fifty yards away from the slab, and more or less exactly where I had been when I had pondered the possibility of their presence earlier in the day. Nice when that happens! I now pondered the possibility that these two birds were close to their northmost limit on the planet. I had read in Seton Gordon's *Amid Snowy Wastes* a chapter on the presence of the purple sandpiper in Spitzbergen. He wrote:

> *All of the larger waders are absent – golden plover, grey plover, curlew, whimbrel, oystercatcher, redshank, greenshank; even the hardy dotterel, which nests on the high Scottish hills does not penetrate thus far north, for suitable feeding grounds for the larger wading birds appear to be non-existent.*

I wondered if climate change would take care of that. Perhaps it already had, and these were pioneer plovers. But as they are among the most totemic birds of wild country to which their voice seems so peculiarly well attuned, I was very pleased to hear them, and for a moment, even in that most precious of landscapes, I felt a pang for the wild places of home – the eternal affliction of the Scot abroad!

★

The entire week was as crammed with incident and encounter as Lofoten is crammed with mountains. They tumble over themselves as I cast among souvenirs in the form of photographs and notebooks and conversations. For a nature writer travelling north, my preferred direction, and tasting new flavours of my very idea of northness, Lofoten was a feast.

The ferry to Skrova, a small island off Austvågøya, largest of the Lofoten islands, was another dream-like venture, horizons characterised by tiers of mainland mountains that paled into distance, and still the heatwave held, still the natives were in a kind of daze at it all. It was memorable for a patch of coastal woodland thick with rowans (redwings on the berries) and a meeting at a distance of about 100 yards with a family group of four sea eagles on top of a low sea cliff. The four rose, again with that chaotic tumult of wings and briefly filling the binoculars, each bird at a different angle, and against a background of that same mountain-strewn sea; an image I will not expect to be eclipsed if I go on eagle watching until I am a hundred. The adult male turned and lingered, and began circling directly overhead, apparently just as intrigued about the human presence. He made twenty slow circles there (you wouldn't catch a golden eagle doing that). Turning to watch him in the glasses for every one of those circles, becoming faintly dizzy, and watching intently how he used his wings and tail to achieve tight turns and wide turns, small fluctuations in height, gliding and soaring (his final gesture, he went straight up with wings battering the air in loose curves then headed out to sea), I felt as if I had been given a personal masterclass in the wiles of sea eagle flight.

Finally, there was the old wooden fishing village of Nusfjord, where accommodation for the second half of the week was in a fisherman's cabin (wonderfully Ikea-ed into the twenty-first century) built on wooden piles out beyond the high-water mark so that the tide flowing into a short, sheltering fjord came in beneath the cabin. Hefty clusters of mussel shells clung to the supporting piles, and tysties nested under the floor. The sound of the sea beneath the bed eased me into sleep. I was never happier inside four walls in my entire life.

Nusfjord is a village whose summers are sung to a soundtrack of kittiwakes. A concession to modern living was an area of decking in front of the cabin, and the perfect place from which to watch the kittiwakes (the Norwegian word is *krykkje*, so that's two Norwegian bird names I know: it's a start) that nested on the cliff across the fjord, about 200 yards away. It will be clear by now that kittiwakes and I go back a long way and that they are among my most enduring and endearing manifestations of summer. Now they were my nearest neighbours in the house of my dreams.

But it was quickly apparent that something was wrong. First of all, there were no more than a dozen nests and faded evidence from empty, whitened ledges suggested that in old summers there had been several times that number. But it was July 22 and there were no young at all.

At the mouth of the fjord was the same evidence on the cliff faces: two more kittiwake colonies, both of them completely abandoned. Yet still the village resounded to the cries of, "Kitt–ay-wake! Kitt–ay-wake!" Something very strange had happened. Kittiwakes had moved into the village. They nested IN the village, ON the timber buildings, on the window ledges and architectural nooks of the general store and the souvenir shop and the oldest houses, and these nests had young. I counted eight twin-chick nests. And two fully-fledged chicks perched side by side on a corrugated roof away from the nests. Nusfjord is a tourist village. Its streets throng with visitors pointing cameras and being loud. It seemed to me the parent birds were distressed, and yet they put up with it rather than using the cliffs a few hundred yards away. Nor did they appear to use their last-resort technique when they feel threatened, which is to throw up a vile liquid at their aggressors, from skuas to sea eagles. If you get it on your clothes, my best advice is to burn them.

Questions. Do the street urchin chicks pass on the habit to the next generation? Will the cliff-nesting habit disappear from this corner of Lofoten? Will the building-nesting habit spread? Will it surface somewhere else? Or will the well-known crisis afflicting kittiwakes all across their range because of food shortage solve the villagers' problem with the sledgehammer of extinction?

Out at the cabin, late in the evening, the sound of kittiwakes still resounds. The relentless daylight drifts past midnight, past 1a.m., and only in the brief twilight towards 2a.m. did I suddenly realise that the voices had stopped. The uncanny silence lasted an hour.

The Arctic has been central to our awareness of the chaotically out-of-kilter climate from the first. The climatologists who first flagged up warming seas and dwindling ice sheets and melting glaciers warned us that what begins in the far north of the world does not stay there.

The process has progressed from there to what we face today: wildfires from the Americas to Australia; the UK's and Europe's hottest ever temperature recorded in the summer of 2019; temperatures in Australia in their summer of 2019–20 edging up towards fifty degrees; polar ice – at both poles – melting at a rate that threatens to reach tipping point, beyond which we can only try to slow down the thawing process but not reverse it.

And in a week of extraordinary beauty in the Lofoten Islands off north-west Norway, a Scottish nature writer with a lifelong thirst for the north of his country and the north of the world, finally crossed inside the Arctic Circle and an airline pilot announced the temperature on the ground was thirty-four degrees, and the first Norwegian I spoke to was the car hire man and his first words were:

"Hi, welcome to Spain."

Forty-two

The Climate Imperative

WHEN SETON GORDON wrote *Amid Snowy Wastes*, he provided a rare snapshot of high summer in the high Arctic 100 years ago. It was almost the first thing I read when I came back from my week in Lofoten, for I was eager to refresh my memory of his reading of that Arctic landscape back then, while carefully bearing in mind of course that he was fully 400 miles further north. I found this in a chapter titled "Summer Weather in Spitzbergen":

The finest month of the whole year is usually June, when continuous sunshine may be experienced day and night, for a week on end; but in June the winter snow still covers the ground to sea level. Indeed, in the Green Harbour inlet it was practically unbroken and lay several feet deep on June 2...Even in the finest summer weather in Spitzbergen it is still chilly out of the sun. At about six o'clock on the morning at Gipps Bay, and not more than fifty feet above the sea, there was black ice on the pools in the shade...Perhaps the most bitter day I remember was June 30. Three companions and I had been floundering all through the night in horrible snow bogs. I shall never forget the bitter wind in which we cowered on the shelterless shore of Richard Lagoon while we awaited a boat from the sloop, anchored over a mile from the shore. It was fully as cold as a January day in Scotland...

In the summer of 2019, Sami reindeer herders made an unprecedented plea to the Swedish government. A combination of protracted drought and wildfires inside the Arctic Circle had created a situation that suddenly became symptomatic of the impact that climate chaos was making in the most unlikely of circumstances. The Sami were seeking emergency funds to provide supplementary fodder because drought and fire had effectively destroyed reindeer winter grazing grounds. By their own reckoning (and few people are so attuned to the intimacies of the Arctic landscape or better placed to make such a judgment), it could take thirty years to restore those wintering grounds. That presupposes that conditions will prevail that permit the land to heal. If drought and wildfire become the summer norm, then the nature of summer in the high Arctic could become very ugly indeed, and a centuries-old way of life is at risk. Climate chaos has also infected winter conditions for reindeer, for rain has replaced snow in many places. Rain at such latitudes creates an ice sheet rather than a soft fleece of snow, and reindeer cannot reach the lichen beneath. The Sami fear that without government help, the reindeer will starve, and given that reindeer are central to the Sami's way of life, then that too is at risk. In the course of writing this entire project, I have witnessed the disintegration of our idea of a wild year divided into four distinct seasons of more or less similar duration. After that first autumn of Storm Abigail, a series of seasons followed that could only really be defined by the dates of the calendar, rather than the weather itself. This, I imagine, is why the Met Office started to announce on its weather forecasts that "tomorrow is the first day of meteorological winter/spring, etc." The summer of 2019 lasted little more than a fortnight in my neck of the woods (yet contrived a temperature of thirty degrees, while the south of England and France achieved unprecedented highs in such a slim window of opportunity), and the world began to catch fire in a worrying, headline-grabbing way; it hasn't really stopped burning since in lands as diverse as the Canadian Arctic, Siberia, California, Bolivia and Australia. By the turn of the year, Australia's summer achieved temperatures above forty degrees in every state in the country, and exacerbated by drought and strong winds, the wildfires grew vast and ferocious, as potent a warning to the whole world that climate chaos is no longer a nightmare: it's here and it's now.

The summer of 2019 was also notable (at least to a Scottish nature writer who had started to be scared by numbers) for the number of scientific reports that devoured an unprecedented acreage of column inches in newspapers and scientific journals, hours of news broadcasts.

They were about the impact of climate chaos on our planet and our wildlife. I was a newspaper journalist in a previous life and have never broken the newspaper habit, nor the habit of amassing a small hillock of cuttings:

A DYING OCEAN: THE ARCTIC AS WE KNOW IT IS ABOUT TO BECOME HISTORY

THE GLACIERS OF ICELAND SEEMED ETERNAL: ONE BY ONE THEY MELT

DRASTIC CHANGES IN RIVER FLOODING AND SPRING GROWING PATTERNS

GREENLAND'S MELTING GLACIERS: 'THAT NOISE YOU HEAR – THAT NOISE IS THE END OF THE WORLD'

ANTARCTIC SEA ICE PLUNGES IN DRAMATIC REVERSAL OF 40-YEAR TREND

MELTING OF HIMALAYAN GLACIERS DOUBLES IN 20 YEARS

IMPACT OF GLOBAL HEATING ON LAND POSES THREAT TO CIVI-LISATION – UN

MIGRATING GEESE SHIFT NORTHWARDS IN RESPONSE TO GLOBAL HEATING

NATURE WARNING SPARKS ACTIVISTS' CALL OVER FOOD

A LAST CHANCE FOR THE OCEAN

These are the cuttings uppermost on my table as I write, what you might call the tip of the iceberg.

I could start with the small numbers. The Arctic has heated up by an average of two degrees centigrade since the pre-industrial era, twice the average for the whole world, and in somze places by four degrees centigrade (the troublingly termed "hotspots", and really the Arctic shouldn't have any of those). Sea ice melts earlier in spring, freezes later in autumn, gets thinner and recedes further in summer. So instead of summer ice that reflects sunlight back into the atmosphere, there is a summer ocean which absorbs the sun's heat and grows warmer, and warmer, and warmer.

Now, here come the scary numbers. Since 1979, when we began to be able to measure such things by satellite, Arctic sea ice has lost forty per cent of its reach and seventy per cent of its volume. Science's best guess: it diminishes at the rate of 10,000 tons *every second*. If the trend remains unchecked, and there is nothing about the behaviour of the world's most influential nations to suggest there is any concerted willingness to impose the necessary drastic measures, ice-free Arctic summers could be the norm in twenty years, which means cruise ships all the way to the North Pole, commercial exploitation, Arctic tourism…or to put it another way: "The Arctic as we know it is about to become history."

*

The newspaper cuttings lie untidily on the table beside me as I write. There is no tidy way to accommodate a pile of newspaper cuttings. For a start, quite a few of them are torn out, so at least one of the edges is ragged. Some are cut so are less than the size of a full page, so they slide awkwardly among the full pages. Some are entire two-page spreads with lots of lines untidily marked in ink.

When I started to write this chapter I moved the pile from the far end of the table to lie beside my laptop. I did not put them down carefully, because I had a coffee cup in the other hand, and they landed awkwardly, partly on a small stack of notebooks. Very slowly, they started to slide, and as they slid they reached the edge of the table and fell on the floor. But they are sheets of newspaper of different sizes and different weights, and as they fell they took on the guise of a slow-motion waterfall, or – the thought struck me at precisely the pertinent moment – a glacier. And on the top of the pile, and held aloft and almost but not quite motionless as the mass of the others slid away beneath it, was the one with the headline that read:

"The glaciers of Iceland seemed eternal: One by one they melt"

I played with the words in my head: "The cuttings of ice lands seemed ephemeral. One by one, they fall." It's the sort of thing writers get up to (some writers, at least; okay, this one writer) when they are temporarily at a loss in the matter of writing something useful for the job in hand. The page with that headline was the last one to fall, although it had been on the top. Just like a melting glacier, I thought, the top is the last bit to go.

The area of the table where the glacier of papers had been was now just a piece of oak table, roughly the same shade of brown as the aerial photograph of what was left of the glacier that sat just above the headline on the cutting. So, suddenly I was preoccupied by glaciers. All the other articles were factual pieces written by environment editors and environment correspondents. This one was on the top because it was quite different from the others. It was a singularly moving piece by an Icelandic writer, Andri Snær Magnason, who in his own words had "grown up with glaciers as a geological given, a symbol of eternity". He had been asked by academics in Houston, Texas to write the text for a plaque to commemorate "the first dead glacier in Iceland". Surely no writer was ever handed a more portentous commission.

As it happens, the only time that I have been on a glacier was in Iceland. To see a glacier, to stand beside one, to touch one, all for the very first time, to watch its inexorable creep from volcanic ice cap to the ocean, is to be hooked for life. The very word "glacier" has grabbed my attention ever since, another powerful component in that thirst for northness that has been with me forever. I had never realised how vocal glaciers are. They groan, grunt, whistle, squeak, growl; you could swear the thing breathes, that it lives, and you try to grasp that its life is a constant process of moment-by-moment journey in actual-time slow-mo that simply never ends. Except that for one glacier in Iceland, ironically named Ok Glacier, it just did. It has been officially declared as "dead ice".

Would you like some more numbers?

Iceland has 400 glaciers. They cover ten per cent of the island. The thickest glacier ice is 1,000 metres. In 200 years, there could be no glaciers at all.

Mr Magnason's article concludes:

'So on the copper plate to commemorate Ok Glacier, we have written to these loved ones of the future: 'We know what is happening and what needs to be done. Only you know if we did it.'

In the greater scheme of things, Iceland is small. If all its glaciers vanished, that would raise sea levels by a centimetre. If its rather chunkier North Atlantic neighbour Greenland lost its ice sheet tomorrow then sea levels would rise seven metres, which would mean... thank you and goodnight, world. It won't happen, not tomorrow. But (one more scary number alert) in August 2019, NASA recorded the Greenland ice sheet's biggest loss of volume in a single day: 12.5 billion tons.

And this is not just happening in the north of the world. The author of one more study – of ice melt in Antarctica – remarked that the Arctic had become "a poster child for global warming", then pointed out that between 2014 and 2018 Antarctica had lost as much sea ice as the Arctic has lost in the last thirty-four years. Antarctic ice had been consolidating for forty years, but in 2014 "something flipped", and nobody knows what.

In the Himalaya, glacier-melt has doubled in twenty years. In the highest mountains in the world, lost ice is not being replaced by snow. A billion people in India, Pakistan and China, among a cluster of nations, depend on Himalayan rivers for, well...for everything. Untold numbers of wildlife species are at the mercy of the same cataclysmic outcomes.

Given all of the above, it came as no surprise that in August 2019 the United Nations Intergovernmental Panel on Climate Change concluded that the Earth cannot handle the current demands of humanity. Or to put it another way: "We know what is happening and what needs to be done." Oh, and by the way, a glacier just died.

Wildlife hardly ever gets a mention in my collapsing glacier of newspaper cuttings. Two that did give me pause for thought involved bowhead whales and barnacle geese. The geese, travelling from Britain to Svalbard, an archipelago halfway between the north Norwegian mainland and the North Pole, have abandoned a feeding stop south of the Arctic Circle in favour of one north of the Arctic Circle where their preferred grass is growing earlier, in response to global warming. The report of this comparatively minor adaptation has something of a sting in the tail. The geese benefitted from a better food source, and the population grew, but in their new Arctic surroundings, the geese were suddenly at risk from something new to them: polar bears.

Something about "the grass is always greener" comes to mind, but so does John Muir's essential truth about everything being hitched to everything else in the universe.

The bowhead whale was an altogether different problem. For thousands of years, the character of the Arctic Ocean has been determined by a band of cold and all-but-fresh water that lies just under the surface of the ocean, a kind of insulation against the creep of warmer waters from the Atlantic that kept the ice intact. That cold layer is disintegrating. Fast. One more study, this time by the Norwegian Institute of Marine Research, predicts that the water will grow too warm for fish larvae and the links of the food chain will start to unravel and fall apart. Whale populations in the Arctic Ocean are in decline already. The bowhead develops slowly, can live to 200 years old, and reproduces only sporadically. A creature that moves to that kind of timescale cannot, simply cannot, adapt biologically to the speed of change and the biological chaos that our impact on the climate is driving.

It just goes on getting truer and truer: everything is hitched to everything else in the universe. Unless we reverse the warming of the ocean and the disappearance of ice in all its major configurations all across the Earth, from Arctic to Antarctic and from Greenland and Iceland to the high Himalaya and the Alps...unless we do that quickly, we undermine the very essentials that have maintained planet Earth as a beautiful and healthy place to sustain life in myriad forms. Biodiversity as we know it – or to put it another way, everything under the sun – will stop working. The bottom line, the very bottom line, is this: nature is all there is.

There isn't anything else, no alternative, no second coming of natural forces. We have to listen to what nature is telling us, or there will be no us left to listen. We have to start putting nature's needs on a par with our own. We have to start facing up to our responsibilities to nature, because whether we like it or not, we are nature too. And the way we know that is because nature is all there is.

"We know what is happening and what needs to be done."

We need to stop using fossil fuels, yet coal is being massively mined in – among other places – China, America and Australia.

We need to reduce drastically our carbon emissions.

We need to reduce drastically our energy consumption.

We need to replace huge areas of intensive farmland with billions and billions of trees, and stop felling the forests that we still have.

We need to find something better than plastic to do all the jobs that plastic does.

We need to satisfy the needs of the big species with which we share the planet, the ones that sustain all the lesser creatures.

And it is no good waiting for China and the United States and the other heel-dragging nations of the world. It is not good enough to shrug and say, "What's the point when you see what's happening in China and America?"

The point is to set examples.

Every nation that does care enough to legislate drastically on nature's behalf sets an example. And if enough do it, then a tide will turn, and the heel-draggers will be shamed into action. And when do we need to start doing this? Well, a glacier has already died in Iceland. We are already late. We have a lot of time to make up. And we have no time left at all to change our attitudes.

For example: in early May 2019, the United Nations more or less launched that frantic summer tsunami of scientific studies when it announced to the world, with as much fanfare as its considerable public relations muscle could muster, that global scientific opinion thinks we are about to preside over the extinction of one million species. The fanfare was loud, the PR muscle did its job well, and the world's media sat up and took notice. Front pages and two- or three- or four-page spreads were the order of the day. But then, two days later, a royal baby called Archie was born and the million species vanished, never to return. They may as well have become extinct. One London newspaper alone devoted twenty-three pages to the royal baby. That's what I mean about having no time left to change our attitudes.

I still shudder at the implications of the million species, and shudder again at the attention span and the priorities of much of the British media. But then nature is not just what I write about, it's where I live, what I breathe, who I am. And before I started to write books about it in

1988, I was a newspaper journalist and I couldn't help noticing then that the media's approach to nature stories routinely involved more puns than biology. Matters can hardly be said to have improved since then.

I heard it first on the radio. My ears said to me:

"Did she just say *one million* species?"

It quickly became clear that she did. And then there was Lofoten when we were coming in to land 120 miles inside the Arctic Circle and the captain spoke first in Norwegian and then in English and one of the passengers said:

"Did he just say *thirty four* degrees?"

I will remember the summer of 2019 as the one when the numbers didn't add up.

Numbers. They are really starting to scare the hell out of me.

Forty-three

The Accidental Kingfisher
and Other Stories

THE SUMMER OF 2019 turned out to be a furtive creature, the summer
that mostly hid its fair face behind mountains of rainclouds, or just
stayed away altogether. One of the results was a summer of demented
rivers and overflowing lochs. When summer did show up it was as
short-lived as snowflakes and I clutched at it as a drowning man
clutches at straws, with much the same outcomes. Yet for a couple
of weeks it bore down with tormenting heat, and just when we were
all lamenting the unprecedented lack of butterflies they all arrived at
once and flooded the land, and hung around until November.

And it was the summer when the swifts stayed away, at least they
did here. I found them eventually, but in the last place I would ever
have thought of looking for them. In fact, I wasn't looking for them
at all when I found them, and now that I think about it, I didn't find
them. They found me. So one way and another, it was an out-of-sorts
summer. And at the very end, it was the summer of the accidental
kingfisher.

It was also the summer I bought a new bike.

A week of rain relented into a sunny June morning. I pointed the
bike north from Callander, a track through the oakwoods beyond
Kilmahog and up the west side of Loch Lubnaig. The out-of-sorts
summer smiled down on me for all of fifteen minutes then compre-
hensively soaked me inside one of the blackest clouds I have seen since
the eruption of Eyjafjallajökull cast its giant shadow over Iceland and
grounded every aircraft in Europe, thereby achieving its own carbon
neutrality at a stroke. The rain cloud thrashed up the loch, contriving a
bit of a gale out of a flat calm as it came and went. After fifteen minutes

more it was gone, the air was calm and smelled of bog myrtle and wild hyacinths. Behind it was summer on a mission. Having soaked me, it set about drying me, and that too was accomplished within about fifteen minutes. It was as if the passing cloud was a cork in the neck of a huge bottle of sunlit heat, and the cork having been popped, the heat poured forth and the land basked. What followed was that summer's finest hour. Suddenly I felt lucky cycling easily along the shore of the loch, and the land wore its most seductive summer sheen, that ultimate, glossy, vivid, early summer green of a Highland forest. The light and the rain had rinsed the air clear and clean and supercharged it; nothing was hidden and everything and anything felt possible on such a day.

A wondrous old holly tree stands in a rough and piecemeal and quite possibly accidental hedge by the side of the track. I have a peculiar fascination for hollies that I don't quite understand because they are rarely shapely or beautiful, and they are dark and shiny and waxy and sharp-edged, but metaphorically speaking at least, they get under my skin in a good way.

There is something "other" about them, and I like that. I can only imagine that this particular holly is old, but I have not the slightest idea how old. I have never seen a tree quite like it, for it appears to have grown round itself and inside itself and into itself, so that branches weave in every direction and the tree wraps itself in hoops and crosses over itself like saltires, and where the branches rub up against each other, which is often, they grow into each other and form bizarre junctions.

The combination of the aftermath of the storm (it had drenched the holly as thoroughly as it had drenched me) and the strong sunlight electrified the sheen on the leaves so that they acquired a hallucinatory edge, rippling surprising shades through that vibrant green. I thought I was investing it with more than was actually there, but I found ally in Hugh Johnson and his book *Trees*:

The best-looking ones are in hedgerows where the wind has a pruning effect: shorter shoots keep the foliage dense and stress the contrast of glitter and darkness that is half the pleasure. For this reason, holly is best in summer when the new shoots emerge so soft and shiny that they look (and even feel) wet. The new leaves glow with pink, brown and purple tones as well as green.

It was such a word-perfect portrait of that trackside holly that I wondered idly if perhaps Hugh Johnson had ever strayed that way and marvelled at that very same tree.

Alistair Scott, a former senior executive in the Forestry Commission, wrote and privately published a remarkable little book in his retirement called *A Pleasure in Scottish Trees*. In it, he pointed out that the holly "is a useful indicator of grazing pressure…it seems to be common only where grazing animals are restricted"; that its leaves "have one of the highest calorific contents of any tree browsed by animals, and are rich in nutrients"; that "the traditional practice continues of feeding stock and deer on the leaves"; and that "woodmen still refuse to fell holly, just in case". He also identified a small wood of hollies on an island in the Fionn Loch in Torridon that more or less avoids the attention of grazing animals and prospers as a result, and that has put in my mind the idea of a small pilgrimage someday soon to see just what a small wood of hollies on an island in a loch in a such a spectacular West Highland setting might look like.

*

The solitary predetermined purpose of my bike ride (as opposed to the non-specific purpose of drinking in whatever turned up) was to check on the nesting season progress – or lack of it – of a pair of mute swans in a reed bed at the head of the loch. In my back catalogue there is a study of that nest site over more than thirty years that fuelled my addiction to the tribe of wild swans. Books, radio broadcasts, that solitary wretched TV film, and hundreds of newspaper and magazine articles flowed from it, and in all that time, no month passed without at least a couple of visits, and during nesting seasons it was sometimes daily.

My visits are less frequent now, but I still like to see for myself whether the birds have been successful or not. The rate of failure is almost off the scale, so desperate that I have often wondered why they stay loyal to the nest site, for it is prone to flooding, and year after year after year I charted the too-predictable fate of one pair of swans in particular over more than twenty years. When the cob finally died, he was over thirty years old, and his mate would have been well into her twenties when she succumbed. It seemed to me that they broke all the rules all the time – they had very little patience with field guide generalisations about "normal" mute swan habitats and behaviour. I learned from them. I knew them as individuals. They recognised me. I could summon them from quarter of a mile away. I learned not just about them but also about all the creatures with which they shared the head of the loch, the reedbeds, the well-treed river that flows into the loch between them, the oakwoods to the west and the spruce forest to the east and the mountainsides above; everything from otters and foxes and pine martens and red squirrels to little grebes and herons to goldeneye and wintering whooper swans, and from surface-skimming clouds of sand martins and dragonflies to golden and sea eagles. The more I watched the swans the more I learned about their fellow travellers and neighbours and the fly-by-nights who just dropped in and were driven out again, for they were two of the most formidably aggressive swans I have ever seen when it came to defending what they regarded as their domain, the extent of which I revised upwards several times over the years; my final estimate was about half a square mile of water.

So edging north towards the reed beds that June day as the heat built and my clothes steamed, I started to look for a pair of mute swans, and the faint hope (it was always a faint hope, the consequence of low expectation born of so much experience) of a brood of cygnets. They were not hard to find. They stood out of the water on a narrow spit of land over by the riverbank and almost surrounded by floodwater. They were preening. They blazed in the sunlight. The grass where they stood shone. The floodwater threw long reflections of the riverbank trees out into the loch, which was far above its natural shoreline. They were surrounded by about thirty Canada geese. If you knew nothing at all of the history of the place and its swans, you might chance on the scene, spare it a passing glance and find it at least agreeable, perhaps beautiful, perhaps a symbol of nature prospering in high summer. But

I knew – from the attitudes of the swans and from the presence of the geese so close to the reed bed that routinely accommodated the swans' nest – that their whole year had been rendered devoid of meaning. The nest was fully submerged by floodwater. There were no cygnets. Again. And June was almost certainly too late for them to start a new nest. I say almost certainly because there was one year when the old cob and pen built five nests in a single season, and a swan nest is a major piece of civil engineering. But that was exceptional.

The situation, or something like it, has played out so often in those last thirty-something years, and much more often than not. To have a trouble-free nesting season, the swans need a gentle and relatively dry April and May; and in the mountainsides of the Highland Edge, there are not many of these. If they had had cygnets, the adults would have had no difficulty herding thirty Canada geese far down the loch, and heaven help any that tried to nest in the riverbank grasses and trees. But as soon as the swans accept – or at least recognise – that the nesting season has failed them again, they drop their territorial guard.

Given how much time and energy I have invested in swans, it is hard not to feel for the birds. It is one of humanity's more likable traits that we mourn the dead and perform the rites of funeral. But one thing of which I am truly certain after all these years is that I don't think like a swan. If they have any sense of mourning at all – and in all the nesting season disasters that I have witnessed at Loch Lubnaig, I have seen no hint of it – it must be as brief as it is undemonstrative.

They will moult, they will feed up, they will defend their portion of the loch against the wintering whoopers that rest up here for a few autumn or winter days or weeks, harass them and drive them as far down the loch as they feel is necessary to maintain their authority. There may be ten or a dozen whoopers, and the mute swan cob will take them all on (the pen may or may not bother to participate; pens tend to be more peaceable) and the whoopers will sail before him, even though they could kill him if they turned on him en masse. But they never do, for swan aggression is almost invariably about territory, and the whoopers have no territorial interest in the winter loch, and they treat the mute swan cob with what looks like grudging respect. They understand territory, too. I saw it at work in Iceland, and was surprised to find that whereas all mute swan disputes are enacted on water, the whoopers resolve them in flight. This year, as so often before, it feels almost as if summer for the mute swans goes on without them.

*

I was far back down the track, almost at the south end of the loch where there is a small Forestry Commission development of timber chalets with a good café, and the café had supplanted the fate of the swans in my mind about half a mile back. All the buildings have eaves, and I was suddenly aware of strange bird activity deep in the shadow of one of the buildings and its surrounding trees. I now saw there was a long puddle at the edge of the track, which was almost all I could make out, that and a series of sporadic white flashes. The bird shapes were dark shadows within dark shadows. The scene had a mysterious restlessness about it, like watching bats in the dusk.

It took a few moments to work out what was going on. Around twenty house martins were flying down from nests in the timber eaves of the chalets to bathe and drink in the puddle, and doubtless to cool off as the day warmed up. I eased the bike as gently towards the puddle as I could but every bird rose at once: a squadron of dark blue and white darts fired into the air, and they all took the same flat-out, tight-cornered route to safety, as if they had rehearsed it many times before – hard right into a space between the café and the trees, hard left round the corner of the café. Dark blue and white never look so good since Denis Law used to wear it.

Did someone say café?

*

A network of narrow farm roads extends west from Stirling, mostly pointing towards the mountains around twenty miles away. It has become a favourite leisurely bike ride, usually a couple of hours respite from a writing shift, ten miles there and back, carrying nothing more than binoculars, camera, sketch pad. These long summer evenings are the best of it, and late June is the longest of the best of it.

This is brown hare country. The thing I like about watching brown hares is their unpredictable nature. There was one sitting back on its hurdies in a field, very much at ease, enjoying the fruits of some of the best grassland in the country. It tipped forward to put its weight on its front feet, ambled forward a yard in a low, curved, head-down-ears-up slouch. Stopped, sat again, ate, filled the binoculars with an over-all coat of deep russet (the evening sunlight giving an illusion of grey-ish-yellow shot through with black).

Repeat.

And again.

Then it came to a bare patch of earth not more than a square yard. Here it lay down, flattened its ears and to all intents and purposes disappeared in plain sight. If it had been lying there when I came along, I wonder if I would have seen it at all. There was no question that the hare was fully aware of me. It stared at me. Eyes of black and gold. A long stillness on the patch of bare earth, matched by a long stillness of my own. I told it softly: "I can do stillness, too."

In the evening quiet, a yellowhammer fizzed on a wire. Ever since I heard someone describe the yellow of yellowhammers as "egg yolk yellow" I have called them eggyolkhammers, which I think of as an improvement, an endearment. It fizzed again. I didn't want to turn to see where it was, somewhere behind me, because I was trying to out-still the brown hare, to see what it did next. It stood, sat back, looked left, looked right, tipped forward again and jogged *towards* me. Unpredictable, see? A few yards from the far side of the field fence, it cut away at an angle to reach the fence perhaps ten yards to the west of me, the way I had been travelling. It wafted through the fence as if no fence existed, and out onto the road, sat back again, stared at me, unblinking stare. This is good. What next?

It turned and started to jog along the road, going west. I eased into the saddle, followed. Fifty yards, a hundred, then it stopped again. Sat. Looked back. Still here, hare.

Turned again and jogged on, a leisurely ten miles an hour. I didn't try and catch up because I have seen a hare do forty miles per hour and Chris Froome doesn't do that, and I was no Chris Froome, even when I was Chris Froome's age, which is not recently. I have no wish to be shown up by a brown hare. The hare used the whole road, ran in curving lines, as though perhaps it was looking for an easy way back into the fields on both sides of the road. Then a tractor materialised a few hundred yards ahead and dispelled that theory. The hare stopped. Stared west at the tractor. I had also stopped when it turned its head to look at me through its left eye. In that position, given the placement of its eyes on the side of its head and its almost 360-degrees vision, I reckon it was watching both me and the tractor at the same time, twin threats from diametrically opposed directions.

It turned through ninety degrees to face a hawthorn hedge. The easier option (as I saw it) was on the other side of the road, a fence I could have got through. The hare ran at the hawthorn hedge, vanished, then reappeared about five seconds later twenty yards inside the field and running. I pulled the bike into the grass verge to let the tractor past, exchanged a wave with the driver. When I looked back into the field beyond the hawthorn hedge I couldn't find the hare. But there were two more eggyolkhammers on the next 100 yards of wire, and they hadn't shifted for the tractor. Or the hare. Or the bike when it passed them, and its rider was looking up at them, smiling.

And then I was looking up smiling at a buzzard. It was a pale phase bird. I have never read a convincing explanation for why the plumage of common buzzards can vary as much as it does. The "standard model" is mid-brown with a pale crescent across its breast. A pale phase bird goes all the way to off-white with a dark brown crescent, or no crescent at all. I pass this way often in the car on my way to Flanders Moss and have got into the habit of slowing down when I drive next to a power line slung from a row of wooden posts, because there is often a buzzard perched there, and not quite as often but more often than not, it will be on the fifth post from the end of the row. Now that I cycle this way as often as I drive, I have started to look out for it more conscientiously. I spotted it from a hundred yards away, assisted by its particularly pale outfit, the thick dark crescent lending its plumage something of the air of an Icelandic sweater. So I slowed right down from 100 yards and the bird stayed put, watching intently. From about fifty yards I started doing my fair impression of a buzzard call.

I have called to buzzards for years, to see if I can get a conversation going, or even lure them closer. Mostly they stay silent, but sometimes it works, it works. The bird changed its attitude only to the extent that it started to watch me side-headed, which I took to be an upping of the intensity of its scrutiny. I was almost at a standstill when I passed the buzzard's pole, still calling, but I knew better than to stop and break the spell. It flexed and fidgeted its wings twice at the last moment, readying for take-off, but it stayed put. I had just passed the bird's pole, no more than ten yards from it, when it called back, just once. I felt greeted, acknowledged. I was smiling again.

★

The summer of 2019 was the one when the International Union for the Conservation of Nature put the swift on its Red List, rating it as officially endangered. Weather conditions had held back its arrival from Africa, numbers appeared to be down, and my summer was impoverished.

A few years ago now, sitting in my garden on a late-summer evening with a beer and a book, I became aware of distant swift voices. Something about the nature of the sound, the way it fell on my ears, was different. Swift voices always grab my attention: I simply love to watch them fly and it is that simple. I put down my book and my reading glasses and looked up. The reason why the sound struck me as unusual was apparent at once. They were very, very high, and there were upwards of 200 of them. This I had never seen before. More remarkably, they hung around more or less directly above my garden, for half an hour. I watched until my neck hurt. Then I went back to my beer and my book and my attention drifted back and forward between the words on the page and the soundtrack in the sky.

In a handful of years they have gone from such spectacular gatherings to internationally "endangered", one more casualty of humankind's increasingly cavalier approach to the world we live in and the creatures with which we share it. I am in the habit of walking most mornings to get newspapers and read them over coffee. My walk takes me along a street I used to think of as an alleyway for swifts. Flat-out squadrons of them dived down from the roofs of big old villas and whipped through the airspace of the street, trailing their high-pitched voices behind them like contrails. Sometimes the most moving and uplifting encounters with nature are in the wildest of landscapes and you share the privilege of becoming part of the landscape, part of that wild world that is as vital to a nature writer as oxygen. And sometimes, nature comes in among us, finds something agreeable in our built-up landscapes and for a few midsummer weeks transforms them into something so season-defining that we cheer their arrival and mourn their departure. So it has always been with swifts and me. Better still are the crowstep-and-red-pantiles of steeply tiered Fife coast rooftops in places like St Monans and Pittenweem, when your wandering footsteps will be stopped in their tracks by the sight of twenty swifts against the sea. In the out-of-sorts summer of 2019, I saw no swifts before July 6, when seven emerged in my neighbourhood street, made two circuits of the rooftops, and disappeared, in complete silence.

I don't like the tendency to dismiss the voice of a swift as "screaming". Screaming inevitably implies the outermost edges of heightened emotions. What you hear with swifts is simply conversation; swift-to-swift communication. There will be an evolutionary explanation for why a swift's voice sounds the way it does, and it may well have something to do with cutting through the air during high-speed flight. "Screaming" is just plain wrong.

The day after that silent seven in a Stirling street, I happened to be in Moffat, and headed for one of my favourite cafés in a wooded garden. A high stone wall flanks one side of the garden and beyond it is a long and narrow cobblestone lane, with terraces of two-storey, slate-roofed cottages on its further side.

I sat down with my coffee and quickly changed the position of my seat because the rooftops and the lane and the sky above were alive with passing showers of swifts. These nineteenth-century slate roofs, with slate-roofed dormers and eaves, are a fixture in the architectural tradition of many Borders towns and villages. There was only one other person in the café garden – as it turned out, a fellow swift fanatic. We lingered there talking swifts and I never spent a more agreeable hour in a café.

Swifts, unlike swift-watchers, don't linger. They are among the latest of migrants to arrive and the earliest to leave. Routinely, they start to move south in early July and are mostly all gone by the middle of August. But that summer, I was back in Moffat on August 24, headed for the same garden café knowing full well that it would be devoid of swifts, only to find that they were still there, thirty or forty of them still making the most of the summer's late heat and its bounty of flying insects.

*

Mid-August, the track between Callander and Loch Lubnaig where it follows the River Leny through oakwoods north of Kilmahog. It contours the slope through the oak woods so that there are trees above and below. The river was in turbulent mood after yet more days and days of relentless rain. It flowed black and white and sunlit, and giving voice. It was a roar of massed whispers, orchestral in their range when you really, really listen and pinpoint its bassiest and trebliest voices and its baritones and contraltos. It rose through the deflecting canopies of the oaks so that it reached me in fragments, yet the fragments cohered to become the whole orchestra, the one river.

The sunlight fell differently on the oaks above and below me. Above the track the sun speared between the tree trunks and through gaps in the canopies in straight lines, broad sunbeams where dragonflies danced. The floor of the wood, with its thick carpet of grass and berries and knee-high hollies and birches and rowans, was splashed with spotlights of yellow where the sun held sway.

But below the path, the effect of the sun on the trees was of extravagant beauty, lit as only an oak wood knows how to be lit. No wood is better at ingratiating itself with sunlight than a summer oakwood. The steepness of the ground – essentially a Highland river gorge – is part of the magic, the deep green of oak leaves is another, and so is a mature oak tree's insistence on making space for itself.

I was still fourteen days away from the end of summer, and it briefly occurred to me that I could stop right now, right here, in this epiphanic moment, head for my writing base and start to try and make sense of the notebooks, the sketchbooks, the photographs, my memories of this and older summers. But who knows what fourteen days might contribute, with the weather set fair and that particular summer's capacity to delight and disappoint and disgust me in more or less equal measure? And somewhere back there I made a promise to nature to see the final season through to the final hour of the final day, for all that it was ever my least favourite season. And writing this book has taught me, among much else, that really there is no such thing, that nature nurtures and mothers them all equally, as all good mothers do with their children.

I cycled back south between fronds of bracken and other more benevolent ferns, shrubby fronds of birch and blaeberry, and the track was everywhere a tapestry of sunlight and oak shadows, and the river cried up to me with its huge voice of whispers, the anthem of the Highland Edge. I was briefly content, a strange and rare state of mind and body, and once again I flirted with the idea of writing *finis* at the foot of a notebook page. And then the understorey at the very edge of the track exploded. For a moment there was nothing louder than the thrum of tiny wings, and as they burst bluntly up and out from the foliage – startled then panicked by the intrusion of my bike – they flew through the sunlight and shadow of the first two feet of airspace above the track, and they were vivid reddish-brown where they caught the sun and just plain brown where they were shadowed. For perhaps ten seconds they flew ahead of me down the line of the track, but then it seemed to occur to them that if they dived back into the understorey they would be safe from me, whatever I might be, whatever threat I might pose. It was a brood of wrens and there were nine of them. I did some simple arithmetic. Surely it was a third brood, to be so newly fledged in the second half of August.

*

The Met Office will have you believe that tomorrow, being the first of September, is the first day of meteorological autumn, which is how this writing adventure began. I am inclined to heave a huge sigh of relief when September dawns and I can start to think autumnal thoughts, but I was suddenly reluctant to take leave of summer and I decided to hang in there for at least as long as the weather did.

The Leny has a sister river just to the south, a little sister that slips more or less unsung into the Leny's mainstream just to the west of Callander. I have cause to love it dearly. In particular, there is a bend in the river where I like to sit, not least because of the view, not least because of the otters and herons and redstarts and goosanders and dippers.

Not least because of the kingfishers.

My seat is on the outside of the bend. On the inside bend of the bank there is a willow tree with seven trunks. Depending on the state of the river, the willow is either perfectly reflected in its dawdling waters, or it fractures into a crazy paving reflection when the river's dander is up. Watch an otter swim by when the river dawdles and see the reflections scatter all through its wake, and then watch the whole upside-down tree magically restore itself over several minutes. It is one of my favourite places to sit and write, and I have tried again and again to draw the willow tree, but never come close to doing it justice. But I'm not done yet.

Beyond the willow and the other trees that line the bank, there is a square mile of floodplain, nothing more than long grass with reedy pools and unguessable peaty depths. Beyond that, the land climbs into foothills, and to the wonderful profile of Ben Ledi.

Late afternoon, early September, and a conviction in me that summer has finally slipped below the horizon, that the light has yellowed beyond anything that summer can contrive: this is autumn's light, and I witnessed the change, sitting there, and I wished them both hail and farewell, for they were the beginning and the end of the greatest adventure of my writing life.

But what happened next is included in this late summer diary to remind you – and me – about the continuity of nature, that there is no division between the seasons, that they feed into each other seamlessly, that the one begets the next, begets the next, begets the next.

Then the kingfisher.

It came upstream, so from my right, and it was as sunstruck and bejewelled and bedazzling as any kingfisher you ever saw, and it took the bend on the inside and for as long as it takes a kingfisher eye to blink I saw its reflection flare among the reflections of the seven willow trunks and then dowse in the same moment. Because at that particular time of day in that particular season, the tree is not only reflected sevenfold in the river, it also casts seven shadows on the water.

The kingfisher seared on upstream then took the next bend, which is a left-hand bend, also on the inside, so you could say it took the racing line. I always sit here with binoculars close at hand for situations just like this one, and as I followed the kingfisher until it vanished round the next bend, something caught my eye on the far bank of the second bend. I focussed on the bank, which for about fifty yards was bare earth and vertical and with tree roots protruding here and there. In other words, it was the perfect place for a kingfisher nest. I had wondered in the past if the local birds might nest there but I had never seen them use it. A kingfisher nest is a messy place. Norman MacCaig caught it nicely:

> ...*it vanishes into its burrow, resplendent*
> *Samurai, returning home*
> *to his stinking slum*...

It advertises its presence with a seabird-like splash of droppings, and that was what caught my eye in the binoculars as the kingfisher vanished. It is a precarious site, for the bank is not high and the river has a tendency to flood, but then as our land warms and floods more and more frequently, digging a nest in any riverbank anywhere becomes a chancier business.

I was about a hundred yards away from the nest, and getting closer is not possible without a canoe and I don't have one. Besides, I don't need to get closer. I used my camera's ridiculously long zoom lens to take two pictures, nothing more than reference images, but the white splash is clearly visible.

It was days later before I looked at them on the screen of my laptop. Only then did I realise I had accidentally photographed a kingfisher I hadn't seen. Not only that, it was about fifty yards nearer to me than the nest, so it was very out of focus. And it was in both photographs. I have good eyesight for this kind of thing. There are days when I think I have worked as hand-in-glove with nature as it is possible for me to achieve. And there are days when I'm nowhere, when I blow it, when – for example – I might pass up a very good opportunity to photograph a kingfisher because I was taking a picture of kingfisher shit.

★

I am inclined to sit on after the kingfisher's disappearance, although I have more or less stopped working again. More or less because I never truly stop. Nature is all around us wherever we are so my raw material is never far from me. My dear departed friend, the artist George Garson, whose ghost has had walk-on parts in all four of these seasons of storm and wonder, once told me that sometimes he craved the darkness because only then could he stop looking. We had been sitting in a bar in Edinburgh, a thing we did often. I asked him what he meant. He pointed out an old fellow sitting on a bar stool, side-on to us so we only saw him in profile.

"I'm painting him in my mind," he said. "Look at him. Left elbow on the bar. Chin in his left hand, reading the racing paper, his sideburns are grey but there are wisps of red hair escaping from the back of his cap. And his cap's blue. How often do you see an old man wearing a blue cap? See how the sun hits the lines on his forehead, and what colour would you reach for for his eye? Could be just the side of his head, and his left arm…don't need anything else, maybe a bit of the racing paper."

He was silent for a few moments. Then the old boy lifted his right hand, subconsciously pushed his cap up so that it moved back a bit on his head. George laughed.

"That's better," he said. "That's much better."

But I don't suffer from George's obsessive personality. He told me that himself. He was an alcoholic. Once, when he talked about that, he said that I would never become one because I don't have an obsessive personality. It's true: I haven't become the one and I don't have the other.

And yet…

Now that I have stopped working, sitting by the bend in the river, something of me still keeps watching in some shape or form.

Late afternoon eases quietly into early evening. My eyes wander all over that so-familiar landscape. I think how much I love the mountain. Then it occurs to me that I have never set foot on the floodplain on the other side of the river, and isn't that strange? At that moment exactly, I know that the accidental kingfisher is summer's final flourish. The day is still warm, the river mutters and swishes at my feet, the seven-trunked willow leans far out into midstream and it is as if the whole landscape turns around that singular tree, as if it directs the course of the river, and places the components of its backdrop – floodplain and foothills, forest and mountain – and gives them their cues of light and shade.

As if it conducts the song of that place.

I close my eyes for a few moments.

Then there is a movement in the long grass out on the floodplain.

It is the head – small ears erect, eyes of deep gold – and the back of a grey wolf.

It emerges from the long grass and comes to sit by the willow. Tree and wolf appear to know each other.

The wolf looks up and downstream then straight across the river at me.

Its gaze rests on me. I have known this feeling twice before, to be the centre of a wolf's attention. There is no feeling quite like it on the face of the Earth.

It looks back at the tree. Then it stands and jumps down onto a patch of solid ground that had briefly been a beaver dam two or three years before. It no longer looks like solid ground, for it has grown over with water-loving plants. But the wolf recognises it for what it is and knows it is still solid.

It steps into the current and swims across, heading for a small bank of gravel just below where I sit. From there, it scrambles easily up onto the bank and shakes itself, and I am anointed by river water discarded from the pelt of a wolf. Then it comes up to sit beside me facing the mountain, as I do myself. We are a yard apart, no more.

We share a kind of natural camaraderie, a deep calm. The river is the only sound.

Then, from far off beyond the floodplain, somewhere near the forest under the mountain, a wolf howls.

The wolf by my side looks at the sound, as if it were visible.

I imagine that howl rising out of the trees like a column of smoke. Smoke signals.

The wolf looks at me. Then it stands and retraces its journey back across to the willow, where it looks directly at the tree, then looks back along its spine, back across the river and finds my eyes again.

Then it simply turns and walks away out into the long grass of the floodplain where it is once again as I had first seen it, just the head and the ears and the top of its back.

It stops once, briefly, tilts its head back so that its muzzle is higher than its ears and howls once towards the mountain.

Answering smoke signals.

It looks back at me again. I stand for a better view and I raise an arm.

Then the wolf turns again and walks off, walks towards the unseen wolf at the foot of the mountain.

A willow with seven trunks on a bend in the river. I always thought there was something special about that.

FOUR IN THE MORNING MOON

Look the four-in-the-morning moon
in the eye
and wonder why
it only ever greets the bruised and broken Earth
with a smile.
Maybe the view from there is blind
to tears and fears
of four-in-the-morning moonwatchers
sees instead only the deep
blue beauty of the world
asleep.

Afterword
Never Forget

ONCE UPON A TIME, a boy of three or four looked up from childhood's garden at wild geese overhead. He never forgot the moment. He still hasn't: he is about to finish writing the book you have in your hands. If that moment can truly claim to be the first time nature tapped him on the shoulder and whispered, "Watch this, pay attention," I can testify on his behalf that whatever his many flaws, he did pay attention and he has never stopped.

When I finally sat down to write a book about autumn, it was that memory that stirred, that first moment of awareness that certain things outside happened at certain times of the year. The evolution of that awareness has led me to this moment as I write, and the long evolution of that awareness within me developed a particular intensity when I embarked on a book about autumn, then on a quartet of books about the seasons. The sense of that quartet evolving into a single piece of work first occurred to me about halfway through the writing of the second book, *The Nature of Winter*, and it grew in importance as the series unfolded. With the publication in 2020 of the final book in the series, *The Nature of Summer*, I remember holding all four books in my hand as if I was trying to weigh the significance of what it meant to me as a nature writer, for the entire project had consumed five years and was by far my working life's most substantial undertaking.

It was late in the evening, the house in silence, and I poured a whisky before leafing through the books – not one by one but jumping from book to book as the memory of writing a particular paragraph prompted a thought about something in one of the other books. I had wanted to talk about the four books as a single piece of work, but any such thoughts were scuppered by Covid. I felt curiously aggrieved, a sense of unfinished business. And moving thoughtfully among all four books, comparing and contrasting, remembering and reliving, somewhere in the course of the next hour the idea was born – a single volume. I started to reimagine the series, removing some of the structure of the individual books, deleting some chapters from each of them so that the result would weigh in at less than 500 pages, allowing the books to flow into each other, distilling and strengthening the impact of the finished product, a bit like the whisky.

Even as the process began, the common thread of climate chaos and human exploitation of nature that had run through the four original books seemed to enter a particularly virulent phase. I had been amassing cuttings and notes about the despoliation of Mount Everest ever since that now famous photograph of the queues on the summit ridge in 2019. In 2022, revelations of cracks appearing in the ice at base camp prompted Nepalese authorities to explore the possibility of moving it down the mountain. (It was also revealed that people urinate 4,000 litres there every day of the climbing season – and what does that do for an already melting glacier?)

At the same time, the Sierra de la Culebra, the setting of Spain's ground-breaking Iberian wolf recovery programme, caught fire just as the new cubs were beginning to explore above ground; one hundred swifts died from exceptional heat in Italy, and for the same reason one hundred million Americans were told to stay indoors; Yellowstone was closed because of unprecedented flash flooding.

And then, much nearer home, the Bass Rock in the Firth of Forth, about seventy miles east in a straight line from where I live, became the setting for catastrophe. The Bass caught the flu. It appears in the "Bass Notes" chapter of this book in the guise of a symbol of nature at its most vigorously spectacular: the world's biggest gannetry. Avian flu, a gift to the world from poultry farms in the Far East, penetrated the gannetry where 80,000 breeding pairs and unknown numbers of juveniles cram the rock's every usable square inch so that it blazes bright white in summer sunlight. I walked two stretches of the Fife coast and began finding washed-up dead gannets every few yards. There was a clear view across the Firth to the Bass, and it was dirty brown. Asian flu was on target to wipe out half the gannet population.

But even as I write these words on a warm July afternoon, news has reached me that the first osprey chick of the year has just flown from the Scottish Wildlife Trust reserve at Loch of the Lowes in Perthshire, about fifty miles north from where I live. The osprey reintroduced itself to Scotland in the late 1950s after decades of absence and, aided by the best efforts of conservation, the UK population is now 300 pairs and rising.

Then an email arrived from the woman who organised my remarkable trip to the Lofoten Islands of Arctic Norway in 2018 (see the two "The Land of Havørn" chapters) to say she was back in Lofoten and had just been swimming in a small lake, where she had shared the water with a very relaxed pair of red-throated divers. And then my heart and mind were suddenly reeling with the wonders of that land-and-seascape beyond the Arctic Circle.

The point is this: The storms can be overwhelming, but we have the wherewithal and the intelligence to mitigate them provided we are willing to divert the resources and, crucially, to apply the will to make it happen. And meanwhile, we must cling to those moments, those seasons, when we meet the wonders head-on, for these are what sustain us just as they sustain nature, and they reveal the essential truth that we are nature ourselves.

I know this for a fact because, once upon a time, a boy of three or four looked up from childhood's garden at wild geese overhead and never forgot.

Acknowledgements

Warm thanks to Kathleen Jamie for her very generous foreword. Coming from such a fine writer, and one with a particularly thoughtful appreciation of nature, her words are very much appreciated. Thanks too for permission to quote in the Introduction from her book, *Sightlines*.

The beautifully atmospheric artwork on the dust jacket is based on a painting called 'Zephyr Dreaming' by Argyll-based artist Lizzie Rose. Again warm thanks for permission to reproduce a work of art that seems to reflect perfectly the spirit of the book.

Given that detailed acknowledgements are published at the end of each one of the four books that gave rise to *Seasons of Storm and Wonder*, it seems sufficient now simply to offer a kind of roll-call of writers, artists and friends. To that generalisation, I should like to make one exception – Seton Gordon. His work is referenced and quoted throughout these pages. The resurgence in nature writing in Scotland today is a river that springs from a single source, and that source is Seton Gordon. His work is long overdue a thoughtful re-evaluation and an infinitely greater recognition. In that context, I am particularly grateful to his great-grandson, James Macdonald Lockhart, for permission to quote from his work.

The following writers, artists and friends have all assisted the cause of this book because, one way or another, my admiration and gratitude for their work and/or their friendship continues to assert benevolent influence on the way that I think about nature and how I write it down: Ansel Adams, George Mackay Brown, Robert Burns, Marion Campbell, David O. Carroll, Paul Cezanne, Frank Fraser Darling, Leo du Feu, Ralph Waldo Emerson, Margiad Evans, George Garson, Violet Jacob, Hugh Johnson, Aldo Leopold, Nancy Lord, Norman MacCaig, Hugh MacDiarmid, Sheila Mackay, Gavin Maxwell, John Muir, Roger Payne, Douglas Culross Peattie, Polly Pullar, Mark Rothko, Pat Sandeman, Holly Schaff, Sandra Dawn Taylor, Mike Tomkies, Charles Tunnicliffe, William Butler Yeats.

Acknowledgements

This book is dedicated to the memory of a great friend, David Craig, a writer and mountaineer of rare distinction, and Britain's first professor of creative writing. He died in November, 2021, at the age of 89. He was my last letter-writing correspondent. His last letter to me, written a few months before he died, enclosed a hand-written copy of "the only poem I have written in the last eight years". This is it, and I can think of no finer way to close *Seasons of Storm and Wonder*.

Spores

Under the armpit of a bracken frond
Its spores are as neatly herring-boned
As hairs on a moth's antennae
Or veins in a pigeon's quill.
I sketched these images on a lime-tree leaf –
The ink dried slowly, glistening in relief,
Black juice on chlorophyll.
I would have gone on writing
But the green page was full.